THE REVOLUTIONARY IMAGINATIONS OF GREATER MEXICO

THE REVOLUTIONARY IMAGINATIONS OF GREATER MEXICO

Chicana/o Radicalism, Solidarity Politics,
and Latin American Social Movements

ALAN ELADIO GÓMEZ

UNIVERSITY OF TEXAS PRESS ⟐ *Austin*

Chapter 5 originally appeared, in a different version, as "Por la reunificación de los Pueblos Libres de América en su Lucha por el Socialismo: The Chicana/o Movement, the PPUA and the Dirty War in Mexico in the 1970s," in *Challenging Authoritarianism in Mexico: Revolutionary Struggles and the Dirty War, 1964–1982*, edited by Fernando Herrera Calderón and Adela Cedillo, 81–104 (New York: Routledge, 2012).

Chapter 6 originally appeared, in a different version, as "Puente de Crystal (Crystal Bridge): Magdalena Mora and Multiple Feminist Insurgencies," *African Identities* 11, no. 2 (2013): 159–184 (published by Taylor and Francis).

Requests for permission to reproduce material from this work should be sent to:
Permissions
University of Texas Press
P.O. Box 7819
Austin, TX 78713-7819
http://utpress.utexas.edu/index.php/rp-form

♾ The paper used in this book meets the minimum requirements of
ANSI/NISO Z39.48-1992 (R1997) (Permanence of Paper).

LIBRARY OF CONGRESS CATALOGING-IN-PUBLICATION DATA

Names: Gómez, Alan Eladio, author.
Title: The revolutionary imaginations of greater Mexico : Chicana/o radicalism, solidarity politics, and Latin American social movements / Alan Eladio Gómez.
Description: First edition. | Austin : University of Texas Press, 2016. | Includes bibliographical references and index.
Identifiers: LCCN 2015050871 | ISBN 978-1-4773-0921-6 (cloth : alk. paper) | ISBN 978-1-4773-1076-2 (pbk. : alk. paper) | ISBN 978-1-4773-1077-9 (library e-book) | ISBN 978-1-4773-1078-6 (nonlibrary e-book)
Subjects: LCSH: Mexican Americans—Politics and government—History—20th century. | Radicalism—Latin America. | Solidarity—Political aspects—Latin America. | Social movements—Latin America. | Latin America—Politics and government—20th century. | Chicano movement.
Classification: LCC E184.M5 G59 2016 | DDC 303.48/40980904—dc23
LC record available at http://lccn.loc.gov/2015050871

doi:10.7560/309216

DEDICATED TO MY MOTHER, ALICIA GALLEGOS GÓMEZ; AND
TO THE MEMORY OF BALDOMERO GALLEGOS AND ESTHER
GALLEGOS ZARATE, GUADALUPE GONZALES, ELADIO GÓMEZ,
AND RAÚLRSALINAS.

CONTENTS

ACKNOWLEDGMENTS

ALL KNOWLEDGE IS COLLECTIVE, even though writers often create during long stints of isolation and solitude. This absence affects all social relationships. The particular ways in which each of the following people contributed to the book—its editing, research, theorization, and critique, as well as the intimacy, conviviality, and friendship necessary to reproduce oneself every day—would constitute its own chapter. To collapse twenty years of relationships into a few lines about specifics would be to radically mischaracterize and misrepresent the depth of appreciation and humility I have for the continued support and friendship of these individuals over the years that opened this century.

Without my mother, Alicia Gallegos-Gómez, and my *abuelos* and *abuelas*, I would not be writing these words. Their support and patience, curiosity and critique—about this book, the political work, and the politics of the university—have been a solace and refuge as well as an impetus animating my drive to research and teach. Their own struggles against racial injustice in South Texas during the post–World War II Juan Crow regime are partly responsible for the analytical questions about power, resistance, struggle, and change that structure this book.

This book was written over ten years, and so my thanks are as much personal as the personal is place-based. On a basic level, tracing the cultural politics of a Chicana/o Left was a consequence of a political need to know a genealogy that influenced the relationship tying Chicana/o communities in the United States to the EZLN and other political movements in Mexico and elsewhere in Latin America. So, I have much appreciation and respect for the folks who agreed to be interviewed for this project and who shared their personal archives.

My thanks, then, to archivists and staff at Stanford Special Collections, especially Polly Armstrong, Tim Noakes, and Robert Trujillo; at UT-Austin's Nettie Benson Latin American Collections, especially Carla Alvarez, Margot Gutiérrez, Michael Hironymous, Kelly Kerbow-Hudson, and Christian Kelleher; at the Harry Ransom Center (also at UT-Austin); and at the Archivo General de la Nación, in Mexico City. Many thanks to UT Press's two readers for their invaluable suggestions and to Kerry Webb, acquiring editor at the press, who helped make this a stronger, more analytically sound, and more readable book.

In addition, I owe a debt of gratitude to many others in various locations. In Texas: Luis Alvarez, Estevan Azcona, Manolo Callahan, Emmet Campos, Alex Chávez, Veronica Delgado, Melissa Forbis, Tamara Ford, Rebecca Gamez, Gloria Garza, Jennifer Goett, Pablo Gonzalez, Daniel Guerra, Cale Layton, Veronica Martinez-Matsuda, Luis Mendoza, Peter Mendoza, Jake Mitchell, Mariana Mora, Haldun Morgan, Jamie Munkatchy, Toni Nelson-Herrera, Vivian Newdick, Alba Peña, Omar Angel Pérez, raúlrsalinas, Gilberto Rosas, Lilia Raquel Rosas, Christina Salinas, Alberto Sanchez, Maryanne Schiffman, Patrick Timmons, Cristina Tzintzún, Geoff Valdés, Rene Valdez, Cristóbal Valencia, and Vincent Vargas. Thanks also to the following organizations with a presence in Texas: MEChA, the Advanced Seminar for Chicana/o Research, the Midnight Art Project, Acción Zapatista, Maneja Beto, Radio Aguascalientes/Caracol, and Resistencia Bookstore.

In New York: Asma Barlas, Sean Eversley-Bradwell, Rosa Clemente, Jason Corwin, Belisa Gonzalez, Beth Harris, Leslie Jones, Richard Keily, Ulises Ali Mejias, Charles Venator Santiago, Alicia Swords, and the Goldsmith and Grady families.

In Arizona: thanks to all the staff and faculty, as well as graduate students I have worked with at ASU, particularly Ed Ableser, Diego Avalos, Sandra Castro, Wendy Cheng, Jeremiah Chin, Marivel Danielson, a de la maza tamayo, Grace Gamez, Kathleen Given, Rudy Guevarra, LaDawn Haglund, Keonna Harris, Pat Lauderdale, Karen Leong, Tami McKenzie, Luis Mendoza, Gregorio Montes de Oca, Erica Ocequeda, Abigail Perez Aguilera, Mary Romero, Santiago Rosas, Mary Stephens, Beth Swadener, Rebecca Tsosie, and Tamara Underiner. My thanks as well to Puente Human Rights Organization, the Arizona Worker's Rights Center, and the amazing HBW crew.

In México: Fernando Calderón, Habana Aleida Campos, Adela Cedillo, Enrique Cisneros, Sandra Amelia Cruz, Mariano Leyva Dominguez, Mercedes Nieto, Ana Ignacia "La Nacha" Rodríguez, Ernesto Reyes, David Roara, Abraham Vidales, and la familia Porras.

And finally, my thanks to many in the extended diaspora: Chuck Armsbury, Victor Bono, Jordan Camp, Antonia Castañeda, Harry Cleaver, Lucha Corpi, Ruthie Epstein, Toyin Falola, Ted Gordon, Charlie Hale, Christina Heatherton, Milton Jamail, George Lipsitz, Toussaint Losier, Alberto Mares, Anne Martinez, Alejandro Murguía, Susan Oboler, Annie Paradise, Olga Talamante, Dionisio Valdés, Helena Viramontes, Rhonda H. Williams, Tiffany Willoughby-Heard, Ruth Wilson Gilmore, Tomás Ybarra-Frausto, and Emilio Zamora.

The last months of finalizing drafts could not have been done without an amazingly creative, patient, and giving support network—friends and colleagues who read drafts, offered analytical suggestions, and created spaces of refuge with food and spirits, laughter, and much-appreciated encouragement: Mom, Luis Alvarez, Manolo Callahan, Leahjo, Berkley, Linda and Doug Carnine, Johnny Roldan Chacón, Nic de la Fuente, Carlos García, Virginia Grise, Crystal Griffith, Caroline Picker and Ada Johnson, Toni Nelson-Herrera, Kyla Pasha, Sarah Suhail, Lola Levesque N'Sanguo, Louis Mendoza, Michael and Sandra Perez, H. L. T. Quan, Brooke Reynolds, Michelle Tellez, Rene Valdez, Geoff Valdés, Mark Van Hagen, Matt Young, and Barley, Benny, Billi, Bizloo, Sabzi, and the late Mozart.

THE REVOLUTIONARY IMAGINATIONS OF GREATER MEXICO

CHICANA/O RADICALISM, TRANSNATIONAL ORGANIZING, AND SOCIAL MOVEMENTS IN LATIN AMERICA

POLITICAL MOVEMENTS IN Mexico and Latin America during the 1970s inspired a Chicana/o Left politics that created nuanced and politically astute forms of international solidarity. This book focuses on how the participants in these trajectories of the Chicana/o movement saw themselves as part of a larger hemispheric and global political community, and how that political perspective led them to intentionally look outside the borders of the United States to create connections with political movements, artists, and revolutionaries that were anticapitalist and anti-imperialist. *The Revolutionary Imaginations of Greater Mexico* uncovers and highlights the contours within the Chicana/o movement that inspired solidarity with political movements and connections between artists in Mexico and Latin America. It addresses what it meant to be Chicana/o in Mexico and Latin America, and how Mexico and Latin America existed in the political imaginations of Chicanas/os in the United States. Through an analytic of international solidarity enacted in local contexts, this book brings together the different perceptions and meanings of the Third World within the Chicana/o movement.[1] It reveals how anticapitalism, socialism, insurgent feminism, radical creativity, and global justice influenced the ideas, imaginary, and political practices of the Chicana/o Left during the 1970s. Exploring transnational connections, cultural imaginaries, and political events, the book's seven chapters focus on the stories of little-known activists and artists, tortured revolutionaries, feminists, gunrunners, labor organizers, poets, journalists, former prisoners, and their "freedom dreams" for social change enacted through diverse and creative forms of solidarity.[2]

International solidarity as concrete actions, and as a political imaginary, conditioned the possibility for the Chicana/o movement such that "the existence of a Chicana/o internationalism . . . was present at the movement's very origins, e.g., solidarity with socialist Cuba and Vietnam."[3] In dialogue with the postnationalist turn in American studies, the influence of Chicana/o and Latina/o studies on Latin American studies, and the highlighting of postnationalist political activity in the 1970s, this book uncovers and examines intimate encounters between activists and artists across borders who shared a socialist-oriented, anticapitalist politics. Specifically, it uncovers Chicana/o participation in the hemispheric movement Nuevo Teatro Popular (New People's Theater); the Revolutionary Proletariat Party of America (Partido Proletario Unido de América—PPUA) in Mexico; and the Marxist-Leninist organization Centro de Acción Social Autónomo.

The solidarity politics of Chicana/o leftists included socialist, anarchist, and anti-imperialist imaginaries and represent different "apprenticeship[s] with Marxism" inspired by political struggles in Mexico, Cuba, and Latin America, as well as a long history of leftist organizing by people of Mexican descent in the United States.[4] Organizing festivals, assemblies, and united fronts; circulating information in newspapers, press conferences, art, and public protests; and directly joining revolutionary organizations during the 1970s, their efforts connected the Chicana/o movement with leftist struggles in Mexico and Latin America. At its most basic, this book is a social history of a political and cultural imaginary and the people, places, events, and organizations that, inspired by this imaginary, produced different articulations of solidarity with the Chicana/o Left.

The late Chicano scholar Américo Paredes inspired the book's title. His concept "refers to all the areas inhabited by people of Mexican culture—not only within the present limits of the Republic of Mexico but in the United States as well—in a cultural rather than a political sense."[5] His term "Greater Mexico," a cultural geography, was also a political imaginary, I argue, a space and place inhabited by people of Mexican descent in an imagined community created through shared cultural and historical pasts, memories, and practices.[6] Solidarity politics inspired revolutionary imaginaries. My use of the term "Greater Mexico" is not intended to center the nation-state, identity, or citizenship. Inhabiting a proto-postnationalist position during the 1970s while merging a critique of racial capitalism in the United States and anti-imperialism, Greater Mexico provides a political and discursive analytic to trace how multiple revolutionary and radical imaginaries that inspired political activity circulated through people and organizations that made anti-imperialism, antiracism, and transnational organizing the center of their political analysis and practice.

A political imaginary and geographic space, Greater Mexico encompasses places where people of Mexican descent lived, worked, dreamed, and struggled to make their lives better. Tracing specific geographic, political (revolutionary), and creative (imaginary) terrains requires consideration of the relationship of people of Mexican descent living in the United States to Mexico and its people as a country or nation-state. This is already a challenging proposition, for the very notions of Mexican identity, citizenship, and race, for example, are highly contested in Mexico with regard to indigenous peoples, peoples of the African diaspora, and the complicated and contradictory history of *mestizaje*—as evidenced in nation-building social policy.[7]

LOCATING CHICANA/O LEFT IMAGINARIES IN THE *AMÉRICAS*

Revolutionary Imaginations, in the plural, emphasizes the multiple ways that an anticapitalist critique inspired solidarity through the creation and deployment of an array of political and cultural practices deeply rooted in everyday relationships of power, and geared toward organizing people for social justice and political change. These cultural and political practices underscore connections between artists and activists that shared an anti-imperialist politics. Together they worked to create a new world, enacting those conceptions in creative labor and imaginings as political projects and political struggles. Political imaginary is also a specific and differentiated way of talking about culture, a specific designation that indicates how a person, organization, or movement understands the relationship between what is considered possible, and how that possibility can, through collective work and struggle, have specific intentional results.[8] The political imaginary functions as a political weapon, analytical tool, and narrative arc: "culture is political because meanings are constitutive of processes that, implicitly or explicitly, seek to redefine social power."[9] By invoking the imaginary, I want to emphasize how political movements created new narratives, experimenting with new (and sometimes forgotten) retrofitted tactics often inspired by previous movements, ideas, theories, and experiences.[10] Counterhegemonic and autonomous (from state and capital) narratives of change can challenge the dominant story and inspire action to change the relationships of power that scaffold and create dominant stories.[11]

By the 1970s, the language of civil rights no longer sufficiently represented the political desires and demands of political movements, which were now composed of constituencies that had new goals and targets and employed a range of different tactics. Changing political laws did not necessarily alter behaviors or lead to equal economic opportunities, nor did reforming rules result in structural changes to access to opportunities, fair treatment, or freedom from state-sanctioned and extralegal violence.[12] As a result, Chicanas/os looked to other Third World peoples in the United States and solidarity with social movements in Mexico and Latin America, as well as inwardly, to challenge the limitations, contradictions, and oppressive characteristics of movement culture.[13]

Leftist politics and international solidarity connected seemingly disparate places that were intimately linked through people in struggle, as well as political and cultural organizations. Connecting experiences and analysis across geographic and political differences, these histories demonstrate how big ideas have a local impact on political and social conditions, historical patterns of change and continuity, and organizational forms and cultural imaginaries. The following chapters emphasize an internationalist perspective that cuts across ethnic and area studies approaches in the context of state violence, geopolitics, and human rights violations on the one hand, and political movements, anti-imperialism, cultural politics, and solidarity on the other. Political movements became internationalized and changed both the terms of engagement with state institutions (police, prisons, schools, the military, state houses, etc.) and themes that were central to the Chicana/o movement. A denser social history of radical anticapitalism and socialist-oriented ideas and politics during the Chicana/o movement paces the narrative, expanding what we know and offering a reconsideration of the significance of these transnational connections.

Similar to how activists and artists crossed geopolitical, cultural, linguistic, and creative borders, chapter 1, "Cartographies of the Chicana/o Left," maps key terms and methods within their historical context. It also introduces some preliminary responses to these questions as a way to situate this remapping of Chicana/o movement history. Chapter 2, "Mexico, Anticommunism, and the Chicana/o Movement," contextualizes the forthcoming chapters within post–World War II US/Mexican/Latin American history, focusing on how solidarity created from below by political movements threatened hemispheric security. By way of introducing the reader to the world of Chicana/o leftists, this chapter also addresses the national question, returning-home narratives of Chicanas/os, and the influence of Aztlán on the Chicana/o imaginary and the Chicana/o movement.

Chapter 3, "Nuevo Teatro Popular across the Américas," examines political solidarity and cultural production through the lens of the Nuevo Teatro Popular in Latin America, in Mexico, and among Chicanas/os in the United States. The chapter tells of Latin American theater festivals, the politics of post-1968 protest art and theater in Mexico, and Chicana/o Theater and the emergence of TENAZ (Teatro Nacional de Aztlán) in 1971.[14] Inspired by the ideas of "art-based community making," cultural workers "sought to push beyond the limits of the nation form, their struggles g[iving] rise to a ferment of aesthetic and cultural innovation."[15] Theater functioned as a social, cultural, and political dialogue. The chapter emphasizes the hemispheric nature of a movement that developed new methods of collective creation, public performances, and audience participation, as well as a trenchant anti-imperialist socialist analysis and political inspiration.

Chapter 4, "'Somos uno porque América es una': Quinto Festival de Teatro Chicano/Primer Encuentro Latino Americano de Teatro," examines a transcontinental theater festival. This unique Chicana/o-driven festival took place in Mexico City and Veracruz, Mexico, during July 1974. The gathering brought together theater groups from the United States, Mexico, and Central and South America, and more than seven hundred actors and artists from across the continent. The festival offers insight into the contentious relationship between revolutionary politics and art as revealed through the discussions, performances, and political encounters that took place during the two-week gathering.

Chapter 5, "'Por la reunificación de los Pueblos Libres de América en su Lucha por el Socialismo': Mexican Maoists, Chicana/o Revolutionaries, and the Dirty War in Mexico," begins by addressing San Antonio's legacy of radical political organizing during an understudied period in Mexico's political history. In 1975, Maoist-inspired Mexican revolutionaries founded the Partido Proletario Unido de América (the United Proletariat Party of America—PPUA), and Chicanas/os from the US Southwest joined the movement. The PPUA was one of more than forty rural and urban guerrilla organizations in operation during the 1960s and 1970s in Mexico, and the only one (so far as we yet know) that included

Chicanos.[16] It was in this context that Chicano activist Ramón Raúl Chacón was arrested, tortured, and imprisoned in October 1975. Chacón was a student and worked as a teacher at the Chicano university Colegio Jacinto Treviño in Mercedes, Texas.[17] Arrested with two others just south of Monterrey, Mexico, Chacón and his companions were accused by Mexican federal police agents of transporting arms to incite revolution in Mexico. The three arrestees and Mario Cantú, a well-known Chicano activist and businessman from San Antonio, who along with Chacón had been politicized while imprisoned in the federal penitentiary at Leavenworth, Kansas, in the late 1960s, were publicly accused of being members of the PPUA. Chacón was tortured into signing a confession. Cantú self-exiled to Europe, where he and other exiled Mexican artists and activists founded the European Committee in Solidarity with the Chicano People, which attempted to take the cases of human rights violations in Mexico and the United States to the international human rights community in Europe. This chapter demonstrates how Chicana/o activists were directly involved in creating a transborder socialist revolution against both the US and Mexican governments, and how the Chicana/o movement expanded to a European context.

Chapter 6, "Puente de Cristal (Crystal Bridge): Magdalena Mora, the 1975 Tolteca Strike, and Insurgent Feminism," examines a 1975 labor strike at the Tolteca Foods factory in Richmond, California, through the writings and political activity of Magdalena Mora. Most of the workers at Tolteca were women from Mexico, many undocumented, who had worked for years at the factory. They had tried to organize with local unions, yet their efforts were ignored by male leaders. The factory's owner, S&W Fine Foods, a subsidiary of the Canadian transnational corporation IMASCO, had purchased the family-owned factory in 1974. The leaders that emerged during the struggle not only sidestepped the union representatives, but also developed their own culture of leadership and organizing. These leaders took the meetings from the union hall to the community center while expanding the political discussion to include issues that directly affected undocumented women outside of the workplace. Local Marxist-identified activists and organizers (members of CASA—the Centro de Acción Social Autónomo—and the October League) were also instrumental in organizing community support for the strike and influential in supporting the development of leadership among the Tolteca workers. One of these participants was Magdalena Mora, a student leader at the University of California, Berkeley, who joined CASA after graduating from college in 1974. The second half of the chapter provides a close reading of Mora's articles and editorials published in CASA's newspaper, *Sin Fronteras*, between 1975 and 1978. Connecting international capitalism, public policy, and union organizing with cross-border movements in Mexico, Chile, and other parts of Latin America, Mora's writings and political work were an example of an insurgent feminism. While the gender politics and participation of women in CASA have been well documented, chapter 6 discusses how the role of undocumented women and insurgent feminist journalism transformed notions of transnational solidarity and community justice.[18]

The epilogue, "Solidarity/Beyond Solidarity," probes the legacy of the Chicana/o Left, exploring how themes in the narrative relate to the present, particularly solidarity in an age of globalization and neoliberalism. The epilogue also explores the uprising of the Zapatista Army of National Liberation in 1994 and how it resonated with Chicanisma/o.[19] Following others, I conclude that we should look at the 1970s for the emergence of what are now referred to as antiglobalization movements in a time of neoliberal security regimes of racial control.[20]

This book is an attempt to circulate these transnational and transcultural histories of solidarity in a manner similar to the way that these movements circulated the struggles at the time. By focusing on the political reference points that oriented peoples, places, events, and organizations, we can unpack and more fully understand the relationship between rhetorical, ideological, and cultural influences and the human dimension of political action and engagement. Political imaginaries, cultural exchanges, and the contradictions of the ideological and human dimensions of international solidarity help reimagine transnational and transcultural mapping of the Chicana/o movement, introducing a political and cultural cartography and a newly recovered genealogy. A genealogy, rather than historical recovery, recognizes that organizations have beginnings, but the influences that are inherited from previous struggles and passed on through people, organizations, ideas, political practices, memory, and experimentation condition the possibility of new social movements in specific moments of rupture.

Whereas the literature on transnationalism is varied and robust, I specifically draw on Inderpal Grewal to emphasize the complex and multiple characters of transnational "connectivities" rather than focusing on specific connections and the autonomous Marxist literature on the circulation of struggle.[21] Exploring how Chicana/o leftists and artists created a variety of strong, weak, and often unevenly connected relations with people and organizations in Latin America simultaneously opens up the category of political solidarity in relation to transnationalism. This, in turn, allows for a deeper understanding of the varied and diverse ways that people enacted solidarity and created the conditions for connectivities and connections—whether at a march or protest, a theater festival, or a land takeover or through textual acts of solidarity in articles, press releases, and artistic production. These connections and connectivities in turn circulated ideas, struggles, and cultures that affected the political analysis of capitalism, for example, or led to further cross-border collaborations. Ideas and struggles circulate through people, through organizations, and in cultural creativity (rather than only through products). These circulating struggles helped shape a transnational imaginary and identity that in turn influenced the political decisions of Chicana/o leftists and the political imaginary of the Chicana/o movement.

PERIOD AND THEMES: SOLIDARITY POLITICS AND THE POLITICS OF SOLIDARITY

While the narrative is paced by the decade and discussion of solidarity, the chapters are neither linear nor specifically contemporaneous. Not all chapters span the entire decade, and chapters overlap and diverge in time, theme, and geographic location. The events in the book happen between roughly 1973 and 1980, years characterized by global political, economic, and social crises. During the transition years to neoliberal capitalism, insights into how Chicana/o leftists interpreted, responded to, and in some cases accelerated the crises reveal significant strains of leftist political, social, and intellectual history in the United States. While events, places, and processes also pace the narrative, the social history approach provides a human dimension to the political engagement, exchanges, and disagreements that made up the Chicana/o movement experience, particularly issues involving solidarity, gender, and anticapitalism.

As in all social movements, there were differences, disagreements, and contradictions. For example, the strategies and tactics by which these changes were brought about; gender roles, sexual violence, and patriarchy in movement politics; issues of sexuality and homophobia; the means and compromises involved in raising funds; and the level of interaction with the state all worked as sites of political tension and possibility. While they have their uses, dichotomies and binaries limit the imaginary that expands what is possible, as "politics is not separate from lived experience or the imaginary world of what is possible; to the contrary, politics is about these things. Politics comprises the many battles to roll back constraints and exercise some power over, or create some space within, the institutions and social relationships that dominate our lives."[22]

I understand solidarity as direct action and a political weapon, a form of praxis, a social tool, and a space of knowledge production. Solidarity can include but is not limited to direct aid, circulating information about struggles, political interventions, and personal and organizational engagement with political movements in other countries. Why do we know so little about the anticapitalist Chicana/o Left? Despite their small numbers, Chicana/o activists from across the United States created organizations, projects, and political cultures inspired by socialist imaginaries that had a significant impact on US social movement history during the 1970s as well as political and cultural movements in Mexico and Latin America. Why did Chicanas/os look to Mexico, Central America, and Latin America, even traveling there to engage with its movements? What did they do once they arrived? How did the experiences of engaging and connecting with political movements from Mexico and Latin America influence, shape, and reshape the political and cultural imaginary, as well as the political practices of the Chicana/o movement? What did the Chicana/o movement look like to activists and artists in Mexico and Latin America? How were Mexican and Latin American leftists influenced by their engagement with Chicanas/os? How and why did Chicana/o artists go global? How did the involvement of Chicanas/os in Mexico and the politics of returning home influence their experiences and political imaginary? How were the different interpretations of the national question among Chicana/o leftists manifested in their political activities? Given that the Chicana/o Left is a "site of gender struggle," how did gender influence the ways that revolution was imagined and solidarity enacted?[23] How did radical and/or revolutionary politics influence gender relations? How did culture, theater, and performance function politically?

Engaging these questions, this book demonstrates how the Chicana/o Left, socialist imaginaries, and the Chicana/o movement changed throughout the 1970s by looking at different forms of solidarity over the decade, not as an evolution or progression, but in regard to the self-activity and collective organizing of openly leftist artists, organizers, journalists, and self-identified revolutionaries. Chicana/o artists and activists were in search of new forms and content, new political inspirations and projects. Inspired by the Mexican and Cuban revolutions and the larger terrain of the Latin American Left, solidarity translated into social justice, anti-imperialist art, and creative political organizing. Mexican and Latin American leftists saw Chicanas/os as potential allies, sources for political support and international solidarity, and voices against empire inside the belly of the US beast, complicating the idea that Chicanas/os are "junior partners" in empire.[24] In addition, Chicana/o leftist politics opened possibilities and inspired the political imaginaries of Mexican and Latin American leftists to include Latinas/os living in the United States as part of their political analysis. To be clear, this book does not propose to provide systematic answers to all these questions, and in fact it intends to generate more questions than answers. Each chapter is part of a whole that offers some first responses to these inquiries. Chapters 2 through 5 are set in Mexico City, several states in Mexico, and central and south Texas, while chapter 6 is largely situated in California.

For folks involved in struggles that aimed to change society and themselves in the process, contradictions were both messy and generative. We cannot and should not romanticize, create heroes from, or pathologize the behaviors and decisions of people involved in political movements with socialist dreams, revolution, or radical politics; nor can alliances and coalitions be assumed to form naturally or "obviously," or to exist without their own contradictions. Solidarity required struggle, and it was a struggle to create and maintain solidarity. Alliances, coalitions, networks, and connections were not characteristics of only radical, revolutionary, or transnational politics. People and organizations that shared a political perspective on power, transformation, and change also cultivated alliances and coalitions, as well as other forms of solidarity politics. A particular identity does not have an a priori relationship with a specific political position, belief, or analysis.[25] Nor does it automatically imply solidarity with other people experiencing similar conditions, whether nearby or far away.[26] Solidarity, alliances, long-term coalitions, and sustained political movements were built through struggle and trust. These networks also circulated struggles, and that presupposes time spent together and collaboration.

The participation of women changed the course of these histories. At the same time, there were many different forms of feminism and anti-feminism within the movement. I focus on insurgent feminists who formed a structural critique of the emerging security state in relation to capitalism, also examining their actions on individual terms. In defining insurgent feminism, I draw from Denise A. Segura and Beatriz M. Pesquera: "a political tradition that contests the social relations of production and reproduction. Women who articulate these sentiments call for Chicana self-determination which encompasses a struggle against both personal and institutional manifestations of racial discrimination, patriarchy, and class exploitation."[27] Insurgent feminism exists in relation to Chicana liberal feminism. The political trajectories of insurgent feminists transformed the view that women had of themselves, of how they participated in spaces, the written analysis, and cultural production and simultaneously created spaces for Chicanas to create and develop their own political imaginaries. In turn, these efforts affected social movement activity, leadership styles and decisions, the political imaginary of what was possible, and how to make those possibilities materialize in everyday life.

An internationalist, leftist political imaginary, characterized by particular political practices and cultural forms, made possible a politics of solidarity. Solidarity is a political relationship that helps reframe social movements as a category. To narrate the category of solidarity through Chicana/o internationalist histories of the 1970s, employing an analytic of circulation of struggles and cycles of struggles, is to reframe the periodization of the Chicana/o movement in relation to the long 1960s in the United States and Latin America and reconsider the impact of 1968 as a global(izing) narrative.[28] This book emphasizes that social movement activity continued in the context of the economic crisis of the 1970s, a decade that witnessed the increased momentum of "law and order" politics, anti-immigrant organizing, the rise of a "New American Right," and the recomposition of global capital.[29] In other words, political movements created and accelerated crisis.[30] The Chicana/o movement, though locating its own origins in the mid-1960s, continued headlong into the late 1970s and early 1980s, a continuity of the civil rights, cultural nationalism, and community power–based organizing characteristics combined with an emerging internationalist and leftist trajectory and a move toward the language of human rights. The point is not to replace 1968 with 1973, or 1975 with 1980, as the "end of the movement," but to emphasize cycles of struggles that recompose civil society and the specific acceleration of historical moments (elongated in years) which condition the possibility that "crisis [will] occur when the social formation can no longer be reproduced on the basis of the previous system of social relations."[31]

Solidarity was a weapon of the US Third World Left, a political strategy, analytical tool, and way of envisioning action and participation on a variety of interrelated levels. The politics of solidarity is a conceptual tool for investigating political connections, social networks, and direct action during the 1970s. To make solidarity observable, and to build on the work of the Center for Convivial Research and Autonomy, I propose that solidarity was a political weapon, a form of praxis, a social tool, and a space of knowledge production about struggle and prefiguring a different society.[32] International solidarity was about the local, even as the imaginary (and the minds imagining) crossed borders, sojourning with new ideas, possibilities, and inspirations.[33] It was enacted locally—in domestic spaces, political organizations, community centers, street corners, restaurants, and the localized politics that were the consequence of national and international political decisions.

Studies of political solidarity must confront its contradictions with its own political histories, including the often unexamined power relations between people situated in different political, social, and economic conditions (as between the United States and Latin America, or in the designation of north-to-south solidarity rather than south-to-south). Examining how Chicanas/os reimagined and deployed the political practice of solidarity during the 1970s helps explain how solidarity is articulated as an intellectual tool, as well as how it is limited if not closely examined for relations of colonial domination—even between people of color and black people in the United States and people in the Third World. Solidarity that does not confront the structural issues of economic, political, and social control can instead replicate notions of charity, infantilization, and relations of colonial violence and domination.[34] Solidarity politics was already conditioned by contradictions—between participants, and often between organizations across borders. These *encuentros*—at festivals, community centers, and homes; in organizational meetings and prisons; or during a land takeover—provided the possibility for new political, personal, and cultural relationships. In narrating the category of solidarity, we have to read through a politics of solidarity at different moments, when the Chicana/o Left could decipher their more prescient questions about capitalism, nation, and revolution.

As a way to open up the category of solidarity as a weapon, praxis, tool, and space to prefigure new possibilities, five elements of solidarity politics highlight the political function and practice of solidarity: (1) direct or indirect aid, (2) active elements/interventions, (3) circulation of information and ideas, (4) the more complicated issue of involvement/ participation, and (5) the moments of articulation of an internationalist solidarity. Moments of articulation, which include the previous four characteristics, specifically focus on how struggles that resonated with and influenced the politics of the Chicana/o movement reconfigure the historical timeline of movement activity. Aid includes everything from printing newspapers and books, to providing weapons and ammunition, to other monetary support, including offsetting travel expenses or supporting the material necessities for organizing festivals, protests, or long-term campaigns. Active elements and/or interventions pertain to the festivals, protests, public performances, press conferences, and other actions done in the name of solidarity. The circulation of information and ideas was a way to inform, educate, and provide the opportunity for people to become more aware of a particular movement or issues through newspaper articles, editorials, theater, community gatherings, or house meetings, but the emphasis is on the content as much as the context (active elements).[35] Rather than levels of participation, the focus is on what people did, how they did it, and the meanings given to their actions. This is the more complicated element of solidarity—participation and involvement. Said another way, the difference between active elements/intervention and involvement/ participation depends on the organization and its intention or mission. The difference is both political and strategic, but it is not about integrity or political astuteness. Interventions could be made by individuals who were or were not part of organized political formations. But to consider involvement and participation in regard to organizational affiliation, specifically socialist anti-imperialist Chicana/o-Mexicana/o organizations, offers analytical and political nuance in understanding the complex and layered elements of international solidarity as they played out between people in organizations. Not everyone in this book engaged or enacted all five elements of solidarity, but those who were part of organizations or artists collectives did have multiple moments of articulation that in turn had numerous and diverse impacts and consequences. Solidarity as a conceptual tool can renovate academic and political debate in the context of globalization.

Solidarity is situated knowledge and political action. It can also be antiblack if it erases the distinct and particular struggles of the black diaspora, specifically the antiblack nature of coalitions and the notion of people of color.[36] Solidarity is also a "site of gender struggle."[37] As H. L. T. Quan specifies in relation to the feminist analysis and methods of the black radical tradition, "gender as an infrastructure of resistance" offers a both political and analytical reading of power and political movements, as well as engaging a feminism without borders that is simultaneously attuned to differently situated people and politics.[38]

As a way to talk about the politics of refusal and the participation of people in international solidarity and leftist political organizing outside of established leftist parties or unions, I use social factory, a political/conceptual tool developed by the Italian autonomist Left in the 1960s and 1970s.[39] The social factory is a way to critically analyze and map how capitalist social relations have attempted to colonize all of life, that is, the time and space when not at work, as well as how people have refused these impositions and in turn created new forms and practices of political organizing. A post-Fordism concept, the social factory is the terrain of political struggle where different types of solidarity unfold and where solidarity is always emerging. The social factory helps to center events and rallies not tied to official parties or organizations, and to look at how people organize with each other in all types of spaces. More complex than building space, the social factory is where people can possibly refuse the imposition of capitalist relationships of hierarchy and coercion, including patriarchy, homophobia, and antiblack racism, simultaneously creating new social relationships, cultural imaginaries, and political possibilities.

A NOTE ON ARCHIVES

This is a subaltern history "from way, way below."[40] Effecting this recovery required investigating a wide variety of sources. At the more formal level, I combed through archives held in special collections at formal academic institutions; at Lecumberri, the federal prison in Mexico City that was transformed into the National Archives; in the homes of former political prisoners in Mexico; and under "pyramids" in Cuernavaca, Mexico. In addition, I sought out and recovered *testimonios*, poems, recordings, posters, remnants of archives created in struggle, living archives, and other forms of memory. Interviews and questions were based on personal and political relationships. These relationships and questions frame not only the "stories for the book" but also the leftist political imaginary that inspired my own politics, hemmed in and limited by contradictions and blind spots. Unless otherwise indicated, all translations are my own. Some quotations are rendered in a mixture of Spanish and English. For primary sources, I have conserved the grammar and the use of accent marks of the documents themselves. Preserving bilingual, bicultural code switching is part of a decolonial methodology.

In 2002 the Mexican government's intelligence agency, CISEN, declassified and made public the archives of the Secretary of National Defense. These archives include extensive, detailed documentation of the Guerra Sucia (dirty war) against political organizations in Mexico during the 1960s and 1970s. "Despite [their] limitations," writes Tanalís Padilla, "these sources . . . are the eyes and ears of the state, the sum of the views of these agents often determined official policy . . . [and] it is possible to glean *campesino* voices from these documents, as infiltrators reproduced speeches, reconstructed meetings, and detailed planned actions."[41] I appreciate the willingness of some of the participants to revisit and analyze these times and to speak about outlawed political activities. Not everyone I contacted responded, and out of respect for their political decisions and lives, I have not named them other than by alias.

The anticapitalism of the past was dismissed by many of the same social forces (and people) that dismiss anticapitalism in the present; whether on the streets, across borders, in the academy, or in the neighborhood, alternatives to the status quo, including Chicana/o Left politics, continue to grow in strength.

LIMITATIONS

This book does not directly address the relationship between Chicanas/os and indigenous peoples in Mexico or the United States. The absence of references or discussion of black people in Mexico within the histories recovered here does not mean that black people—Afro-Mexicanos—were not present. Though way beyond the scope of this book, and though race plays out in different ways in Mexico with regard to indigenous and (denied) black populations, the views that Chicanas/os had of México Profundo—indigenous and black Mexico—are vital to any scholarship that would build on the recent studies of multiracial alliances between African Americans and Latinas/os in the United States.

CHAPTER 1

CARTOGRAPHIES OF THE CHICANA/O LEFT

Chicana was really an inclusive term . . . it really included all of Latin America.

OLGA TALAMANTE

WHY DO WE KNOW so little about the Chicana/o Left? That we know little is partly "understandable because of the small size of the Third World Left relative to the larger nationalist movements," but in her book *Black, Brown, Yellow, and Left*, Laura Pulido argues that this unfamiliarity "*reflects an ambivalence, at best, toward anti-capitalism.*"[1] At the same time, not everyone that identified with leftist anticapitalist politics has shared the same vision of struggle and organizational needs, or even the same analysis. Chicana/o internationalism has been part of a longer genealogy of leftist-inspired organizing by people of Mexican descent in the United States. The 1970s was a time when solidarity deeply influenced the political imaginary and social movement activity. Inspired by the Cuban Revolution, anticolonial struggles in Asia and Africa, and the momentum of Black Freedom struggles and the US Third World Left, Chicano/a leftists expanded their political activity to engage with political movements in Mexico and Latin America. Transnational solidarity was imagined and enacted in local contexts and cross-border political projects, providing for an alternate political, ideological, and geographical mapping of the Chicana/o movement. I propose that the Chicana/o Mexicana/o Left played an important role connecting the US Third World Left—the Black, Red, and Yellow power movements—with the Latin American Left. By engaging a politics of solidarity, the Chicana/o Left drew on a longer history of anticapitalist politics among the communities of Greater Mexico during the nineteenth and twentieth centuries.

One really key thing that happened is that I became very involved in third world alliances, cross-ethnic alliance building, [and] coalition building. . . . It wasn't that well received by some people in MEChA and within the Chicano movement, but I just really saw that we needed to be, and in fact we were, part of a larger reality . . .

So it was like we were part of this continental reality. I would say that's one of the political realizations and stands that I began to take coming back. . . . I pushed for alliances with African Americans and Asians and Native Americans in terms of the struggles that we had at the university level. I think that's how it affected me. I absolutely found myself identifying as a Chicana as a political identity; and I saw that Chicana was really an inclusive term, that it really included all of Latin America. That's not how people generally see it.

OLGA TALAMANTE, 2005

Hermano Nicaragüense
hermano salvadoreño
eschucha el clamor Chicano
que te canta un carnal Aztleño
Desde las trieras meshicas
hasta la punta de Chile
de las nieves Alasqueñas
a las islas del Caribe
En Aztlán, como en Puerto Rico,
y también en Panamá,
llevamos el mismo sueño
de encontrar la libertad.

Pero hay un pesadilla,
Que nos roba unidad,
Pa'que ese sueño precioso
Se nos puede realizar,

Porque hay un pesadilla
Que nos roba unidad
y de ese mal sueño yanqui
Es tiempo despertar (bis)
"PESADILLA YANQUI" (YANKEE NIGHTMARE), IN
EL TRIO CASINDIO, BY JOSÉ MONTOYA (LETRA)[2]

INTRODUCTION

Before Olga Talamante was tortured and imprisoned by military and security agents of the Argentinian state from 1974 to 1976, she had traveled for three years throughout Mexico, Central America, and South America.[3] By the age of twenty-two, Talamante had lived, worked, studied, and been politically active in several countries, enacting various forms of solidarity. Born in Mexico, Talamante worked in the agricultural fields of California and was active in the Movimiento Estudiantil Chicano de Aztlán (MEChA) and United Farm Workers (UFW) boycotts. In 1970, a political/research trip to Mexico with other Chicanas/os in a Volkswagen van changed her life. Having seen the Mexican theater group Los Mascarones perform in Santa Cruz, California, she sought them out in Mexico City. The meeting never took place, as Los Mascarones were hiding from the authorities in the aftermath of the government paramilitary group Los Halcones's attack on a peaceful protest in June 1971.[4] As they traveled through central Mexico to Chiapas, and later to Central America, the group was stopped, interrogated, and almost deported in Honduras for carrying "subversive literature." On this and subsequent trips, Talamante engaged with artists and political movements in Mexico, Central America, and South America, experiencing the state violence of dirty wars in the United States, Mexico, and Argentina firsthand. Talamante intentionally pursued solidarity politics across a number of registers, creating and expanding connections between political movements, organizations, and people in the different countries and regions of the *Américas*. In her analysis she connected the policies that created the conditions of life south of the US-Mexican border to US policies that conditioned the possibilities of her own life, as well as the lives of her family members and community, during her time as a farmworker in California in the 1960s. Her experiences south of the US-Mexican border (predating her torture and imprisonment in Argentina in 1974) influenced Talamante's political outlook upon her return to California to finish a bachelor's degree in Latin American Studies at the University of California–Santa Cruz. Talamante centered anti-imperialism, feminism, and solidarity in her politics, creating coalitions with other Third World students and Chicana feminists. As a result, she came to understand "Chicana as an inclusive term that included all of Latin America."[5]

The lyrics, arrangement, and affect of "Pesadilla Yanqui" are a different iteration of international solidarity. Political movements in Mexico and Latin America influenced culture and cultural production by Chicana/o artists during the *movimiento*. Poets, muralists, musicians, novelists, and *teatristas* were inspired to experiment and, in experimenting, to create an internationalist imaginary of political struggle. For example, "songs of solidarity"[6] circulated word of struggles while inspiring the political imaginary of people involved in social movement activity, in this case, hemispheric/continental solidarity against the common enemy: Yankee imperialism. José Montoya, Chicano poet, musician, and artist, and one of the original members of the Royal Chicano Air Force, a multimedia art collective formed in Sacramento, used the lyrics to "Pesadilla Yanqui" to emphasize how continental unity and solidarity is a nightmare for the *yanquis*. This political insight signaled the urgent need to wake up from the nightmare of US imperialism and create a new political reality through solidarity across the Spanish-speaking world. Inspired by the "necessary theater" of Teatro Campesino, the Rebel Chicano Art Force, later called the Royal Chicano Air Force, was an art collective founded in 1969 as part of the larger Chicana/o arts movement of the time.[7] Montoya had been a member of the San Francisco Bay–area Mexican American Liberation Art Front before founding the RCAF.[8] An example of cultural production grounded in anti-imperialism and hemispheric solidarity that emphasized the connections between struggles across the Américas, "Pesadilla Yanqui" locates Chicanas/os in Aztlán as an active part of the Latin American Left and helps us reimage the political and cultural cartography of the Chicana/o movement. The cultural knowledge and political analysis communicated through the lyrics and sentiment of "Pesadilla Yanqui," a clamor for continental solidarity similar to Talamante's message, reflected this inspiration.

Talamante and Montoya saw that uniting across borders amounted to both a refusal of US imperialism and the creation of cultures of resistance and politics of world building. For Talamante, Montoya, and the many other voices in this book, Chicana/o as a political identity engaged *a larger reality*, one that conceptualized Chicana(o) *as an inclusive term that included all of Latin America*. To include all of Latin America required the political, cultural, and intellectual labor to create both a political imaginary and a strategy for organizing and connecting movements. Talamante's reference to the reticence and pushback from some people in MEChA and within the Chicano movement, a point she also makes in regard to the response to feminism by some people within the Chicano movement, attests to the organizing work necessary to connect the struggles of Chicanas/os with ideas and people that emerged from political movements in Mexico and Latin America.

To fully understand the trajectories and importance of the Chicana/o Left in the 1970s, Chicana/o, US, Mexican, and Latin American history must all be considered. The political and cultural imaginary of Latin America, Mexico, and Cuba influenced early Chicana/o movement activists and organizations. Elizabeth "Betita" Martínez, Enriqueta Vasquez, and Luis Valdez all visited Cuba in the first years of the revolution, and each was inspired to apply that influence to the Chicana/o movement. Betita Martínez, known at the time as Elizabeth Sutherland, wrote the first book that took an intersectional approach, analyzing class, gender, and race in Cuban society.[9] Martínez and Vasquez would cowrite *Viva La Raza* in 1974, centering the varied labor, student, and land-based movements of the time while emphasizing a critique of racial capitalism. Valdez, openly inspired by the Cuban Revolution, infused the San Francisco Mime Troupe with his own life experiences, creating the initial stirrings of a Chicana/o theater movement.

Because I trace a particular genealogy of the Chicana/o movement that is different from *how people generally see it*, it is necessary to provide an overview of the "worldview" of the Chicana/o Left, the historical conditions in which decisions were made, and the historical struggles that influenced how they imagined what was possible. In other words, because the Chicana/o Left was not separate from the broader Chicana/o movement, ideas and politics (revolutionary or otherwise) can be seen to overlap in the narratives of how the Chicana/o Left influenced the Chicana/o movement, and how the Chicana/o movement was influenced by Mexico and Latin America. That attempts at Third World alliances, as well as Talamante's and others' feminist politics, were not well received by some people within the Chicano movement highlights the stakes of remembering and recovering these stories of the struggle to create solidarity.[10] This was a complicated endeavor given the tumultuous and ever-changing geopolitical and economic relationships among countries in the Americas, especially during the twentieth century, but it had roots in the previous epochs and the hegemonic influence of US economic and foreign policy toward Latin America. The deep resentment many Latin Americans felt toward the imposition of US culture and politics across the continent was akin to Chicana/o rejection of US Anglo-Saxon cultural norms, further complicating how we understand these hemispheric/continental connections.[11]

Extending this framework, Alicia Schmidt Camacho writes,

> By the 1930s . . . in the wake of new immigration policing and the mass deportations that followed, a new generation of Mexican American and immigrant activists and writers questioned the primacy of the national sovereignty over the historical claims of Mexican people to the border territories. Out of their histories of border insurrection and racial terror, these intellectuals elaborated visions of "Greater Mexico" that superseded the national boundary.[12]

This work picks up Schmidt Camacho's trajectory of Greater Mexico and the leftist-inspired freedom dreams of the Chicana/o movement during the 1970s.[13]

A political imaginary is as much about a vision of something different as it is about effecting that vision. A political imaginary animates across different, overlapping registers: it reconsiders the personal and local in terms of community power and power relationships between people, while connecting struggles across political, cultural, and imagined borders. A revolutionary imaginary critiques the roots of capitalist power, the structures of political domination, and the relationships of control within society. Most importantly, it envisions a different society with alternative values and social relations, and takes action to create that society. To be sure, leftist political imaginaries can inspire and influence, but they do not necessarily lead to revolutionary politics and practices. In other words, movements must be "built and organized."[14]

EL MOVIMIENTO: CRISIS, RUPTURE, AND OPENINGS IN THE 1970S

The 1970s are characterized as a time of decline for the cycle of social movements that had begun in the post–World War II period. The commonly rendered narrative is one of a lost decade: "Americans during the 1970s commonly described their world and their future in a language of loss, limits, and failure."[15] The 1970s were years of shifting terrains, strategies, and goals, always understood within the context of increased state violence and the recomposition of capital—in direct response to these very movements.[16] The struggle for economic and political equality in fact intensified. New political formations, a recomposing working class, the circulation of struggles across political and geographic borders, and increasingly localized activity and political organizing centered on community power, self-determination, and creative projects that reflected the worlds people wanted to create as much as the worlds they were critiquing. Some scholars claim that these movements fractured the American Left by focusing on "identity" issues that displaced class as a category of analysis, therefore allowing the political Right to increase in power and appeal.[17] Others have argued that the movements transformed protest into policy and therefore the struggle ceased to have the same urgency.[18] Scholars across disciplines have already observed that there is no simple "1960s" narrative.[19] Periodization, thematic issues, analytical perspectives, and other theoretical questions continue to both characterize and challenge the historiography of this time period, reminding us that historical narratives are politics by other means.[20]

The year 1968 has become synonymous with global rebellions on every continent. The consequences of the "eros effect" of 1968 were felt in the 1970s, the same decade when the US Third World Left emerged.[21] During the 1970s the global political and economic system of Keynesian capitalism and liberal governance was challenged as anticolonial movements gained independence and global economic recession spread as a consequence of this political upheaval. These crises, a result of political movement activity during the previous four decades, were the terrain on which people created new organizations and social relations.

Though the Chicana/o movement had its origins as a generational struggle in the mid-1960s, the movement's expansion was most evident during the early and mid-1970s. This book is about the Chicana/o Left and solidarity politics, but without a general understanding of the Chicana/o movement and its relationship to the US Third World Left, it is difficult to situate the influence of Mexico and Latin America on the political imaginary.

The Chicana/o movement can be understood as people of Mexican descent organizing for social change, political power, community control of resources, cultural pride, economic equality, and dignity.[22] Cross-class and intergenerational, the various political causes advocated by people of Mexican descent were "a social movement that began in the late 1960s and ran its course through the late 1970s. Although certainly influenced by the rise in social protest actions in the United States and throughout the world, the Chicano movement itself arose in response to a unique set of social, geographic, and economic experiences."[23] Overall the movement shared a general struggle for liberation from different oppressions: structural racial and class domination; everyday forms of state and economic violence; internal issues within the movement of the interconnected oppressions of sexism, patriarchy, and homophobia; and concerns with cultural authenticity. "A diffuse movement," Jorge Mariscal writes, "cross-cut by regional, gender, [sexuality] and class issues, the Movimiento . . . was a mass mobilization dedicated to a wide range of social projects, from ethnic separatism to socialist internationalism, from electoral politics to institutional reform and even armed insurrection."[24]

Anticapitalism, or at least a critique of the US economic order, existed within the movement and was coupled with a critique of white supremacy and Jane and Jim Crow in the US South and Southwest.[25] The influence of anticapitalist and anti-imperialist organizations that connected a political analysis of capitalism with specific organizing strategies and solidarity politics increased as the 1970s unfolded. The Chicana/o movement was not just against oppressive structures and exploitation. People organized to imagine and create a different world in which community power, control of resources, and local self-determination were manifest in organizations representing the needs and struggles of different sectors of the Chicana/o-Mexicana/o community.

The "acceleration in a different register" of the Chicana/o movement began in the 1950s and was rooted in the organizing within the labor sectors and communities where Mexican people lived.[26] In the following decade, Filipino and Mexican laborers founded the United Farm Workers in 1962. The Plan de Santa Barbara and Plan de Aztlán, both written in 1969 and presented to Chicano/a students at the Denver Youth Conference, served as ideological documents and historical markers that inspired students, labor organizers, *pintos* and *pintas* (Chicanas/os in prison), and cultural workers. Together, these markers introduced some cohesion to a deeply complex and emerging movement.

People and movements, communities in struggle, and organizations for change all need usable pasts. As Lee Bebout argues, "The concept of Aztlán as a Chicano nation moved to the foreground of Chicano political discourse, becoming a dominant ideological and rhetorical trope."[27] The Plan de Santa Barbara and Plan de Aztlán charted a particular course for the Chicano movement, providing "a means of imagining community and mediating the heterogeneity of the movement" that permitted Chicanas/os to organize around broadly understood concepts of home, nation, gender, and sexuality and to push back against the limitations of the nationalist imaginary.[28] The plans were diagnostic and prescriptive, blueprinting a historical retrofitting as well as the specific goals that the Chicana/o movement writ large should pursue. Aztlán connected imagination and process, possibility and sometimes conflicting goals; it "functioned as a commitment mechanism, allowing activists engaged in different strategies and struggling toward disparate goals to rally around a singular, if often multivalent, concept."[29] It offered a commitment mechanism that both organized community imagination and set limits on what folks should imagine, forcing the question: a past usable for whom? From the 1960s onward, Chicana feminists as well as gay and lesbian Chicanas/os challenged the nationalism and heteropatriarchy (though "sexism" and "machismo" were the terms used at the time) of the movement's cultural nationalist origins and the founding documents relied on to construct a usable past.

The Chicano Moratorium against the Vietnam War first took place in 1970, with some thirty thousand people organized to protest US imperialism in Indochina. In 1971, Francisca Flores founded *Regeneración* (named after the Magonista PLM newspaper published from 1900 to 1918), and Anna Nieto Gomez and Adelaida Del Castillo founded the feminist journal *Las Hijas de Cuahtemoc*, both pioneering publications in Chicana feminist thought. These journals, as well as the newspaper *Sin Fronteras*, the majority-female editorial collective of the New Mexico–based movement paper *Grito del Norte*, and the production of Chicana/o theater, also demonstrate the centrality of print culture to Chicano/a radicalism.[30] These touchstones are not arbitrary. They highlight the connections between farmworkers, students, antiwar organizing, labor struggles, and insurgent feminisms that help remap the narrative of the Chicana/o movement within the context of cultural nationalism and international solidarity. Cultural nationalism, as an idea and a political project, deeply influenced the Chicana/o movement. "Cultural nationalism or ethnic pride ('Brown Power')," writes Jorge Mariscal, "functions as the site of a community's collective identity, organization, and passage into praxis as a historical agent."[31] Cultural nationalism, with an "underpinning of compulsory normative Chicano family romance" that emphasized male authority, nationalism, and specific familial roles, reflected the externalization in public politics of the internal dynamics of the assumed heteropatriarchal family order.[32] Yet rather than rely on a primary ideology from which others emerged, the Chicana/o movement was informed by "multiple ideologies."[33]

MEXICO, AZTLÁN, BORDERS, AND HOME

Mexico existed as an imaginary, a place, an inspiration, and a memory, before and sometimes simultaneously with Chicanas/os actually living in Mexico.[34] The context and content of these experiences in turn influenced that imaginary and how it inspired actions and the meaning given to actions. Mexico was a meaning-making place that inspired Chicanas/os to dream, to create possibilities, and to act politically. For some who had family in Mexico and who perhaps visited often, their image and understanding of that nation was different from that of someone who had never visited, did not speak Spanish well, or grew up in US society being taught history from the perspective of the winners. In the 1960s young people of Mexican descent adopted "Chicana" and "Chicano" to reclaim a pejorative term and honor their Mexican roots while demanding a place in the political, social, and cultural publics running counter to US citizenship and assimilation narratives. For Chicanas/os and Mexicanas/os who knew about, supported, or were directly involved in political movements, Mexico was both the homeland and an international political destination.

Simultaneously, the Plan de Santa Barbara and Plan de Aztlán centered a nationalist male culture within the very concept of Aztlán.[35] Aztlán is considered to be the homeland of the Nahuatl-speaking peoples that migrated south to the valley of Mexico, Tenochtitlan, in the eleventh and twelfth centuries. From this view, Chicanas/os and people of Mexican descent living in the United States represent a return-to-the-source narrative. So in a sense, we are talking about a triple return: from Aztlán to Tenochtitlan, from Mexico to the United States, and from Aztlán back to Mexico.

Aztlán as a concept and a geographic space, as myth and history, consisted of the recovery of an indigenous past and present combined with an open and defiant refusal of the terms of assimilationist, citizenship-based identity politics. Striking back against assimilationist citizenship narratives, the Plan de Aztlán and Plan de Santa Barbara grounded "the embrace of a proud cultural heritage forcefully resist[ing] the idea that success and upward mobility would be accomplished through melting pot assimilation . . . [making] evident that narrative of myth and history operate as an alternative site of struggle, a discursive space through which psychological colonization can be contested and decolonization can emerge."[36] As the foundation for retrofitted memory as political project and imaginary, Aztlán, Los Planes, and the movements that involved people of Mexican descent (in the factories, fields, prison yards, streets, stages, classrooms, or occupied land) were alternative sites of struggle, political strategies, and different ways of imagining the world. Aztlán could be anticapitalist, even if not theorized or imagined in that way, but perhaps most importantly, "amidst this Chicano post-modernist reconstruction, Aztlán touched a deeper spiritual core that addressed the profound need of the Chicano to find a spiritual homeland."[37] These were more than questions of identity, nation, and culture. Aztlán can be understood as the spiritual element of the Chicana/o movement that proposed an alternative set of social, political, and economic relationships. These diverse meanings enriched the struggle even as they came into conflict with Marxists and socialist-inspired Chicana/o leftists, and particularly Mexican and Latin American anti-imperialists.

To be clear, the breadth and depth of the Chicana/o movement cannot be reduced to specific struggles, ideological positions, issue-based politics, or cultural nationalism. Instead, I understand the *movimiento* as a complex and contradictory history of people of Mexican descent creating organizations to engage in political activity that improves conditions for communities and individuals. The *movimiento* existed wherever people of Mexican descent lived, worked, played, and dreamed, in prisons, schools, factories, and fields; on street corners and in homes between families and lovers; in community centers and across borders. The difference for Chicana/o leftists was in a clear anti-capitalist analysis that led to new political practices and a collective cultural creativity that helped foster an imagination made real through international solidarity.

THE CHICANA/O MOVEMENT AND THE US THIRD WORLD LEFT IN THE 1970S

The Chicana/o Left was distinctive in its anticapitalism and its radical approach to the national question, cultural nationalism, and Aztlán. In referring to the Chicana/o Left, I specifically mean people, organizations, imaginaries, and projects that advanced a critique of capitalism and (US) imperialism, while focusing their political activity on local struggles concerning labor rights, community power, human rights, socialism, and international solidarity. Though I emphasize a distinction between the Chicana/o Left and the Chicana/o movement, the former emerged from and within the *movimiento,* but also had longer roots in twentieth-century leftist politics.

The Chicana/o Left emerged from the interstices of the Chicana/o movement's cultural nationalism, the radical history of Mexican labor organizing, and the localized politics of community control. Consequently, the Chicana/o Left offered new analytical tools and different solutions to issues of police brutality, economic exploitation, political solidarity, and multiracial organizing. It critiqued and then moved beyond the demands stemming from the War on Poverty initiatives for resources and community control.[38] A politics of solidarity led Chicanas/os to engage in creating a socialist state in the United States, Mexico, and Argentina. During the 1970s the Chicana/o Left emphasized responses to police brutality, foreign policy, and human rights violations in the United States, to the victims of the Dirty War in Mexico, and to US collusion with dictators in Latin America.

The Chicana/o Left formed part of the larger US Third World Left, which was committed to "eradicating colonialism, imperialism, racism, class exploitation, and, in some admittedly rare instances, homophobia and misogyny."[39] The term "Third World" denotes a particular political consciousness linking race and capitalism in the context of the national and international implications of a Cold War fought to control territory and ideological influences across the globe.[40] Chicana/o leftists were similarly "[f]orged between the New Left and the civil rights movement, between the counterculture and the Black arts movements[;] [as part of] this US Third World Left [they] created cultural, material and ideological links to the Third World as a mode through which to contest U.S. economic, racial and cultural arrangements." In her book *Soul Power,* Cynthia A. Young explains, "This appellation *Third World* served as a shorthand for leftists of color . . . signifying their opposition to a particular economic and racial world order."[41] The Third World Left in the United States was one of the most compelling manifestations of these impressive efforts to organize in the face of the era's political and economic tumult. Chicana/o leftists and the US Third World Left both inherited and (re)created a "project" with a longer history than the 1960s: the Third World.[42] The organizing necessary to make this project a reality in many different nations united activists across borders of all types while creating new cultural practices in music, art, theater, and literature, as well as in the exploration of "how . . . ideas, political strategies, styles, cultural practices, and rhetoric mutate and adapt across multiple diasporas."[43] Chicana/o international solidarity against US imperialism connected the movement to global anticolonial struggles and the longer genealogy of leftist and anti-imperialist–inspired political organizing by people of Mexican descent.

Lorena Oropeza locates 1971 as a pivotal year in the acceleration of Chicana/o Left politics.[44] The Chicano Moratorium march against the Vietnam War marked an escalation in Chicana/o militancy. A number of factors immediately situate the expansion of Chicana/o Left politics in the 1970s. First, the police violence during the march and the murder of Chicano journalist Ruben Salazar amplified the anger toward law enforcement, further demonstrating the long history of legal and extralegal violence against Chicanas/os.[45] Second, the limitations of political reform were revealed by the "inability of La Raza Unida Party to achieve interregional unity and electoral success beyond southern Texas," which in turn "set the Chicano movement into decline and provided Marxist Leninists with an opportunity to advance an ideological alternative to Chicanismo among Chicana/o activists."[46] Third, deepening economic crises in capitalism, shrinking and shifting labor markets, limited options for safe housing and education, and heightened neighborhood policing increased urban social tensions. Fourth, connections expanded between Chicana/o students and artists and their counterparts in Mexico and Latin America. Most significantly, a long history of leftist political movements by people of Mexican descent in the United States, in combination with these shifting social, political, and economic forces, conditioned the possibility for the Chicana/o Left in the 1970s.

Chicana/o leftists concluded that US imperialism was a global political and economic system that had to be destroyed. Analytically and historically, it is important to differentiate between straightforward, formal, established, and institutionalized colonial relations through direct political, economic, and legal control of colonies and protectorate states, and a more informal colonialism that relies on a collaborating capitalist class of national elites, "markets" and trade agreements, diplomacy and cultural exports, and military strategies to induce coercion and cooperation.[47] By legalizing policies that had disproportionately affected the working-class and indigenous populations of Mexico and Latin America, the United States saw itself as benevolently applying its moral authority to create order and "shape the economic and political institutions of poor countries to the advantage of U.S. lenders, investors, traders, and manufacturers."[48] Not simply political or economic, informal imperialism reveals how these two realms were essentially about culture, about the "available" reasons and meanings that explain how a group, nation, or people are subordinated, dominated, and controlled.

Chicana/o leftists proposed "that Chicanismo was capitalistic separatism, that it did not take into account the inter-connectedness of the world, and that it incorrectly focused on racism, when capitalism was the true source of their oppression."[49] While this implicated the larger movement as having a limited, narrow, and insufficient economic analysis, nationalists decried the European origins of socialist ideas for failing to recognize the unique differences and histories of Chicanas/os in Mexico and the Southwest, and often emphasized indigenous and/or Mexican resistance to Anglo domination and US intervention in Mexico. Cultural nationalism emphasized gaining liberation by attacking and resisting the colonial racist state as a united people with a shared culture and history, whereas Chicana/o Marxists argued that the system of capitalism was the problem and required a class analysis, as well as an understanding of international politics and economic imperialism, that in turn translated into international solidarity. In this milieu, the Chicana/o Left was "another world in the making."[50]

GENEALOGIES OF THE CHICANA/O LEFT

Clearly, Mexican leftists organizing in the United States during the twentieth century is not a 1970s phenomenon. Tracing their genealogy helps to historicize transnational social movements and make apparent the deeply intergenerational character of leftist politics.[51]

Perhaps the most influential organization in the political imaginary of the Chicana/o movement in general, and the Chicana/o Left in particular, was the Partido Liberal Mexicano (Mexican Liberal Party—PLM), in existence from 1900 until 1911. I do not want to reduce the influence of the PLM to its leader, Ricardo Flores Magón, or suggest that the PLM was a singular organization (the Magonistas were always the most radical trajectory), but the histories of struggles and organizations are often learned at first through the legacies of key individuals. The influence of the PLM has been thoroughly documented elsewhere, but the basics of the story follow.[52] Born in the southern state of Oaxaca, Mexico, the Magón brothers (Ricardo and Enrique) were exiled to the United States in 1905 after numerous imprisonments and years of agitating against the government of Porfirio Díaz. Connecting struggles for land and liberty across borders, they continued to organize against Díaz, collaborating with US socialists and communists and working at various times in San Antonio and Laredo, Texas, as well as St. Louis and Los Angeles. The influence of the PLM on the US Left and on people of Mexican descent in the United States was widespread, anticipating the political solidarity of the Chicana/o Left. The Industrial Workers of the World (Wobblies) and the PLM had overlapping members and worked closely together on union drives, strike organizing, and armed rebellions.[53]

Socialist- and anarchist-inspired mutual-aid societies, radical mining unions, and revolutionary journalists circulated the revolutionary ideas that reflected a cross-border analysis of capitalism while emphasizing the urgent necessity of international solidarity. Through the newspaper *Regeneración*, edited by Ricardo Flores Magón and others, that circulated across the United States and Mexico, people learned about labor struggles, strikes, revolutionary movements, and the crimes of capitalists in both countries. A propaganda tool, *Regeneración* anticipated stories that would create solidarity and inspired journalists and activists in the Chicana/o movement to do the same, connecting labor, feminist, and internationalist struggles.[54]

In the first decades of the twentieth century, activists such as Sara Estela Ramírez, Jovita Idar, and Leonor Villegas de Magnón worked out of San Antonio and Laredo, founding newspapers and writing articles and editorials critical of capitalists and their political puppets and in support of workers' and women's rights. They organized with other women to found organizations like La Liga Femenil Mexicana, actively participated in the PLM, attended to soldiers as revolutionary nurses in La Cruz Blanca, read *Regeneración*, and provided examples for Chicanas and Chicanos of strong women struggling for the rights of their people.

The Congress of Spanish Speaking Peoples (El Congreso), founded through the organizing efforts of Luisa Moreno in December 1939, was another important reference point for the Chicana/o Left. Born in Guatemala to an elite family, Moreno moved to Florida and organized with Latin, black, and Italian tobacco and cigar workers. She then joined the Congress of Industrial Organizations (CIO) and became an international representative for the UCAPAWA (United Cannery, Agricultural, Packing, and Allied Workers of America) in California. In the 1930s, Moreno worked in San Antonio with Emma Tenayuca, then secretary of the Texas Communist Party (though she later identified as an anarchist) and a member of the Workers Alliance, to organize workers in the pecan industry, a labor sector employing primarily Mexican women.[55] A brilliant organizer, strategist, and negotiator, Moreno "distinguished herself as an educator, agitator, and mobilizer by focusing on the relationship between individuals and their communities."[56] Moreno activated the networks and resources of established organizations and unions, including the Communist Party USA, of which she was a member, to support campaigns that included workers from all backgrounds, regardless of citizenship.

El Congreso was an attempt to unite Latinas/os from across the United States in an organization to change the economic, political, and social conditions of Spanish-speaking peoples. Moreno took a leave of absence in 1938 from the UCAPAWA to meet with Spanish-speaking communities throughout the United States, perhaps the first time such an ambitious tour had been attempted. Moreno sought to build on the work of the PLM, which had also organized Spanish-speaking communities around leftist ideas earlier in the century. An initial founding meeting in Los Angeles in December 1938 established the Los Angeles Congreso, and was to be followed by a national gathering in Albuquerque, New Mexico, in March the following year. After massive preparations and endorsements from organizations across the country that represented a wide swath of the political spectrum, the meeting was not held due to red-baiting in New Mexico prior to the gathering. Instead, the founding Congress was held in Los Angeles, a city more capable of sustaining a Left-inspired organization due to a long history of radical labor politics in the city and in the rest of California.[57] Delegates arrived from Spanish-speaking communities in every region of the United States, as did representatives from Mexican labor unions aligned with the ruling party (Partido Revolucionario Institucional/ Institutional Revolutionary Party—PRI). The political agenda varied. From encouraging people to vote, to criticism of capitalism and the relationship between the United States and Latin America, the "delegates at the Los Angeles convention stressed an internationalist perspective, especially concerning relations with Mexico and other Latin American nations. El Congreso . . . warned against reactionary efforts to have the United States intervene militarily in Mexico on behalf of American oil interests," in the aftermath of the nationalization of the Mexican oil industry by President Lázaro Cárdenas in 1938.[58]

Josefina Fierro de Bright was one of the main organizers of El Congreso in Los Angeles. Nineteen years old at the time of the founding of El Congreso, Fierro de Bright was born in Mexicali, Mexico. Her mother, Josefa, was a Magonista, and her father had fought in the Mexican Revolution with Pancho Villa. Raised by her mother in Los Angeles, Josefina attended UCLA and soon met John Bright, a radical Hollywood writer. With access to the support and resources of Hollywood radicals, Fierro de Bright organized a successful boycott of a Los Angeles brewery that had refused to hire Mexican workers. When Moreno heard about this young organizer, Fierro de Bright was immediately recruited to organize the Los Angeles convention. Though no documentary evidence exists that El Congreso was a communist party front, it was clearly a progressive organization, bringing together socialists and communists with labor unions, liberals, and moderates to focus on the economic, educational, social, political, and health issues facing Spanish-speaking communities. The Communist Party USA at this time favored popular front politics that emphasized coalitions between leftists and liberals against fascism and "support for a liberal welfare state."[59] El Congreso's intimate knowledge of conditions within Spanish-speaking communities inspired their radical political genealogy. Perhaps the best-known campaign involving El Congreso was the Sleepy Lagoon Case, involving a group of Mexican American youths accused of a murder in Los Angeles in 1942.[60] The efforts of these organizers clearly represent the insurgent feminist politics that Denise A. Segura and Beatriz M. Pesquera identify as anticapitalist and antiracist, and were geared toward community power and organizing for workers' rights for not only Mexicans but all workers, a politics of solidarity across borders.[61]

Workers from the fields, factories, and mines in Colorado, Texas, Arizona, and California gathered in Phoenix on February 12–13, 1949, to found the Asociación Nacional México-Americana (ANMA). Initially proposed by Mexican workers in the Mine Mill union, a militant element of the CIO eventually expelled from that organization in 1950, and labor leaders in the CIO, ANMA raised the possibility of "a second Mexican-American left leadership and organization."[62] ANMA membership included Mexican nationals and Mexican Americans united through language, culture, and history. Together they organized as a broad-based civil rights organization influenced by ANMA's base in the "labor-left movement of the Southwest" that emphasized class struggle, exploitative labor conditions, and racial and ethnic discrimination and violence.[63] Chapters emerged wherever there were people of Mexican descent. In the late 1940s, local, regional, state, and national conventions brought workers together to establish goals, share their successes, and continue to struggle for equal treatment, labor rights, and community dignity. The continuity between El Congreso and ANMA is visible in the "popular front strategies and multi-issue program on such issues as the peace movement, workers' struggles, the plight of Mexican undocumented workers, housing needs in the southwest, education, Mexican-American political representation, youth work, the promotion of Mexican-American culture, and police brutality."[64] Like El Congreso and the PLM, ANMA also built solidarity with political movements in Mexico and Latin America.

One of the main organizers for ANMA in northern California was Bert Corona. Corona was born in Chihuahua, Mexico, in 1918, and like Fierro de Bright he had a father who had fought in the Mexican revolution with Pancho Villa and was a member of the PLM. His mother was an educator and a Protestant. Corona was attracted to radical ideas from a young age. After moving to Los Angeles to attend USC, he began to organize workers from different labor sectors, eventually taking a position as a CIO organizer. When the CIO provided support for the founding of El Congreso, it provided an important spark for Corona's future political plans. Investigated and harassed by Congress in the 1940s because of his political views, Corona joined the recently founded ANMA after World War II. In 1951, his experiences as ANMA's representative to an international gathering of mine workers in Mexico further solidified his beliefs in leftist organizing and international solidarity. Corona organized workers and critiqued class exploitation, emphasizing international solidarity and cross-racial alliances while focusing on the politics of the working class and Mexican people in his political efforts.[65]

In 1968, Soledad "Chole" Alatorre and Corona worked together to found Centro de Acción Social Autónomo-Hermandad General de Trabajadores (CASA-HGT), an immigrants-rights group based on principles of mutual aid and labor rights, community power, and localized organizing. Alatorre was born in San Luis Potosí, Mexico, where her father was a Railroad Workers Union official. With her husband and sister, Alatorre immigrated to the United States at the age of twenty-seven. On a job as a swimsuit model, Alatorre met many garment workers, which led her to advocate for their rights and eventually become a negotiator with employers and unions. Over the next decade, Alatorre worked with the teamsters union, the Maritime Union, the United Auto Workers, and the United Farm Workers. These experiences, and her own treatment in US society, led to the founding of CASA-HGT. Corona and Alatorre would influence the leftist politics of the Chicana/o movement throughout the 1970s, particularly in regard to the rights of undocumented workers in the United States, workers in Mexico and Latin America, and immigration policy.[66]

El Congreso, ANMA, and CASA-HGT were all established by people of Mexican descent—workers organizing for their rights. Influenced by the radical elements of the CIO in the United States, these organizations inherited the genealogy of the previous generation's revolutionary and anarcho-syndicalist struggles in Mexico, and of women's political leadership and intellectual creativity, as well as labor organizing, in Latin America. They paved the way for the Chicana/o Left. With regard to the HGT, Alatorre and Corona would be present at the founding of CASA in 1968.

The ability of these organizations to connect domestic policies with international issues and to build solidarity along the lines of political movements and organizations rather than political class revealed the depth of pre- and post–World War II leftist politics within Spanish-speaking communities in the United States, as well as the continuity of struggle through intergenerational organizing. "It was leftist unions, whether Communist Party or Socialist Party unionists and the internationalist ideologies they practiced," Antonia Castañeda argues, "who sought to organize workers of color, especially farm labor and related agricultural industries, who along with domestic workers were excluded from the National Labor Relations Act of 1935."[67]

THE NATIONAL QUESTION

One of the most significant theoretical and political discussions on the Chicana/o Left across the twentieth century has been the national question. Depending on which organization is examined and at what time, people of Mexican descent in the United States, Chicanas/os, were (1) an oppressed minority, (2) part of the Mexican Left, (3) part of the US Third World Left, (4) part of the Latin American Left, or (5) some combination therein. Are people of Mexican descent in the United States a nation, and therefore should have the right to decide about self-determination? Or are Chicanas/os a US national minority, part of the US working class, and with strong tendencies toward international solidarity? The national question as posed by Vladimir Lenin has very particular components.[68] In 1913 Joseph Stalin published *Marxism and the National Question*. In this text, written before the Russian Revolution in 1919, Stalin discusses the Bolshevik perspective on issues regarding how to politically organize the many ethnic minorities within Russia, and what their relationship would be to the revolutionary nationalist movement. The theory emphasized that a people indeed formed a nation as "a historically constituted, stable community of people, formed on the basis of a common language, territory, economic life, and psychological make-up manifested in a common culture." When twentieth-century anticolonial, revolutionary organizations have discussed national movements and the relationship between culture, nation, and revolution, they have looked for insight to determine their own conditions of struggle; the relationship of a people who share a language, culture, and history of struggle and exploitation to a national liberation movement; and the relationship between national liberation movements and international solidarity. Stalin wrote:

> The solution of the national question is possible only in connection with the historical conditions taken in their development. The economic, political and cultural conditions of a given nation constitute the only key to the question *how* a particular nation ought to arrange its life and *what forms* its future constitution ought to take. It is possible that a specific solution of the question will be required for each nation. If the dialectical approach to a question is required anywhere it is required here, in the national question.[69]

For leftists of Mexican descent in the late nineteenth and twentieth centuries, the answers have varied. Alaniz and Cornish provide a thorough examination of the national question in the twentieth century, tracing varied interpretations from the writings and organizing of Emma Tenayuca and Homer Brooks as part of the Communist Party's position on the "Mexican question" through ANMA, El Congreso, and other organizations throughout the 1970s.[70] Aztlán further complicated the national question. The national question was about not identity but rather what Marxist analytic drove a particular ideological or organizational position and how people of Mexican descent in the United States with leftist politics understood, gave meaning to, and changed their relationships to Mexican and Latin American leftists.

In 1939, Brooks and Tenayuca published "The Mexican Question in the Southwest." Inspired by the national question, the essay's goal was to analyze the conditions of workers of Mexican descent in the Southwest in the context of whether Mexicans in the United States had the right to self-determination. At the time, both of the essay's authors were members of the Communist Party in Texas; as mentioned, Tenayuca was deeply involved in organizing pecan shellers. In the article, Brooks and Tenayuca clearly "regarded all Mexicans north of the border as one people. They endorsed political unity between Mexican Americans and Mexican nationals since the majority in both groups represented working-class people bound together by a common history, culture, and oppressed conditions."[71] They concluded that people of Mexican descent in the United States were not a nation, as they did not possess "either the economic or territorial base for a nation," and therefore did not have the right to struggle for national self-determination under the terms identified by Stalin. Though they were one people on two sides of a political border, Mexicans in the United States were part of the US working class.

During the 1970s the national question provided Chicana/o leftist groups with a provocative and constructive discussion for how to organize, with whom to organize, and for what purposes. In 1976 the Centro de Acción Social Autónomo (CASA) declared itself a Marxist-Leninist organization, and there was a parting of ways between Corona and Alatorre—the original founders of CASA, who continued to work at the grassroots level—and the new organizers, who wanted to take the struggle to an international level guided by the principles of Marx and Lenin in terms of analysis, cadre, and party building.[72] Because chapter 6 provides a discussion of CASA and the politics of solidarity and feminist insurgencies that places CASA within the larger context of the Chicana/o Left in the 1970s, I will forgo the discussion here.

Though CASA, due to its size and influence, has received the most scholarly attention among leftist organizations, "many Chicano leftists disagreed, sometimes vehemently, with CASA."[73] In 1974 the August Twenty-Ninth Movement (ATM), a national Marxist-Leninist formation, emerged out of the labor committee of La Raza Unida Party in Los Angeles.[74] The committee consistently represented a leftist perspective, eventually coalescing with other Chicana/o leftists in ATM in 1974.[75] Named after the date of the Chicano Moratorium on the Vietnam War and the murder of journalist Ruben Salazar, ATM developed support through a national campaign with posters, discussions, meetings, and other gatherings, work that "spark[ed] a lot of discussion around the character of the Chicano liberation struggle and its relationship to the larger working class's struggle for socialism."[76] For ATM, Chicanos were an oppressed nation, not an oppressed national minority, and "they felt it was dangerous to deny the existence of the Chicana/o nation."[77] This was a different stance, according to Pulido, than that of most other New Communist Movement organizations. On the one hand, ATM challenged CASA on the national question, dismissing CASA's denial that "Chicanos were a distinct people with a history of their own in the United States" and insisting "on the existence of the Chicana/o nation" as CASA proposed.[78] On the other hand, CASA accused ATM of being a Maoist formation. ATM was a nuanced organization with an analytical perspective that combined a critique of US racial capitalism with a developing anti-imperialist politic, an "analysis of the Chicano struggle [that] was an advance over previous formations . . . [in which] most leftists had simply applied Lenin's and Stalin's ideas of the nation . . . with unsatisfactory results."[79] Though ATM recognized Aztlán from a Marxist perspective and located anti-imperialism as part of their ideological formation, "it paid less attention to the international working class, stressing instead the subordination of the Chicana/o nation by the United States."[80] For ATM the Mexican War of Independence, the nineteenth-century liberal reform movements, and the Mexican revolution had resulted in the creation of the Mexican nation. Chicanas/os did not, as a group or in any real numbers, participate in these revolutionary moments, so Chicanas/os "as a people developed under different historical circumstances, those of colonization and national oppression within the borders of the U.S."[81]

A less-known example of cadre building on the Chicana/o Left was the Communist Collective of the Chicano Nation, a Marxist-Leninist formation founded in 1973. It took the position that Chicanos were an oppressed minority with a shared culture, economic foundation, and land base to fit the conditions to justify a struggle for self-determination as a national minority. Their propaganda arm, "El Amanecer Rojo," allowed them to circulate their ideas. Attending the Conference of National Marxist Leninists in 1973 in Albuquerque, they declared, "The Chicano nation was southern Colorado, New Mexico and South Texas, precisely because Chicanos were a nation . . . communists should unite."[82]

In addition to CASA, the August Twenty-Ninth Movement, and later the League of Revolutionary Struggle, during the late 1960s Chicanos in the Leavenworth federal prison organized with Native American, black, radical white, and Puerto Rican political prisoners for civil and human rights.[83] Their internationalist revolutionary politics, inspired by the same documents and struggles occurring during this time outside the walls (the student rebellions, labor strikes, organizing mothers, and politicized artists of the Chicano movement), were transformed through contact with the Puerto Rican freedom fighters—

Rafael Cancel Miranda, Irving Flores Rodríguez, Andrés Figueroa Cordero, and Oscar Collazo. raúlrsalinas would refer to the incarceration of Third World peoples in US prisons as a "backyard form of colonialism, juxtaposing the larger meaning given to Latin America in US foreign policy, to the space of unfreedom that prisons represented during this time."[84] These men were part of the cycle of prison rebellions taking place at the time all across the country—in Attica, New York; San Quentin, California; Marion, Illinois; and Bedford Hills, New York, for example.[85] Embracing an anti-imperialist politics centered on an analysis of the prison as a colonial institution, and emphasizing international solidarity and multiracial organizing, men like Ramón Chacón, Alberto Mares, Mario Cantú, Ramón Tijerina, raúlrsalinas, and others began organizing inside the prisons, challenging treatment of prisoners, creating political organizations, publishing newspapers, and organizing strikes. Upon release they all continued to work in progressive and revolutionary struggles, some of which are told in chapter 4. *Pinto* leftists connected the revolutionary politics that emerged in conditions of unfreedom and theorized in collaboration with imprisoned anticolonials in the Chicana/o movement.

Despite all these efforts, according to Oropeza, "neither vigorous condemnation of U.S. foreign policy nor genuine enthusiasm for the Vietnamese and Cuban revolutions necessarily translated into immediate support for socialism or communism among *most* movement participants." Given that "the Chicano movement always remained predominantly a cultural-nationalist movement," there were often tensions between Marxist-oriented organizations and actors and those grounded in "a narrative of civil rights, ethnic diversity, and US liberalism."[86] These were varied and intense efforts, yet "even at the height of the *movimiento*, the idea of a socialist Aztlán, which took revolutionary Cuba as its primary model, did not attract a significant segment of the Chicana/o community."[87] Yet despite limited numbers, Chicanos and Puerto Ricans participated in the founding convention of the League of Revolutionary Black Workers Congress in Detroit in 1969, while Chicanas/os played an important role providing material resources and community support to the Puerto Rican independence movement in Chicago and California.[88] In addition, Mexican youth participated in the Young Lords Party in Chicago.

Efforts to build a multiracial Communist Party that included ATM, the Communist Collective of the Chicano Nation, and the League of Revolutionary Struggle characterized the landscape of the Marxist,

Maoist, and Guevarrista-inspired politics in the United States during the 1970s. From anti-imperialism to localized socialist-inspired projects, Chicanas/os shaped the US Left while contributing an anti-capitalist and internationalist politics to the Chicana/o movement.

Chicana/o leftists inherited and created an internationalist politics of solidarity during the 1970s. The ideological perspective on reform, capitalism, or the national question mirrored discussions and debates among US black leftists and anticolonial struggles across the globe. These movements grappled with questions concerning leftist ideas, cultural history, what constitutes national community, the relationship between racial or national minorities, and the right to self-determination. Chicana/o Left organizations struggled to find an analysis of capitalism and power that also directed and inspired particular ways to organize politically. "All of these organizations," Mariscal argues, "struggled to distinguish themselves from competing groups, a process that produced doctrinaire charges of collaborationism and reformism and then insistence on a 'correct party line.'"[89] Though distinctions may have inevitably led to divisions and disagreements, it is also important to recognize the generative and significant history of struggle and intellectual analysis that emerged during this period. At the same time, the prevalence of the continental and hemispheric politics of the Chicana/o movement—leftist or otherwise—was limited in number relative to the movement as a whole, while the internationalist imaginary reflected deeper trends in the Chicana/o movement as activists across the political spectrum were inspired in different ways by struggles in Mexico, Latin America, Cuba, Africa, and Asia.

Chicana/o leftists were part of the larger global struggles against imperialism and in support of socialism, engaging in the national arena within the United States as well as establishing links with movements south of the border. A continental/hemispheric Chicanisma/o is helpful in rethinking and reframing the post-1968 context and 1970s neoliberalism, the longer trajectory of Chicana/o radicalism. The next chapters explore different types of solidarity politics introduced by the ideas and imaginaries represented in the words of Olga Talamante and José Montoya quoted at the beginning of the chapter: "Chicana/o included all of Latin America." That was not only the Yankee's worst nightmare, but also, as the next chapters demonstrate, the nightmare of governments in Mexico, Central America, and South America's Southern Cone.

CHAPTER 2

MEXICO, ANTICOMMUNISM, AND
THE CHICANA/O MOVEMENT

This problem in Latin America is reflected within American society itself in the Mexican-Americans and Puerto Ricans and other racial minority groups. Therefore either we find balanced economic solutions to these issues or [the communists] will gain ground in Latin America and that will have repercussions inside your own borders.

LUIS ECHEVERRÍA ÁLVAREZ, PRESIDENT OF MEXICO (1970–1976), TO RICHARD NIXON, JUNE 1972

The group [Los Nakos] was very clear. What interested us was to keep questioning the [Mexican] state. Continue denouncing what the state was doing. We rolled with the comrades from Poli [National Politecnic Institution] and would sing about those we admired, Che Guevarra, Lucio Cabañas, we were interested in the women's movement, the political prisoners, all the prisoners of 68.

MAILO COLMENARES, CO–FOUNDING MEMBER, LOS NAKOS

Implicit in the myth of Mexico's social stability is the idea that official violence was relatively absent. While it certainly never reached the levels seen in many Central and South American military regimes, repression undergirded the PRI's rule.

TANALÍS PADILLA, *RURAL RESISTANCE IN THE LAND OF ZAPATA*

RESISTING THE DIRTY WARS OF EMPIRE

This chapter offers a discussion of political and economic contexts in Mexico in the post–World War II era, especially after 1968. It demonstrates that state counterinsurgency terror and violence were hemispheric and international, and that the organized resistance against them was part and parcel with establishing solidarity to create a different world. Of particular importance are US-Mexican relations and the manner in which both governments used anticommunist language to argue that the connections between social movements threatened hemispheric security. Such language provided the political cover for targeting political movements. "Cold War ideology provided a nationally and internationally legitimizing framework for government repression in Mexico and throughout Latin America," Tanalís Padilla argues. "Leftist groups, likewise, interpreted this repression within the Cold War context and speculated about Washington's involvement." During the second half of the twentieth century, rural and urban movements in Mexico "acquired a more militant tactical and programmatic nature in response to government repression."[1]

NIXON AND THE ECHEVERRÍA DOCTRINE: "MEXICO AS THE BRIDGE BETWEEN THE US AND LATIN AMERICA"

During the 1960s, Mexican and US officials both expressed concern over people and organizations that were making connections across the international border. The FBI kept files on many sectors of the Chicana/o movement, including La Raza Unida Party (LRUP) in different parts of the country; CASA; the connections between the Black Power and Chicano Power movements in Los Angeles, San Antonio, and Denver; the political activities of Chicanas/os who traveled to Cuba, Mexico, or other Latin American countries; and the Chicano college Colegio Jacinto Treviño in Mercedes, Texas, to name but a few examples.[2] In Mexico, the Dirección Federal de Seguridad (Federal Security Directorate) produced a report titled "Political and Social Investigation of Current Principal Problems in Mexican-American (Chicano) Communities." Though more a general assessment than a nuanced study, it "addressed a series of questions about the nature of the racial, cultural, and ethnic identity, social status, and diversity within Mexican American communities."[3] Connections between political activists in the United States and Mexico concerned Mexican president Luis Echeverría Álvarez (1970–1976). A CIA asset and ambitious political operative, Echeverría had influenced the direction of national and foreign policy since at least 1964, when he served on the cabinet of president Gustavo Díaz Ordaz.[4] In a 1972 meeting with US president Richard Nixon, Echeverría discussed a wide range of topics, including US-Mexican relations, Mexican relations with Chile and Cuba, international communism, water issues, and, at the end of the conversation, transnational political connections between African American, Chicano, and Mexican activists.[5]

The context of this discussion, and Echeverría's access to Nixon, were of great political import in Mexico. Whereas the first two years of Echeverría's presidency were focused on internal issues, particularly his role in the violence against political movements, "beginning in 1972, when he wasn't able or didn't want to solve the internal problems, the internationalist vocation was born. Thus began his meteoric and insignificant career as a redeemer on international injustices and champion in the struggle against imperialism, especially that of the United States."[6] Yet this anti-imperialist posturing was not apparent in the discussions with Nixon. The diverse agenda reflected the salient geopolitical concerns of both leaders at the time. It also underscored the interconnectedness between dissidence and foreign and domestic policies in the United States and Mexico. A good portion of their conversation is worth consideration at this point:

> ECHEVERRÍA: Tell Mr. President that in the speech that I will deliver to the joint session of Congress within the hour, I will reiterate my principles of the Third World vis-à-vis the great powers of the world. Because . . .
> NIXON: [Interrupting] The Echeverría Doctrine.
> ECHEVERRÍA: Yes—because if I don't take this flag in Latin America, Castro will. I am very conscious of this.[7]
> ECHEVERRÍA: We in Mexico feel—and I sensed this also when I was in Chile and it can be felt in Central America, and among young people, among intellectuals—that Cuba is a Soviet base in every sense of the word, both militarily and ideologically, and that this is going on right under our noses.
> ECHEVERRÍA: [. . .] We are also aware of the fact that Dr. Castro and Cuba are instruments of penetration into the United States itself, not to mention Mexico and the other countries of Latin America. They are unceasing in their efforts, using one path or another.
> ECHEVERRÍA: And I believe, Mr. President, that it's obvious that with the large subsidies he receives [from the Soviets] and his very deep complicity, he seeks to project his influence into groups within the United States and Latin America. And if we in Mexico do not adopt a progressive attitude within a framework of freedom and of friendship with the United States, this trend will grow. I have sensed this not

only in Latin America, but in certain groups within the United States as well.

ECHEVERRÍA: He [Castro] has had no scruples whatsoever about sacrificing his own country and eliminating all freedoms there just to be a tool of Soviets; at this very moment he is making a grand tour of many of the smaller socialist countries in Eastern Europe.

ECHEVERRÍA: And this poses a huge problem for all of Latin America, in this time of population growth, unemployment and social tensions aggravated by international communism. That's why I believe that it is extremely important and this is something of great personal concern to me—that we take their flags away from them by making real efforts to cooperate at the highest levels of government, as well as with private initiatives and technology.[8]

After positioning himself in contradistinction to Castro and Allende, Echeverría used Chicano political activity to point out a vulnerability within the United States. Concern over cross-border solidarity was central to the discussion at the highest government levels:

ECHEVERRÍA: This problem in Latin America is reflected within American society itself in the Mexican-Americans and Puerto Ricans and other racial minority groups. Therefore either we find balanced economic solutions to these issues or [the communists] will gain ground in Latin America, and that will have repercussions inside your own borders.

ECHEVERRÍA: There is no doubt whatsoever that President Nixon's meetings in China and Russia were great successes, but at the same time anything that China and Russia can do to cause problems, they will do—and in Latin America we feel that directly. I have observed this in Mexico. I saw it in Chile directly and in every Latin American country in one form or another.

[TRANSLATOR]

NIXON: Well I think that, ah—first, the President's analysis is very perceptive about the problems of the hemisphere. And second, I appreciate the fact that he is taking the lead—speaking up not only for his own country, which of course is his first responsibility [. . .]—but he's taking the lead in speaking up for the whole hemisphere. Because Mexico, as he said earlier, provides not only the U.S. border with Mexico but the U.S. border with all of Latin America. And Mexico also, you could say, is the bridge—the bridge between the United States and the rest of Latin America. I think for the President of Mexico to take a leading role in speaking about the problems of the hemisphere is very constructive. . .

ECHEVERRÍA: When I was about to leave from Mexico for this trip, Mr. President, I was informed by my various people that groups of Mexicans had been in touch with friends of [black activist] Angela Davis in this country. And that we were aware of the plans of the organization that Angela Davis heads to mount a key demonstration in protesting the existence of political prisoners in Mexico. All of this is connected to people in Chile, with people in Cuba, with the so-called "Chicano" groups in the United States, with certain groups in Berkeley, California—they're all working closely together.

ECHEVERRÍA: As soon as the plan existed that she would go to San Antonio to a demonstration in protest of internal affairs of Mexico with this idea of saying that "all political prisoners in every country should be released," we were immediately informed.

ECHEVERRÍA: They are working very actively—and again, these events that take place in Latin America have repercussions within the borders of the United States.[9]

Echeverría's concerns are revealing in both their specificity and context. First, his comments came eleven days after jurors in the trial of "the dangerous terrorist, Angela Davis" [Nixon's words], who was found not guilty on counts of murder, kidnapping, and conspiracy.[10] Second, earlier in the conversation, Echeverría had presented himself as a loyal supporter of the United States in Latin America, criticizing Castro and Allende (though he publicly supported them) and promising to work with US companies and Mexican businesses to promote increased economic integration. By strategically mentioning the links between such a high-profile figure as Angela Davis and Chicano and Mexican organizations within the context of international communism and the need to promote economic integration and development in the hemisphere, Echeverría made a stronger case for himself as a trusted ally. Moreover, he argued for increased security and financial cooperation between the two countries by pointing to Chicano alliances with African Americans and organizations in Mexico as a shared problem. Echeverría's intelligence was accurate. Four days later, when he traveled to San Antonio to inaugurate the Instituto Cultural de México as a resource for Chicano groups with whom he had previously established contact, he was met with protests organized by Mario Cantú, Angela Davis, and others demanding freedom for political prisoners and an end to the dirty war.[11]

HEMISPHERIC TERROR

During the post–World War II period, political movements in Mexico and the United States were deeply impacted by government repression—infiltrations, kidnappings, disappearances, and assassinations. In discussing repression in the United States, Mexico, and Latin America, it is important to keep in mind that state violence should not be a comparative measurement, as each situation is different and conditions the possibility of what can be unacceptable within a given society. Parsing "levels" of terror (rather than a taxonomy of democratic terror) dissuades a critical eye and creates epistemological and political blind spots as we begin to traffic in commodifying and quantifying "scenes of subjection" that diminish the violence and refocus the gaze yet again on the state.[12] Instead, the overlap in techniques and political reasons employed to justify such widespread violence reveals the relationship across geopolitical borders of the logics of law and order.

The actions employed in the United States, in Mexico, and across Latin America were partly the result of counterinsurgency strategies developed by the US military and intelligence institutions that in turn trained other such organizations throughout Latin America.[13] In addition, politicians and leaders of urban police departments shared techniques, policies, and ideologies with counterparts in Latin America and Mexico.[14] That said, state counterinsurgencies against transnational leftist social movements date back to the early twentieth century along the US-Mexican border; in the interior of the United States against radicals from Mexico, Europe, Asia, and Africa; and among workers in the mines and agricultural fields of the US Southwest.[15] The FBI's surveillance and infiltration operations, directed in one form or another by J. Edgar Hoover, dated back to 1924 with surveillance of Marcus Garvey and infiltration of the Universal Negro Improvement Association and African Communities League (UNIA-ACL). These operations, which targeted political movements to "expose, disrupt, misdirect, discredit, neutralize or otherwise eliminate" leadership and support, should be understood in relation to the state violence in the Americas.[16] The COINTELPRO operations were made public in 1971 after antiwar activists liberated documents from an FBI office in Media, Pennsylvania, and leaked them to the press. COINTELPRO targeted students, unions, civil rights organizations, pastors and churches, black freedom movements, the Chicana/o movement, the Communist Party, and New Left organizations. The evidence of infiltrations, surveillance, planted stories and use of journalists to manipulate press coverage, assassination plans, and all types of disruptive and illegal activities revealed the types of crimes the FBI committed in the name of national security.

These counterinsurgency efforts also resulted in the creation of COINTELPRO's Border Coverage Program. In response to public exposure and the Church Committee hearings in 1976 that found numerous constitutional violations (despite severe limitations on the scope of the investigation), FBI leaders swore under oath that these programs no longer existed. Yet the same tactics continued to be used against the American Indian movement; the Black Liberation Army; the solidarity movement within the United States to support people's movements in El Salvador, Nicaragua, and Guatemala; and the US-based exile community from Chile. By obscuring the political and social function of state terror in the United States and in turn pathologizing state terror as something that happens only in developing countries, the ideological, political, technical, and social connections between the forms and functions of state violence were camouflaged. This political, historical, and psychological obfuscation has inoculated the public from considering state violence in the United States along the same register and analog as state violence in other parts of the world.

To read about COINTELPRO and the lesser-known CIA and Defense Intelligence domestic operations is to read how a democratic state sought to "expose, disrupt, misdirect, discredit, neutralize or otherwise eliminate" political dissent, suggesting that the relational political violence of the state across the Americas is paramount in understanding the nature of governance during the Cold War.[17] This is not to ignore the intranational cooperation between countries in the Southern Cone. The best-known campaign of violence and terror, Operation Condor, involved intelligence agents spread across Uruguay, Paraguay, Chile, Bolivia, Brazil, and Argentina, and even in Europe and the United States. In other words, as much as the organized violence of the various dirty wars against people in Latin America was a product of US/Latin American Cold War geopolitical collaborations, so too must COINTELPRO operations in the United States be seen as a dirty war against political activity and understood in the context of US support for right-wing governments on every continent during the Cold War.

ON THE MEXICAN MIRACLE AND POLITICAL VIOLENCE

Just as the particular characteristics of repression and terror crossed borders, so too did the underlying reasons. Violence undergirded the myth of the Mexican economic, political, and social miracle, where an Import Substitute Industrialization (ISI) model of development created a burgeoning urban middle class and, so the story goes, increased economic opportunity for all classes.[18] In an apparent exception to other Latin American countries, Mexico achieved unprecedented success in the post–World War II era through democratic elections that institutionalized the revolution in the official political party (PRI—Partido Revolucionario Institucional/Institutional Revolutionary Party). Yet graft, violence, and rigged elections aggregated wealth and political power through the structures of corporatist governance, while rural campesinos and the urban poor were left out of the model—except as exploitable labor to make the plan work.[19]

The massacre at Tlatelolco in 1968 was not the beginning of the Mexican dirty war, though it marked a significant watershed in Mexican and global history.[20] For Chicanas/os, the first connections between students and the Mexican Left were established during the time immediately following the massacre. Yet the beginnings of the modern dirty war can be traced to post–World War II responses by the Mexican state to organizing efforts by the teachers union, railway workers, and miners. Their mobilizations and general strikes were met with repression from the Mexican military, causing numerous deaths and the incarceration of leaders.

Starting in at least the late 1950s, the Mexican state targeted political movements that emerged demanding democracy, liberty, and land. From peasant land occupations, student movements, and cultural organizations to labor unions, teachers, and rural and urban armed self-defense and guerrilla movements, people organized against exploitation and violence. In addition, land occupations and peasant movements inspired by Emiliano Zapata, the Revolutionary General of the South, were most clearly embodied by the Jaramillista movement led and organized by Rubén Jaramillo from the 1940s to 1962 in Morelos (discussed in chapter 6). Specifically, in 1962, Jaramillo, his wife, Epifania, and their three children were assassinated by the military on orders from within the upper echelons of PRI power in Mexico.[21] The level of violence from the mid-1950s to the late 1970s "reveals the nature and extent of the Mexican government's use of repression," historian Tanalís Padilla points out. "Implicit in the myth of Mexico's social stability is the idea that official violence was relatively absent. While it certainly never reached the levels seen in many Central and South American military regimes, repression undergirded the PRI's rule."[22] These political movements and the violent response by the Mexican state suggest that we have to widen our analysis to understand how the Mexican Miracle and state violence were two sides of the same coin—a contradiction that Mexican civil society would highlight during the 1970s.

Anticommunism was a hemispheric politics, often consolidating conservative, right-wing regimes into a reactionary force to combat the "red menace" by extralegal and legal mechanisms, essentially collapsing the distinction between the two. The Cold War played out in local neighborhoods, farms, factories, universities, and homes where people were abducted and then taken to other local neighborhoods to be tortured, imprisoned, and "disappeared." Fighting communism could also explain the police and military actions necessary to maintain law and order. Mexican presidents from Miguel Alemán Valdés (1946–1952) and Adolfo Tomás Ruiz Cortines (1952–1958) to Luis Echeverría Álvarez (1970–1976) and José López Portillo (1976–1982) all actively used anticommunism as a rationale to target internal political movements and make alliances in foreign policy with the United States. "At the same time as the United States was promoting modernization," Grandin explains, "it was also invigorating Latin American militaries and centralized intelligence agencies in an effort to counter real and perceived insurgent threats."[23] Echeverría's meeting with Nixon in 1972 clearly demonstrates ideological agreement.

While the United States was invigorating militaries, creating, supporting, and benefiting from political and economic crises abroad, domestic movements in Mexico accelerated their opposition. Antiimperialist movements worked to put US hegemony and the power of ruling national elites in crisis by demonstrating that "counterrevolutionary terror was inextricably tied to empire."[24] Political movements in rural and urban Mexico became particular targets for counterrevolutionary attack from 1971 to 1978, with a particular escalation in 1974–1975. People from all sectors of society were targeted. "According to the report on the 'disappeared' released in late 2001 by the National Commission on Human Rights," writes Kate Doyle, "abductions of Mexicans by government agents were at an all-time high, with over 350 documented cases between 1974–1978."[25]

THE AFTERLIFE OF 1968: "NO SE OLVIDA"?

The Mexican government and political and economic elites had hope that the 1968 Olympics would provide an opportunity to display the economic success of the Mexican Miracle to a global audience. The 1968 Olympics were the first global games to be held in a developing country. In the months leading up to the games in October, growing social unrest in Mexico and the ever-present yet prodigiously hidden specter of state violence rumbled to the surface.[26]

The confrontation with the Mexican state in the summer of 1968 emerged during a seemingly innocuous dispute between student groups at two preparatory schools (the equivalent of secondary schools in the United States) over a game of American football. Riot police beat protesting students to discourage dissent and maintain "public order." Subsequent confrontations between students and *granaderos* (riot police) continued throughout the summer, culminating with a bazooka being fired at the Preparatory Number 2 in the center of Mexico City, which was answered with the March of Silence on July 26. This response drew special attention to the violent reaction of the state, solidifying support from a conservative Mexican society.[27] From that point on, students worked at exposing the illusion that hosting the Olympics signaled progress for Mexico. They did this by juxtaposing the elaborate spending of public funds for Olympic preparations with the increase in the cost of education that was passed on to the students.[28]

The Universidad Nacional Autónoma de México (UNAM) was located in southern Mexico City, and students were largely middle class, as public subsidies for education were limited at best. Students from the Instituto Politécnico Nacional (IPN), located north of downtown Mexico City, often came from working-class backgrounds.[29] The working class, middle-class students, sometimes their families, and their supporters pushed back and made evident the violence of the Mexican state and the PRI regime. They organized the General Strike Council with representatives from various schools, the UNAM, and the IPN, and issued a series of demands. At the same time, conservative families supported the decision of the Mexican state to respond with force to maintain law and order.[30]

Throughout the summer, the stakes escalated on both sides: "both the students and the government continued to remain in a dialogue with one another hoping to reach an agreement whereby the students would return to the revolutionary family and the patriarchs would yield to the political demands of their children."[31] For their part, students were able to communicate the specific issues of their struggle and the demands for reform through hundreds of *brigadas* (brigades). These *brigadas*, which comprised ten to twenty-five people and constituted the primary units for the student movement of 1968, fanned out across Mexico City and the country, organizing *mitines relampagos* (lightning meetings).[32] The students embraced the brigade model as a weapon for combatting the vilification of their movement by the *prensa vendida* (sellout press), as many activists called the media. For example, a musician would sing and play the guitar while someone else passed out literature and a third person made a speech. There was always someone whose sole responsibility was to watch for the police, who were always close by. These roles were often interchangeable. Fanning out across Mexico City on the buses and recently constructed state-of-the-art subway, and across the entire country and parts of the United States, they went directly to the people, using music, poetry, theater, and conversation to explain why they were protesting. Direct contact was the most effective tool for circulating information about the movement.

The brigades were innovative, adaptable, and effective in communicating the justice in their movement.[33] This would be a critical political formation that theater collectives would use during the 1970s. "The disruption of the Olympic Games in the hope of implementing a socialist society in Mexico might have been echoed in numerous autonomous brigades," Pensado argues, "but such radical ideas never received the overwhelming support from the students."[34] Many of the brigades continued to exist in other forms after 1968, either as affinity groups that engaged in a variety of political activities or as confederations and fronts (*frentes*) of artists inspired by the liberation fronts of anticolonial groups.

The Tlatelolco massacre, which occurred on the afternoon of October 2, 1968, when students, parents, and other supporters gathered for a (relatively) small meeting at the Plaza de las Tres Culturas (Plaza of the Three Cultures), sparked disbelief, condemnation, and anger across the globe. The protesters were listening to a student speaker and were surrounded by military tanks and personnel when what appeared to be fireworks went off overhead. Bengal lights dropped from helicopters hovering above signaled a volley of gunshots from the rooftop of a nearby church and the windows of apartment buildings in the vicinity. The military fired in response to what they assumed was an attack by the students, killing many of the students and parents who had gathered peacefully in the plaza. Those who fled to the neighboring apartments for refuge were pursued, arrested, and imprisoned. We still lack an accurate tally of the number of dead and wounded that night, but estimates generally agree on approximately three hundred. Some met their death while in custody. While the movement included the participation of numerous sectors of the working class, particularly students from the INP and high schools, Tanalís Padilla points out that "Tlatelolco is remembered primarily as a student massacre. The shock of the attack is thus compounded by the middle-class origins of many of its victims."[35] Like students in France, Germany, Italy, Chile, Argentina, and other countries, Chicanas/os mounted a protest at the Mexican Consulate in Los Angeles. Echeverría was secretary of the interior at the time. Subsequent research and publications, as well as a federally sponsored investigation more than thirty years later, found that he had coordinated with the special presidential security forces and the military to organize the sharpshooters firing from the church roof.[36]

The conservative support for state violence deeply impacted the momentum and reach of political movements after 1968 that continued to focus on the state and publicly criticized Echeverría's contradictory domestic and foreign policies.[37] The hegemony of the PRI's "revolutionary" legacy limited the Left's scope; still, "though budding, scantly populated, and lacking social and political embeddedness, the Left in 1960s Mexico was nonetheless restless, studious, and determined."[38] This restless and studious determination would grow stronger as the result of consistent agitation and organizing in the early years of the 1970s. Social movements drew out the contradictions of the social pacts of PRI corporativist control, revealing deeper fissures in the regime as the 1970s opened.

The legacy and meanings of '68 are still contested: "Regardless of the strike's massive demeanor, the movement never achieved a truly popular or national dimension," argues Pensado, while Raúl Garín, one of the student leaders of 1968, emphasizes that it was "not [only] a student movement, but one that was eminently social."[39] The fruition and continuity of the 1970s evoke clarity about the consequences of these leftist-inspired brigades, and about how resisting state violence and US imperialism led them to create solidarity connections across Mexico and the Americas.[40]

THE 1970S AND ECHEVERRÍA'S *APERTURA DEMOCRÁTICA* (DEMOCRATIC OPENING)

Luis Echeverría Álvarez was born in Mexico City in January 1922. An intellectual, teacher, and PRI political operative, he married into the wealthy Zuno family. In the 1970s he saw himself as the new Latin American man, putting forth what he called the "Echeverría Doctrine," his "principles of the Third World vis-à-vis the great powers of the world."[41] Political movements had challenged the efficacy of the Mexican Miracle over the previous two decades. Political movements and artists questioned, challenged, and rejected the PRI's ability to absorb sectors of society by distributing social goods, services, and access in return for political loyalty. Beginning in 1970, "the presidency (sexenio) of Luis Echeverría Álvarez was the first big push to correct the deficiencies of the regime that had come to light with the student movement of 1968."[42] Yet when the state acted, it exacerbated rather than managed the crisis.

In June 1971, one year into Echeverría's presidency and two and a half years after the Massacre of Tlatelolco, government-paid and -trained agents attacked a peaceful silent march organized in celebration of the Cuban Revolution and in support of the struggle to maintain university autonomy in Monterrey, in the northern border state of Nuevo León. The march was the first public gathering to bring together recently returned political exiles and released political prisoners. It functioned as an impromptu assembly for dissident political activists, labor organizers, intellectuals, and artists who continued to agitate against state violence. Shortly after the march began, the paramilitary group Los Halcones, armed with kempo sticks, pistols, and rifles and trained in martial arts, attacked the participants. Beatings and deaths accompanied the detainment of a large but unknown number of students. Like the White Brigade (La Brigada Blanca) and the Jaguars (Los Jaguares), the Halcones, created during the Díaz Ordaz presidency (1964–1970), were paramilitary shock troops directly tied to various federal security agents whose sole purpose was terrorizing political movements and their supporters in Mexico throughout the 1970s.[43]

Though Echeverría came to power "obsessed with reform," the contradictions of the democratic opening played out on national and international fronts. On the one hand, state-sponsored terror devastated political movements, attempting to arrest political organizing, while on the other hand, political rhetoric limited policies that were

ostensibly aimed at reincorporating the Left and expanding the corporatist Mexican state. Even as Echeverría created a nominal space for
political leaders from the 1968 generation within the existing copora-
tivist system, these gestures were contradicted by his actions regarding
political movement activity during the 1970s.[44]

In 1971, as a gesture of reconciliation to the Left and Mexican society, Echeverría released more than two dozen political activists (never
recognized as political prisoners in public) incarcerated during 1968.
In addition, he appointed former students and other social movement
leaders to government posts. Echeverría openly supported the right for
countries in Latin America to determine their own destiny—ostensibly
without the influence of the colossus to the north. Herrera and Cedillo
write:

> First, the myth of the *pax priísta* aims to minimize moments of
> upheaval. Studies of this period tend to focus on populism, election
> frauds, the failure of land reform, moderate economic prosperity, the
> rise of the middle class, peaceful social movements, counter culture,
> and international relations. None of these works takes into account
> the gravity of the Dirty War or how this period offers a window onto
> socio-political and cultural issues after 1968.[45]

Padilla argues convincingly, "State violence and popular resistance
emerge here as an escalating dialogue: each act of state repression was
answered by popular organizing and militancy." It is also important to
consider that each act of popular organizing and militancy was not necessarily "seeking . . . some radical alternative, but [often] the fulfillment
of the 1917 Constitution. It was only when the state responded with
repression that these groups became radicalized."[46] As the next three
chapters demonstrate, state violence directed at political movements
accelerated the pace of organizing in Latin America and the United
States.[47] Organizations took up arms, students went to the mountains
for training or organized small urban guerrilla cadres, and artists radicalized their message. While the political movements of the 1960s and
1970s may have grown in large part as a response to the repressive mea-
sures, historical context is not causality. In Mexico, the dirty war reflected the profound political crisis in the corporatist system.

In this "more insurgent new Left" of the 1970s, artists played an important role in reimaging rebellion and creating political organizations,
spaces that conditioned the possibility for social change.[48] After 1968,

numerous poets, *teatristas*, filmmakers, photographers, and musicians forged new organizations with openly leftist and antiauthoritarian politics. Artists not only resisted repression but also began to identify as cultural workers, centering the labor of the creative process and their work with popular movements of the time as themes for their creative work and inspirations for political organizing. For example, artists, musicians, and writers that established the Frente Artístico Revolucionario Organizado (Organized Revolutionary Artistic Front, FARO) in late 1968 were directly connected to the struggle to establish CLETA (Centro Libre de Experimentación Teatral y Artística) in 1974.

THE UNITED STATES, MEXICO, AND COLD WAR COUNTERINSURGENCY

During the 1970s Cold War, the Echeverría administration played a crucial role for the United States in Latin America. The US government viewed Mexico as a stable democratic regime during a time when political, economic, and social instability—oftentimes caused by governments that the United States supported—dominated domestic conditions in other Latin American countries. Mexico was the only country in the Western Hemisphere to maintain relations with Cuba, opposing Cuba's expulsion from the Organization of American States in 1962. Cuba, in turn, denied direct or indirect support for political movements in Mexico, while simultaneously training revolutionaries from across the socialist world. Urban and rural armed formations had to look to China and Korea for ideological and military training, with numerous combatants traveling to both countries in the 1970s. This politics of solidarity dates back at least to the presidency of Lázaro Cárdenas (1934–1940).[49] Cárdenas provided political asylum to Leon Trotsky, and later to political refugees from the Spanish Civil War.[50] Luis Echeverría followed the precedent, extending asylum to dissidents from Brazil, Chile, Argentina, Uruguay, Guatemala, Nicaragua, and El Salvador—many of the countries that were part of Operation Condor, as well as countries where the United States supported repressive governments. As Calderon and Cedillo argue, "welcoming political exiles reveals a number of contradictions within Mexico's foreign and domestic policies. By providing asylum, the PRI supported, for 'humanitarian' reasons, guerrillas abroad while persecuting in the name of patriotism anyone who questions its revolutionary nationalism at home."[51]

The CIA's interventions in Mexican politics began in the 1950s and steadily increased during the late 1960s and the 1970s.[52] Beginning in the early 1960s, the CIA station chief in Mexico, Winston Scott, recruited twelve high-ranking PRI officials and businessmen as intelligence assets under the program code-named LITEMPO. This recruitment program also included Presidents Díaz Ordaz and Echeverría, the latter since his time as secretary of the interior. Relying on these informants affected the US interpretation of events in Mexico, as the United States received a narrative essentially created by Echeverría, among others, throughout the 1960s.[53] This close relationship between US intelligence agencies and high-level Mexican officials during a time of heightened security issues with Cuba and Chile would prove key to the United States' ability to maintain its hegemonic position in hemispheric politics and provide international cover for Mexico's foreign policy toward Cuba. As Kate Doyle points out, because of Mexico's and Cuba's revolutionary experiences, "the historical relations between Mexico and Cuba, on average, are a legend that both nations have tirelessly promoted since 1959."[54] This legend obscured a secret pact. Declassified documents "offer new evidence that the tolerance that the United States had for the intransigence of Mexico was based on a secret pact between the leaders of the Mexican state and their counterparts in the United States."[55] As a result of the direct reports from two Mexican ambassadors to Cuba—Fernando Pánames Escobedo and Miguel Covian Pérez—to the US Embassy and CIA office in Mexico, the United States had access to intelligence data from Cuba. This made Mexico a centrally strategic ally in the Cold War during the 1970s.

In this context, there was special interest in social movements and organizations that were making links across borders, most evidenced by the least known of the FBI COINTELPRO operations, the Border Coverage Program (BOCOV). One of six COINTELPRO initiatives, the Border Coverage Program focused on the political links between organizations in the US-Mexican borderlands. Of all the COINTELPRO initiatives, we know the least about BOCOV. Given the geopolitical implications of US engagement in espionage and counterinsurgency in Cuba, through Mexico, and along the US-Mexican border, these operations could have fallen under the purview of the CIA. Given the heavy reliance on Mexican elites for analysis of Mexico's politics prior to the 1970s, the United States had a deeply skewed view of conditions across the border. During the 1970s, the US government, through both diplomatic and intelligence reports and denunciations of the violence by Chicanas/os and Mexicanas/os living in the United States, was well aware of the dirty war against political opponents, activists, and family members that was taking place in Mexico.[56]

With historically close diplomatic and economic relationships ranging from the Good Neighbor Policy to the economic support provided by US banks and investment of US oil companies in the Mexican state-run oil industry, the United States needed Mexico to maintain these ties as part of the extensive reach of US intelligence services during the Cold War.[57] Meanwhile, on the ground, people struggled to expose the ideological and political connections between US and Mexican business and political elites as proof of the negative consequences of imperialism, using politics, theater, creative organizing, and armed struggle to build solidarity across borders.

CHICANO FOREIGN POLICY AND THE MEXICAN STATE: "LOS DOS MÉXICOS"

From the perspective of the Mexican state during the presidencies of Echeverría and López Portillo, Chicanas/os were politically expedient and their usefulness situational. Echeverría's politics toward the "Chicanomexicana" community were twofold: establish a stable working relationship with key (male) Chicano leaders and attend to the binational issues like migration, water rights, and immigration that were more relevant than ever because of growing Mexican communities in the United States. His relationships with Chicano leaders would lead to disagreement among Chicana/o organizations, particularly in regard to Echeverría's role in the Tlatelolco massacre in 1968 and again in the "Halconazo" of 1971. "For understandable reasons," Arturo Santamaría Gómez explains, "Mexico has held a magnetic attraction for the Chicano community, and at the same time Chicanos and the events occurring in the southwestern United States have influenced the opinions and politics of Mexico."[58] In addition, because Echeverría had his own agenda as a self-styled "progressive" left-leaning leader in Latin America, he approached foreign policy issues, particularly relations with the United States, strategically as an opportunity to increase Mexico's influence in Latin America and his own power within Mexico and internationally.

For example, as word of the massacre of Tlatelolco spread through student and political movement networks, and particularly Chicano movement newspapers, student activist and labor organizations protested at the Mexican Consulate in Los Angeles. Building on movements that targeted the consular institutions in the United States, these were perhaps the first sustained protests by Chicanas/os during this time period in solidarity with political movements in Mexico, creating the reference point for later political solidarity.[59] This action of "Chicano students . . . in response to what happened in '68, speaks to their interest in the future of the country of their parents and at the same time demonstrates their word for Mexican politics."[60] Solidarity with Mexico transcended political ideology, "whether their philosophical base with liberal humanism, indigenous culture, or socialism, movement leaders, artists, and intellectuals stress[ed] the importance of solidarity with Latin American social movements."[61]

Building on this solidarity of protest, "[t]he first visible and productive attempts by Chicano activists to unionize undocumented workers coincided with the student, farmer and labor movements in a post-'68 Mexico that created the atmosphere for a coming together of 'Los dos Méxicos.'"[62] The first visit between Chicano/a students and functionaries of the Mexican government took place in the months after October 1968. Though Echeverría was questioned about the Tlatelolco massacre, the record regarding his response is unclear.[63] Reies López Tijerina had first engaged President Díaz Ordaz in 1964 concerning land grant issues in New Mexico. Tijerina traveled from New Mexico to discuss compensation from the Mexican government for violations of land grants. On orders from Díaz Ordaz, Echeverría, attorney general at the time, had Tijerina deported. Before the 1970 presidential elections, a group of approximately two hundred Chicano/a students that included members of MEChA visited Mexico City. Rather than meet with political elites, the delegation, organized by the lawyer Frank Ortiz, gave students the opportunity "to meet with the struggle committees of the UNAM, specifically the law school committee. The assemblies of Mexican *universitarios* [members of the university community] and the visits to *ejidos* and popular neighborhoods was an important political learning moment for the young Chicanos."[64] The law school had some of the strongest and most persuasive leaders and included the only two women to be part of the General Strike Council—Roberta "La Tita" Avendaño and Ana Ignacia "La Nacha" Rodríguez. Antonio Rodríguez was one of the students on this trip in 1970; he later joined CASA in Los Angeles and became one of the people involved in CASA's shift toward a revolutionary Marxist-Leninist position in the 1974–1975 period (see chap. 6). Rodríguez made important connections in 1970 with José Jácques y Medina and Carlos Arango, who as law students had participated in the student rebellions in 1968. Medina and Arango worked on immigrants' rights issues with CASA in Los Angeles in the mid-1970s, while also fighting their own deportation back to Mexico.

In south Texas the Chicano college Colegio Jacinto Treviño was inspired by Mexican social movements, particularly student and rural campesino organizing efforts, political education, and grassroots organizing.[65] The Colegio Jacinto Treviño eventually played a key role in support for the PPUA (discussed in chap. 6).

Solidarity protests against political repression and circulation of news about the massacre that was not covered in the US or Mexican mainstream press pointed to nascent connections between political movements. They also highlighted an emerging analysis that combined a critique of racial and economic politics in the United States with an analysis of US relationships with Mexico and Latin America. According to Santamaría Gómez, the process of building lasting connections was impeded by "[t]he lack of resources, the volatility of student movements, and the limited definition of their agreements, in addition to other various reasons." At the same time, these experiences and direct connections raised the possibility of future engagements from some of the same people who were on the delegations, as well as others influenced by connections made through international solidarity. Mexican students were influenced by the engagements with Chicana/o activists and the experience of living in the United States: "it was through the struggle committees that they were able to begin a relationship with MEChA, the vision that they had of North American society was substantially modified."[66] Yet "while Chicanos looked toward Mexico, especially after '68, Mexicans did not do so in the same manner; few students, intellectuals, and social and political leaders paid attention to Aztlan before 1972."[67]

1972: "CARTA DE LECUMBERRI" (LETTER FROM LECUMBERRI)

The summer of 1972 was an important time for Chicana/o-Mexican solidarity. Echeverría visited San Antonio on three occasions during the 1970s, twice in 1972 and again in 1976. A few days after his meeting with Nixon, he inaugurated the Instituto Cultural de México in San Antonio. While local political and economic elites received the visiting dignitary, San Antonio restaurateur and activist Mario Cantú enlisted the support of Angela Y. Davis and the National Alliance against Racist and Political Repression (NAARPR), Clyde Bellecourt from the American Indian Movement (AIM), and some forty others to protest Echeverría's visit. Three hundred protesters met Echeverría in Los Angeles a few days later on the same trip for a similarly coordinated action.[68] Those who had gathered condemned the existence of political prisoners in Mexico and Echeverría's complicity in the violence against students the previous year in the Halconazo on June 10, 1971. The protesters were also seeking support for a boycott of lettuce to back farmworkers on strike in Texas. On this issue Echeverría was clear: his intention in Washington, DC, was to discuss the water issue concerning the Colorado River, not internal US policy. On the second day of the protests, Echeverría agreed to meet with the delegation if they would call off a protest scheduled for that afternoon. In the meeting, Echeverría denied that there were political prisoners in Mexico and agreed that a delegation of Chicanos could visit Lecumberri in Mexico City.[69]

The following week a delegation of Chicanos traveled to Mexico City. It appears that two groups visited Lecumberri in the week after Echeverría's visit: one from San Antonio, and a few days later "Two Chicanas" from San Diego who requested anonymity in a letter to *La Raza* explaining their experiences.[70] According to the "Two Chicanas," during the visit, they "discussed both the Chicano and Mexican movements. We learned of the similarities of the two struggles due to the fact that our common enemy is the United States imperialism."[71] There was some concern on the part of the prisoners that in San Antonio the Chicano protesters had been "fooled by Echeverría's blatant lies."[72] The prisoners in cellblock M, where some political prisoners were held together, handed over a collective letter originally drafted to the Chicana delegation from San Diego.[73] The letter provides important insight into how elements within the Mexican Left understood the struggle of Chicanos north of the Rio Bravo.

Directed to the Chicano/a community, the letter, "Carta de Lecumberri," was published in the magazine *La Raza* (San Antonio, Texas), *El Grito del Norte*, and other *movimiento* publications. As a political manifesto and gesture of solidarity, the letter emphasized "el parentezco historico chicano-mexicano" (the historical bonds between Chicanos and Mexicans). Drawing similarities between the dominant politics of the United States and Mexico, the letter explained, "Chicanos and Mexicans are united for a common historical inheritance and by a just struggle against a common oppressor. We are struggling against an enemy that stole a part of our National Territory and that condemned a sector of our population to live under a foreign government."[74] Contrary to Echeverría's claims, political prisoners existed, and they were reaching out to Chicana/o allies north of the border. They understood that Chicana/o struggles were related to other Third World political struggles and therefore sought connections with their international counterparts.

> To speak of Nationalism, here in Mexico, is to make it clear that no imposed frontier, by a foreign aggressor, can separate our people. When speaking of Mexican culture, language, tradition, and patriotism, the Bravo River is only a gash on our peoples' hearts and never a barrier between our common historical heritage, we must not forget our wounds suffered at the hands of a common enemy . . . it is this common enemy, U.S. imperialism, that from across the river sustains the most monstrous system of oppression and exploitation upon the shoulders of its oppressed classes, fundamentally with the working class, within which exists super-exploited strata (Chicanos, Blacks, and Puerto Rican workers), and who, on this side of the border, supports an oppressive ruling class which serves its interest.[75]

The letter emphasized that the international bourgeois class created the structures of colonial rule in Mexico *and* that Chicanos in the United States were Mexican by nationality but simply lived "on the other side of the border." The letter indicated that Chicanos were a national minority confronting a system that denied their right to self-determination: "Chicano is a word which has come to mean a struggle for self-determination. That struggle and the struggle for self-determination for the Mexican people merge into a common commitment of those struggling on both sides of the border."[76] When combined with the language and politics of solidarity conveyed in the letter, the series of events that led to this historic meeting between Chicanas, Chicanos, and Mexican political prisoners is important for several reasons. First, an alliance of Third World activists, organized by Chicanas/os in Texas and California, forced the president of Mexico to concede to a visit by a Chicana/o delegation investigating the conditions and treatment of political prisoners at Lecumberri prison in Mexico City. Second, it forced Echeverría to publicly deny that there were political prisoners in Mexico, and then disproved his denial by visiting the prison and publishing the letter. Third, the delegation itself was significant, as it provided direct contact between Chicanos/as and Mexican political prisoners. Fourth, the letter from the political prisoners offers insight into an anti-imperialist analysis of Chicana/o history from the perspective of the (imprisoned male) Mexican Left that understood Chicanos as an oppressed minority struggling for self-determination, in other words, as an anticolonial struggle (from an internal colony). Fifth, according to the political prisoners, Chicanos/as were Mexicans who lived in the United States, workers fighting against a global imperial system that uprooted them (or their parents) from their land in Mexico, and a national minority struggling for self-determination.

The prisoners called for solidarity: "This unity [we call for] must be a unity of two peoples, side by side, against both ruling classes; it must be unity against two dominant classes; it must be a union against Imperialism. The struggle of the Mexican people will only achieve victories if, under the leadership of the working class, it stands for complete popular unity and knows who are its enemies." Though recognizing a cultural and/or national link between Chicanos and Mexicans, "the struggle of Chicanos against national repression is also of interest to the working class of North America."[77] For the prisoners in Lecumberri as well as the Chicano internationalists in Texas, Mexican and Chicano workers were part of the same imperialist system. Because a geopolitical line divided them, this demanded a politics of *Sin Fronteras* (No Borders).

There was no single Chicana/o foreign policy toward Mexico. The walls and mirrors of a socialist imaginary among Chicanas/os and Mexicanas/os in the United States revealed the range of meanings attached to revolutionary movements in Mexico, Latin America, and Cuba and challenged notions of the limitations to making long-term political connections.[78] Even the idea of a foreign policy assumed engaging with the governments of other countries rather than with political movements. Differing perspectives on the relationship between supporting the Mexican state and/or supporting political movements in Mexico and Latin America reveal differences among sectors of the Chicano movement. For example, when Olga Talamante was arrested, tortured, and imprisoned in Argentina in October 1974, she did not notify the US Embassy, she did not act as an American in need of protection, and she did not accept the sentence that would have allowed her to be deported. Instead, Talamante, guided by an insurgent feminism that advanced a critique of class, race, gender, and nation, appealed the decision in solidarity with her comrades. As a consequence, she remained imprisoned. Magdalena Mora's insurgent feminism inspired her political organizing and intellectual writings, newspaper articles, research essays, short stories. Focusing her analysis on US imperialism and collusion with national elites in Mexico and other nations, she aligned herself with political movements rather than state governments, organizing with other Mexican workers. Mario Cantú emphasized at the time, "We need to move history . . . we should identify with feelings and struggles, and not with the government . . . a lot of Chicanos want to have a 'foreign policy' position . . . [that] we should identify with Mexican government. This is incorrect. . . . We should identify with the people, with the struggle of the people."[79] Cantú, Ramon Chacón, Olga Talamante, Magdalena Mora, and others were intentional and adamant about making connections to the people of Mexico rather than politicians.

José Angel Gutiérrez of La Raza Unida Party held a different perspective on the relationship between Mexican politics and Chicanos, in many ways mirroring Echeverría's policy of political expediency in this matter. "For Chicanos, contact with the world began with Echeverría," explained Gutiérrez in his memoir. "This president also raised the reputation of Chicanos in Mexico. The rich and upper-middle-class Mexican doesn't think of us at all. To members of these social classes, Chicanos are an embarrassment because we don't speak Spanish, don't know Mexican history, and often, are poor imitations of gringos."[80] In an interview published in 1975, Gutiérrez explained:

> We have also achieved, and this is probably the most important issue (publicly declared by the President of Mexico) that Mexico has finally recognized that Chicanos form an internal colony of the United States and that they are part of the Third World. This has been publicized and Echeverría admitted that Chicanos exist and that we are oppressed. . . . Chicanos should not look toward Wall Street or Washington to find their destiny. Our destiny is in the south with a *pueblo* like ours. We are a family without borders, we are a family without orphans. I'll remind you in case you're forgotten that we are not sons of the Immaculate Conception or the statue of Liberty. We are sons of *Mexicanos*.[81]

In addition to the formal political recognition of the Chicano movement by the president of Mexico, Gutiérrez worked to garner resources such as two thousand books donated to the library in Cristal City by the Mexican government, a statue of Benito Juarez, and the Becas de Aztlán

(Scholarships for Aztlán) as part of a larger "Chicano foreign policy" that he envisioned.[82] The scholarship program, a collaboration between the Mexican government and the University of Houston, was initially for Chicanas/os interested in studying medicine. By the end of the decade, the program included social sciences and fine arts. Sylvia Orozco was the first Chicana/o to study art in Mexico under this program. The experience led her to change her self-identification from Chicana to Mexicana:

> In the beginning we were all Chicano, [now] a lot of people in the becario [scholarship] group feel that they are Mexicanos, that they are not Chicanos anymore, that the word Chicano itself is just another word to separate us more. *What makes us different is that we have been living in this environment* [emphasis added]. And the things that make us different are negative things; being very individualistic, competitive, being very aggressive to an extent that it is harmful. We just disagree with that. We are trying to get things back that have been taken from us. We don't want to separate us any more from Mexicanos.[83]

The scholarship program reflected La Raza Unida Party's vision of Chicano power and nation building. "I knew we had to have a foreign policy," Gutiérrez explained. "We could not have pretended to be an alternative political party if we did not have an alternative foreign policy."[84] It made sense for a third party in the liberal electoral arena to establish these connections. At the same time, this relationship limited what issues could (or would) be discussed in the meeting with Echeverría. In a certain way, Chicano Power, through third-party representation, also created an opportunity for Mexican politicians to increase their influence on the US government. Echeverría, and later López Portillo, recognized the political expediency of reaching out to male leaders.

In 1976 a changing of the guard in the PRI ruling party brought José López Portillo to the presidency, where he "adopted a different approach in the selection of targets within the Chicano community . . . [taking] advantage of the fact that a new crop of moderate Chicano leadership and organizations, such as the Congressional Hispanic Caucus, MALDEF, NCLR . . . [and] LULAC, had developed a deeper and broader interest in foreign policy, including economic matters and immigration."[85] It is worth considering that these organizations would not have been focusing on economic matters, immigration, and relations with Mexico had it not been for people and organizations putting forward the importance of these issues from an anti-imperialist rather than strictly liberal reformist perspective, before 1976 (when López Portillo and Carter both came into power). Gutiérrez mentions in his memoir a meeting on the night in 1976 when Echeverría, after consulting with party leaders, tapped his successor for the PRI candidacy for president. According to Gutiérrez, Echeverría counseled that "Chicanos were the single most important people outside of Mexico . . . the future of Mexico rested with the Chicano people and that his successor would be well served to pay attention to relations with Chicanos."[86]

Sons and daughters of Mexico did not agree about their parental relations, or how to respond to events in Mexico without supporting the very government responsible for repressive acts, or the terms of the relationship to the political movement in Mexico as opposed to the Mexican state. On the one hand, organizations like CASA, the August Twenty-Ninth Movement, and the Crusade for Justice; newspapers like *El Grito del Norte* and *Sin Fronteras*; and individuals like Olga Talamante, Magdalena Mora, Mario Cantú, and Ramón Chacón were not interested in making connections with the Mexican government. Instead, they consistently protested the violence of Latin American regimes, including Mexico, against labor and people's movements that they supported and were involved in.

In an unanticipated sense, Gutiérrez's description was accurate: "Mexico has finally recognized that Chicanos form an internal colony of the United States and that they are part of the Third World." Echeverría characterized Chicanos as a threat to national and international security in the same breath that he distanced himself from Cuba and Chile.

Diplomacy and reciprocity, though a successful formula for exacting support from Echeverría and bolstering the individual power of leadership, created limitations as to what could be brought up for discussion. Perhaps Gutiérrez and other Chicano leaders were allowed access because they were not publicly critical of the internal politics of Mexico. In broaching the touchy subject of government repression, Gutiérrez limited the possible concessions that could be gained from Echeverria: "I didn't see my dialogue with the Mexican president in that limited sense [accountability for state repression]. We needed resources from wherever we could get them and we needed to be legitimized by the leaders at the highest levels of our other mother country."[87] Echeverría had a similar view of Chicanos: they were politically expedient, and a desire for power directed his strategic alliances.

The process of creating political alliances implied responsibility for the decisions of each party involved. Because Echeverría's hands were stained with the blood of two massacres and an escalating dirty war against political activists and ordinary citizens who were part of social movements—a war that included the torture and imprisonment of Texas-based Chicanos Rubén Solis and Ramón Chacón—the decision by male leaders of the Chicano movement to engage in "diplomatic" relations with the Mexican government is complicated at best, particularly given the travel to Cuba and Libya by LRUP leaders in the mid-1970s. To his critics, Gutiérrez explained, "They could not see beyond the massacre of students at Tlatelolco, nor could they understand why it was important for us to have contact with other governments such as Mexico. They could not see what there was to be gained . . . for Chicanos to have an independent position in foreign affairs and, more importantly, our own voice and contacts abroad."[88] For La Raza Unida Party, it made sense to cultivate relationships with heads of state to demonstrate political power within the electoral arena, garner monetary support (as Gutiérrez was accused of doing by taking resources from the Echeverría government), and bring some resources back to the movement in the form of scholarships, books, and other cultural exchanges.

An alternate Chicana/o foreign policy, a politics of solidarity and anti-imperialism, defined the Chicana/o Left. The point is not to decide which perspective was correct, but to emphasize that the consequences of engaging the Mexican state and/or social movements in Mexico (whose proponents were themselves refusing the authority of the state and exposing its violence) were not the same for all US-based Chicana/o political organizations. These differing perspectives are further examples of how interpretations of solidarity with Mexico and Latin America varied within the Chicana/o movement.

THE IDEOLOGICAL GLUE OF ANTICOMMUNISM

Nixon's response to Echeverría served as a political anointment of the Mexican president: "In other words, let the voice of Echeverría rather than the voice of Castro be the voice of Latin America."[89] Nixon's words must have elated Echeverría. Nixon emphasized that Mexico had to be safe for investors and that private enterprise was to be protected in order to avoid the flight of capital that Chile was experiencing (as a consequence of direct, indirect, and clandestine intervention in internal Chilean politics and economic subversion supported by the CIA). Nixon then encouraged Echeverría to take a leadership role in the Organization of American States, while assuring promotion of Mexican markets among US companies that were seeking a safe investment terrain. All this was to be done to prevent "the Cuban tragedy to infect the rest of the Caribbean and eventually the rest of Latin America. And frankly, to be quite candid, I think it would be very detrimental to all of us to have the Chilean experiment spread through the rest of the continent. It will be a very unhealthy hemisphere if that will be an element—the wave of the future."[90] This was a quintessential anticommunist Cold War US–Latin American moment. The president of Mexico, with aspirations of a career at the international level, used multiracial alliances as the foil for Mexico's (and his own) ascension in the hierarchy of US allies.

The question is not whether Echeverría, Nixon, or Kissinger (who joined the conversation toward the end of the meeting) feared these alliances. The governments of both countries used fear to manipulate public opinion and actions against perceived political threats. The question is, what did Echeverría gain by mentioning these events in his discussion with Nixon? Where did he get his information? How commonly was counterintelligence shared between the US and Mexican governments? These questions contextualize the following chapters, emphasizing the threat of transnational connections to the foundations of intrastate power relations. Two days after the meeting with Nixon, and two days before the protest in San Antonio, a burglary took place by members of the Committee to Re-Elect the President (CRP/CREEP) at the Democratic offices in the Watergate Complex in Washington, DC. This event was the beginning of revelations that uncovered levels of corruption and deceit in the Nixon administration that led to his eventual resignation. At the presidential level, Echeverría would need a new ally. Yet his warning, and the concern behind it, would portend the increased cross-border solidarity of the coming years.

CHAPTER 3

NUEVO TEATRO POPULAR
ACROSS THE AMÉRICAS

"No Hay Arte sin Ideología"
FRENTE ARTÍSTICO REVOLUCIONARIO ORGANIZADO, 1969

REVOLUTION, THEATER, AND STATE REPRESSION:
MANIZALES AND THE FRONT OF LATIN AMERICAN
CULTURAL WORKERS

Latin American *teatristas* convened their first continental/hemispheric gathering in 1968 at Manizales, Colombia. Connecting *teatros* from across the continent, the Festival de Teatro Latinoamericanos was organized at different locations in the following four years. *Teatristas* shared works in progress, techniques and pedagogies, workshops on acting and directing, and the latest developments in their evolving and changing roles as cultural workers. They worked to deemphasize professionalization and remuneration while experimenting with ideas of collective creative processes and organized leftist political activity. By 1973, Latin American groups had met on five occasions, with attendance ranging from five thousand to ten thousand people a year. The Manizales gathering drew theater groups from Europe and Africa, connecting the influential Latin American theater movement across the hemisphere.[1] At the 1972 gathering, attending groups formed the Frente Latino Americano de Trabajadores de la Cultura (Front of Latin American Cultural Workers—FLTC). The founding document of the FLTC reflected the need to make connections across different political and geographic borders: "The fundamental base of its activity is: communication between different theater and cultural organizations and groups with the goal of breaking through the barriers traditionally imposed in our countries."[2] The FLTC grounded its politics in a critique of imperialism, particularly the domination of the hemisphere by the United States, and in international solidarity between left-inspired artists. In the same vein as economists proposing a *dependentista* model to explain the economic crisis in Latin America, the FLTC emphasized that underdevelopment of Latin American countries was a result of colonial and neocolonial economic and social structures.[3] The signees were a who's who of Nuevo Teatro Popular in Latin America. The Frente pointed to low levels of education or educational opportunities for the marginalized and poor; the "mercantilization" of culture, resulting in "the progressive loss of our own cultural characteristics"; and a brain drain of technical knowledge and experts. Finally, in what is both the language of anticolonial struggles and, in the 1990s, the antineoliberal language of social movements, the FLTC identified global capitalism, transnational corporations, and structural adjustment programs—with support from national elites and the selective use of cooptation and violent coercion—as the causes of underdevelopment, poverty, and inequality:

> Concerning the political economy, the extensive sacking of our natural riches combined with the permanency of monocultivation, and together with the archaic feudal structures, leads to a surge in industrialization with deformed tendencies concentrated in the emergence of large multinational monopolies and dominating foreign investment. As the national rent of our countries increases, so too do irregularities in distribution: the exploitation of the work of the people continues to increase. This type of situation is beneficial for the large foreign corporations (with a majority being North American) and in the second place, for the local bourgeois intermediaries, who in order to better fulfill their function, make up the servile government and fascist dictators.[4]

The remainder of the communiqué called for recognition of a shared history of struggle and experimentation (out of necessity) with alternative ways of bringing theater, culture, education, and politics to the populations marginalized by mainstream cultural and social norms.

Victor Fuentes, representing the Teatro de la Esperanza from Goleta, California, described the transformative power of theater. Fuentes was an exile from Franco's Spain in 1944 who studied and later taught drama and Spanish at the University of California–Santa Barbara. Fuentes was in Manizales, where he had been studying prior to the festival, with the Colombian Enrique Buenaventura's Cali Experimental Theater (Teatro Experimental de Cali—TEC) group. According to Fuentes, the days were filled from morning until night with events—"cargadisimos" (supercharged). As he explained:

> For ten days Manizales was converted to the cultural center of the country, and those that make theatre in Latin America. . . . But for the hundreds of people that come for the festival, for the participants and large sectors of the population, and especially the workers that open their union meeting halls to the presentations, their homes to the "artists," the party has a profound meaning, something that is also the essence of theatre: Manizales is a place where it is possible, maybe just for a few minutes, maybe more, for a communion: an encounter.[5]

Fuentes emphasized that the very essence of popular theater, a people's theater, was its ability to engage and represent the lives of ordinary people. These festivals provided the opportunity for collective statements about the relationship between art and politics and the necessity of creating a united front against US imperialism. Finally, Fuentes lamented the absence of Chicano *teatro*, but emphasized that the decision to hold El Quinto in Mexico City and link up with Latin American *teatros* was readily anticipated: "There is a lot of interest among the groups from Latin America about our [Chicano] theatre, of which they already have a strong reference. Hopefully for the next festivals Chicano representatives will attend."[6] The wait wouldn't be long. The following year, the gathering of *teatros* from across the Américas would take place in Mexico City, simultaneously marking the third gathering of the FLTC.

Anti-imperialist struggle was not fought with only guns and military tactics. Art, music, and theater were also weapons in an ideological and political war against cultural imperialism. Artists used popular theater as a weapon against political repression. It was a tool for cultural survival, an organizing strategy, a medium to communicate political ideas, and a platform for a political critique of culture. Art functioned as both a political weapon to counter hegemonic worldviews and prescribed beliefs and a way to imagine different outcomes for political change.

Whereas chapter 4 specifically narrates the social history of the Quinto Festival/Primer Encuentro, including a discussion of the theater and its performance aspects, this chapter offers a political history of cultural movements in post-'68 Mexico, highlighting the influence of the Chicana/o movement on Mexican theater: the Mexico that the Chicanas/os might have imagined and then encountered in the summer of 1974. If, according to Diana Taylor, the period from 1965 to 1970 was one of crisis, with political and economic systems in Latin America clamoring to maintain power in a time of revolutionary fervor across the continent—a "turning point between life and death, regeneration and repression" on the one hand and a yet-to-emerge political culture where "new ideas had not yet congealed into a seamless, integrative ideology" on the other—then the early 1970s in Mexico provide insight into the lives of people inspired to create these emerging ideas. They pushed back against the political winds shifting right across the continent and used culture to defend against US imperialism and the "colonial" Mexican elite that facilitated continued US political and economic influence in Mexico. Simultaneously, the historical ethnographic elements of the chapter reveal that "theater [was an] arena for ideological confrontation and struggle."[7]

NUEVO TEATRO POPULAR: HEMISPHERIC ANTI-IMPERIALISM

The Manizales festivals and the FLTC were two examples of how theater and art served as a unique arena for contesting imperialism. While military dictators and repressive goverments established power throughout Latin America during the 1960s and 1970s, artists continued to play a vital role in critiquing the status quo, creating an alternate political imaginary and prompting people to take action. Coming from working-class backgrounds, these artists created Nuevo Teatro Popular (NTP), the political theater movement of the people that grew out of the repression of the time.[8] Part spectacle, part political intervention and disruption, simultaneously didactic and polemical as well as a collective celebration of working-class culture, NTP was not in the auditoriums and salons of the bourgeois and elites. It drew crowds in the union halls, community spaces, the streets, and the homes of the working class, the same communities from which many of the cultural workers had come. These cultural workers were not attendant to political movement activity. Rather, their creative works and labor to build organizations and projects made them central to political activity during the 1970s. NTP was a way to transmit ideas and provided a particular means for imagining creative processes and creative influences.[9] This meant theater was a multifaceted tool and creative practice that helped people to imagine what changes were possible. For people to see their own lives and experiences represented in the story offered the possibility of a different ending. Popular theater reminds us that different social classes have their own cultural practices and rituals, with their own ends, methodologies, and cultural assumptions.

Invoking Paul Gilroy's *Small Acts*, specifically concerning the ways that cultural expression (creation, production, and circulation) and the political economy are reciprocally and integrally linked, NTP represented an antidote to the developmentalist narratives of Western modernity.[10] Nuevo Teatro Popular "first of all evokes the idea of non-commercial theater, created *by* and *for* popular classes, a theater with limited resources, and whose purpose to promote popular cultural values is generally complemented by other political and social values."[11] The theater collectives that emerged at this time under the larger banner of NTP combined a critique of bourgeois culture with a political imaginary in the service of social justice.[12] NTP sought to make the connections between political economy and culture more transparent in the public sphere, and to consciously organize the idea and practice of collective performance. Given that NTP emerged during a time of revolutionary fervor in Latin America, and specifically in the context of targeted dirty wars, political performances about these themes on buses, in the streets, or on a stage connected state violence and art in unique and unanticipated ways. Grounded in an oppositional politics, local cultural conditions, and the influence of European avant-garde artists (who were in turn influenced by the art emerging from anticolonial movements), NTP circulated political struggles and provided the people and organizational infrastructure to create connections across borders through the FLTC.

In *Theatre of Crisis: Drama and Politics in Latin America*, Diana Taylor acknowledges that "Latin American Theater is a relatively unknown field" while emphasizing that to speak of *"a* Latin America, and hence a Latin American theatre or theory, is in itself misleading."[13] On the one hand, theater of the absurd, theater of the oppressed, theater for social change, popular theater, street theater, epic theater, or theater of cruelty emerged and comingled as aesthetic and political influences within artistic communities in Latin America. Yet "rather than squeeze this theater into the so-called 'Western' tradition (the term alone relegates Latin Americans to the nonspace of the non-Western) and continue to analyze it as an offshoot of . . . [European-inspired political theater (as a general term)], it proves more productive to relate this discourse to other minority or marginal discourses inside and outside the West: to black South African theater, or to black and feminist and Hispanic-American theater in the United States."[14] Taking up this point, NTP was a hemispheric movement of radicalized theater artists who were astute and creative in their political organizing and sought to transform "the role and function of oppositional theater in highly inflammatory sociopolitical contexts."[15] For NTP-inspired groups, Chicanas/os and the larger US Third World Left were connected to Latin America and Africa and Asia, politically and aesthetically. Chicana/o theater was already part of NTP before the Quinto Festival/Primer Encuentro in Mexico City brought together artists from across the continent.[16]

In contrast to previously published scholarly and journalistic writings about Chicano theater in general and the group El Teatro Campesino specifically that were "chronological, text-centered, and male-centered," Yolanda Broyles-González emphasizes the "Mexican working-class tradition of orality and oral culture. . . . Within this greatman/text-centered/chronological-linear approach to history many dimensions of the company's history recede into oblivion: the reality of collective creation; the contributions of women (and other men); the entire Mexican working class experience and popular tradition of performance."[17] For our purposes, this reshifting of the gaze to the "entire Mexican working class experience" first and foremost centers on Mexico and Latin America rather than the United States and examines how that context conditions Chicana/o theater. NTP engaged thousands of people across the continent to participate in creating original theater. These experiences allowed young people to experiment with new ways of being, to experience new social relations upon leaving home for the first time—experimenting with psychedelics, having a lover, creating political organizations, traveling—all acts that challenged and pushed back against the established social and cultural norms of the time.

The Cuban revolution and Latin American Marxism deeply influenced the ideological and artistic development of NTP. Chicana/o theater and NTP were "in their essence, performative acts of redressive rebellion."[18] Throughout these years, many artists in Chile, Argentina, Uruguay, Brazil, Mexico, and other countries were forced into exile in Europe and the United States.[19] While researchers have emphasized the influence of Bertold Brecht, Antonin Artaud, and others on Latin American theater, the specific contemporary economic, social, and political conditions in each country, the governance of an emerging political/economic elite, and a local and nationally centered cultural politics influenced the direction, style, and trajectory of NTP.[20]

Hardly an exhaustive list, these are but a few examples of *teatros* that made the NTP movement a widespread phenomenon that attracted young people in almost every country in Latin America. The Cuban writer José Triana's *Night of the Assassins* was a "crisis" moment in Latin American theater.[21] Written in the early years of the revolution, Triana's critique of the political class caused turmoil, a rupture that influenced the political imaginary from which NTP emerged as an art form of oppositional politics.

Perhaps the most well-known artist associated with oppositional theater during this time was Augusto Boal. A contemporary of Brazilian revolutionary educator Paulo Freire, Boal joined the group Teatro de Arena in 1956. Boal had studied engineering and theater at Columbia University in the 1950s. His work with theater and political movements made him a target of the Brazilian government. In 1971, Boal was tortured and imprisoned for four months before going into exile, first to Argentina and later to Europe. Returning to the United States in 1971 on a State Department–sponsored tour, Boal visited El Teatro Campesino in California and built a connection between Brazilian popular theater and Chicana/o theater.[22] Boal also "spent time in Central America and France, where he created the Institute for Theater of the Oppressed."[23] Also in Brazil, Amir Haddad directed the theater group T'Na Rúa, which participated in the Manizales festivals and was a founding group in FLTC. In Colombia, Enrique Buenaventura and the TEC developed collective techniques of writing and production. Buenaventura had been fired from his position as director of the Fine Arts School of Theater, along with other collaborators in the late 1960s. Also in Colombia, Santiago García of the group La Candelaria was important in connecting *teatros* across the continent. In Argentina, Griselda Gambaro, now one of Argentina's most celebrated dramatists, produced plays during this time that examined (and predicted) the consequence of organized state violence, incorporating unexpected bizarre scenes and modified characters while disrupting visual expectations on the stage.[24] In Nicaragua, Alan Bolt and the group Nixtayolero made history for their innovation and political scripts—yet this group was not founded until 1979, demonstrating the longevity and influence of NTP throughout the 1970s. In Guatemala, El Teatro Vivo and the Rabinal Achí collectives led protest activity and incorporated anticapitalist themes in the context of the everyday lives of workers and farmers. In El Salvador, El Sol del Río 32, Roberto Salomón's ActoTeatro, and the Maíz collectives worked closely with Justo Rufino Garay and the Teyocoyani collectives.[25] In Uruguay, Teatro El Galpón, founded in 1951 and directed by Atahualpa del Cioppo, was eventually forced into exile in 1976. Other theater groups associated with NTP that emerged during this time included the troupe Escambray from Cuba (1968); the Teatro de la Resistencia from Chile; and in Mexico, Los Mascarones (post-1968), El Zopilote, el Teatro Cooperative Decuncia de Felipe Santander (The Denunciation Theater Cooperative), Matlatzincas, el Grupo Cultural Zero, Tepito Arte Acá, Zumbón, and independent organizations like FARO and CLETA. Although this is not a complete list of Latin American popular theater groups of the 1960s and 1970s, these collectives were central in the work of the larger Latin American cultural and political Left.[26]

CHICANA/O THEATER AND NTP

The 1974 Quinto Festival/Primer Encuentro Latino Americano in Mexico was not the first time that Latin American popular theater groups had come together with Chicana/o artists. According to Martínez, "the 1969 World Theatre Festival in Nancy, France, provided the forum for the first encounter between *Teatro Chicano* and NTP."[27] This experience inspired Luis Valdez, a founder of El Teatro Campesino, to organize the First International Chicano Theater Festival in 1969 in Fresno, California.[28] The festival attracted thirteen Chicana/o *teatros*, Los Mascarones, and El Nuevo Teatro Pobre de las Américas from Puerto Rico. In all, some 250 people participated.[29]

After graduating from San Jose State University, Valdez traveled to Cuba in 1964 with the first Venceremos Brigade. This experience in the new socialist experiment would affect Valdez's political and artistic decisions in the following years. "Perhaps prompted by the 'international' aspect of the Nancy Festival," Martínez writes, "Valdez invited *Grupo los Mascarones* from Mexico City to attend the festival, an exchange that marked many Chicano *teatristas'* first exposure to a *teatro* from the Mexican *Nuevo Teatro Popular* movement."[30] Returning to the Nancy Festival in 1972, El Teatro Campesino and Valdez connected with Enrique Buenaventura from the *TEC* in Colombia, "establishing an important bridge between [men involved in] *Teatro Chicano* and the Latin American NTP Movement."[31]

Political theater is an act of necessity, of survival, and it is a way of giving meaning to struggle, of naming what was killing people and creating the possibility of change. Similar to NTP in Latin America, Chicana/o theater also had roots in redressive and revolutionary soil. Echoing the intentions and political imaginary of the Chicana/o movement, Chicana/o theater intended "to create an alternative to the dominant mode of production of mainstream theater, to make theatre accessible to working-class Chicano audiences, and to create an accurate theatrical representation of Chicanos' historical and social experience."[32] Teatro Chicano as a conscious, self-defined political movement traces its roots to El Teatro Campesino (ETC), a theater group that began as part of the movement of the United Farm Workers (UFW) in 1965. ETC's history has been told elsewhere.[33] In 1967 it split from the UFW organization, but it still worked closely with the UFW movement.

Exploding onto the scene, the Chicana/o theater movement emerged "from the physical memory of a dormant collective tradition: the Mexican popular performance tradition. Chicano theater emerged from localized roots, in neighborhoods and community centers, in universities, factories and the fields, alternative schools and inside prisons. . . . With an orally based culture, memory and the body are the sites of a community's self-knowledge."[34] This tradition of popular performances included the *carpa*, which was a kind of vaudeville, with traveling performers who connected small rural towns in a network of public art and engaged theater. Theater was used to communicate struggle, challenge relationships of power, and inspire action. The artistic explosion during this time included a significant number of Chicana/o theater groups. Though largely composed of young people and creating a youth culture of political engagement, the theater groups were an intergenerational effort that refused to accept the economic and political status quo or the cultural norms of US society.[35] Theater groups sprang from universities, community centers, political organizations, schools, barrios, agricultural fields, factory floors, and prisons. According to Jorge Huerta, a founding member of Teatro de la Esperanza and TENAZ (Teatro National de Aztlán), "prior to 1965, Chicano theatre was mostly Christian, reflecting the teachings of the Jesuits and Franciscans who had founded missions in Aztlán and employed theatre as an educational tool."[36] As more people were inspired to experiment with theater to represent their own local struggles and artistic talent, *teatros* emerged in all places where Mexican communities existed.

By 1971 and the founding of the umbrella group TENAZ, many other *teatros* had emerged, with heavy representation from California. These *teatros* included the following:

Teatro del Piojo, Seattle/Tacoma
Teatro Aztlán, Northridge, California
Teatro de Esperanza and Teatro Chicanito de Tiburcio Vasquez, Santa Barbara, California
Teatro Popular de la Vida y Muerte, Long Beach, California
Teatro Urbano and Teatro Pequeño, South El Monte, California
Teatro Machete, Los Angeles
Hijos del Sol, Berkeley
Cucarachas en Acción, San Francisco
Teatro Calcetín, Oakland
Teatro de los Barrios, San Antonio
Teatro Cucarracho, Brownsville, Texas
Teatro Bayuco, Houston
Teatro Estudiantil, Crystal City, Texas
Teatro de los Pobres, El Paso, Texas
Teatro del Chicano, Del Rio, Texas
Teatro Chicano, Austin
Teatro Rascuachi, Colorado Springs, Colorado
Su Teatro and Teatro Tlatelolco, both in Denver
Teatro Amigos, Tucson, Arizona
Teatro Indio, Douglas, Arizona
Teatro de la Calle, Albuquerque, New Mexico
Teatro Norteño, Las Vegas, New Mexico
Teatro del Barrio, Chicago
Teatro Desengaño del Pueblo, Gary, Indiana
Teatro Libre de Las Américas, Detroit
Teatro de los Estudiantes, Ann Arbor, Michigan[37]

Many of these *teatros* performed at or attended the festival in Mexico City in 1974.

Bringing fresh ideas, energy, and enthusiasm, theater reflected the everyday life experiences of Chicanas/os who were, for the first time, protagonists in their own plays. To explain the historical continuity linking the *teatros*, Broyles-Gonzalez locates a "working-class memory system allow[ing] for reliance on a common performance vocabulary based primarily on collective and improvisational creation."[38]

FIGURE 3.1. Members of Teatro Aztlán from Colegio Jacinto Treviño in Mercedes, Texas, at the federal penitentiary in Leavenworth, Kansas, circa fall 1971. raúlrsalinas is second from the left, wearing black glasses. Raúl R. Salinas Archive, MO774, box 13, folder 10. Courtesy of the Department of Special Collections and University Archives, Stanford University Libraries.

This working-class memory system was not necessarily nationalistic or based on the nation-state, but rather was often translocal in that it was situated on the US border and had cultural and political ties to Mexico, Latin America, and indigenous peoples. Collective improvisation was about life and survival, given that the theater was about art and politics. By the early 1970s, "it is safe to say that Teatro Chicano [was] a living, viable weapon in the struggle against Gabacho oppression in Aztlán."[39] Theater collectives like Las Cucarachas en Acción from the San Francisco Bay area, directed by Dorinda Moreno, were centered on Chicana perspectives and issues, casting women actors in roles as women, a contrast to ETC, which often cast women in either male roles or as nonhumans (the dead) and animals.[40] Incarcerated Chicanos in the federal prisons at McNeil Island in Washington State and Leavenworth in Kansas experimented with theater. At McNeil Island in the early 1970s, Chicano *pintos* worked with Seattle's Teatro de Piojo and Tomas Ybarra-Frausto, while Chicanos in Leavenworth hosted the *teatro* from the Colegio Jacinto Treviño (fig. 3.1).

Cultura and politics overlapped across the hemisphere, as "*Teatro Chicano* and *Nuevo Teatro Popular* shared a number of important and formative elements, including histories of *mestizaje* (mixed Amerindian and European heritage), colonialism, language, political affinities that embraced postrevolutionary Cuba, Marxist-Leninism, the rejection of US political-economic expansionism, and Christian and indigenous religious syncretism that the Chicanos called *Indigenismo*."[41] These shared characteristics highlighted the similar experiences of racism and foreign economic domination that existed in the internal colony and the proverbial backyard colony of Latin America. That said, *teatros* were not homogenous in their political conclusions regarding the role of spirituality in revolutionary struggles, the relationships between culture and politics, or the taking up of arms—issues discussed at length at the Quinto Festival in 1974. These shared characteristics provided a bridge connecting Chicanas/os with Latin American influences: "These similarities—and the two groups' parallel rise and decline—suggest *Teatro Chicano*'s greater resemblance to its Latin American counterpart than to mainstream or popular/political avantgarde US-American theater."[42]

LOS MASCARONES AND POST-'68 MEXICO

Although it attracted young people in the decade preceding 1968, theater in Mexico at that time was characterized by formal high-culture theater imported from Europe and the choral poetry performances of groups like Los Mascarones (LM). Founded in 1961 at the Prepa No. 6 in downtown Mexico City, the group began with five members, including Humberto Proaño, Eduardo López Martínez, Fernando Leyva, and Lourdes Pérez Gay, and was directed by Mariano Leyva Domínguez. It soon grew in size, inspiring other young people to form their own groups. Its name was derived from the *mascaras* (masks) that bordered the entrance of the building, La Casa de los Mascarones (the House of Masks), in which the school was housed.[43] The group's first performances in 1962 were the Russian playwright Anton Chekhov's *Sobre el daño que hace el tobacco* and *Farsa y Justicia del Corregidor* by the Spanish poet and playwright Alejandro Casona. At first they performed more traditional, primarily choral, theater, reciting poetry in layered and overlapping, cycling, and rotating chorus. Traveling extensively through Mexico, they took to the stage at universities and public theaters in Veracruz, Oaxaca, Puebla, and Morelos. LM also offered continual performances in Mexico City. The group won various awards, including a first prize in stage setting for *Lyrical Indigenous Poetry* from the National Institute of Mexican Youth in 1966 and first prize for best director, best actor, best actress, and best group for *The Invaders* in 1966.[44] By 1968 they had expanded to eight people and settled into the recital style of choral poetry.

Initially, the success of Los Mascarones resulted from its touring schedule and mesmerizing delivery of choral poetry—a style largely attributed to the young director Mariano Leyva. Once they were winning awards, they refused the federal support that had sustained them "and began an independent life producing and distributing recordings of their own work."[45] LM eventually became established in a collective house in Mexico City's southern artistic district of Villa Coyoacán (made famous by the artists Frida Kahlo and Diego Rivera, as well as Leon Trotsky), living and performing collectively. Martha Ramirez-Oropeza, a Chicana from Los Angeles who at the age of nineteen was beginning an apprenticeship with David A. Siqueiros, the master muralist, met the Mascarones during 1971:

> I was invited to live in the commune. During those first few months, the rules in the commune were to participate in the daily seminars we had on Marxist philosophy and the history of theatre and the student movement. The latter was of more importance as we the group had a play called "Volveremos" (We Will Return), a show that paralleled the slaughter of indigenous people by the Spaniards in 1521 to the slaughter of students by the government in 1968.[46]

Olga Talamante, passing through Mexico City on her way south to Chiapas in the fall of 1970, sought out Los Mascarones at their collective art commune after having met the group when they performed in Santa Cruz earlier that year. Missing them on her way to Chiapas, Talamante was able to meet up with them on her return trip in June the following year. Talamante arrived shortly after the Massacre of June 21 while Los Mascarones members were on the run, hiding from the Dirección Federal de Seguridad.[47]

SIN FRONTERAS

By 1970, Los Mascarones had a national and international reach. The group had performed across Mexico, in Europe, in Latin America, and in all the Chicano Theater Festivals since their inaugural gathering in 1969. In fact, the engagement with Chicano theater groups was a major catalyst for the continued internationalization of Los Mascarones. At first they were reticent to come to the "belly of the beast." As Fernando Hernández commented on his first trip to the United States,

> At first we didn't want to go to the United States because of all that was implied, over there were the imperialists and we had yet to realize that there was a part of our compatriots from Mexico, from all of Mexico. Later we understood the importance of having been there. Arriving in San Diego I realized the symbols, the importance of the indigenous question. That is when I began to be more interested . . . because I was somewhat interested in theater and poetry—which was what we were best at, and indigenous poetry, but I repeat, it was there that I recovered more of my identity with the Chicano *compañeros*. Most important was that we re-nourished ourselves. I mean, we didn't go to compete with anyone, or criticize. It was a really cool *encuentro*. We both learned a lot.[48]

For Hernández, the trip to the land of the "imperialists" and the exchanges with Chicanas/os allowed him to reflect on his own life, his artistic choices, and his personal and political identity. Hernández "recovered more of [his] identity with the Chicano *compañeros*," a nourishing experience. The Chicana/o narrative of returning to the "homeland" to recover a stolen language, culture, and history was common within the political context of the Chicana/o movement, and many *teatristas* anticipating travel to Mexico would characterize their expectations in that way. Hernández's experience of reconnecting with his indigenous roots through his interaction with Chicanas/os brought the cycle of discovery full circle. This also would be true of UNAM students who came into contact with Chicana/o MEChistA's (members of MEChA) in Mexico City in 1974 and went on to form a MEChA chapter at the UNAM. These students in Mexico were inspired by the Chicana/o recovery of an indigenous past, as they too were interested in the struggles of farmers and their cultural and historical relationship to indigenous communities.[49]

Until 1973, Los Mascarones, particularly Mariano Leyva, were the primary contact between Chicana/o and Mexican—and, by extension, Latin American—theater groups. As Betita Martinez's letters underscore, Chicanas/os revered Los Mascarones for their political radicalism and international solidarity, history of performance, technique and style, and mixture of indigenous pasts with anticapitalist presents. This reverence led many to refer to them as Los Más-cabrónes.[50] Aside from participation in the TENAZ meetings, theater groups were involved in a number of exchanges. In December 1970, for instance, Los Mascarones performed *Las Calaveras de Posada* and *Danza Azteca* at the University of California, Berkeley, having been invited by the Chicano Studies Department.[51] They had come from a previous performance at Sacramento State College sponsored by the Associated Students of Sacramento State College.[52] The following year, Jorge A. Villamil, subdirector of the Preparatoria Popular, invited Martin Dale Montoy and Ruth Robinson of the Teatro Mestizo to perform at the school in Mexico City: "We believe that for the people of Mexico and the student sector to have the opportunity to see your theater would be important so that they could have the chance to appreciate for the first time your dramatic expressions that speak about your people, whose roots are also ours."[53] Similar to the Colegio Jacinto Treviño in Mercedes, Texas; La Escuela Tlatelolco in Denver; Lincoln-Juarez University in Austin; and La Universidad del Barrio in San Antonio, La Preparatoria Popular represented a community mobilizing to solve their own educational needs, provide localized knowledge, and offer a curriculum grounded in people's history and political struggle.

In November 1971 these exchanges continued in Texas. Guadalupe Saavedra, a prominent cultural worker from Texas and director of Teatro Atahualpa, invited Lourdes Gay and Mariano Leyva to lead a series of workshops on "technique, politics and theatre for children" at the Colegio Jacinto Treviño in cooperation with Teatro de los Barrios (San Antonio), Teatro Chicano (Austin), Teatro Estudiantil de Aztlán (Edinburg), Teatro Atahualpa (Kingsville), and Teatro Juvenil (Weslaco-La Feria-Mercedes).[54] The following summer, El Colegio Jacinto Treviño and La Raza Unida Party sent students to Mexico to study history, culture, and sociology as part of the Becas de Aztlán (Aztlán Scholarships) educational exchange set up between the president of Mexico and José Angel Gutiérrez (see chapter 2). Mariano Leyva was the official representative in Mexico.[55] In 1972, Mario Cantú invited Los Mascarones to perform in San Antonio for the celebration of "La Semana de la

FIGURE 3.2. Members of Los Mascarones and El Teatro Campesino, San Juan Bautista, California, June 26, 1973. "To the right, the man standing is filmmaker José Luis Ruiz, cameraman for the production. Seated below him is Luis Valdez, director of El Teatro Campesino. To the left, standing and pointing down, is filmmaker Jesús Treviño. Below him, seated, is Mariano Leyva, director of Los Mascarones." Text from Jesus Treviño; photograph by Gayla Treviño.

Raza," held at the Ruben Salazar Cultural Center. In a letter dated October 15, 1972, John Dauer from the American Friends Service Committee thanked Los Mascarones for their participation and assured them that the collaboration would continue, as "many people are still talking about your performance in San Antonio."[56] The AFSC was not the only group interested in the participation of Los Mascarones; the FBI also took note of their presence.[57]

From San Antonio, LM traveled to Leavenworth, Kansas. At the invitation of the group Chicanos Organizados Revolucionarios de Aztlán, and facilitated by Mario Cantú, they performed at the federal penitentiary where Ricardo Flores Magón died, and where raúlrsalinas, Ramón Tijerina, and Ramon Chacón were already planning revolution. In 1973, LM toured California and were present for the founding of TENAZ. A production of *Somos Uno* (We Are One), a weaving of Chicano theater and Los Mascarones plays into one, was produced for film by Chicano cinematographer Jesus Salvador Treviño (fig. 3.2).

THERE IS NO ART WITHOUT IDEOLOGY

In post-1968 Mexico, people involved in political movements reinvented themselves and their organizations. Three important yet little-known political organizations, composed primarily of cultural workers and political activists, were founded after the student movement of 1968 and played an important role in creating the possibility for continued mobilization of activists and artists: FARO, or Frente Artístico Revolucionario Organizado (Organized Revolutionary Art Front); the closely related CARM, or Comité Artístico Revolucionario Mexicano (Revolutionary Mexican Artistic Committee); and, in 1973, CLETA (Centro Libre de Experimentación Teatral y Artística), which came out of the occupation of a university-affiliated theater. These organizations served as vehicles for political organizing that used art and culture to communicate ideas about power, change, justice, and the impact of creative expression.[58] In turn, they connected the generation of '68 to the radical 1970s in Mexico. The Quinto Festival/Primer Encuentro was a consequence of, and further deepened, the political solidarity that Los Mascarones, FARO, and CARM provided to CLETA and the connections that these artists had in Latin America and with Chicana/o theater groups.

FARO was at the center of political and artistic organizing after 1968. The collective was composed of a variety of organizations that rejected offers from the Echeverría administration for cultural posts, fellowships, grants, and other corporativist largesse. Founded sometime in 1969, one of FARO's slogans was "First I am a revolutionary, then an artist. There is no art without ideology."[59] FARO was made up of a number of independent organizations: the Cooperativa de Cine Marginal, Grupo Arte Colectivo en Acción, Grupo Crepúsculo, Grupo de CCH, Grupo Diez de Junio, Grupo Hoz, Martillo y Libro, Grupo Héctor Jaramillo, Grupo Libertad, Grupo Mascarones, Grupo Matiatzincas, Grupo Nakos, Grupo Nueva Voz Latinoamericana, Grupo Plaza de Sitio, and Grupo Poder Popular. The artists that organized under the banner of FARO were the originators of the "frente de arte popular callejero" (front of popular street theater).[60] FARO-affiliated political artists included the musicians playing *la nueva canción*: José de Molina, Amparo Ochoa, Judith Reyes, León Chávez, Oscar Chávez, and others whose music would circulate through the networks of radical politics. Reyes and Molina especially would develop close ties to Chicana/o movements in Texas, New Mexico, Arizona, and California, supporting the campaign to free Ramón Chacón in 1976.[61] Los Nakos also played a vital role in the founding of CLETA in 1973. Founded in 1968 by students and artists, Los Nakos represented a rejection of Onda Chicana. Its compositions were a mix of traditional Mexican music—*trova*, Huapango, *corridos*—with rock and roll protest music, *la otra canción*, and other styles, and the lyrics were fun, critical of power, and animated by rebellion. Essentially composers of acoustic parodies, Los Nakos were a product of the cultural brigades of 1968, born out of urgent necessity and creative urgency.[62]

Both a political organization of artists and an artistic movement of and for the people, FARO protested against government repression, advocated free speech, and agitated for socialism while simultaneously declaring international solidarity with Chile and Cuba, as well as with Chicanas/os in the United States. FARO emerged in the same political milieu as the political prisoners in the Mexican prison Lecumberri in 1972 who wrote the letter to the Chicana/o community, connecting anti-imperialist struggles across borders. FARO performed in support of labor strikes and campesino land takeovers, among other acts of political solidarity. Representing their own interests as cultural workers and musicians, they were an integral part of the political and cultural movements organizing in Mexico. Less is known about CARM, although it included some of the same artists as FARO, as well as numerous other writers, painters, cinematographers, sculptures, architects, and poets.[63] Whereas FARO was composed of organizations, CARM had individual members. But there was considerable overlap between the two formations. These cultural workers were at the center of a revolution in political culture in Mexico. Where the state succeeded in squelching mass protest during the violence of a dirty war, cultural workers created new political imaginaries. More than the cultural arm of a political movement, FARO and CARM, as organizations and individuals, were political forces in and of themselves.

The Centro Libre de Experimentación Teatral y Artística was founded in February 1973 as a result of the ten-day occupation of the El Foro Isabelina, a university space affiliated with UNAM in downtown Mexico City. Initially a student protest, the occupation was a reaction to university officials in the Drama Department shutting down a theater production on the grounds that student or independent groups could not present their works in university establishments outside the campus. Some of the participants were not affiliated with either UNAM or the National Institute of Fine Arts (Instituto Nacional de Bellas Artes—

INBA). Although it seemed that a university policy was the primary issue, the radical content of the dramatic production in question and the possible implications of the shutdown for free expression and the autonomy of UNAM led artists to organize. On the one hand, the existence of the Foro and the resources invested in the arts—whether at the university level or through INBA—represented one element of Luis Echeverría's *apertura democrática* (democratic opening) to incorporate the generations previously agitating for social change into the corporatist system. On the other, the closure of the Foro for what appeared to be spurious reasons had more to do with control, policy, political perspectives, and generational differences, representing yet another in a long line of contradictions in regard to the democratic opening.

The collection of artists, writers, musicians, and community supporters that came together as a result of the occupation decided in assembly that their temporary Foro, or open meeting, should be converted into a community cultural center. CLETA's view was that artists and intellectuals were commodifying Mexican culture and representing only the viewpoint of the bourgeoisie, a gaze turned to Europe and the United States. A rejection of the previous generation of theater actors, directors, and the larger artistic communities in Mexico, CLETA challenged all sectors of the cultural establishment. "New ideas" emerged in these times of crisis, and political organizing was also essentially experimental. CLETA was an experiment inspired by a political imaginary that broke out of the confines of Mexican theater, the focus on the director, the centering of the text, and the institutionalization of the creative process. Inspired by a revolutionary imagination catalyzed by the Cuban revolution as well as socialist-inspired revolutionary movements in Mexico, CLETA was established through a takeover of a government building in Mexico City at the height of the dirty war.

CLETA brought together the diverse experiences of artists and their equally diverse ideological positions. Some, like the members of FARO, had lived through and participated in the events of '68 and the repression that followed. Others, like Mercedes Nieto, Abraham Vidales, and Enrique Cisneros, were new to the movement, yet excited and willing to sacrifice themselves to the struggle. At the same time, new meanings were being created that worked to redefine the relationship between gender and political participation. As Mercedes Nieto explained:

[As women] we were activists! Trying not to be irrelevant, trying to build consciousness of what it meant to be a woman in those years of transition. To be young, trying to be independent and take care of yourself . . . live the experience of being a woman. At all levels: as a worker, as a partner, in your sexual situation. Trying to take care of yourself, to maintain that independence and the right to decide. I believe that has been the characteristics of the majority of women who at this time participated. Trying to be ourselves.[64]

Women worked to make CLETA a space where political and artistic decision making was not limited solely to the men in the organization. Nieto's rendering of how men responded to the participation of women is worth quoting at length:

Because we really did try to make clear a certain perspective of "you and me" with men. I remember many occasions when there was an attempt to silence me in the assemblies. "Oh, no, that one is going to speak, and who knows what else." [Ay, ya va a hablar esa, que no sé que.] Well, I'm sorry, you will let me speak because I have asked to do so. Maybe politically I am not developed, even less then. . . . We lacked serious study. To see things for how they really were. We wanted, more than anything, to learn how to live in a different way. This also played out at the foro. When we wanted to protest something, [in a deeper voice] "This, no, no, no, if you do not know what you are talking about . . ." Even if I don't know, I need to speak because this is where this issue is bothering me and we need to talk about it. Maybe I don't know how to give a rant like you all do, nor does it interest me. [Imitating voice again] "But there are questions that need to be dealt with, that we see you all are on the wrong path. The problem isn't where you say it is. You are not seeing other options. You are not seeing this or that consequence." It was difficult, still very difficult to change the situations.[65]

As Nieto explained, women demanded respect on an individual basis—one on one—as well as in the larger assemblies where issues were discussed and decisions were made. One way that men disqualified women was to claim that they didn't know what they were talking about. This generally implied that they were not "well read" or knowledgeable about "political theory," and that men by definition were knowledgeable and knew what they were talking about. Men assumed that they were the only ones qualified to participate in discussions, and that the experiences of men were the only place for political imaginings.

The political importance, as Nieto explained, was that women had something to say, period. All the talk about masculine-defined political preparation was irrelevant, as Nieto was not interested in "ranting," or following some predetermined correct political line, but wanted to express her ideas about the situation at hand. Nieto locates an important element of how leaders navigate and try to control political spaces through manipulation of language, ideas, and the parameters of acceptable and appropriate topics for discussion. In what often amounted to a Marxist lexicon reduced to the bare minimum of political categories, men accused women (and sometimes other men) of not analyzing social relations, not taking into consideration the right variables at a particular conjuncture, not seeing "this or that option" or "this or that consequence," all to silence critique and maintain authority. Implicit in the critique is not only that women were unprepared, but that political strategizing was a male endeavor. For Nieto, the "political rant" was not a useful form of communication. Rather than trying to replicate the "rant" as a woman, she wanted to be listened to and respected.

CLETA functioned as a liberatory space for artists in Mexico at the height of the dirty war. This is significant. CLETA also provided women the opportunity to speak out and be part of the larger public political culture, but as Nieto pointed out, men within CLETA did not always respond as openly. As is the case with all social movements that carry with them the gender relations of the larger society, it seemed that the "permanent and organized struggle" against censorship had to begin at home.[66]

TENAZ (TEATRO NACIONAL DE AZTLÁN): TENACIOUS THEATER

With these political and artistic influences, and a flourishing national theater movement that was a central part of the larger Chicano movement, Chicana/o theater groups established a federation known as TENAZ in 1971. TENAZ originated from a hemispheric imaginary situated in local contexts. It was founded in Fresno, California, a week after the second annual Festival de los Teatros Chicanos ended in Santa Cruz, California. The TENAZ founding meeting included representatives from nine *teatros* that agreed to (1) establish communication between *teatros*; (2) provide a means for sharing materials, for example, actors, songs, and so forth; and (3) establish a summer workshop for representatives of as many *teatros* as possible.[67] The humble proposal called for communication, collaboration, and a yearly gathering. TENAZ was the sum of its parts. From its inception, it was predicated on the belief that "because there are too few Chicanos in theatre programs in colleges and universities . . . it is therefore difficult for neophyte groups to organize and perfect their art which requires some sense of theatre."[68] Cultivating autogestion (self-management) and a marked distinction from institutions, even as participants were involved in universities as students or teachers, the Fresno Manifesto read,

> En el Espíritu de Aztlán . . .
> Nosotros . . . Los Chicanos
> nos juntamos aquí en Carnalísimo
> con hermanos de nuestra Raza
> para celebrar
> con orgullo y con sabor
> la vida cotidiana del pueblo del sol
> nuestra herencia
> miles [*sic*] años de magnífica cultura
> y de su Renacimiento en estas tierras colonizadas.[69]

Colonization, brotherhood, celebration, pride, daily life; all these themes connected Chicana/o theater with Nuevo Teatro Popular. Moreover, the founders included cultural workers from Mexico: the founding of TENAZ was also a moment of transnational engagement and cultural solidarity that influenced the political imaginary of the Chicana/o movement. The name "TENAZ" was proposed by Mariano Leyva, director of Los Mascarones: "For the name that the organization was going to take, it occurred to me, I said to Luis [Valdez], TENAZ, the name has to be TENAZ, because you have been tenacious, because you have endured and have had the tenacity of Huiltzilopotchli."[70] Playing on the word "tenacity" or "tenacious" (in Spanish, *tenacidad* and *tenaz*, respectively), Leyva's designation emphasized the resilience of surviving and thriving in the "belly of the beast."

The ETC played an important role connecting Chicana/o theater groups with Los Mascarones and, through Los Mascarones, with theater groups in Mexico and later elsewhere in Latin America. According

to Hernández and Leyva, one day in the summer of 1970 an unidentified person knocked on the door at the Mascarones "house" in Coyoacán with an envelope that contained an invitation from Luis Valdez to
come to California and funds to pay for the trip. They accepted and traveled to California for the first time that year, but they needed visas.[71]
Procuring visas meant going to the US embassy in Mexico City. The US
official had not taken kindly to a trip that Los Mascarones had made
to Cuba in 1968, and after five hours of interrogation only four of the
fifteen members were given visas, as only four had any official identification. As Levya explained, "No one else in the company had papers
. . . not even birth certificates. We were undocumented in our own
country."[72] Los Mascarones subsequently participated in the first four
TENAZ festivals. These exchanges led to and provided the possibility
and opportunity to connect with a variety of organizations throughout
the Southwest. These included activists from El Colegio Jacinto Treviño and the Ruben Salazar Cultural Center in San Antonio, as well as
Chicanas and Chicanos from New Mexico, New York, and throughout
California. They even performed at the prison in Leavenworth, invited
by the Chicano *pinto* organization CORA on a trip arranged by Mario
Cantú. As Elizabeth Martínez, speaking on behalf of *El Grito del Norte*,
a movement newspaper published out of New Mexico, wrote in a letter
to her "Queridos Compañeros" in 1972, "Compañeros, Los Mascarones
are very well known by all Chicanos and it was a true inspiration for
our *gente* here."[73]

TENAZ's foundational documents reflect these broader efforts to
establish connections across borders. In 1973, for instance, TENAZ
members issued a new manifesto that incorporated Mexican indigenous history and identified the Chicano theater movement within the
larger Latin American popular theater movement. The manifesto also
merged a well-defined working-class memory system with a particular
indigenous identity:

El Teatro Chicano was born of the social struggle of la raza; given birth
by trabajadores [workers]; who remain trabajadores [workers]. Este es
un renacimiento: de lo viejo sale lo nuevo. Teatro es el espejo y espiritu del Movimiento. Es el espejo de Tezcatlipoca que ilumina the evil
we are surrounded by; es el Espiritu de Quetzacoatl en que hallamos la
bondad y la Esperanza de la Raza. Teatro es la voz de los barrios, de la
comunidad, de los de abajo, de los humildes, de los rasquachis.[74]

By invoking important stories of Tezcatlipoca and Quetzalcoatl, two of the central figures in Aztec, *Mexica*, and Mexican history (not mutually exclusive or the same), TENAZ activists were invoking a spiritual awakening with cultural nationalist tones, in part influenced by the Concheros de la Santa Cruz, led by Andrés Segura Granados. TENAZ remained philosophically and linguistically tied to the struggle of working-class Chicanos:

> The workers of TENAZ are committed to a way of Life/Struggle helping the people understand the why of their social and individual problems. . . . So that our theatre will be the human rainbow: let it create Theater for children, young people, elders, women, students, workers, farmers and even the ones who aren't interested. It should be strengthened by the cultural roots of our ancestors to then plant seeds of liberation in the present and for the future harvest of the victory of our peoples.[75]

The manifesto also reflected the radical language of liberation struggles, anticipating the fifth gathering in Mexico City: "La organización de TENAZ, which will work with all oppressed peoples must develop a humane revolutionary alternative to commercial theatre and mass media. It is also necessary that we work and unite with all theatres struggling for liberation donde quiera [everywhere], particularmente en Latinoamerica. It should serve as a tool in the Life/Struggle of la Raza by developing Teatros as community organizations."[76]

Chicana/o theater was creative, fun, and intergenerational, organizing communities for "human revolutionary alternatives" that would lead to liberation and connections with people south of the Rio Grande. Solidarity was a clear point of emphasis—in terms of supporting political movements, sharing the process of creating art in times of war, and coming together to share these ideas and struggles across borders. Nuevo Teatro Popular was a form of both political solidarity and artistic experimentation.

LA TRADICIÓN (THE TRADITION) AND TEATRO CHICANO

Centering the indigenous past and present in the project to create Aztlán, an imagined community, animated many young Chicanas and Chicanos and played a central role in the development of an idea of nationalism, family, community, identity, and struggle. The influence of

Aztlán and Teatro Chicano can be traced in part to Andrés Segura Granados. At the first festival in Fresno in 1969, Mariano Leyva introduced ETC and Luis Valdez to Segura, a "Mexican Aztec/Mayan spiritual leader" who emphasized *indigenismo*, the recovery of an indigenous past in the present (re)created through *danza*, a dance that re-creates, celebrates, and actually conceives the movement of the universe.[77] In 1972, Segura would give a presentation in English about his teachings that outlined an "individual spiritual foundation that taught indigeneity as a personal religious practice." Segura's influence on ETC, Chicana/o theater, the Chicana/o movement, and Chicana/o spiritual practices is profound and revered. Prior to Fresno, "Segura had been traveling to the US to teach Chicanos how to integrate the heritage of Nahuatl culture inherent to the roots of the Aztec, Mayan, Toltec, and other ancient civilizations with the militant traditions of La Raza. Called *la tradición*, this spiritual philosophy blends Catholic, Christian, and *Indígena* culture."[78] The basis of this spirituality is dance, *la danza*—rich in symbols and symbolic movements, astronomy, oral tradition, a "non-literate historical tradition of dance-theater." These ideas, rituals, and traditions would have a significant influence on Luis Valdez and the direction of ETC. During the Quinto Festival, these influences were the focus of intense discussions about the role of spirituality and religion in political movements and artistic creation as ETC brought this spiritual "non-literate historical tradition of dance-theater" to a gathering of folks from across the continent, many of whom rejected religion altogether. Given this spiritual-political quest, La Raza and many *teatristas*, poets, playwrights, and political leaders embraced Segura's teachings of *la tradición*, finding in this work the spiritual-religious meaning lacking in the dogma of the Chicano movement. *Indigenismo* became the hidden narrative of the Chicano movement, as evidenced in the manifestos of the 1969 Plan Espiritual de Aztlán and the language of the TENAZ festival manifestos.[79] Segura circulated and expanded the meaning and practices of a spiritual Aztlán: "The concept of Aztlán moved from myth to reality, to important cultural metaphor, to the Chicano Nation and beyond, because of Andres Segura. . . . If there has ever been a spiritual leader of the Chicano Movement . . . it would have to be Andres Segura."[80] The influence of Segura's teachings "not only aligned themselves perfectly with the Chicano's philosophical concepts of Indigenismo and Chicanismo as a basis for national identity formation and nationalism, they made the Chicana/o aware of their relationship with all *Indigenas* and mestizos across the Americas."[81]

Yet these different influences, like the different interpretations and manifestations of NTP at a hemispheric level, began to divide TENAZ from its inception, a division that would come to a head in Mexico City. TENAZ was created to unite Chicana/o theaters, yet "TENAZ began to suffer almost immediately from an ideological split: the radical Marxist-Leninist *teatros* versus the *Indigenistas*. By the TENAZ Third Chicano Theater Festival (1972), this fractionalization caused significant stress in the organization."[82]

NTP encouraged working-class youth to create, imagine, and experiment with new ways to be in the world. Leftist-oriented artists "use[d] theater to create shared performance-scapes," and theater, like art in general, was a way to create, represent, and invigorate an analysis of gender, class, nation, and race in which cultural production could expand the political imaginary.[83] Theater and live performance functioned as a unique conduit for internationalism and solidarity while also galvanizing local support for political struggles—whether the farmworker movement in the United States or actions by radical artists in Mexico. Form communicated content as much as content impacted form, conditions of production, and the relationship of artistic creation to the communities in which these cultural workers lived. Theater was a way to engage people in struggle and perhaps change what was imagined as possible in everyday life—a celebration as much as a political statement. In the context of state violence and a political terrain increasingly more reactionary and conservative, NTP challenged the capitalist politics of individual artists creating alone, the capitalist production cycle and process, and the circulation of art and theater through official channels, stages, and theaters. Centering working-class populations in struggle, the theater groups associated with NTP performed anywhere and everywhere, organizing artists' collectives and founding political/cultural organizations.[84] A tool of critique and a weapon against intolerance and imperialism, NTP contested, challenged, and reassigned political meaning to social relationships, working conditions, and the international political economy. Through a process of collective creation, *teatristas* cultivated a culture of resistance and prefiguration for a different world.

Members of FARO, CARM, and CLETA remembered their experiences in the student brigades of 1968 and demonstrated that these national and international networks were vital to creating and maintaining organizational power and cultures of resistance. For Mexicans and Chicanas/os alike, crossing political, cultural, and geographic borders meant challenging and recasting parochial ethnic nationalisms to go beyond the limitations borders placed on what was imagined as possible. These artists were not attendant on a political party. Even as one of the political struggles inside CLETA was to align with state-recognized unions and parties, or to maintain political and economic independence, artists organized to transform society and the static ideas concerning the relationships between politics and art, revolution and social change.

As the next chapter demonstrates, though many of the NTP groups that came together in Mexico City shared a critique of US imperialism and the repressive conditions in each country, their distinct experiences as well as the overlapping histories of their respective nations influenced the content of their performances and their political perspectives on the relationships among theater, politics, art, and solidarity. Chicanas/os were inspired by the idea of Mexico as much as they were by the political and cultural movements that they learned about or had direct contact with through organizations or individuals. While this chapter was a bit of a departure from the Chicana/o Left, it offers insight into the political terrain of the Mexican Left (with regard to theater and politics) during the 1970s, with its struggles that influenced the Chicana/o imaginary as much as the ways in which Chicanas/os imagined that Mexico influenced political solidarity. Nuevo Teatro Popular in Latin America, Mexico, and the United States remaps Latin American, US, and Chicana/o theater history as acts of social identity, political solidarity, community memory, and the "politics of the possible."[85]

"SOMOS UNO PORQUE AMÉRICA ES UNA": QUINTO FESTIVAL DE TEATRO CHICANO/PRIMER ENCUENTRO LATINO AMERICANO DE TEATRO

It was teatro night after night and meetings during the day. Discussions about where the Chicano movement was going and what it needed and what teatro could say about that. . . . I really got drenched politically by means of teatro . . . I came back really transformed."
ANNETTE OROPEZA[1]

El Primer Encuentro Latinoamericano y El Quinto Festival de Teatros Chicanos was to try to embrace all of Latin America and part of the United States in a festival that bound all of the currents of independent theatrical expression in Latin America . . . everyone thought we were a "bunch of crazies." . . . In reality, the political line was not the only interest, that is why we were able to bring together so many currents of thought; that is why so many people joined with us at that given moment."
MERCEDES NIETO[2]

INTRODUCTION

If the target was empire and theater the weapon, then in 1974 the battle-fields were Mexico City, the ancient pyramids at Teotihuacán, and in El Tajin, Veracruz, Mexico. Chicana/o movement theater, and the movement of Chicano theater, to paraphrase Tomas Ybarra-Frausto, take us to Mexico, where artists attempted to build new worlds through theater. Against the backdrop of an escalating dirty war in Mexico and deepening political, economic, and social crises in the United States, more than seven hundred cultural workers from throughout the Americas came together in Mexico City and Tajín, Veracruz, for two weeks in June and July 1974 for some three hundred theater performances, dialogues, and exchanges as part of the Quinto Festival/Primer Encuentro Latino Americano. This event was both the fifth time that Chicano theater groups had convened an annual gathering and the first time that South American, Central American, Mexican, and Chicano theater groups came together in an organized manner. For almost two weeks these political artists ate, breathed, and dreamed theater. They also critiqued each other, creating significant connections that would evolve throughout the decade. With nonstop performances each night at two different theaters in Mexico City, the morning ritual of analyzing and discussing the previous night's performances, the government surveillance, and the internal dynamics within CLETA (as described in the previous chapter), there was an intense urgency to the gathering. But first and foremost, the festival was an attempt to bring together different currents of popular theater from across the continent. *Encuentro* means a coming together, an encounter *as* purpose and *for* a purpose. The gathering was more than a festival of theater performances; it was an attempt at unifying—if only for a few days—a Third World theater of the Americas. A political history of cultural workers and a cultural history of politicized artists, this chapter situates connections between Chicanas/os and Mexican and Latin American revolutionary artists within the context of increasing state repression in both countries—from the moment that Chicanas/os arrived in Mexico City, they were followed, an extension of the infiltration of and surveillance against CLETA.

The Mexican government was concerned about the potential that this gathering held for creating international solidarity, but it also recognized and aggressively pursued the possibilities of co-opting the festival for its own ends. In this complicated and contradictory situation, Chicanas/os were transformed by the festival. In lieu of providing a detailed textual reading of the plays presented in this chapter (though there are brief discussions within), the goal is to focus on a social history of the festival: its everyday occurrences insofar as what happened, how it happened, and what folks said about what happened.

THE LOGISTICS OF ENCOUNTER

Chicanos arrived within a Latin American political context that was swiftly moving to the right. The installation of military dictatorships, with the tacit and open support of the US government, accelerated throughout the decade.[3] These regimes employed widespread use of repressive state violence that included kidnappings, detentions, torture,

and murder, all done with total impunity and in parallel with neoliberal modes of economic reorganization bequeathed on the world by
Milton Friedman and his militant disciples.[4] Put another way, the appli-
cation of economic models that were imported from the United States
to roll back spending demanded that governments maintain the appearance of law and order to facilitate "safe" investment markets. The
political economy of US–Latin American relations represented a new
set of social and economic relations between citizens, the nation-state,
and corporations that became the hallmarks of neoliberalism during
the transition decade of the 1970s.

The festival took place less than a year after the democratically
elected president of Chile, Salvador Allende, was overthrown in a US-
backed coup d'état led by Augusto Pinochet on September 11, 1972, and
just two short years after the establishment of a nationalist revolutionary military regime in Ecuador under the control of Guillermo Rodríguez Lara. In Mexico, Echeverría was in the midst of a dirty war, and
the United States was still entrenched in a lost war in Southeast Asia
and aggressive foreign policy toward Central America and the Middle
East. By 1974 the Chicana/o movement had claimed several victories. In
1974 the Farah boycott led to a contract with the Amalgamated Cloth-
ing Workers Union of America, ending a two-year struggle by Chicana/
Mexicana workers for better conditions and pay.[5] Also in 1974, the various political movements that would come to influence the Marxist-
Leninist direction of the Centro de Acción Social Autónomo in Los
Angeles were coalescing around community-based struggles against
police brutality, the sterilization of women, drug addiction, and other
health and safety concerns (see chapter 6).

The idea behind the Quinto Festival emerged during the final day
of the fourth TENAZ Festival in San Jose in 1973. Organizing a two-
week gathering required a massive dedication of time and collective
creativity, as well as a reliable measure of patience and commitment
to social change. The organizers' inspiration to connect with artists
across the continent animated the work, which involved arrangements
for housing, performance sites, food, travel, and program development.
Meetings to organize the Quinto Festival were held in California and
Mexico City. Through the TENAZ network, Chicana/o theater groups
from across the United States were kept abreast of plans while they
organized their own local groups for the trip to Mexico. This involved
raising funds from community members, universities, and other institutions; many students used their financial aid money. These grass-

roots efforts were a vital and often-overlooked element of the creativity within the political movements.

In Mexico, the planning of the festival was done in committees of two or three people that overlapped with the already existing committees within CLETA. The "Budget and Administration" committee focused on the logistics of transportation to and from Mexico City. The committee was coordinated by María Acosta, a Chicana from the University of California at Northridge who been working with Los Mascarones since 1971.[6] On UNAM letterhead, the committee sent requests for various types of support to universities in Mexico City, Puebla, Guerrero, and Zacatecas; to rural schools; and to labor unions and individual artists and academics. Luis Cisneros spearheaded the correspondence. They contacted all manner of media outlets: radio, television, newspapers, and magazines. Enrique Ballesté arranged advertisements in Radio Universidad and Radio Educación, while Mariano Leyva planned the calendar of performances. This required securing theaters and arranging for Teotihuacán to be the inaugural site for the Quinto Festival, which in turn meant discussion and negotiations with government officials of the corporatist PRI state.[7]

In March 1974, CLETA established an office at the Foro Isabelina to coordinate the festival logistics and serve as a meeting point during the festival. Luz Maria (Luzma) Espinosa managed the offices.[8] In a letter, Espinosa explained the initial efforts, giving insight into the amount and pace of preparations:

> In the month of August, the office for the V Festival de los Teatros Chicanos was established [in California]. During that time, CLETA-UNAM has been working on (1) organizing itself, (2) looking into fundraising projects, and (3) establishing a permanent office for the TENAZ festival. At the present time we have been working on transportation, room and board, obtaining lists of all newspapers and television and radio stations for publicity for the festival.

Demonstrating how organizing the festival was a transnational project in itself, Espinosa continued:

> However, as you well know, it is not an easy task to organize a festival and cooperation from the groups de TENAZ is needed. The type of help which would benefit us is 1) all types of information you can send us on TENAZ so that we may use it for publicity. 2) an estimate of how

many people are planning to come from each group (Family included for those who are married), 3) an estimate of cost up to the border, 4) an estimate of cost to Mexico City for those planning to bring cars, 5) an idea as to how you would like to see the workshops organized, and what you would like the workshops to include.[9]

The invitations were sent across Latin America and Aztlán through the connections and networks established over the previous years. The letterhead gives some insight into the political imaginary that inspired the preparations and expectations. It had a border with a serpent whose head and body met at the bottom of the page. At the top left corner, inside the serpent border, was a symbol of a shield, and at the right corner, the symbol for the Mayan expression "In Lak' Ech," which means "You are my other me." Enrique Cisneros and Aaron Abde organized correspondence with Latin America, while Luz Maria Espinosa, Martha Ramirez-Oropeza, and María Acosta corresponded with Chicana/o theater groups.[10] Special invitations were sent to Augusto Boal, who was best known for his Theatre of the Oppressed, a pedagogical approach to theater that was related to the radical educational philosopher Paulo Freire; Enrique Buenaventura, founder of the Teatro Experimental de Cali (Colombia) and a close collaborator of Boal; Luis Valdez of Teatro Campesino; and Jorge Huerta from Teatro de la Esperanza, who was a founder of TENAZ. Each was invited to give workshops on various aspects of theater, while Valdez and Huerta were invited to attend and give workshops at the Primer Encuentro Nacional in Mexico scheduled for early 1974, before the Quinto/Encuentro.[11]

The organizing committee also secured state-subsidized transportation from Ferrocarriles Nacionales de Mexico—but only for the Chicana/o participants.[12] Theater groups from Latin America would be on their own in terms of travel arrangements. In an interview with Alma Martínez, Chilean photographer Alejandro Stuart, who was living in the San Francisco Bay area at the time, remembered, "Many people came in carreta, bote, balsa, en tren, hitchhiked from very far away. There are people who came overland from the south cone [Latin America]. They slept on the side of the road, even eating worms to get to the Festival."[13] The high costs of travel were prohibitive for many *teatros*, while others were supported by CLETA: "The situation of *Teatro de La Candelaria* from Colombia illustrates the problem. Held up for several days, this group missed its early scheduled performances. They finally crossed the border only after the intervention of CLETA, who drove a bus to the Mexico-Guatemalan border to pick up the *teatristas* and deliver them to the festival."[14] Though Martínez does not indicate who drove the bus, nor does Enrique Cisneros specifically mention this occurrence in his memoir (he does mention driving many of the *teatros* from Central America and South America back after the festival, encountering numerous challenges along the way), it may well be the case that Cisneros was behind the energy to make the long trip—at least twenty hours each way.

The Ferrocarriles Nacionales de México, the state-owned railway system, offered round-trip, full-passage, first-class transportation for 260 people at 359.90 pesos each and 25 "medios boletos" for round-trip first-class for $178.45. These costs were in addition to the beds, sleeping cars, and mileage for transporting the props, baggage, and other items. The total estimate was 131,834.52 pesos.[15] The Food Committee requested support from CONASUPO, explaining that "as new organizations they did not have an adequate budget to subsidize all the Festival expenses."[16] To serve the food three times a day for ten days (the final three days were to be spent in Veracruz), the Food Committee also requested help from Abel Boza, who was in charge of the Centro Social de la Unidad Tlatelolco, a government housing project in the area near the Plaza de las Tres Culturas where the Massacre of 1968 had occurred. The committee asked for a special rental rate.[17] Boza agreed, and CONASUPO offered coffee, bread, and fruit for breakfast; salad, cold cuts, *aguas frescas*, coffee, and bread for *almuerzo*; and soup, salad, rice, a main course, bread, *aguas frescas*, and coffee for the dinner.[18] Enrique Cisneros arranged for a 50 percent discount at the Hotel Casa del Maestro, the same hotel that would be used to house those attending the Encuentro Nacional in early 1974. In the end, a few months before the festival, a TENAZ report communicated what to expect: "The housing situation is still tentative . . . maybe setting up a tent city . . . whatever is picked to use, BRING YOUR SLEEPING BAGS OR BLANKETS!!!!!!!!" Most participants would sleep on the floor of a gymnasium at the National Polytechnic Institute, near the location of the massacre of Tlatelolco in October 1968. Two different ideas emerged in CLETA: to work with local neighborhood committees and the Prepa Popular schools to provide food and shelter or to use resources from various government institutions for transportation, housing, and other needs.

SPIRITED PREPARATIONS IN AZTLÁN:
"A POLITICAL ACT BECOMING MYTH"

Expectations for the Quinto Festival animated Aztlán, as many of the letters from Chicano groups attested, offering insight into notions of home and hopes for the festival. Katia Pana, counseling psychologist and lecturer at Merrill College and the University of California–Santa Barbara, for instance, explained, "It will be a historic moment for the Chicano searching for their roots and the universal in the specific."[19] Mario Matollana from "El Quetzal" Movimiento Artístico del Pueblo in San Jose, California, expressed similar sentiments: "For you [CLETA] and for Latin America, this encuentro is another triumph and a positive step to a more profound union."[20] Rediscovering ancestral roots was also a stated expectation for Antonio Perales, director of "Artistas del Centro Cultural de la Gente," also in San Jose: "As a cultural educational organization, we think that this event is important for our people here in Aztlán to learn about their cultural and historical roots."[21] For Luis Valdez, the meeting promised greater unity: "[We travel to] the capital of Mexico, the land of our roots, to share with the people of Mexico the message of unity and love that all the Chicano brothers and sisters carry in their hearts."[22] Los Mascarones and Mariano Leyva had made the most contact with Chicanas/os over the past years. This closeness was reflected in their perspective that the Quinto Festival represented "the return of the Chicanos from Aztlán to Tenochtitlan, the return of the 'prodigal sons.'"[23] The Aztec creation story came face to face with their return. Yet the experiences were hardly that simple, as some Chicanas and Chicanos had different expectations of the accommodations and food; unable to adjust, some actually returned to the United States shortly after arrival. As Martínez writes, "The Chicano's mythical homeland of Aztlán continued to dissolve in the face of the grave contemporary social realities of Mexico City and the racism, sexism, and political repression."[24]

A three-page document, written in code-switching Spanish and English, appeared in the 1974 *Chicano Theatre Three* and promoted the return myth to the prospective Chicano participants as part of the unifying effort:

> La Jornada de Teatros Chicanos is . . . a political act becoming myth. Teatro becoming ritual. It is a journey into the very heart of unity. Unidad. UNIDAD con pueblos hermanos de America. UNIDAD con

los teatros. UNIDAD con los teatro populares de liberacion. UNIDAD con nuestra lucha social continental. UNIDAD con nuestra causa espiritual internacional. UNIDAD con nuestras raices indigenas. UNIDAD con nuestro Corazon Amerindio. Un continente y una cultura. Somos uno. Marchamos desde los cuatro vientos para juntarnos en el Corazon de America, en Teotihuacan. La Ciudad de los Dioses, donde comenso nuestro destino, aqui en esta tierra, es este Quinto Sol. Nuestra lucha revolucionaria tienes sus raices cosmicas en la infinita Guerra de Nuestro Padre Solar de la Noche. We struggle against the forces of darkness. Against the forces of ignorance and disease. Against hatred, violence and exploitation. Against disunity.[25]

Invoking the migration of the Aztecs from the present-day southwestern part of the United States to Anahuac (present-day Mexico City) in the twelfth century, the codices reveal that Aztecs had searched for the island in the middle of a lake where an eagle was devouring a serpent on top of a cactus. The festival marked the return of the Chicanos to Mexico, "the very center of the American continent." The plumed serpent Quetzalcoatl figured prominently in the images invoked in the conference documents, as he represents the myth that unites the Americas. For the TENAZ organizing committee, Quetzalcoatl (Mexico) would unite all peoples of the Americas, and they would rediscover their true identity as Mexicans: "El SER HUMANO IS A FEATHERED SERPENT, uniting all the contradictions of life in his being. Every human being on earth is a Mexican. America will never be totally free, nor totally united until it discovers its *mexicanidad.*"[26]

After another five paragraphs invoking indigenous cosmologies, the document explained how revolution and spirituality were a necessary syncretic myth for Chicanos:

El verdadero camino revolucionario is the path with heart. It is the aesthetic of compassion. It is the love of creation (not destruction). It is the struggle to achieve unity with all life, to balance all contradictions in a single, powerful overwhelming CREATIVE MOVIMIENTO. And that is what the Quinto Festival is hoping to do: to unite all the teatros in Mexico . . . to converge on a single point in the middle of the circle of America, and then to explode outward! To spread north, south, east and west in a single thrust with all the energy and creativity two weeks of encounter can create.[27]

Returning to the wellspring of destiny, a "new beat, a new cycle," the
Quinto Festival was a pilgrimage and convergence with an aesthetic
of compassion: "The myth of the Mexica from Aztlán to México-
Tenochtitlan to Conquest to Colonization to Immigration to Aztlán
again is the entire history of the Chicano in one heart beat."[28]

Though the document reflected the cultural nationalism of the
times, it was more complicated, mixing indigenous, Chicano, and
Mexican discourses on struggle and change with revolutionary "cosmic" socialism. Struggling for "a Cosmic Socialism" through an "aesthetic of compassion" that would characterize a new "Amerindia," colonization had forced an internalized racism that led Chicanas/os to lack
faith in their own lives and experiences and to look to the "outside" for
the seeds of change.[29] Experimenting with myriad symbols, languages,
and political perspectives, the document ends by positing the possibility of a universal identity through a "movement" that claimed a unifying working-class identity and a spiritual cause of the soil:

> The impression we leave is rasquachi and intellectual, political and
> spiritual, inspired and clumsy, but we are alive and growing, or alive
> and dying, and none of us are standing still. We are exploding in
> every direction, around the central core of our UNITY IN SOCIAL
> STRUGGLE. . . . Somos los de abajo, de los trabajadores, y de los jodidos
> [we are the underdogs, the workers, the screwed], and we are discover-
> ing our universitility [sic] by getting to know our faults and virtues in
> struggle. In el trabajo, en la casa, en la calle [at work, in the house, and
> in the streets], the political vision of AZTLAN is making us interna-
> tional and universal. Nacido del CORAZON DE LA RAZA, Chicano
> theater is united with its Creator. It is as political, simple, colectivo,
> rasquachi, cosmic and powerful as the number ONE.[30]

This mix of spirituality, ingenuity, and strategies for survival and
struggle from those from below—the exploited, the marginalized, the
worker, the student, the warrior—contained within it the various elements of the Chicano movement. Cultural pride and an idea of a collective struggle; a view from below that changed the perspectives creating
projects for social justice; a nationalism within a continental indigenous cosmology; a *rasquachi*, do-as-you-can-with-what-is-at-hand aesthetic—these were the major symbols that Chicano theater would have
to defend in Mexico.

FISSURES IN THE PYRAMIDS:
CHICANAS/OS IN TENOCHTITLÁN

By early 1974, two positions emerged within CLETA concerning the resources to cover the costs of the Quinto/Encuentro. Through relationships CLETA had established with labor unions, students, and neighborhood organizations, one possibility was to organize with these new allies and provide housing, food, and transportation without any influence or resources from the Echeverría administration. The central question was whether to subsidize the gathering with government funds and facilities for the performances or to finance it with community and neighborhood support and through alternative educational initiatives like the Prepa Popular and the UNAM-affiliated Colegios de Ciencias y Humanidades (CCH).[31] Los Mascarones and Mariano Leyva represented the former view, while other groups within CLETA leaned toward the latter. In addition, Leyva created controversial alliances with the state-affiliated Partido Socialista de Trabajadores (PST) and the tobacco workers union, led by the agrarian organizer Cesar del Angel Fuentes, that was part of PST.[32]

These opposing perspectives came into conflict in the days leading up to the Quinto/Encuentro. The differences, however, were not limited to financial sponsorship. Other disagreements became apparent in the political discussions during the morning critique and analysis sessions: Did accepting support from the state mean consenting to Echeverría's brand of Third World politics of solidarity? Would accepting help from CONASUPO and the Ferrocarriles Nacionales de Mexico constitute collaboration with the state? What would be the consequences of affiliation with or support from the PST, an organization that claimed an independent status but was affiliated with the official labor unions? Affiliation also meant opening up CLETA to infiltration by government surveillance agencies.

On May 1, Los Mascarones (in the name of CLETA) agreed to march with the PST in front of the National Palace. Not everyone within CLETA agreed. Leyva insisted that the PST was made up of independent campesino organizations, tobacco (*tabacoleros*) unions, led by Cesar del Angel Fuentes. This was not the first time CLETA or Los Mascarones collaborated with the PST. On March 7, CLETA and the PST, along with students and members of the Union Sindical Española, the Spanish Communist Party in Mexico, Comisión Sindical Voluntaria de España y México, the Patronato de la Cultura Gallega, Unión Nacional de Mujeres Mexicanas, and the Ateneo Española de México organized a demonstration with some 250 people in front of the offices of the Spanish Embassy in Mexico, protesting the death of a Spanish student, Salvador Puig Antich.[33] On March 30, 1974, CLETA performed for the inauguration of the Constitutional Assembly of the PST in Poza Rica, Veracruz.[34] Cesar del Angel was from Veracruz, and he represented and advised the Asociaciónes Agrícolas Productores de Tabaco de Papantla, Espinal y Álamo Temapache. He was also a leader of the PST's work in the municipalities of Papantla, Coatzintla, Castillo de Teayo, Coquille, Coyntla, Álamo Temapache, Chicontepec, Ixhuatlán de Madera, and Tihuatlán, all in the state of Veracruz.[35]

Practical concerns regarding resources and finances brought pragmatism and ideology into a creative tension, although the challenges were also eventually divisive. The issue of whether to accept government support—either directly through grants or subsidies or indirectly through organizations and institutions of the state—raised questions about the function of the state in society and became a measure of one's revolutionary credentials. At the time, as part of the *apertura democrática*, Echeverría pursued several progressive agrarian reform policies, redistributing land and funding land improvements.[36] To finalize the plans, a meeting was scheduled with Echeverría. Echeverría did not personally attend but was represented by one of his assistants, who made it clear that "the President supports as much as he is able with the only condition that the Chicanos leave with a good impression of the nationalist government of Echeverría."[37] A "good impression" for supporting the festival would appeal to Chicanos by providing an example of his dedication to supporting left-leaning groups who were critical of US influence. In emphasizing his nationalism and loyalty to the *patria*, while publicly aligning with other Latin American countries, Echeverría's support can also be seen as a continuation of established relationships with male leaders in the Chicano movement (see chapter 2).

For CLETA, a collective composed of diverse groups and people, the issue of state support led to the first of many reconfigurations. As an organization, CLETA identified US imperialism as the scourge of the continent, and as previous chapters have shown, it consistently protested the collusion between Mexican political elites and US policy makers, as well as US domination in Latin America. CLETA favored extending Mexican solidarity into the political imaginary of greater Latin America. At the same time, there were different perspectives on the role of the Mexican government within CLETA, and this was the main reason behind Los Mascarones's insistence that the decision to take money from Echeverría was not a contradiction of political beliefs. For Los Mascarones, the enemy was US imperialism, and therefore an alliance with the Mexican government was an acceptable, if not necessary, strategic decision, even as Echeverría also (privately) aligned with US political and economic interests.[38] Other groups within CLETA had a different perspective that rejected any collaboration with a regime in the midst of a dirty war against social actors. In their opinion, because imperialism was a global system, it needed national elites to cooperate in the spread of capitalist social relations.[39] The solution that emerged from the meeting involved the PST in an agreement as shady as it was complicated. Cesar del Angel and the *tabacoleros* union he led had an "outstanding monetary debt to the government."[40] In the meeting, instead of offering direct monetary support, "Echeverría allowed Leyva, representing CLETA, to deduct the costs for the use of Teotihuacán . . . from the Tobacco Union['s debt]."[41] This decision would come to haunt CLETA and Los Mascarones. While the negotiations took place, non-Mascarones members of CLETA established direct contact with Chicanas/os in the United States for the first time.

Mariano Leyva had been the primary contact with the Chicano theater movement, and as a result, the ideas that CLETA and other organizations had about Chicanos were mediated through Los Mascarones. In addition, the primary goal for LM was to successfully organize the festival, as it was a compromise. Like a promise, a *compromiso* implies a certain conviction based on a relationship of solidarity and trust that has built over time, and/or based on one's word or honor. Politically, the festival was a powerful project that offered many possibilities for connections, organizing strategies, sharing of techniques and analysis, and making of friends. But as the festival took shape, members of Los Mascarones such as Leyva, who had promoted a more favorable—one could argue romanticized—view of Chicanos, were no longer the sole contacts with the *hermanas* and *hermanos* north of the Río Bravo.

In May 1974, Enrique Cisneros traveled to San Jose for the final organizational meeting. This trip brought him face to face with the reality of Chicano theater that had previously been mediated by Leyva and other members of Los Mascarones. Guillermo Loo, director of Teatro Primavera and openly critical about the use of religion, spirituality, and politics in theater, reportedly challenged him by asking, "Have you also come to make us sick with the Quetzalcoatl and Virgin of Guadalupe?"[42] This initial challenge from a Chicano director within CLETA revealed that not all Chicano theater groups were the same. Loo must have assumed that, like Leyva, Cisneros agreed with the trajectory of Chicana/o theater that embraced a syncretic Catholic-Indigenismo. Cisneros explained to Loo that the only information they received in Mexico was mediated by Los Mascarones, who he said simply thought that "Chicanos are like children and it would be unjust to take away their romantic vision of pre-Hispanic Mexico; it would be like taking away their only lollipop."[43] This new information "made more acute the internal contradictions of CLETA that had originated with the flirting of Mariano Leyva with the nascent Socialist Worker's Party, a relationship that translated into manipulations and actions that contravened the internal alignments of our organizations."[44] A week before the festival, "positions could not be reconciled."[45] A tacit agreement was made to hold off on engaging with these issues until after the festival. But the issues would not wait for the people to decide when to engage them; they were already influencing the discussions and adding to the urgency of efforts at political and artistic solidarity.

MORE THAN THREE HUNDRED PERFORMANCES IN TWO WEEKS: "SOMOS UNO PORQUE AMÉRICA ES UNA"[46]

The festival was not only the largest and most representative gathering of *teatristas* from all parts of the Américas but perhaps the most expansive in performance and scope. The participation by Chicanas/os was one of the most distinguishing characteristics of the conference. Other Latin American festivals had taken place in San Francisco (1973) and New York (1972), but never had so many Chicanos/as gathered with their *compañeros* and *compañeras* from the south. Mexico City, the center of the hemisphere, the navel of the moon (Nahuatl meaning for Mexico), received people from North, Central, and South America, including Brazil, Uruguay, Chile, Argentina, Peru, Colombia, Honduras, Ecuador, Venezuela, Paraguay, Panama, Costa Rica, and Nicaragua. Chicanos/as from all parts of California and the states of Illinois, Texas, Michigan, Colorado, New Mexico, and Washington also participated. They joined with CLETA-affiliated *teatros* and groups from Guadalajara, San Luis Potosí, Mexico City, and Jalisco. The San Francisco Mime Troupe was the only non-Chicano theater group invited to Mexico City, and the only group to arrive by plane. Chicanos/as arrived by train from Calexico, California, and Laredo and Reynosa, Texas.

Teatro Mestizo departed from Calexico and Teatro de la Universidad de los Barrios of San Antonio left from Nuevo Laredo, while El Teatro Jacinto Treviño departed from Reynosa, Mexico. The train from California came by way of Guadalajara and arrived on Saturday, June 22, 1974, at the Buena Vista station of the National Railroad in Mexico City. The groups from Texas arrived the following day, along with the South and Central American groups—who had been picked up by a CLETA bus, as they did not have enough resources to finish the journey. "For the Mexican government, and the more conservative segments of the Mexican population, Martínez explains, all young *teatristas* and student activists—particularly those sporting long hair and non-conservative attire—were considered militants, anarchists, 'hippies,' drug users, and sexually promiscuous and/or sexual deviants."[47] As a precaution, the organizing committee warned travelers to be careful about what types of materials were being brought and "took extra precautions to insure the safe crossing of Chicanas/os and *Latinoamericanos* into Mexico City."[48]

At the Buena Vista station just north of the Zócalo in the center of Mexico City, those arriving by train were greeted by mariachi bands playing "Son de la Negra" and banners that demanded freedom for political prisoners and demonstrated worker support for the festival.[49] Among the mariachis, Chicanas and Chicanos, and the bevy of Mexican activists and *teatristas* were agents of the Dirección Federal de Seguridad (DFS), who may have even traveled on the trains. If we remember Echeverría's conversation with Nixon, the confrontations in San Antonio and Los Angeles by black, Chicana/o, and white activists, and the ongoing dirty war in Mexico at the time, the festival was another chance to use a two-pronged approach to diplomacy: support the festival through various means, while also using it as a chance to gather intelligence and infiltrate.

Given the divisions within CLETA, and with Los Mascarones staking out the lone pro-PST position, the descriptions of the arrival differ depending on the source. In two documents, the first attributed to Los Mascarones and probably written by Mariano Leyva, and the second to Luis Cisneros in the name of CLETA, the different meanings given to the arrival of the Chicanos is clear. For the Mascarones, the characterization by CLETA of the arrival at the train station was wrong. "Un caso fue, cuando al recibir a los compañeros que llegaban por ferrocarril, los chicanos, se escondieron las banderas hechas por el propio CLETA, por el 'atroz delito de ser rojas' iguales a las del PST y esto, para ellos era la prueba clara y contundente de la prentendida manipulación a que se prestaba los Mascarones (aún que Mascarones no intervinó en la hechura de las banderas)."[50] The statement goes on to explain how, from the perspective of Los Mascarones, Felipe Galván, Luis Cisneros, and Carlos Escobar took it upon themselves to "save the organization" and rallied support to counter the presence of the PST. The FSI responded and, according to the document, were the ones who brought the banners demanding freedom for political prisoners. This caused the secretary of the interior to close the southern border, "putting in danger, irresponsibly, the Festival. Another event comes to view: the ignorance and lack of political preparation of these controlled 'activists,' overlooking that in Mexico, so-called political prisoners are not only from the left, but also the right."[51] For the author of the document, these "activists" were confused "sheep" blindly following the orders of "los salvadores de CLETA." The tone of the document is condescending, terse, and dismissive. Luis Cisneros offered this recollection:

> As the first day of the Festival got under way, they [Los Mascarones] blocked CLETA's base, hiding from them the arrival date of the first contingent of Chicano compañeros at the train station Buenavista, reserving for themselves the "right to know." Nevertheless, they did communicate it to the leadership of the PST so that, before the press, said organization appeared as if it were the organizer of the Festival. This day also initiated an open war; CLETA's base discovered the dishonest action of "Los Mascarones" and hundreds of red and black flags, symbols of the dirty party, began to disappear, while also closing the Foro Isabelina.[52]

In a 2004 interview, Leyva insisted that the red and black flags were for not the PST but rather the United Farm Workers, and the lack of understanding on the part of CLETA members about the actual conditions in which Chicanos/as lived resulted in the assumption that the flags were the PST's. Leyva's personal investment in and relationship with the Chicana/o *teatristas* led to his efforts to welcome them in a grand fashion. For Enrique Cisneros, and CLETA in general, the relationship—personal or political—with Chicanas/os north of the border was different, and the issue was about the relationship between CLETA and a government-affiliated organization in the midst of a dirty war against social activists. Regardless, the welcoming was grand and truly did reflect the different political perspectives in Mexico—even as tensions were high.

MASS, MITOS, AND REVOLUTIONARIES:
FROM THE CHURCH TO THE PYRAMIDS

Before the inauguration of the festival took place on June 4, a syncretic Indigena/Catholic mass/ceremony was held at La Iglesia de la Noche Triste/Iglesia San Hipólito, Tacuba, near central downtown Mexico City.[53] Danzantes and Andrés Segura shared the altar with Catholic priests (fig. 4.1). A contrasting mix of cassocks and feathered headdresses, copal and myrrh, and music and hymns characterized the ceremony, after which Segura knelt and kissed the hand of a priest, saying, "This ceremony, combining the Catholic/Spanish-European religion and Aztec-Mayan/indígena thought, represented the racial and cultural syncretism of the Chicano and Latinoamericano." Teresa González of the Teatro de los Barrios in San Antonio recalled, "That morning we had a Mass that aroused some controversy. Lots of people were hesitant and suspicious about attending, but it proved to be a very unusual kind of Mass. The priest was a revolutionary priest, and the Mass declared the oppression of the people."[54] As Alma M. Martínez writes, in the layered political and cultural contexts of Mexico and Latin American Nuevo Teatro Popular, "Marxist-Leninists saw both parties, both religions, as antithetical to NTP and Teatro Chicano Movements."[55]

From the church, the participants traveled by bus north of Mexico City to the pyramids of Teotihuacán. Once a thriving city known as the birthplace of the gods, Teotihuacán figures prominently in indigenous and Mexican national history, with Nahua, Toltec, Otomi, and Totonoc creation stories tied to the area. The mall where the various pyramids were located was vast, with smaller pyramids ringing it and connecting the perimeters of the larger Temple of the Sun and Moon. Participants sat on the ledges to watch the performances below. Leyva had been key in negotiating use of the area with the National Institute for Anthropology and History, another sticking point within CLETA. Expecting instead to use the Temple of the Sun, "the participants, according to Segura, were not spiritually prepared for the amount of energy that would be invoked by holding the ceremony at the most powerful of all pyramids at Teotihuacán."[56] Segura warned against a ceremony at the Temple of the Sun on the day of the summer equinox, given that

FIGURE 4.1. Opening ceremonial mass for Quinto Festival/Primer Encuentro Latino Americano de Teatro, Catedral, Mexico City, June 24, 1974. Andrés Segura is on the right holding his hat. Alejandro Stewart Photography Archives, MSS Photos. Courtesy of the Department of Special Collections and University Archives, Stanford University Libraries.

the colliding energies might be much too powerful and intense; he suggested instead the Temple of the Moon. Approximately two thousand people attended the event. The participants were met with the sounds of Andrés Segura and the ritual dance of Los Capitanes de la Danza.

The welcoming document of the Quinto Festival, read at the base of the Pyramid of the Moon on the day of the summer solstice, called for unity in the Americas against imperialism and totalitarianism in Latin America:

Compañeros de América

As we welcome you to Mexico, we give you the memory of the "pensamiento Americano" that has been produced in the theatre the last few years, as well as some political documents.

The ancient Indians of our continent used the tablets to transmit to the coming generations the memory of things, customs and art, so that the roots of the people be embedded in the soil.

Study and analyze those documents, because this Festival wants to set the basis so that our nations will be one in the future together with our people that fight for their liberation against the *yanqui* imperialism. Mexico is your home. Our people have been waiting for you since long ago. Here, we have kept with love the culture of the continents. Let us be a thousand thoughts but one single heart.

We wish to finish this welcome greeting with the words of a great liberator of America, Jose Marti: "The people should try to hurry up to know each other like they were going to fight together."

Chicanos, Indians, Mexicans, Latinamericans, Anglos. We inhabit and live this continent: our América. We have been isolated but now the time has come to be ONE, to unify our strengths, our hearts.

Our people, today more than ever suffer the massacre, the torture, the murder, especially our brothers from Chile. Our solidarity with them which has to become action.

The spirit of Salvador Allende and Victor Jara, as well as our liberators Bolivar, Hidalgo, Morelos, Marti, San Martin, Zapata, Che, they should illuminate us so that our results should be the best.

Un Continente, Una Cultura

Por un teatro libre y para la liberación[57]

The welcome brought together anti-imperialism, indigenous cosmologies, and continental solidarity. As part of the program, and reflecting the broad-based support from the art community in Mexico, festival participants were also given a fifteen-page pamphlet by the cartoonist RIUS, the pen name of writer and cartoonist Eduardo del Rio, best known for the series *Los Supermachos* and *Los Agachados*, which were both critical of the Mexican political class and elite society. The illustrated pamphlet contained the goals of the meeting, a description of popular theater, and a brief history of Latin American, Mexican, and Chicano popular theater. RIUS provided an illustrated explanation of how popular theater was different from elite theater, explained the history of Latin American popular theater, and discussed the Quinto/Encuentro for social movement across the continent.[58]

Luis Cisneros read a *corrido* in Nahuatl and Spanish, and welcomed the *hermanos de la raza* from the United States, Mexico, and Latin America. In Spanish, English, Portuguese, Nahuatl, and "dialects,"[59] he called for unity based on the idea of "One Continent, One Culture," adding,

We recognize our common cultural struggle as people of this continent. That is why, as cultural workers, we will unite today in our effort to bring about social, political and spiritual liberation of La Raza throughout the Américas. Therefore, emphasis of this Festival will be on our common Indigenous roots and tradition, as well as current political and social realities facing Chicanos and Latinoamericanos.[60]

In the context of tensions within CLETA, the indigenous characteristics of the opening ceremony reflect the influence of Los Mascarones and the close coordination between Segura and Los Capitanes de los Danzantes with Los Mascarones and TENAZ. Fifteen groups that performed various mitos, or creation stories, followed the opening ceremony. They included El Teatro Campesino (El Baile de los Gigantes), Las Cucarachas (Ix, Diosa de Cozumel), Teatro Mestizo (untitled), Los Topos (The Human Zoo, la jaula de Moctezuma), Teatro Razita (untitled creation myth), El Teatro Urbano (untitled), Comunicación Aztlán (La Palabra), Teatro del Piojo (El Aguila), El Teatro Quetzal (El Quetzal Nunca Muere), Teatro La Gente (untitled), and Teatro de los Niños (Elias en Chibalba). Teatro Campesino was the first to perform. Different CLETOS (group members of CLETA) also performed.[61] The inauguration ended with "El Grito del Universo" and a ceremony and offering by the "Servidores del Arbol."[62] The initial performances met the familiar controversy over the spiritual and political messages of teatro. According to Teresa González, a member of Teatro de los Barrios from San Antonio, "a lot of people se aguitaron [discouraged]. Mitos just didn't turn them on. They wanted to see something they could benefit from, so they could go back home and take it to the Raza, to help the Raza. But they felt that mitos wouldn't help."[63] Among Chicanos/as, Aztlán, indigeneity, and ceremony were not necessarily shared beliefs even as they functioned as shared references and shared usable pasts. Another participant had a similar impression: "There was a feeling among most festival participants that theatre should deal more directly with social-political problems, that it should designate the oppressor and the oppressed, that it should clarify the issues of the class struggle."[64]

Apart from the mass, the inauguration in Teotihuacán, and the closing ceremonies in Veracruz, all other events took place at El Teatro Comonfort and El Teatro Negrete, both in the central district in Mexico City; the latter was, according to Teresa González, an "upper class sort of theatre."[65] Performances in the two theaters were organized in two-day cycles: that is, the plays at El Teatro Comonfort were presented the following day at the Negrete, and vice versa. Every night three groups would perform at each theater, while "roughly, half of those who weren't performing went to each of the two theatres."[66] Musicians, including Judith Reyes and José de Molina, performed songs that celebrated the working class and attacked Yankee imperialism and the violence of the Mexican government. Other artists denounced injustice against Chicanos in the United States; rejected the submissive, reproductive role of women; and called for feminist liberation. Still others critiqued the Mexican government for its dependent relations with the United States and condemned fascism and repression in South America.[67] El Teatro Quetzalcoatl from San Jose focused on repression by the Border Patrol before an audience of 350 at El Teatro Negrete. The Paraguayan group Tiempovillo performed *De lo que se Averguenzan las Viboras*, addressing colonialism and Europe's continued exploitation of indigenous lands.[68]

Las Cucarachas, from the San Francisco Bay area and directed by Dorinda Moreno, presented the complex issue of gender equality in relation to white feminists and the historical strength of Mexican women through a new form—*teatropoesia*—with the script *Collage Chicano*.[69] Las Cucarachas prepared a pamphlet for the festival concerning the role of Chicanas in the movement, "stressing the perpetuation of family life as well as the recognition of India/Latina women who have passed into history for their participation in the liberation of their people . . . [,] representations of women as revolutionary subjects demanding equality with men in relation to images of women as Earth Mother/Tonantzín, symbol of fertility and mainstay of the strong, united family."[70]

Although much unanimity was demonstrated, the diversity of experience produced great thematic variety. Solidarity of shared conditions, as much as solidarity in the struggle to create new cultural forms and content, can be seen in the diversity of theater presented. Solidarity was a political relationship, as well as a weapon against empire and to create alternate possibilities. The theater groups from across Latin America drew from their experience of military dictatorships, state terror, and US complicity. Teatro Universitario from Costa Rica performed *Libertad, Libertad*, directed by Juan Salcedo, a musical and testimonial presentation that explored different definitions of liberty while making reference to the general strike in Chicago in 1886, the French and Mexican revolutions, US interventions in Latin America, the economic exploitation of Latin America by US transnationals, and the war in Vietnam.[71] The Venezuelan group Zuliz presented *TO 3*, which also emphasized the capitalist exploitation of the working class and the need for workers to organize independently of state-affiliated unions.[72] Students from the Bachillerato de Artes in San Salvador performed *Los Miton Indígenas*, tracing struggles in El Salvador against foreign control beginning during the conquest. El Triangulo from Venezuela performed *Búfalo Bill en Cledulilandia*. They told the story of the US-supported coup against Allende.[73] The Colombian group Teatro Experimental de Cali (TEC) brought their well-toured plays *La Denuncia* and *Soldado*, both directed by Enrique Buenaventura. TEC focused on the exploitation of Central American farmers by the United Fruit Company, and the complicity of the army in repressing union organizing. La Candelaria, also from Colombia, performed *La Ciudad Dorada*, which spoke to the conditions of Colombian campesinos who were trying to escape exploitation by fleeing to Bogotá, where instead of improving their condition, they suffered even more due to their lack of "urban" knowledge.[74] Teatro Universitario Trujillo (TUT) from Peru performed Boal's *Torquemada* (directed by Henry Romero), while the TEUM from Honduras presented *Don Anselmo*, which examined the apparatuses and mechanisms—scientific, medical, and educational commissions— by which the United States extended its imperial rule.[75] Finally, traveling from Argentina, Nuquen presented *La Vaca Blanca*, a musical fable with anthropomorphic animals, emphasizing how easily power can be used to control desire.[76]

Teatros from Mexico also focused on US economic and cultural imperialism, as well as the repression of the Echeverría years. In all, of the twelve groups from Mexico, eleven carried the suffix CLETA, with nine claiming Mexico City and the other two, Zopilote from San Luis and CLETA-Jalisco, reflecting CLETA's national reach. Only El Teatro Ambulante de Puebla was not directly affiliated with CLETA. The Mexico City–based CLETA groups and their respective performances included: Fantoche/Laboratorio (*Crucificado*), La Calle (*Espiritu Araucano*), Los Mascarones (*Maquinas y Burgesas*), Xicotencatl (no record of their performance), Taller de Cine (no record of their performance), Minicalzetin—children's theater by children (*Actos*), Azotea (*Los Desplazados Cuarentena*), Katarsis (*La Madre*), and Los Perros Nopaleros—children's theater by children (*El México*).

Chicana/o theater groups also focused on their own lived experiences, including struggles against racism, poverty, lack of educational opportunities, police brutality, and cultural genocide. They celebrated a Chicano culture that was thriving in the context of the social, political, and economic challenges that they faced. Of the forty Chicano groups that mailed applications to TENAZ, nineteen performed. Some of the performing groups included: El Teatro Urbano from Dallas (*Actos*); El Teatro Quetzalcoatl from San Jose (*Collage Latino*); Los Topos from San Francisco (*Yankees Go Home*); El Teatro de la Esperanza from Goleta, California (*Guadalupe, Un Pueblo*); El Piojo from Seattle (*Capriotada de los Espejos*); Movimiento Primavera from Los Angeles (*Tlatelolco del Barrio*); Teatro Mestizo from San Diego (*Historia de un Chicano*); Cucarachas en Acción from San Francisco (*Collage Chicano*); Teatro de la Gente from San Jose (*Flor y Canto*); Teatro Mezcla from East Los Angeles College (*Revolucionaria*); Teatro Espiritu de Aztlán from Placencia (*La Gran Carpa de los Desplazados* and *Y Asi Morí*); Teatro Conciencia (*Trampa Sin Salida*); Teatro de los Barrios from San Antonio (*El Alamo*); Su Teatro from Denver (*Kiko Incident*); and Teatro Aztlán from California State Unviersity, Northridge (*Ejecución de un Hombre*). Similar to the anti-imperialist themes of the South and Central American theater groups, Chicanos and Mexicans played with the contradictory relationship between US economic and geopolitical interests and the needs of the working class and marginalized groups.

THE POLITICALLY SYMBOLIC

To provide a clearer sense of the content of their performances during the Quinto Festival, the next section will briefly examine three groups: El Zopilote from San Luis Potosí, El Teatro Ambulante from Puebla, and El Teatro Campesino. I have chosen these particular works in order to compare the themes, use of symbols, and political critiques embedded in the stories. By comparing these various elements and then moving forward to the morning gatherings where the previous nights' performances were discussed, we can get a better sense of the political and artistic dialogues, disagreements, and disenchantments that were taking place.

El Zopilote joined CLETA during the planning for the First National Encuentro held in February 1974. Their name at the time was La Asociación de Ideas. Self-identified anarchists, they had a significant role in developing CLETA's critical perspective. Founded in 1967 in San Luis Potosí and led by Ignacio Betancourt, El Zopilote produced a syncretic mix of deeply critical and political work with innovative methods, techniques, and stage direction. Betancourt had won the National Poetry Prize given by UNAM in 1974 for his poem "Punto de Partida" and the 1976 Short Story Prize given by the INBA.[77] Their productions were also controversial. In one version of the play *El Gran Circo de los Hermanos Gandalla*, the first scene begins with one of the actors masturbating while reading from the magazine *Alarma*, comparing politicians to devils with forked tongues and despicable morals.[78] In a presentation at La Jornada de Amnistia International in March 1973, they decided to challenge the "elegant ladies and pseudo-revolutionaries of Amnesty International" by slaughtering a sheep and splattering the audience with the animal's blood. According to an observer, "various members of Amnesty left the room vomiting" and criticizing CLETA.[79] Despite or perhaps because of these outlandish tactics and their acerbic political commentary, El Zopilote was considered among the best in Latin American popular theater.[80] Their creative energy and consistent presence transformed Zopilote into one of the pillars of CLETA. In addition to their scandalous presentations, they performed as clowns and comedians, leading one commentator to declare that their collective spirit "deeply influences the other members of the organization."[81]

At the Quinto Festival, El Zopilote performed *El Cico* at El Teatro Jorge Negrete and El Teatro Comonfort. Instead of masturbating while reading *Alarma*, however, the protagonist wiped his behind with pages torn out of the Mexican Constitution. Explaining that something "smells bad," the actors looked around the stage until they uncovered the Mexican flag, with a wrestler as the centerpiece instead of the Eagle and Serpent. They then stated, "The schools teach the students to respect the national flag so that they can later see how the authorities trample it as well as the people."[82] In a direct insult to Echeverría, Nixon, and Kissinger, they highlighted the fact that Mexican politicians consistently violated the Constitution while killing social activists in its name. They then criticized the open repression against social movements in the service of capitalism and Yankee imperialism. In the next scene, the cast appeared armed and fighting desperately, "emphasizing that it can give power and impunity, but in the end, the person who possesses it commits suicide."[83] Finally, the play ended with workers with thirty years of experience staging a strike and soldiers sent by the government arriving to kill them.[84]

Throughout 1974 El Zopilote performed for audiences throughout central Mexico, again demonstrating how theater could be used to bring an accessible and entertaining critique of those in power to more people—telling a relatable story that was familiar and presented from the perspective of the working class, not from the narratives of the elite.

Teatro Vendedores Ambulantes (traveling or street vendors—TVA) from Puebla also sparked controversy and received widespread praise. Puebla was one of the most conservative Mexican states, located east of Mexico City. TVA both represented the everyday experiences of exploitation and oppression in Mexico and, like all of the *teatristas* at the festival, actually lived the events: they were actors and artists that worked as traveling vendors, cultural workers of a different sort. Founded in 1963, they organized for the right to work and to be respected as workers and artists. The constant repression against them reached a high point on December 29, 1973, when the police attacked them, killing some of their *compañeros*. Instead of backing down, they regrouped, taking over an abandoned lot and establishing a people's market ("mercado popular").[85] The untitled performance was essentially a rendition of their lives and struggles as campesinos and street vendors against "imperialism" and the abuses of the police and "public administration." Beginning with protest songs, they acted out their struggles with the local authorities over the right to sell their products on the street. Finally, they made a call to those present to support their demands for dignity, respect, and the right to work.[86] According to an observer, their performance was polemical: "While Augusto Boal had his mind blown, others proclaimed that this wasn't even theatre."[87]

Extending the reach of the festival outside of El Teatro Negrete and El Teatro Comonfort, Vendedores Ambulantes performed on a Sunday afternoon in the open-air theater at Chapultepec Park, "El Casa del Lago," which had been occupied "[f]or six months [by] CLETA-UNAM . . . presenting every Sunday, . . . [a] forum by the people and for the people, a continual program of teatro, poetry, *cantos*, dance, etc."[88] Traditionally, Sunday was the day that Mexican working-class families congregated at Chapultepec Park, enjoying the performances, or possibly the zoo or museum, with food and family in the sun. Abundant snacks and full meals were readily available; there were clowns, an amusement park, and acres of space to run and play and sleep and eat: it was (and is) an urban escape for children and families. The performance resonated with the working-class crowd, while the critics of Chicano theater's use of religion and indigenous mitos used the Vendedores Ambulantes as an example to emulate—it was "true popular theater." The use of El Casa del Lago by a decidedly non-UNAM-affiliated group, in this case a *teatro* group made up of workers, increased the already existing tensions and strained relations between CLETA and the UNAM.

MITOS VERSUS REVOLUTIONARIES

Following the protocols established at previous Chicana/o theater festivals and previous gatherings of Nuevo Teatro Popular groups at Manizales, the mornings began with discussions analyzing the previous night's performances (fig. 4.2). Gathering at the Club Antonio Caso in the public housing unit Nonoalco-Tlatelolco, these discussions were followed by workshops focusing on acting techniques, stage design, mask making, play writing, political education, directing, and women and theater.[89] All of the morning sessions involved critical discussion, with analyses of style, performance, execution, storytelling, and message. The morning gatherings became a place where disagreements were voiced and lessons were shared and debated. More often than not, men discussed with each other the meanings of political acts; the radical or reactionary nature of a play; and the proper function of art and creativity in political movements—hypermasculine either/ or distinctions that assumed a linear and directed process of political awakening.[90]

The discussions about religion, *lo indigena*, and Marxism-Leninism have been the focus of much that has been written about the festival— both in the immediate aftermath as well as in subsequent years.[91] The discussions typically centered on the question of what exactly characterized popular theater. What were the appropriate themes? How could it be used as a tool for social change or revolution? While the debates over the work of the Chicano theater addressed the conventional topics, they also incorporated tense perceptions of Chicano, South American, and Mexican *teatristas*.[92] The discussions that took place on the morning of July 1 between the Marxist-Leninists and the *Indígena-spiritualista* adherents were as much about the relationships between politics and art as they were about the larger context of the festival in Mexico and Nuevo Teatro Popular in Latin America. They also reflected the internal politics of CLETA and TENAZ. On one side of the proverbial divide were Boal (Brazil); Enrique Buenaventura (Colombia); Ulises Estrella (Ecuador); Santiago García, Atahualpa del Cioppo, and Maria Escudero (Argentina); and various members of CLETA, including Guillermo Loo. On the other were Leyva, Valdez, Segura, and the poet Alurista. "Given the confluence of popular/political theater artists and intellectuals in attendance," Martínez writes, "this could have been the beginning of the first united Pan-American popular/political theater front. Instead, after the *foro* on July 1, following ETC's La Gran

FIGURE 4.2. A morning-after gathering to discuss the context, execution, and other dramatic and political elements of the theater presentations, Foro Isabelino, Mexico City, circa July 1, 1974. Alejandro Stewart Photography Archives, MSS Photos 210. Courtesy of the Department of Special Collections and University Archives, Stanford University Libraries.

Carpa de Los Rasquichis (Tent of the Underdogs), the future took another direction entirely, reinforcing the groups' differences rather than their similarities."[93] *La Gran Carpa* further exacerbated already existing distinctions within CLETA that in turn represented disagreements within NTP.

La Gran Carpa told the story of Jesus Pelado Raquachi, a Mexican family patriarch who leaves his mother and brother in Mexico to cross the US border, and the subsequent challenges and indignities he and the family survived. Describing the performance as "a choreographed dance, rather than a conventional screenplay," Alma M. Martínez writes that "the use of the *corrido* and emphasis on working class values and the 'classical' archetype of Chicano Theater: the devil, death, the Virgen of Guadalupe, and the working class male protagonists, located *La Carpa* as quintessentially representative of Chicano theater at the time."[94] *La*

Carpa calls for Chicanos to gain empowerment through political organizing and participation in movement activities, combined with spiritual strength through a syncretism of *indigenismo* and Catholicism.

The connection between political and spiritual empowerment was
not the spark that lit the fire but the wind that fanned embers into
flames. The discussion that morning, though focused on *La Gran
Carpa*, also touched on the themes of the opening ceremony and the
influence of a syncretic mix of indigenous and Catholic iconography
that for many Latin American leftists was contradictory at best, and
counterrevolutionary at worst. I would add, in concurrence with Mercedes Nieto, that the pontificating and posturing by (primarily) men,
and the process by which these differences were communicated and
discussed, limited the possibility for anything other than confrontation, particularly when combined with the simmering differences
within CLETA.

I present excerpts in the order that they appear, with little commentary, to convey as closely as possible the flow of the discussions. There
was much anticipation of the morning discussion as "[t]he 200-plus *teatristas* who attended this *foro*, Chicanos and Latinoamericanos alike,
were anxious to speak publicly on the subject of *Indigenismo*. . . . [Poet
and writer] Juan Felipe Herrera remembers that the political climate
had built to a fever pitch. Bruce-Novoa recalls Alurista, who anticipated the onslaught of criticism, telling Valdez, 'just be clear' (Bruce-
Novoa interview) . . . [while] some ETC members, anticipating a heated
debate, asked colleagues to attend in solidarity (Herrera interview)."[95]
Luis Valdez began by explaining the context and idea behind *La Carpa*.
Invoking Paulo Freire, Valdez "creat[ed] a common link between Chicano campesinos and the poorest communities in Latin America."[96]
He then shifted to directly address the issue at hand, explaining how
"he saw the syncretism of *Indigenismo* and Marxist-Leninism as two
complementary rather than oppositional philosophical factions." And
though Valdez agreed that religion was not revolutionary, he makes
"one important distinction," according to Martínez: "The Virgen de
Guadalupe rises in answer to this oppression. She has been with our
community since she first appeared in 1531, and she continues to be
with us to this day. She has participated in all the struggles of our community."[97] Reminding us of what Yolanda Broyles-González refers to
as working-class memory systems, Valdez explained the everyday life
of many Chicanas/os and Mexicanas/os living in the United States and
the role that the Virgen de Guadalupe specifically, rather than Catholi-

cism in general, played in connecting them to struggles in Mexico: that of a shared spiritual and proletarian mother-figure. Put another way, the discussion concerning religion and revolution took place not only between these two groups that emerged on different sides of a line but between and within political movements across Latin America. That the discussion focused on a very specific example of performances and their use of art and politics that caused consternation and strong disagreement, and that this happened during the festival, is as much about the larger context as it is about the diverse ideas that congregated in art and theater. In addition, such a public discussion, in front of so many people and after so much buildup, also contained a deep element of performance; that is, the discussions themselves were already scripted, as this was a continuation of an ongoing disagreement. Valdez's opening statement was electric: his "remarks sparked an explosion of energy that had been building since the syncretic mass." The audience was eager to speak, and the moderator, Aáron Abend from Brazil, faced a new situation.

Augusto Boal spoke next. Though not performing (he had been invited to give workshops), he was concerned with what he considered the uncritical syncretic use of religious and indigenous symbols, as well as the abstraction in the themes presented. Admitting little knowledge about Chicanos or the Chicano movement, Boal "explained that he did not want to take an antagonistic position toward faith or religion, nor did he want to change anyone's mind or position. Neither did he expect people to leave the *foro* with a false sense of consensus, when they knew they all had distinct ways of working."[98] Boal was equally critical of CLETA's insistence on maintaining its independence from the "revolutionary and popular" government of Echeverría.[99] A primary criticism was that the arguments and themes of Chicano theater were very localized rather than visualizing the problems of all of the Latin American people together.[100] Four specific issues concerned Boal: the use of religion; the relationships between theater, consciousness, and revolution; the significance of words and language; and the belief in the Virgen de Guadalupe as having *material* influences on the world. For Boal and others, religion was symbolic, not literal. In their political reading of Marx, the Bible was heuristic myth. Boal ended by quoting Brecht: "The duty of an actor is not to show the truth, the duty of the actor is to show how things really are." And there, Boal said, "lies all the difference."[101] Valdez responded, but only after taking a question from the audience. Rather than continue with a detailed discussion of the response by Valdez here, his overall message was that "the scientific and spiritual are neither inseparable or immutable."[102]

Although some participants leveled severe criticism against the focused view of Chicano *teatros*, in other instances they suggested more complete political appraisals and a broader form of politics by pointing to their realities and the radical political ideas that naturally flowed from them. Estrella from Ecuador, for instance, noted the problem of military dictatorships in Latin America and pointed to the necessary role of *teatro* in changing such conditions:

> So, the fascist dictatorship is established and the friends from the Chilean theater are dead, incarcerated, or are being persecuted. Here is where the problem emerges: In Peru there is the danger of fascism, in Brazil, fascism, in my country Ecuador, the danger of fascism. Therefore, theatre people are not only theatre people, they have to be selective about their actions, they have to select their possibilities to say what needs to be said in the little time that we have left. And from there my friends, theatre is not an end. Theatre is not the final objective that we can obtain, but the means by which our process and action as political men; theatre is a way, and is precisely the manner that this truth is transmitted. Which truth? The truth of the people.[103]

A young and exasperated (unidentified) Chicano responded with an exhortation that called for understanding of different experiences and politics that had been waged in the United States:

> I say this for all my compañeros Latinoamericanos, from here in Mexico and South America. It's a reality that has to be recognized that the political awareness that exists here and in Sur America as countries, it's very different than the political awareness that is in America. When the compañero [Genaro Vasquez] Roja[s] had his revolution happen here in Mexico recently in the mountains, there was not a level of awareness in America [United States] that brought revolucionarios Latinos of any kind coming down to the *frontera* to see how they could help. It would lead one to understand that there are many interpretations of revolution in North America. If there is one interpretation while I give this response, my evaluation of the *Carpa* [theatre], it is this, that for me revolution is defined clearly, and [it] honestly means quick change. Recognized throughout Latin America, Teatro Campesino has been foremost in bringing a quick change of awareness for

the problems of the Chicano. It has to be accepted. I don't care if you agree with the concepts or not, they have been the most received and consequently have received the most recognition. I am not saying they are the best or the worst, but they are the most received.[104]

The unidentified speaker then addressed the Chicanos who were present with a reminder that their special reality in the United States required that they rediscover and reclaim their group identity: "The main problem with the Mexicano is, *que es Mexicano* [that he is a Mexican], and because he is so affected by the *sistema* [system] in the *Estados Unidos* [United States] that he has lost respect for what he is—*Mexicano Americano.*"[105] The speaker continued with his defense of Chicano theater, but he also critiqued its leadership for their self-aggrandizing and sometimes conservative ways and challenged the Latin American revolutionaries for their embrace of armed struggle. He added a defense of Chicano theater's use of religious symbols, suggesting that their use was required in order to connect with the people and to recover their culture. "I am not a Marxist-Leninist; I'm a cultural worker," he said.

During his statement, whistles and other forms of expression reflected opposing views on the observations by the unidentified Chicano speaker.[106] The catcalls that some in the audience directed against him were especially noticeable when he spoke in Spanish, particularly when he switched from Spanish to English, mispronounced Spanish words, or confused word meanings. This response to the particular vernacular of Chicana/o Spanish disregarded the observation that the speaker had made regarding policies and practices of cultural erasure and the imperative to recover Chicanas'/os' identity as an important basis for their political work. Seen another way, this view of Chicanas/os was as much about assumptions regarding appropriate cultural identities as it was a misunderstanding or lack of understanding of the conditions and everyday lives of Chicanas/os living in the United States. Misunderstanding and miscommunication characterized these and other exchanges, made more challenging as much by language differences and the dynamics of men contesting who was more revolutionary as by the creation of new connections and exchange of cultural ideas and shared political solidarities.

Next, an (unidentified) Mexicana speaker brought the conversation back to the Chicanos' use of cultural symbols, offering a nuanced understanding of the Chicana/o experience. She warned of the blind embrace of culture. At the same time, she implied that Chicanos were doing more than using culture to identify with the people and to promote change:

> Indeed the *Carpa* does reflect the problem of the Chicanos or Mexicanos in the United States, and from a technical point of view there are not any criticisms to make. But we have to analyze some of the language being used because we run the risk of not being accurate of the meaning we give to this language. For example we can't confuse faith of the Mexican, Campesino, or Chicano with the experiences *parapsycologicas*. It's okay if the reality is that the Chicanos believe in the Virgen, that is fine, but present[ing] faith as the solution . . . as the supreme value, faith in god, unity . . . we commit the same error, that's to say, we run the risk of converting ourselves into . . . a minority that defends an exterior reality, but at the same time cuts off the possibility of action. We have to be careful because often we are converted into the best allies of imperialism because we are separated from reality and are trapped in a dream.[107]

In response to the statement against armed action, she noted that it could not be ruled out a priori. Experience influenced decisions, as well as the meaning given to them:

> You propose nonviolence. Nonviolence toward the growers, nonviolence in response to the slaughter at Tlatelolco—no, *compañero*, when you have been here, when you have seen your *compañeros* killed in front of you, when you have seen how they have cut off their heads, cut off their ears, how they have dragged children . . . perhaps [peace and love] is valid for you in the US. . . . Perhaps for you it is very difficult to fight against napalm bombs, against atomic bombs, against nuclear bombs, but in South America, in Latin America, in all the Third World, we must stand up and fight, and that fight cannot be nonviolent, absolutely not. It must be planned, examined objectively, and be carefully analyzed.[108]

In one of her final observations, the speaker acknowledged the problem of cultural divisions as obstacles to unity in the Americas, although she did not accede to the emphasis that the Chicano speaker gave to cultural identity: "The major triumph of colonialism and imperialism is to divide us internally, referring to cultural colonization or the culturalization of *el pueblo*. Instead of paying attention to the consequences, we need to pay attention to the causes."[109]

Maria Escudero, director of the Free Theater (Libre Teatro Libre) in Cordoba, Argentina, then emphasized that nonviolence was a choice not everyone had: "To preach nonviolence is not realistic for my country (Argentina)." Enrique Buenaventura and Ulises Estrella, both of whom reiterated and built upon previous critiques while emphasizing the need to better understand the situation in Latin America, followed Escudero's comments. Their critique amplified that the political analysis had clear limitations: "What Estrella [Boal, Buenaventura, and others] could not see or understand is how Valdez's struggle constitutes a deeper psychological and spiritual battle against internal colonization."[110]

When Mariano Leyva took the microphone, many in CLETA no doubt heard his words within the context of the pending discussion of the accepted support from the Echeverría administration. Leyva first emphasized that ETC had developed its own style, recognized around the world, and that it expressed a particular relationship between style and ideology. Teatro Chicano emerged from struggle; it was an artistic expression of the conditions of its own production, and therefore it could not be understood outside of those conditions. Explaining the reasons for organizing the festival, Leyva remarked, "I feel that the critiques that are being given are taking us in a destructive direction and to division [protests, whistles and grumblings are heard from the audience]." He went on to emphasize the importance of recognizing and understanding differing experiences, and observed that the festival was intended to "fill a void that festivals in South and North American have not been able to fill." For Leyva, it was an "extraordinary theatre," religious, Marxist, and idealist. He added that separating form from ideology is the dead-end labor of an idealist. No one could deny that the Chicano theaters' style allowed them to make an immediate connection, using space, music, language, and symbols to "capture" the audience. All this could not be separated from the "ideology of identity." Leyva then made the important observation that an ideology of identity could lead to a more "concrete ideology," and that "the artistic product does not depend on a correct or incorrect ideology. The correctness or incorrectness of ideology does not guarantee the quality of an artistic work."[111] In a defense of Chicanos as much as a direct critique of "the bad blood in some *compañeros* who are speaking . . . [who] have their remarks plotted out," Leyva insisted that unity should be a goal, "because if we do not leave this festival with the foundation for a true uni-fication . . . then we will be playing into the *yanqui* imperialist's hands, who is our primary enemy." This is similar to the argument Leyva had previously made when faced with criticism about taking money, re-sources, and other support from the Echveverría administration: that the real enemy was US imperialism.

In the midst of whistles and protests from the audience, Leyva con-cluded with an obscure discussion between Lenin and Leo Tolstoy about the playwright Gorky that contained within it a critique appli-cable to the present situation: "Even with the wrong ideology, extraor-dinary art is still possible."[112] Leyva was perhaps the one who had been most enthusiastic about the political and personal relationships with Chicanos. And to be sure, Los Mascarones were influenced by their experiences working with Chicanos. Yet Leyva's last words indicate a certain tension that bordered on condescension. Remembering that the audience came from across the continent, he seemed to be staking out a neutral middle ground. Leyva lamented that the only thing that would satisfy the majority of those in attendance (the ones launching the criti-cisms, one would presume) would be a "total break with religion and traditions, something that he and many who thought like him were not ready to do." Valdez affirmed that he was a believer [*creyente*] and that this kind of tradition unified the family.[113] After Leyva spoke, Guillermo Loo took the microphone. Loo was "director of Movimiento Teatro Primavera, [and] represented one of the hard-line Marxist-Leninist tea-tros in TENAZ."[114] The tensions between Leyva and Loo were obvi-ous. Irma García from *El Teatro Primavera* insisted his comments were planned at a meeting attended by Boal, Loo, and others prior to the morning *foro.* Within TENAZ, Loo "was one of the most vocal Chicano teatristas advocating against Valdez's use of Indigenismo and Catholi-cism in Carpa, a conflict that pre-dated the festival."[115]

Teresa González, a recent high school graduate and a member of El Teatro de los Barrios from San Antonio, reflected, "According to the play, religion will be the solution to our problems. This was very heavily criticized in México because many teatros there are very revo-lutionary and very experienced and aware and they simply don't think that religion is going to be any kind of solution. So they really hit them strong on that—'How can Quetzalcoatl help the campesinos!' But Luis Valdez answered that no matter what they said, he believed in it and felt it to be the right way."[116] Fernando Hernández, one of the early mem-bers of Los Mascarones, added his own observation: "That is where we have to see if we came together to divide ourselves or what happened? Because that was a break with the South American radicals who came with a cemented Marxist-Leninist position and they weren't able to understand why Luis Valdez used religion how he did."[117] Yolanda Broyles-González's assessment of the relationship between indigenous knowledge and the politics of theater helps frame the parameters of this discussion: "The Teatro Campesino did not regard the cultural and mythical in any way separate or outside of the social and historical context of Chicanas/os. The challenge, however, rested with convincingly bringing the holistic Theater of the Sphere to life within performance practice. What critics overlooked was that the Teatro Campesino did not perceive indigenism (i.e. the Theatre of the Sphere) as an alternative to anti-imperialist struggle, but rather as a way to differentiate and refine that struggle."[118] Much more could be said about this issue, as the relationship between art and politics is an old one. But what is apparent from the festival and the discussions, experiences, memories, and inspiration that came from it was that a diverse set of experiences across the entire span of the Americas shared a common critique of US imperialism. At the same time, wrote Juan Bruce-Novoa and C. May-Gamboa in 1975, "the political tensions between Marxists and nationalists also transcended the Chicano–Latin American categories, a fact that was most apparent in the attacks on Valdez and the *Teatro Campesino* by Chicanos who decried nationalistic tendencies [emphasis added]. The different perceptions and meaning of the Third World caused further splits and fragmentations."[119] In a 2002 interview, Valdez reflected on the festival: "It was en explosive meeting because there were different points of view. We argued that we were *de la pansa del monstro* [from within the belly of the beast] and the other people were attacking the *monstro*, so they started attacking us. And I said, 'No, no, we just live in the *pansa*, we are not the *monstro*.'"[120] After more than ninety minutes of discussion, someone in the audience reminded the crowd that it was not practical to focus only on Chicano theater and lose sight of other objectives at this multifaceted festival of diverse perspectives.[121] Good advice for our story.

VERACRUZ, TAJÍN, AND THE PST

The closing ceremony for the Quinto/Encuentro was to have taken place in Mexico City at the Palace of Fine Arts. A few days before the date, Antonio López Mancera, director of the Department of Techni-

FIGURE 4.3. Closing ceremony for the Quinto Festival/Primer Encuentro Latino Americano de Teatro, El Tajín, Veracruz, Mexico, circa July 14, 1974. Alejandro Stewart Photography Archives, MSS Photos 210. Courtesy of the Department of Special Collections and University Archives, Stanford University Libraries.

cal Production at the National Institute of Fine Arts (INBA), canceled the event. At the last minute the secretary of public education, Victor Bravo Ahuja, requested the Palace in order to hold the graduation ceremony of the National Polytechnic Institute. El Teatro Comonfort was the default site, but it was not available.[122] Irony emerges unexpectedly from history. CLETA arose as an alternative to the institutionalized programs of the UNAM and the INBA, and as the festival drew nearer, divisions that had developed within CLETA were put aside. The cancellation of the event at the Palace of Fine Arts and the collaboration with the PST for the closing ceremonies constituted the final straw for some CLETOS. As a result of the cancellation, the closing ceremony for the festival was held in Veracruz at the ancient indigenous site Tajín (fig. 4.3). This had been arranged by Cesar del Angel Fuentes through the general director of the National Institute of Anthropology and History, Guillermo Bonfil Batalla.[123]

Seven hundred *teatristas* boarded buses for the seven-hour drive, made longer by rain and mudslides.[124] They divided into groups of five to seven *teatros*, and on the way each group visited a different *pueblito* to perform and stay with a family.[125] The PST welcomed the participants at Tajín. According to González, "that Partido really has the campesinos organized in Vera Cruz."[126] On the PST side, the festival was seen as an opportunity to recruit members from the neighboring pueblos. We know this for certain because agents of the Investigaciones Políticas y Sociales (IPS) infiltrated the PST. In a DFS document, the infiltrator reported that the PST meeting scheduled for Sunday July 6 would be canceled so that everyone could attend the closing ceremonies of the Festival Chicano and try to recruit members.[127] This was exactly the fear of some members of CLETA: that they would be used as the *brazo cultural* (cultural arm) of a political party or union affiliated with the PRI ruling party.[128] The experience of spending even a short period of time with indigenous campesinos (farmers) was powerful, offering an alternate understanding of the returning-home narrative. As Martínez points out, "The physical context of González's experience at Tajin [referenced above] seems to frame her understanding and appreciation of *Indigenismo* in a new light. For González, as well as many other Chicano *teatristas*, the experiences in Álamo and Tajin were the 'most important' of the festival because of their personal contact with the Mexican *campesino*, first staying in their homes then the closing ceremony itself."[129]

ASSESSING THE IMPACT: "UNIRNOS PARA DESUNIRNOS"

Coming from across the continent and sharing a politics of solidarity, these artists communicated the ideas and dreams of their struggles through theater as well as music, graphic arts, and poetry. Their public performances and the creation of new cultural organizations, however, also represented a distinct social/political movement with its own history, issues, points of connection, and disagreements. Emphasizing people's theater, Néstor García Canclini explains that "theater, sculptures and cinematographers are changing the social function of art, extending it to new publics, that look for non-conventional channels of communication, and open their art to the participation of the spectators."[130] Popular theater democratized art and exposed the contradictions of power, responding to changes in society, economics, and culture to allow for possible popular participation, "replacing individualism with collective creation" and transforming art into a product of the "cultural and material conditions of each society."[131] At the same time, popular theater was a form of solidarity with people in struggle. Performance was a way of calling together different perspectives, personal experiences, and community memories. Nuevo Teatro Popular was transgenerational and complicated, and it generated a political imaginary of international solidarity that connected specific local struggles across geography and political perspective.

The participants in the Quinto Festival/Primer Encuentro used their experience, imaginations, and art to interrogate what they identified as instruments of economic, political, and cultural domination from Europe, the Mexican political class, religion and spirituality, and the hegemonic impulse of the United States on Chicana/o and Mexican theater. They had created counterhegemonic organizations and cultural forms that challenged the dominance of state-affiliated art institutions and the cultural influence of the United States. In other words, through popular theater presentations on the streets, in plazas, on the subways and buses, in factories, on occupied land, and in community centers and parks, artists uncovered and rebelled against neocolonial domination facilitated by the collusion between Mexican and US political and business interests.[132] They were not artists that were part of a movement, but artists with a radical politics—from a critique of US racism, state violence, and economic exploitation to anti-imperialist and feminist Third World politics. They were also organizers and artists that understood communication and expression as a central organizing strategy capable of translating struggles within and across borders and creating new social relationships. For many Chicanas and Chicanos, the festival was part of a returning-home narrative. Another issue to consider was language. Chicanas and Chicanos, whose Spanish was different from, for example, the Spanish spoken in Mexico City, or Argentina, or New Mexico, or New York, also had a challenging time navigating their stay in Mexico. In other words, for Mexicanos and Mexicanas, Chicanas and Chicanos were coming to Mexico, while for Chicanas and Chicanos, Mexico was a place to return to, even if one had never actually lived or traveled there before. As Martínez writes, "The Chicano's mythical homeland of Aztlán continued to dissolve in the face of the grave contemporary social realities of Mexico City and the racism, sexism, and political repression."[133]

Assessments of the Quinto Festival agree that the very act of coming together from across the hemisphere as radical artists and political actors was the most significant result. Annette Oropeza, a Chicana from California who would later form part of Olga Talamante's Defense Committee,[134] explained her experience: "It was *teatro* night after night and meetings during the day. Discussions about where the Chicano movement was going and what it needed and what *teatro* could say about that. . . . I really got drenched politically by means of *teatro* . . . I came back really transformed."[135]

Enrique Cisneros offered a similar perspective:

> The Festival was beautiful. . . . For the first time in the history of theatre of Our America groups from the United States and groups from south of the Rio Bravo came together, everyone working together. There were two weeks of intense activity, day and night, night and day there was theater, political and aesthetic discussions, shared experiences, acts of love; day and night . . . There had been other prior Latin American events in Mexico and we learned much from them. After, other groups have come from which we have also learned, but that Festival was distinct, it was ours, the theatres from across the continent.[136]

In hindsight, Valdez thought the festival was premature in that Chicano theater had yet to solidify itself as such:

> I think it influenced the way that Teatro Chicano took a turn in the late 70s. Some groups disbanded, actually, they couldn't take the exposure. And other groups just got stronger. The work changed because of the exposure. *Se profundizó,* as they would say in Mexico. It got more profound. So what it did was, it extended the Chicano movement into México and made contact with brothers and sisters from Latin America—all artists, all teatro people, but nevertheless, all political theatre. So it was a political embrace.[137]

Mercedes Nieto characterized the festival in similar terms:

> El Primer Encuentro Latinoamericano y El Quinto Festival de Teatros Chicanos was to try to embrace all of Latin America and part of the United States in a festival that bound all of the currents of independent theatrical expression in Latin America. . . . Everyone thought we were a "bunch of crazies," how could a small group, some twenty crazies, try to organize a festival of such importance? Nevertheless, it was pulled off right. There were crazy proposals that were heard and inspired action. It was a situation where we let anything happen because we all had the desire to make it happen, to make sure it took place. At that

moment, we didn't question whether or not it was politically correct; we knew it was necessary to do it, to give testimony to the things that we wanted to make known at that moment—and we did it. In reality, the political line was not the only interest; that is why we were able to bring together so many currents of thought, that is why so many people joined with us at that given moment.[138]

"The reaction of critics and many Chicano theaters" writes Nicolás Kanellos, "was so politically and emotionally charged that a rift developed between them and El Teatro Campesino that has never been healed. El Teatro Campesino virtually withdrew from the theater movement, and from that point on the Chicano theaters developed on their own, managing to exist as agitation and propaganda groups and rag-tag troupes until the end of the decade."[139] Struggles and disagreements over political uses of culture, the cultural politics of social movements, and the contested relationship between art and politics created a "basic contradiction which faced Chicano [Mexican, and Latin American] artists within the movement; how to remain true to the demands of their art while responding to the political exigencies of the moment."[140]

These testimonies are echoed in the words of historian Robin Kelley, who reminds us of the importance of redefining how we narrate and measure the "success" of social movements, a redefinition that brings up questions about the relationship between change and reform, between revolution and the violence of the state, between transformation and change. "Unfortunately, too often our standards for evaluating social movements pivot around whether or not they 'succeeded' in realizing their visions rather than on the merits of the visions themselves," Kelley writes. "By such a measure, virtually every radical movement failed because the basic power relations they sought to change remained pretty much intact. And yet it is precisely these alternate visions and dreams that inspire new generations to struggle for change."[141]

FARO, CLETA, TENAZ, the *teatristas*, and even younger children who also participated in the theater groups represented a localized political formation that cultivated an international solidarity—whether in the various states north of the border or the various countries south— that resonated across the hemisphere. Creating solidarity through theater, and using theater as a weapon against imperialism, the gathering impacted the artistic and political imaginaries of the participants, while providing concrete forms of solidarity. They were part of a larger circulation of anti-imperialist political movements, contributing to the struggle for an antiestablishment theater and art that did not reflect the experiences of the social majorities, but was itself a form of experience.[142] In other words, the performances were based on everyday experiences to the point where improvisation, rehearsal, and life were melded together, not in the Shakespearian "all the world's a stage" sense, but as part of a process that gets at the essence of experience—lived as familiar, remembered because one's life is almost impossible to forget, and even the forgotten—or intentionally not remembered—lives as ghosted presents.[143] The efforts of these cultural workers transformed theater into a social force. As organized artists, they were a social force to transform society, cultivating international solidarity, the development of innovative techniques and collective methods of creation, and consequently a view of a possible different world. All these experiences led to disagreements and difficult discussions: "For many *teatristas* this was the painful turning point when they knew that the differences between north and south were ultimately too complex for the dreams of the *Quinto Festival* and the new *Frente de Trabajadores de la Cultura de Nuestra America* ever to succeed."[144]

After the festival was over, and as most of the Chicanos returned home, CLETA underwent important changes. First, Chicanas/os that stayed in Mexico City, such as Nita Luna Luján, Lucy Rios, and Estevan García, or with students from the UNAM, including Ernesto Reyes, and that had attended or participated in the festival formed a MEChA group at the UNAM. Throughout the fall they continued to do "guerrilla" theater on the subways and buses and in front of factories. In turn, some of these younger members of CLETA established contacts with the Liga 23 de Septiembre, an urban guerrilla organization that became the primary target of government repression and led the creation of the Brigada Blanca, named as a testament to its specific mission, to destroy the "red brigades" of La Liga.[145] La Liga was one of dozens of urban and rural armed defense and revolutionary organizations that emerged during this time and were subsequently targeted for annihilation by the Mexican government—the subject of the following chapter. CLETA decided to officially distance themselves from the UNAM in their everyday work, most notably by changing their name from CLETA-UNAM to CLETA in 1975. This signaled a shift to focus specifically on creating and strengthening already existing political relationships between campesinos, workers, and community organizations.

In contrast to the arrangements made for the Chicanas/os to return to the United States by train, the theater groups from Central and South

America did not have such an easy time returning home. There was confusion about how these *compañeros* were expected to return. In *Si me permiten actuar*, Enrique Cisneros explains that Leyva had promised (without the knowledge of other CLETA members) to return them by plane. In various interviews I conducted, there were discussions of these post-festival confusions, but no one could or would say definitively what had been promised. What is clear is that shortly after the festival, Los Mascarones spent two weeks in Cuernavaca, the "city of eternal spring" two hours south of Mexico City in the state of Morelos. They would eventually relocate there permanently. As a result, CLETA had to scramble to provide a return passage to the now stranded *compañeros* and *compañeras* from South America. In the same manner that he had hustled resources to participate in Maninzales the year before and driven to the Guatemalan border at the beginning of the festival, Cisneros began to organize. The Autonomous University of Guerrero, courtesy of the progressive Rector Eli Gortari, loaned two buses to CLETA; again the caravan was off, but before they left there was the matter of Los Mascarones.[146]

The differences of opinion concerning working with state entities and directly with the president, the relationship between cultural/political organizations and organized political parties, and the role of cultural workers in social movements were all deciding factors in the split. Depending on one's perspective, either Los Mascarones were expelled by the larger group or they resigned, or both. Either way, Los Mascarones parted ways with CLETA, and CLETA with Los Mascarones. In a recent interview for the fortieth anniversary of the festival, Luis Cisneros clarified that Los Mascarones were not expelled, only Mariano Leyva.

Mercedes Nieto offered an insightful perspective on the meaning the split had for CLETA as well as some of the internal politics, particularly the perspective of women on the divisions and splits provoked by government infiltrators: "From the beginning, we as women were against the expulsions of groups from the Foro Isabelina. You know, I feel that this was one of the questions that tore us apart and it was a product of the people who had infiltrated the movement. The separation of the groups, the political questioning of the groups so that in the end each one went their own way, what this did was disperse us, to create rifts, and eliminate the movement. We as women were against the expulsions."[147] But men did force the decisions, and took lines and defended them, and in Nieto's view these posturings and hard-line positions led to splits that also dispersed power among more people and organizations. In this and many similar moments of encounter and possible collaboration, political discussions—largely but not exclusively between men—limited the outcomes. The divisions and expulsions (exacerbated by infiltrations) and the need for a correct political line or political rectification led to dispersed movements rather than increased solidarity. As discussed in the next chapter, because international solidarity was a site of gender struggle, political power and gender could both open and limit possibilities for solidarity in a struggle against imperialism and in the collective creation of new social possibilities.

In the end, Los Mascarones left. The following year, the Sexto Festival de TENAZ was held in San Antonio. Even though CLETA was invited, they received no help to cross the border and were forced to argue their way into the country. By the time they arrived in San Antonio, the festival was over.[148] The festival itself, according to Martínez, "would become the forum for the continuing and final debate between Marxist-Leninists, represented by Guillermo Loo and Teatro de la Gente and the *Indigenistas* represented by Valdez and ETC. At the end of this volatile encounter, Valdez and ETC would formally withdraw from TENAZ."[149] Los Mascarones returned to Cuernavaca, where they have remained ever since, setting up a collective space in Ocotopec, Morelos, designed to replicate in smaller scale the Pyramids of the Sun and Moon.

Theater functioned to intensify the struggle against the violence of the Mexican state and the influence of US imperialism by revealing contradictions in the system and by rethinking and reimagining the relationships between performance, politics, and social change. Music, graphic arts, and poetry were also central to communicating the struggles and dreams of political movements. Public performances transformed art into a tool for cultural, political, and economic decolonization—of the imagination, social policy, and relations of domination between nations, people, and movements.

Artistic labor was a social and political act. Political organizing was also creative (dare one say even artistic?). Solidarity was a social relationship between people who shared similar ideas and took creative action toward connecting and circulating these ideas. Some engaged in direct actions and protests in their local areas to demonstrate solidarity with struggles elsewhere. Others traveled across borders to directly engage in personal and political collaborations. Challenging the tendency within Western liberalism to view politically engaged art as simple propaganda, US Third World leftists developed *new aesthetic techniques and vocabularies*—brigades, bus theater, collective creative processes, communal living, international solidarity, and the creative mix of politics and art. That is not to say there were not individual protagonists and leaders. These new approaches often emphasized collective participation and local community control over decision making, a contrast to a single-leader model and the central role of directors, institutional support, and the tyranny of the text. This was true for Chicana/o artists and the rasquache socialist aesthetic that developed out of what was at hand, techniques developed in struggle. Mexican and Latin American *teatristas* influenced by the student brigades of 1968 developed techniques to engage people in political discussions using theater on public transportation. Insurgent feminists like Mercedes Nieto and Dorinda Moreno, who worked out of San Francisco with Las Cucarachas, formed a critique of systemic and personal oppression and emphasized an internationalist politics of *sin fronteras*—without borders—grounded not in political rhetoric or analysis, but in the everyday struggles of creating new social relations. There was a need for new techniques, vocabularies, and political practices to create a different world, and artists helped shape and influence that political imaginary.

The question is not only what role did art/theater play in the Chicana/o movement, but how was theater a political movement? Chicana/o theater was a political language. Their cultural production and expression created visual expressions of communities in struggle for a dignified life, as well as audible, tangible representations of movement and struggle. Creativity was about senses, affect, and content; it was a way to connect people, organizations, movements, emotions, intellect, and political organizing through evolving forms of political solidarity. A "collective repertoire" emerged from political struggle, bus theater, and brigades; improvised and readapted scripts were the embodied memory of tactical decisions for collective creative production.[150] CLETA (and FARO before it), TENAZ, Los Mascarones, and others held that "rather than subordinate art to politics . . . art itself as a social practice could build and sustain community."[151] "As artists and activists sought to push beyond the limits of the nation form," writes Alicia Schmidt Camacho, "their struggles gave rise to a ferment of aesthetic and cultural innovation."[152] Expressive cultures and social movements engaged in a creative retrofitting of political and cultural history that included a politics of solidarity and the international political imaginary of the Chicana/o movement. Theater and performance were accessible and powerfully calibrated ways to communicate political ideas to the general public, inventing new techniques, content, and methods out of necessity and in a process of collective creation. The festival illuminated clearly that culture and politics were not separate; that radical cultural production was a critical terrain of transnational organizing; that the cultural workers in Mexico who identified with leftist politics were diverse; and that anti-imperialist theater was international.

The next chapter examines the continuity and strengthening of these networks in Texas, specifically between Chicano radicals and those involved in armed struggles in Mexico, a collaboration initially facilitated by Mariano Leyva. When Los Mascarones and CLETA traveled to San Antonio in 1975 for the Sexto Festival, Chicano activists in San Antonio were solidifying their relationship with the revolutionary formation of armed campesinos in central Mexico, the Partido Proletario Unido de América.

"POR LA REUNIFICACIÓN DE LOS PUEBLOS LIBRES DE AMÉRICA EN SU LUCHA POR EL SOCIALISMO": MEXICAN MAOISTS, CHICANA/O REVOLUTIONARIES, AND THE DIRTY WAR IN MEXICO

We are poor people armed and organized as the P.P.U.A. Our party is made up of workers, farmers, and a few revolutionary intellectuals. As part of the poor people of Mexico and the world, we have not taken up arms because of a love for war, but we have seen that it is the only way that the rich will leave us in peace.
PPUA

If they [PPUA] need money or guns . . . if I can I will give it to them. My participation is to arm the people of Mexico, protect them, and defend the sovereignty of Mexico.[1]
ALFREDO DE LA TORRE, "ENTREVISTA CON MARIO CANTÚ"

ON THURSDAY OCTOBER 2, 1975, at a military checkpoint in Vallecillo, just south of Monterrey, the state capital of Nuevo León, Mexico, Mexican federal police agents arrested and accused Ramón Raúl Chacón of Mercedes, Texas, Andrés Pablo de la O. Castarena of México, and Elsy Morales of Colombia of traveling in a vehicle with a false compartment of weapons.[2] Chacón, who was a prisoner's rights activist with the Puerto Rican Independentistas (freedom fighters), black radicals, and other Chicanos while incarcerated at the Leavenworth federal penitentiary in the late 1960s, was taking classes at El Colegio Jacinto Treviño, an Antioch-affiliated Chicano college in South Texas.[3] All three were taken to the Monterrey office of the Dirección Federal de Seguridad (Federal Security Directorate), or DFS, the primary intelligence-gathering and political police institution in Mexico at the time. Chacón and de la O. were accused of transporting arms with the intention to incite rebellion, as well as membership in the Partido Proletario Unido de América (United Proletariat Party of América) or PPUA, a transnational Maoist-inspired guerrilla organization founded in 1975 in central Mexico in the wake of the military occupation of the Colonia Rubén Jaramillo, a squatters camp in Cuernavaca, Mexico, established in 1973.

Mexican print media and DFS officials claimed that Chicano activists in San Antonio—specifically Mario Cantú—were founding members of the PPUA, and that the PPUA was part of a larger "global terror network" called the Alianza Internacional de Terroristas (International Terrorist Alliance, AIT). Reports from *El Norte* compared the PPUA with the Symbionese Liberation Army (the group responsible for the kidnapping of newspaper heiress Patty Hearst). They also alleged that de la O. was connected with the Black Panthers, had traveled throughout the southwestern United States to raise funds and purchase munitions, and was part of the Mexican Communist Youth (Juventud Comunista Mexicana), allegedly transporting guns for Pablo Gómez Alvarado, secretary general of the Communist Party in Mexico.[4] Chacón and de la O. were tortured into signing confessions, known as "amplifying the declaration." During a transfer from one holding cell to another, and for some reason unrestrained, de la O. somehow escaped, shirtless and barefooted, in a daring dash from the Federal Security Building through the streets of Monterrey. During the chase, a DFS officer shot at and missed de la O., instead killing a young boy.

Chacón was imprisoned for eighteen months. The particular state violence he endured exemplified broader counterinsurgency wars against political movements throughout North, Central, and South America during this period. From the FBI, CIA, and Defense Intelligence counterinsurgency programs in the United States to the dirty wars in Latin America, revolutionaries who engaged in international struggles were the targets of state terror in several nations. Chacón's story—his journey from Leavenworth to South Texas to a prison in Mexico and the influence his prison organizing had on his political work outside the walls—offers insight into the radical politics in central and south Texas in the early 1970s, particularly in San Antonio. It also illuminates how a group of Chicano men gave meaning to their participation in revolutionary activities inside Mexico. It weaves Chicana/o and Mexican social history together by uncovering connections between former *pintos*,[5] members of a landless people's movement, and a rural guerrilla people's army in central and southern Mexico. These contours of international solidarity within the Chicana/o movement in

San Antonio led to direct engagement with armed peasant movements in Mexico. This chapter outlines connections between people and organizations in Texas and radical and revolutionary social movement organizations in Mexico within the context of state repression in *both* the United States and Mexico. It also describes US–Mexican geopolitical relations during the 1970s. For some on the Chicana/o Left who also saw their political activity as part of the larger Third World Left, armed struggle was viewed as an acceptable path to liberation—socialist, anti-colonial, and anti-imperialist. Whereas armed struggle gained momentum across Latin America as one component of a larger socialist anti-imperialist project struggling against an onslaught of violence from dictatorial regimes, Chicanas/os supporting revolutionary movements and armed struggle in the United States were fewer but nonetheless a considerable force in the 1970s.[6]

Recognizing the multiple crosscurrents of radical histories between Aztlán and Mexico not represented in this chapter, the goal is to sketch the contours of a "countertopography" of Chicana/o radicalism during the 1970s. This countertopography negotiates a radical trajectory not fully contained by the Chicana/o movement but that finds articulation within it through armed struggle in Mexico.[7] That said, political work, especially underground activity, demanded secrecy and small groups, and the depth of discussion with regards to internal politics of the PPUA, or among Chicanos who were involved in these movements, is dependent on available evidence and the willingness of still-living participants to discuss these events. There were other Chicanas and Chicanos involved in these movements in Mexico that are still living; I leave it up to them to also tell their own stories. This chapter moves back and forth between Mexico and Texas, tracing parallel chronological trajectories of radical political movements in both nations, as well as the moments and connections of solidarity politics and direct collaboration. It is organized in four parts: Radical San Antonio; the Colonia Rubén Jaramillo in Morelos; the emergence of armed struggle; and the torture of Ramón Chacón.

RADICAL GENEALOGIES: THE CHICANA/O MOVEMENT IN SAN ANTONIO

During the week of September 11, 1971, an unprecedented and unexpected unity formed among Mexican American and Chicana/o organizations in San Antonio at "an extraordinary but little noticed political event" called La Semana de la Raza (Week of the People). Sponsored by Mario's Restaurant (owned by Mario Cantú), the League of United Latin American Citizens (LULAC), the GI Forum (Mexican American veterans organization), and Murguía Printers, La Semana de la Raza brought together groups from across the political spectrum for cultural events, rock bands, educational presentations, and political speeches from a who's who of the Chicana/o movement across the state and throughout the country. Representatives from the community defense organization the Brown Berets, the student organization MEChA, United Farm Workers, La Raza Unida Party, and the Mexican American Youth Organization came together with cultural workers from Mexico to commemorate the massacre of Tlatelolco and the murder of the Chicano journalist Ruben Salazar. Cantú chaired the celebration, and the imprint of his radical politics is evident in the programming.[8] The FBI also took note of the gathering, particularly the presence of Los Mascarones from Mexico City, identifying them as "a group of students that are socialist oriented."[9]

Historically, San Antonio has been situated at a crossroads of radical imaginaries and revolutionary political movements. The Alamo as a symbol of the freedom of Texas and rugged individualism did not have the same meaning for all inhabitants of the city. For the Mexican population, San Antonio represented struggle against Anglo American racism and economic labor exploitation, from the battle of the Alamo to the Mexican Revolution and the pecan shellers' strikes in the 1930s.[10] Since the late nineteenth and early twentieth century, radical socialists, the Industrial Workers of the World (Wobblies), the anarchist PLM (Partido Liberal Mexicano, or Liberal Mexican Party), and other transnational labor and political leftists organized in central Texas and left their imprint across the Southwest. The Flores Magón brothers and the Partido Liberal Mexicano had an important influence on not only the Mexican Revolution but also the political culture of San Antonio, the southwest borderlands, and the entire spectrum of the US Left at the turn of the twentieth century.[11] In 1913, for example, Charles Cline of the IWW (Industrial Workers of the World) and Magonista supporter Jesus Mari Rangel were imprisoned in Carrizo Springs, Texas, while on their way to join Emiliano Zapata's army. They were later tried in San Antonio.[12] The PLM at one time or another organized out of Texas, St. Louis, and Los Angeles. After his imprisonment at Leavenworth in 1924, Ricardo Magón continued to be politically active even as his health deteriorated while prison authorities ignored his problems.

Magón organized study groups with other imprisoned leftists and labor leaders, maintaining a "university of radicalism" as one of his last political acts before his death.[13] Radical labor and revolutionary movements in Mexico inspired activists and journalists like Sara Estela Ramírez and the Idar family of Laredo, along with Luisa Moreno and Emma Tenayuca (labor organizer, one-time member of the Communist Party, and self-declared anarchist) in San Antonio. They actively organized for the rights of workers, women, and others in the Southwest.[14]

As a result of this cross-border solidarity, the US and Mexican governments targeted many of these organizations for surveillance, infiltration, and elimination. As Chicano historian Manuel Callahan explains, "As part of the radical labor movement of the early twentieth century and the 1910 Mexican Revolution that spilled over the border into the US Southwest, [there was] severe repression against labor organizations, anarchists, and the Mexican population of the Southwest by local, state, and federal authorities." Highlighting the transnational and privatized apparatus of surveillance at the turn of the century, Callahan emphasizes, "Assisting local law enforcement were the US Bureau of Investigation and the Mexican Secret Service, as well as private detective agencies such as Pinkerton, Furlong, and Theil."[15] This marked a significant precedent for surveillance of transborder political organizing. Echeverría's discussion with Nixon in 1972 concerning Mario Cantú, Angela Davis, the American Indian movement, and the threat to hemispheric security had its origins in the transnational surveillance and infiltration of transnational organizations working along both sides of the US-Mexican border. The targeting of Mexican revolutionaries on both sides of the border happened contemporaneously with the Red Scare and Palmer Raids in other parts of the country.[16]

During the Chicana/o movement, San Antonio was characterized by a wide spectrum of political influences and organizations that echoed the political diversity within the larger movement. In addition to the above-mentioned organizations, the Universidad de los Barrios, Colegio de los Batos: School of Freedom, a community-based education outreach center, brought university students, Brown Berets, gang members, and other youth together. The Centro de Acción Social Autónomo (CASA), later renamed TU-CASA, organized for labor and migrant rights. The south Texas Valley–based Texas Farm Workers Union had a strong base of support in San Antonio.[17] As in other cities in the Southwest and Midwest, folks organized civic engagement projects, community groups, labor rights campaigns, protests against racial segregation in housing and education, and protests against police brutality and lack of drainage infrastructure.[18] San Antonio also had a vibrant Chicana/o arts community, including muralists, poets, actors, playwrights, and painters, and it was home to the cultural and political magazine *Caracol: La Revista de la Raza* (1974–1979).[19]

PRISONS AND REVOLUTION

Ramón Raúl Chacón was born in Delany, deep in south Texas, on January 5, 1942. Chacón was "raised among the poor and suffered the consequences: racism, exploitation and oppression."[20] After graduating from high school, he worked at various local jobs. In 1967 he was arrested and sentenced to sixty-six months for drug trafficking.[21] Chacón identified as a Magonista and an anarchist, and was considered a radical political theorist in Leavenworth. This is significant on at least two levels: Magón inspired Chacón's political theories and his ideas for social change as revolution. In a larger sense, Magón inspired many radical prisoners to keep his revolutionary spirit alive in Leavenworth.[22] Magón died in Leavenworth on November 21, 1922 (many accused the prison of neglecting his diabetes). While in Leavenworth, Chacón was also inspired by other revolutionary theorists, like George Jackson and the Martinique-based anticolonial intellectual Frantz Fanon. According to Raúl Salinas, Chacón is "how we got to . . . *Wretched of the Earth* by Frantz Fanon. Where he got it from, I don't know. Who his peers or his mentors were, in there or out, before he appeared into our midst . . . I guess we never bothered to ask. And so, you know from Fanon to Amilcar Cabral—the struggle in Guinea Bissau; seriously looking at Mao and what was going on down there; Vietnam . . . "[23]

Chacón and fellow Chicano *pintos* Salinas, Mario Cantú, Alberto Mares, Victor Bono, Beto Gudino, and others organized with Puerto Rican Independentistas, Black Muslims, Black Liberation Army members, Native Americans, and radical whites as part of the prison rebellions taking place across the country in the early 1970s.[24] As a group they studied Mao, Lenin, Magón, and the *Plan de Aztlán* and *Plan de Santa Barbara*, as well as Pedro Albizu Campos, Ernesto "Che" Guevara, and the struggles in Guinea-Bissau. In the early twentieth century, socialists, anarchists, and war resisters incarcerated at Leavenworth, including Ricardo Flores Magón, formed a "university of radicalism"; Leavenworth was again transformed into a hotbed of radicalism during the 1970s.[25] Together Chacón and the others organized cultural history classes, published a newspaper, and established the political organization Chicanos Organizados Revolucionarios de Aztlán (CORA). As a result of this political activity, Chicano *pintos* developed an analysis of society from the perspective of a "backyard-form of colonialism" that emphasized solidarity in act and word with Third World peoples everywhere.[26] Los Mascarones from Mexico and El Teatro Jacinto Treviño, the theater group affiliated with El Colegio Jacinto Treviño, both visited and performed at Leavenworth. These were the experiences and memories that Chacón brought with him to Texas. Organizing inside the federal prison system with other men influenced by anticolonial movements and revolutionary theory shaped the political imaginary of these men who later joined or supported the PPUA.

Upon release from Leavenworth in 1969 after seven years of imprisonment, Mario Cantú returned to San Antonio to run the family's restaurant. Cantú continued to support his comrades at Leavenworth, ensuring there was a steady supply of newspapers, audio recordings, and visitors who brought information about social movements across the United States and Latin America. After their release, Cantú provided them with the means to engage in political work, helping to finance numerous projects and organizations. It was Salinas who connected Chacón and Cantú: "Another brother who is about to get out soon has gone to the 'hospi' in Ft. Worth. His name is Ramón Chacón and I would like for you to send him a few lines. He knows of your correspondence with us, heard the records, read the materials, etc. He is one of the brothers who taught us the most about politics and progressive thought."[27]

Cantú identified as a Chicano Marxist.[28] Politicized in prison much as Chacón had been, particularly through his contact with radical thinkers and revolutionaries like the Puerto Rican Independentistas, Cantú also identified his experiences growing up in the Mexican barrio as important to his understanding of police violence, racism, and injustice. After his release, Cantú immersed himself in local, national, and international politics. The restaurant gave him access to resources as well as an established place where people could meet for organizational gatherings, strategy sessions, or socializing. Cantú gained a degree of freedom and an absence of accountability, as he was not beholden to any organization per se. The resources and networks allowed him to support movements on both sides of the border. Cantú believed "we need to move history . . . we should identify with feelings and struggles of the people of Mexico, and not with the government . . . a lot of Chicanos want to have a 'foreign policy' position [that] we should identify with Mexican government. This is incorrect."[29]

Mario's Restaurant was a "hotbed of political intrigue" in San Antonio. Everyone from mainstream politicians and community organizers to government agents and gunrunners gathered at Cantú's place.[30] In 1969, Cantú established the Centro Cultural Rubén Salazar (CCRS), which served as a cultural center, meeting space, and training area. The CCRS was also an international destination for the radical Left traveling between the United States, Latin America, and Indian Country.[31] Cantú traced his family ancestry to Lucio Blanco, a revolutionary leader from Tamaulipas. Cantú would adopt "Lucio Blanco" as his nom de guerre during his time with the PPUA.[32] Both Cantú and Chacón took the ideas they were exposed to behind bars and applied them to struggles in Texas and later in Mexico.

In addition to supporting local and statewide struggles like La Raza Unida Party (LRUP) and the Texas Farm Workers Union (TFWU), Cantú used his resources to connect San Antonio political activity with a variety of other movements, such as the American Indian Movement, the Crusade for Justice (Denver), the local Brown Berets, the Committee to Free Angela Davis, the Committee in Solidarity with the Chilean people, and cultural and revolutionary movements in Mexico.[33] He helped organize marches, rallies, and other mobilizations on behalf of immigrant rights, against police brutality, and in support of political prisoners in the United States, Mexico, and Latin America. When Cantú encountered legal challenges to his defense of immigrants' political rights in Mexico, respected movement lawyer William Kunstler worked on his defense team. The Mexican human rights activist Rosario Ibarra de Piedra traveled to San Antonio to testify on Cantú's behalf in a 1980 parole violation hearing stemming from his arrest in 1977 for "shielding undocumented aliens" at his restaurant—making him the first person to be tried and convicted under this statute. Ibarra de Piedra was one of the founders of Comité Eureka (Eureka Committee), the group of "mothers of the disappeared" that organized the hunger strike of 1978 demanding the release of all political prisoners and the reappearance of all the disappeared during the dirty war.[34]

Cantú did not hesitate to publicly declare his position on the Mexican government or his critique of US imperialism in Latin America. He organized protests of Mexican presidents, demanding justice for political prisoners and targets in the dirty war. On the one hand, Cantú represented the politics of the Mexican and Latin American Left, exposing the paramilitary violence organized by the Mexican government against students, farmers, and workers and emphasizing the urgency of supporting Mexican social movements rather than the Mexican government. On the other hand, like Chacón, Cantú worked with few people, and his outspoken personality and access to resources made him both well liked and a force to be reckoned with. Perhaps he worked alone because he intended his contribution to political solidarity to be arming movements in Mexico. But that had not come yet, and in his hometown of San Antonio, Cantú moved between political classes and movements. While Cantú and Chacón, both considerably older than the students and youth often associated with political movements, were participating in movement activities, landless people in central Mexico were preparing to take over abandoned land to create their own community. By 1974, Chicanos from San Antonio and elsewhere had joined the underground revolutionary movement that emerged from the land takeover. It is in this context that Ramón Chacón was arrested, tortured, and imprisoned.

LA COLONIA RUBÉN JARAMILLO—CUERNAVACA, MORELOS, MEXICO

At 7 p.m. on March 31, 1973, six families occupied abandoned development lots that belonged to the son of the governor of Morelos, Felipe Rivera Crespo, in the La Villa de las Flores area in Temixco, Mexico, south of the capital, Cuernavaca, in the central state of Morelos. The occupation was an assertion of personal dignity and an expression of the need to solve the critical problem of finding sufficient land and shelter. Seven hundred families had agreed to the takeover at an assembly of the Asociación Nacional Obrero Campesina Estudiantil (National Worker, Farmer, Student Association), or ANOCE, the previous week, but they did not show up at first. Florencio "el Güero" Medrano Mederos, one of the organizers, tried to convince families to come and mark off their piece of land, despite the police patrols in the area.[35] As more and more people came, the land was quickly occupied and marked off, with each claim measuring four hundred square meters. By the end of the week there were some fifty families; by the following month there were thousands. The immediate response by federal and state officials was to send in police and infiltrators. Even so, the emerging community held strong during the first week. Soon thousands of people had joined the occupation. In the first general assembly, held on April 2, 1973, the new *colonos* agreed on the name of Colonia Rubén Jaramillo (CRJ) for their new community, in honor of the agrarian leader killed by the government in 1962. The Comité de Lucha (Struggle Committee), the primary decision-making body of the community, eventually engaged in multilevel negotiations with regional, state, and federal officials over land titles and social services.[36]

Land occupations are a basic strategy of poor people's movements. Land struggles by campesinos in rural areas and campesinos that move to urban areas in search of a livelihood and living space are related in need and action. After the end of the Mexican Revolution, President Lázaro Cárdenas (1934–1940) made some twenty million hectares of land available to campesinos so that by 1940, more than 50 percent of Mexico's agricultural production came from communal *ejidal* lands.[37] Land occupations were a continental and global phenomenon, with movements of landless peoples occurring across Latin America. For example, in Chile there were 340 land seizures in 1969 and 1970; by 1971 the number had risen to 1,300.[38] After World War II, private interests began a process of enclosing communal land; by the 1960s massive amounts of Mexican agriculture had turned into private commercial agriculture.[39] From the 1950s onward, Cuernavaca, the city nearest La Jaramillo, was at the center of a development strategy for the area that included industry, timber, and tourism—all benefiting the wealthy classes from Mexico City and abroad. The "city of eternal spring" was beautiful, and the labor to keep it so came from exploited landless peasants and day-laborers. Previous land takeovers in the 1960s included La Lazaro Cardenas, the Colonia Antonio Barona, and the establishment of Palmar Grande.[40]

Morelos, the land of Emiliano Zapata, is considered a sacrosanct cradle of the Mexican revolution. As part of the *apertura democrática*, Echeverría had redistributed more land than any president since Cárdenas during the 1930s. Yet for many, the redistribution remained insufficient, and numerous organizations rejected the corporatist strings attached to the land. According to Padilla, "The official rhetoric of this period celebrated a national character whose tenets included on the one hand, modernization, middle-class prosperity, and consumerism, and on the other, traditional values such as a commitment to the family and female domesticity."[41] These were urban issues, with their own rural manifestations, and whereas urban middle classes appeared to benefit from the "economic miracle," systemic "underdevelopment manifested itself not only through the continued existence of poverty, but through the deterioration of living standards for a significant portion of the population, especially in the countryside."[42] The bottom line was that need for land outpaced the PRI's political will to redistribute it. So people took matters into their own hands.

Rubén Jaramillo was a political and military leader from Morelos who throughout the twentieth century was a central figure in political movements in central Mexico. Jaramillistas inherited the banner of radical agrarianism raised by Zapata. Born in 1900 in Tlaquiltenango, Morelos, Jaramillo joined the ranks of Zapata's Liberation Army of the South at the age of fifteen. A short two years later he was in command of his own regiment. After the revolution, Jaramillo dedicated himself to the long struggle of realizing the rights to land enshrined in Article 27 of the Mexican Constitution. He not only organized grassroots land invasions but also was a stern negotiator with government officials, meeting with two different presidents to solve political stalemates. Jaramillo ran for governor and organized with workers from a variety of sectors. In 1943, after a strike at the sugar mill in Zacatepec in which Jaramillo supported the workers, he was pursued by the military and fled to the mountains to mount an armed resistance, a tactic he would take up again in 1953. His supporters provided consistent discipline and determined leadership in expanding the movements to different labor sectors. Jaramillo's followers "twice engaged in electoral struggle, on three occasions took up arms, and explicitly organized around women's rights, spearheaded a massive land takeover, and attempted to forge alliances with groups at the national level."[43] In 1962, shortly after meeting with president Adolfo López Mateos, Jaramillo was assassinated by the military, along with his wife, Epifania, a revolutionary leader in her own right, and three of their four children. This act shocked the country, and though never investigated, it spurred the Jaramillistas to continue the struggle for land and labor rights throughout the 1960s and 1970s. Jaramillistas were a continuation, in a slightly different register, of Zapatismo. Both were part of the same revolutionary tradition in Morelos: "The Jaramillista struggle had its origins in Zapata's agrarianism, took form with [president] Lázaro Cárdenas's populism, and was transformed with the renewed hope for radical change inspired throughout Latin America by the Cuban Revolution."[44]

Florencio "Güero" Medrano Mederos was born in Limón Grande, Guerrero, to a poor campesino family. Despite the presence of Pacific tourist destination Acapulco, Guerrero was one of the poorest states in Mexico, and would become an epicenter of armed self-defense groups and revolutionary guerrilla formations throughout the 1960s and 1970s.[45] Early experiences with the power of rural landowners and their pistoleros marked Medrano's life: "The light-skinned one did not learn to read and write until later on and his vocation as a guerrillero can be traced to his experiences as a young boy when he was in a ditch holding his first magnum under his body and he heard how the soldiers took his uncle Martín Medrano who had led an uprising and as a result the army had almost finished off all the Medranos in Palma Grande."[46] Unlike Genaro Vázquez, the leader of Asociación Civica Guerrerense (Civic Association of Guerrero), and Lucio Cabañas Barrientos, leader of El Partido de los Pobres (the Poor Peoples' Party), who were formally trained teachers, Medrano grew up working odd jobs, first in Guerrero, then in Mexico City, and later in Cuernavaca. Medrano was part of Ramón Danzós Palomino's Independent Peasant's Union (CCI) and worked with Genaro Vázquez in the ACG. From 1964 to 1966 he joined a Maoist formation in Cuernavaca, the Partido Revolucionario del Proletariado de México (PRP), but he left over differences with Javier Fuentes, one of the main organizers. Yet he still remained attracted to Maoism. The experience with Fuentes led to a strong dislike of intellectuals, who had always "tried to impose their ideas on me."[47] At one point Medrano was almost expelled from the PRP, when he refused to travel to the Yucatan Peninsula to recruit, simply because "the intellectuals" were following the Chinese guerrilla strategy of a prolonged war. During this time Medrano spent a month in jail in 1966 for a land invasion in his hometown, organized by Jaramillistas. Through the PRP, Medrano traveled to China from June to December of 1969 as part of a delegation where he received ideological and tactical training. In addition to spending time in Mexico City and China, Medrano visited Ciudad Juárez, Los Angeles (where he was jailed for unknown reasons), Eagle Pass, San Antonio, and the Colegio Jacinto Treviño. Along with students and radical teachers, Medrano founded ANOCE in 1973 with the explicit purpose of putting the ideas he learned in China into practice within the agrarian radicalism in Morelos, Guerrero, and Oaxaca. The goal was to create the base for a people's revolutionary movement.[48]

Drawing directly from his experiences in China and with rural agrarianism, Medrano set out to establish the first "popular commune in the Mexican Republic" to demonstrate that "a group of people can oppose the government but also convert itself into a political force."[49] Unique to La Colonia Rubén Jaramillo was the goal of establishing a land base from which to launch and sustain a Maoist-inspired people's war that would emerge from a particular set of conditions in the Mexican countryside. Speaking to possible recruits, Medrano explained, "Our job is to organize the campesinos, the workers, the students, and honest intellectuals who are willing to fight for a revolution in Mexico. . . . We're for the workers who are exploited by the capitalists, and against the landlords who, with their White Guard gunmen, have disposed the villages of their common properties."[50] The neighbors (colonos) formed into collective work brigades to build houses and infrastructure for CRJ. They also established their own internal community security, known as "La Guardia Roja" (the Red Guard), which would form the core of the armed movement.

Representatives from La Jaramillo were sent to various parts of Morelos and across the country, particularly Guerrero, Oaxaca, and Mexico City, to share the news of the land takeover and garner support. The takeover inspired activists in other regions. Students volunteered and were inspired to find themselves on liberated land. Students from the National Autonomous University of Mexico (UNAM), the National Polytechnic Institute (IPN), and a host of other schools joined cultural workers, campesino leaders, labor organizers, and others to participate in the collective labor effort throughout the summer called the Brigadas de Cansancio (Exhaustion Brigades) and Domingos Rojos (Red Sundays). In addition, groups like CLETA and Los Mascarones performed and distributed literature about socialism and struggles in other parts of the world. Word reached San Antonio about the takeover and the need for support.

According to an interview with Cantú in 1978, the connections between Chicanos in Texas and the CRJ were established "thru [sic] activities in progress, [when] we had contact with el 'Güero' when he was working openly in the Colonia Rubén Jaramillo."[51] Whereas Marxist-Leninist ideas had influenced the direction of Los Angeles and National CASA during this time, a Maoist political formation attracted Cantú, raúlrsalinas, Chacón, and others in Colorado, California, New Mexico, and Washington to support armed peasants south of the border in their dream of a socialist revolution. During the summer of 1973 Cantú, raúlrsalinas, and Chacón met for the first time outside of prison. After a poetry reading at the University of Texas at Austin, raúlrsalinas led a discussion about Chicanos in prisons and then traveled to San Antonio. There he met up with Cantú, Chacón, and a group of Brown Berets at the CCRS. From San Antonio, Chacón took raúlrsalinas to

FIGURE 5.1. raúlrsalinas, left, with Ramón Chacón, somewhere in Mexico, circa 1973. Raúl R. Salinas Archive, MO774, box 14, folder 13. Courtesy of the Department of Special Collections and University Archives, Stanford University Libraries.

Mercedes and the Colegio Jacinto Treviño, and then on to Mexico (see fig. 5.1).[52]

As solidarity events, workdays, and negotiations with the government continued at La Jaramillo during the summer of 1973, police agents and members of the military garrisoned nearby continued to harass the inhabitants. On September 24 the military ambushed a delegation from the CRJ. The military claimed the delegation was traveling to Tepecuicuilco, Guerrero, to meet with representatives of El Partido de los Pobres. Primo Medrano, el Güero's cousin, was killed; Rafael Urióstegui and Carlos Rosales were gravely wounded; and five others were detained—including one woman who was pregnant.[53] Four days later, on September 28, almost six months after the first families had arrived, elements of the army and state and federal judicial police forces led by brigadier general Francisco Andrade Sánchez invaded the CRJ and arrested fourteen people, including members of the Struggle Committee. Medrano escaped with other members of the Red Guard. The army did not leave until 1981. Though government agents had already infiltrated the CRJ, the confrontation gave the government added reason to pursue Medrano and his supporters as an armed group. As had been the case with Lucio Cabañas and Genaro Vásquez, state repression of a political movement led to armed struggle. Pedro, one of Medrano's brothers, went into exile to California: "When the squatter camp fell Güero told him 'somebody from our family has got to survive, so I want you to go to California.'"[54]

NACE EL PPUA

Though an initial gathering of some forty representatives of various revolutionary formations was convened on September 28–29, 1974, in the city of Puebla, Mexico, to discuss the formation of a political party and a people's army, it was not until January 10, 1975, that the Partido Proletario Unido de América had its founding congress. In addition to el Güero Medrano, those present included Aguileo Mederos; Simón Elizondo, alias el Nevero; Celia (previously known as Elena), partner with Medrano; Cacarizo (alias); el Chivas Regal (alias); Canario (alias); Eufemio Hernández (a) el Tintán; and "three students from the CCH who never showed up again."[55] Lucio Blanco (Cantú's alias) is listed as a founding attending member from the United States. As stated in the founding documents of the party, the guiding principle of the PPUA was to take power through armed struggle: "The rich use violence to exploit the people. The people will use violence to liberate the people."[56] An editorial titled "¿Quienes Somos?" ("Who Are We?") explained how the decision to take up arms was made:

> We are poor people armed and organized as the P.P.U.A. Our party is made up of workers, farmers, and a few revolutionary intellectuals. As part of the poor people of Mexico and the world, we have not taken up arms because of a love for war, but we have seen that it is the only way that the rich will leave us in peace. We have proven this every time that we have tried to change things through peaceful protests, marches, strikes and written manifestos. The response has always been the same: the government has sent us its army and police and we have

been assassinated in cold blood in the streets, in the factories, in the fields and in our own homes.[57]

In the sixteen months after the military invaded La Jaramillo and the Struggle Committee went underground, efforts to form a revolutionary party and a people's army came to fruition as Medrano expanded and deepened his influence across three states—Morelos, Guerrero, and Oaxaca, with a specific focus on the state of Oaxaca.

The Central Committee's position was clear. Their attempts to peacefully enact a form of local socialism with the creation of the Colonia Rubén Jaramillo and the various committees organized to maintain social life had been met by state repression. In 1975 the dirty war was in full force against social actors, and their reasons given to take up arms were not far-fetched. The PPUA's statement located it within a longer trajectory of Mexican revolutionary movements, yet a distinction was drawn between guerrillas isolated in the mountains without support from the people and an army of the people: "We do not believe we are making a revolution *for* the people, but *with* the people. . . . In our struggle, not only will young men and young women participate, but also the elders and children."[58] Because workers, students, and farmers made up the vast majority of poor people in Mexico and across the globe and everyone is affected by the imperialism of the United States and its colonial allies in developing countries, solidarity was the answer: "If they [capitalist countries] are united to exploit us, we must also realize only by uniting and coordinating our struggle with the struggle of all the peoples of America and the world, will we be able to defeat our powerful enemies. . . . For the Reunification of the Free Peoples of America in their Struggle for Socialism!"[59]

The "Fundamental Program" of the PPUA was "to achieve the defeat of the bourgeois, the *terratenientes* [large colonial landowners] and all exploiting classes of Mexico through armed struggle and substitute the bourgeois dictatorship with a Gobierno de Trabajadores."[60] Through armed struggle and with support from a variety of base communities of workers and farmers, as well as support from Chicanos in "el norte" who would adhere to ideas of self-organizing and liberation, the PPUA would help prepare the people to take power. The PPUA's General Program then provided a brief history of struggles in Mexico, identifying "Yanqui" imperialism as the scourge of the continent. It also emphasized that the PPUA was a disciplined cadre of dedicated revolutionaries who would not fall into the same ideological infighting that, in their estimation, had characterized the Left in Mexico. For the PPUA, their ideology "coincided with the thought of Bolívar, Artigas y San Martín: Liberty and the Unification of all of América. . . . The resistance against foreigners began ever since they [Spaniards] arrived in America, was continued with brilliance by Tupac Amaru and now we continue the struggle."[61] The PPUA had three main goals: (1) organize and develop a clandestine Party across the country; (2) organize and develop a clandestine "People's Army" in rural areas that would eventually expand to the cities, rather than begin in the cities and move to rural areas; and (3) strengthen mass organizations at a national level by developing the Frente Amplio Nacional Democrático Antiimperialista. In the event of an armed invasion by imperialists from the United States, Mexico would be ready to unite all social classes under the direction of the PPUA. To achieve these three goals, the PPUA would consolidate forces and support bases in the liberated zone. These zones would in turn form a guerrilla rear guard that would eventually be converted into centers of provisional revolutionary governance, "the embryo of the Proletariat State."[62] Though it is beyond the scope of this chapter to analyze the documents of the PPUA, there are some obvious tensions between the "continental" perspective of struggle and nationalism in the face of US imperialism. The PPUA was not just about revolutionary talk and hypothetical liberated zones; it had a plan about how to bring about a socialist revolution with eleven main themes.[63] The PPUA's literature explains the responsibilities of members, the geographic organizing strategies (local, municipal, regional, and national), and the organizing strategies of the People's Army.[64]

FUNDING REVOLUTION

Clandestine organizing demanded reliance on allies for support—whether money, food, itinerant housing, information, an automobile, or any number of other necessities. For example, the printing of the General Program and the PPUA newspaper *La Lucha del Pueblo* was done in San Antonio with the help of Mario Cantú.[65] Cantú also supplied other resources, tapping networks across Colorado, New Mexico, California, Washington State, and other places.[66] Like other clandestine revolutionary formations, the Ejército Popular de Liberación Unido de América (EPLUA), the armed wing of the party, took part in the kidnapping of wealthy "capitalists" and politicians, revolutionary expropriations (thefts from institutions to be used for revolutionary ends), and aggressive persuasion of prominent political figures. In the year between November 1974 and December 1975, the PPUA participated in three kidnappings, a series of robberies of small and medium-sized businesses, and numerous armed confrontations with federal and state authorities in Morelos, Mexico City, Puebla, and the state of Mexico. This is not the place for an analysis of all these actions, though I will give a brief résumé of one of these actions that directly involved Chicanos. What is important to emphasize is that the state was faced with challenges by the PPUA on different fronts in a number of states.

On November 13, 1974, two weeks after the Puebla gathering, the commando Miguel Enriquez of the EPLUA kidnapped Sara Martinez de Davis, the wife of a wealthy American investor, Thomas Davis.[67] The commando group was made up of Andrés Pablo de la O. Castorena, Pedro Vargas, Lorena Guevara, and Pedro Moreno. In exchange for the safe return of Mrs. Davis, the EPLUA demanded 20 million pesos ($80,000) in supplies for families and 10 million pesos ($40,000) in cash. They also demanded that the titles to lands in the neighborhood Santa María be turned over without charge, as well as demanding tax exemptions for the inhabitants of the neighborhoods surrounding Cuernavaca, including Satélite, Flores Magón, Las Delicias, and La Jaramillo.[68] Some of the lands belonged to the Davis family, while others were perhaps government owned. Either way, the demands reflected a strategy behind the kidnapping: fund the revolution and expand EPLUA's land base and support for the people.

The action had been planned from "Casa de los Conejos" in the Iztapalapa district in Mexico City. Four communiqués were sent to Thomas Davis in December, none of which were answered. Sergio Méndez Arceo, "el obisbo rojo" (the red bishop) from Cuernavaca, was the intermediary for these exchanges.[69] In late December, Davis wrote to his wife to explain the delay in payment (banks were closed until January 2), promising that by January 7 "everything will be in the hands of the Obispo [Bishop] so that you can obtain your liberty."[70] Finally, in early January, Medrano sent Simón Elízonda, alias el Nevero, to deliver a fifth communiqué. As ordered, el Nevero left it in a trash can in front of the Palacio de Cortés in Cuernavaca. The following day el Nevero returned to the House of Rabbits (Casa de los Conejos), an EPLUA safe house, where Medrano charged him with the task of delivering a sixth correspondence to Thomas Davis. This time, the message was to be taken to the supermarket La Madrileña in downtown Cuernavaca. The daily *Diario Matutino de Morelos* was notified by telephone, and they retrieved and published the demands. Medrano then sent el Nevero back to Cuernavaca, where he was finally given four packages wrapped in white paper by Bishop Méndez.

Davis was released on January 30, 1975. el Nevero then returned to the Casa de los Conejos. After knocking and waiting, he was about to leave when Aquileo arrived to take him to another safe house on Telye-hualco Avenue, where they met up with Elena (a) Celia, Tania, el Chivas Regal, Sin Fronteras, and Medrano's family members, as well as three Chicanos. "In front of everyone, el Güero opened the packages and began to count the bills. When he reached the sum of forty-thousand dollars he explained half was so that the Chicanos could organize the PPUA in the north of the country."[71] Three days later judicial police officials picked up el Nevero in Mexico City near the exit of Los Pinos, the presidential palace. He and his family were tortured, and el Nevero was sent to the state penitentiary in Morelos.[72]

THE TORTURE OF RAMÓN CHACÓN

The surveillance files on the PPUA begin with documents concerning the arrests of Ramón Chacón, Pablo de la O., and Elsy Morales just south of Monterrey. Of course we cannot assume that the state lost track of el Güero in late 1973 when he fled the Jaramillo. What is certain is that after late November 1975, the war against the PPUA escalated and the confrontations were internationalized. The three were arrested on a Thursday. On Friday, October 3, 1975, the day after the arrests, the front page of most major newspapers in Mexico and Texas broadcast the news of a US-born Chicano arrested for smuggling guns and ammunition to "terrorist" groups in Mexico and Latin America. They also reported that Mario Cantú was one of the founders of a new political party in Mexico. The Monterrey-based newspaper *El Norte* reported that Chacón and de la O. were commandos of the PPUA, and that the PPUA was part of the "International Terrorist Alliance." The newspaper not only compared the PPUA to the Symbionese Liberation Army but also alleged that de la O. was connected with the Black Panthers and had traveled throughout the US Southwest to raise funds and purchase munitions. De la O. was also accused of having previously transported guns for Pablo Gómez Alvarado, secretary general of the Communist Party in Mexico.[73] Wild accusations made for great copy and sales.

On October 2 the DFS—in conjunction with the police in the city of Nuevo Laredo—arrested Salvador Abundiz Guzmán at a local hospital (he suffered from hepatitis), along with his wife, Silvia Fuentes, accusing them of forming part of the AIT.[74] The newspapers reported that they were found with weapons similar to those Chacón and de la O. were accused of transporting, lists of contacts in Guadalajara and Mexico City, and a "large quantity of subversive literature."[75] *El Norte* also reported that Abundiz did not contest the accusations against him when he was presented before the judge on October 10. Instead, according to the newspaper, he identified Cantú as a founder of the PPUA.[76] While Abundiz was kept in prison, his wife was deported. It is noteworthy that Silvia Fuentes and Elsy Morales, both women, were deported, in contrast to how the Mexican state arrested, tortured, and incarcerated the men who were captured. During the 1970s, the violence of the dirty war was directed at both men and women in armed confrontations or during torture sessions.[77] Neither Fuentes nor Morales were Mexican citizens, so it would seem appropriate to deport them, but Chacón was not a citizen either.

Seven days after his arrest, Ramón Chacón told his side of the story for the first time. On October 9, Ernesto Chacón, head of LRUP in Wisconsin, visited his brother in prison.[78] A US consulate official accompanied Ernesto. Ramón told his visitors that after he was arrested, he was held incommunicado for three days, during which time he was stripped naked, beaten, and tortured. One of the techniques involved simulated drowning: "[Chacón's] hands and feet were tied, [he was] knocked down, mouth gagged, [and a] water hose down his nostrils."[79] Another method included using a cattle prod on the underside of his arms, his groin, and his chest. Ernesto reported that he saw the bruises on Ramón's stomach: "My brother looked tired, weak and worried. He said he had signed some kind of statement under pressure."[80] During this time he was interrogated by a person with an American accent who was interested not in the charges of gunrunning, but in Chacón's activities in the United States.[81] During the time between his initial arrest and his meeting with his brother, charges of inciting rebellion had been added to the charges of transporting guns.[82]

The security documents and the "confession" that Chacón signed offered more information than had been released to the press. Of course we cannot ever be sure what Chacón really said or what the authorities themselves decided to include. And that is not the point. Revolutionary movements understand this fact. People are inhuman to other humans;

there is a threshold for pain. The information was scattered and non-sensical, though a pattern can be discerned—that of misdirection. Chacón was forced to talk, but he was not being entirely clear. According to the reports, he admitted that he had been bringing guns to Mexico since June. De la O. was his contact in Mexico, while Mario Cantú and Luis Levano were the financiers of the project. Whereas Chacón and de la O. had planned the gun shipments together, de la O. and Morales had met by chance in Nuevo Laredo at the Hotel Calderón, with the former convincing the latter that he could get her across the border but that they would have to go first to Mexico City. The remainder of Chacón's "confession" outlined the current terrain of the Chicano movement in the United States, information that would have been available in the newspaper or contemporary books concerning the issue. But in the eyes of authorities it was damning evidence, as it provided proof of the argument that Echeverría had been making to Nixon, as well as to the Mexican people: that agitators were importing a foreign ideology and arming movements in Mexico.[83] When Chacón spoke to his brother, he insisted on his innocence and that the confession was the result of his treatment, arguing that the arrest was a setup, and that the authorities waiting at the checkpoint knew his name and had extensive files on his activities.[84]

Chacón was not the only Chicano/a to be tortured in Mexico. The previous year Rubén Solis García, also from Texas, was arrested, accused of sedition and transporting arms, and tortured. Solis had been the LRUP candidate for state treasurer in 1972 and had worked with CASA. He was also a history teacher at the Colegio Jacinto Treviño. On July 1, 1974, he was arrested along with Joaquin Vite Patiño in Tamaulipas and accused of smuggling weapons into Mexico to arm movements in Mexico City and Guadalajara. Solis's case was very similar to Chacón's. He was transported to Monterrey, where he endured twelve days of torture before he "confessed." After eight months of incarceration, he was notified that he had been sentenced to four years in prison. On appeal, his sentence was reduced, and he was finally deported in February 1975.[85] Chacón's and Solis's arrests and torture provided yet another example of the transnational surveillance of Chicano movement activists. In the press, the cases were presented as linked.[86]

Cantú was on the defensive, and rightly so given that he was being accused of participating in a hemispheric "terrorist organization." Denying that the PPUA even existed, much less that he was a leader of it or had ever transported arms to Mexico, he also focused on defending

Chacón as a dedicated activist who had nothing to do with the charges against him. Narciso Aleman, a teacher and coordinator at El Colegio Jacinto Treviño, and Rubén Solis joined in the public defense of Chacón.[87] By October 15 they were putting pressure on Echeverría and the US State Department to investigate the torture of Chacón and Abundiz.[88] For his part, Cantú called the allegations "lies" and insisted that the Mexican authorities "used torture to force Abundiz and Chacón to sign statements that they were gunrunners to discredit the Chicano farm workers movement in the United States."[89] Cantú also accused the FBI and the CIA of being involved.[90] But the accusations against him continued, particularly in *El Norte*, which even reported that the FBI was investigating him, a charge the FBI's San Antonio bureau denied.[91] In late November, *El Norte* published two front-page stories. The first was titled "Caen Agentes de ATI aquí y en Venezuela," while the second was "Documento secreto revela plan de PUA [*sic*]." The former told of the arrests of two Mexican citizens, Silvia and Lorenzo Carrasco, in Venezuela. They were reported to be members of the AIT and the Servicio Internacional Nueva Solidaridad. In the second article, *El Norte* had acquired a copy of the aforementioned "Programa General" and published the sections concerning political strategy. Finally, the "Caen Agentes" article infers a link between drug trafficking and arms smuggling, a line of accusation that continued to haunt Cantú and defined the foreign policy parameters between the United States and Mexico for decades to come.[92]

Three months later, at a press conference on January 3, 1976, Cantú changed the story, offering new details on the accusations, Chacón's arrest, and his own involvement. Cantú presented the program of the PPUA "to correctly inform the public and clear up whatever misunderstanding that might exist as a result of what the press in Mexico and the U.S. has published."[93] He also would address the position of the party in relation to the Chicano movement. It was a bold move, one imbued with the bravado of masculine revolution. It was also bold in that he was admitting to believing in and struggling for political change through armed struggle. At the same time, Cantú's forthrightness could also be seen as politically irresponsible given Chacón's continued imprisonment.

From the beginning of the press conference, which he began with the phrase "me and my party," Cantú made it clear that he was speaking in the name of the PPUA.[94] Cantú admitted that most of the accusations against him were true, except the existence of the AIT. He read from a prepared document, "The Truth about Gun-Running, Guerrilla Forces, and Drugs in Mexico." In it, Cantú connected the PPUA to a larger global movement:

> The United Poor People's Party of America, with its program envolved [sic] from the old struggle of the poor and oriented for a total liberation, accepts full responsibility for the importantation [sic] of the people's weapons confiscated. . . . But the U.P.P.A. resolutely rejects and condemns any relation with the drug traffic notion implyed [sic] in the press. The UPPA makes known its existence as part of the ever growing struggle for liberation. The fundamental program of the United Poor People's Party of America [meaning the Americas] coincides with Bolivar, San Martin, Jose Martí, Jose Maria Morelos, Ricardo Flores Magón: Liberty and the Unification of the Americas. In actuality we can forsee [sic] an awakening in the Americas against the impose colonization. The U.P.P.A. . . . . unites resolutely with all revolutionary movements that have such a purpose.[95]

Cantú responded to all the media coverage about torture, his participation in a revolutionary political formation, and the recent articles linking guns and drugs. He made clear that the Mexican authorities had tortured Chacón and Abundiz during their interrogations. He explained the lawlessness and impunity reigning in rural areas, as well as the suppression of information about social movements in Mexico and the corruption and hypocrisy of the United States in relation to drugs and Latin America. Citing the case of John Thomas Jova, the son of the US ambassador to Mexico who was arrested in England in possession of a large amount of cocaine sewn into his clothes, Cantú emphasized the disparately light punishment Jova received. Cantú then announced that the PPUA, "through its chosen representatives and sympathizers in the U.S.," demanded that the US ambassador be recalled, citing the case of Great Britain recalling its ambassador to Chile after the Pinochet coup; that Chacón and Abundiz be released from prison; that the suppression of the Jova case by the US media be investigated; that the Mexican government "reinstate" freedom of the press by allowing the magazine ¡Por Qué! to be published; and that the return of all political prisoners in exile be accepted. Cantú's explanation of his actions and his comments about the PPUA are worth quoting at length, as only his words can convey how he understood the events that had taken place:

When the news appeared in Mexico that a group of Chicanos were apprehended and charged in Mexico with "possession of firearms" and "inciting to rebellion," and that under torture had confessed to charges and, in addition, had linked me and others to a revolutionary party of the people, my first position was to defend the clandestine nature of the Party's function in Mexico and here. At that time [October 13, 1975] my denial of having any relationship with the P.P.U.A was the most appropriate limited position I could take on my own. Today, three months after the name of the party [Poor People's Party of America] was made public, and after communication, group discussion, analysis and evaluation, advice from attorneys and friends, a decision has been made to clarify the circumstances surrounding the whole issue. It is not the decision of a single person nor friends; it is a decision arrived at through the collective function of the party and through myself and family whom I love as I do all the exploited and oppressed everywhere.[96]

To this Cantú added a critique of how the US press was confusing the public with stories about the "dope for guns" connection when they should have focused on the crimes of the CIA, particularly that agency's role in the "S.E. Asia heroin connection during the Vietnam adventure."[97] Cantú then shifted to discuss the reactionary immigration policies that blamed immigrants for economic problems that are really a symptom of US capitalism. According to Cantú, instead of accusing immigrants of being a burden on taxpayers and assuming they do not pay taxes, US society should look to the economic policies behind inflation, the rising cost of living, the shrinking value of real wages, and the role of large corporations in maintaining Mexico's condition of "underdevelopment."[98] Cantú's press conference touched on most of the topics that would dominate US-Mexican relations for the next thirty years: drugs, immigration, corruption, and the power of social movements. Though Cantú claims to have discussed this issue extensively with members of the PPUA, announcing the existence of a revolutionary party in Mexico (one that Mexican authorities had recently detected) still posed a series of issues and risks.

Chacón was still in prison. Cantú's acknowledgment of not only the existence of the PPUA but also its responsibility for the guns and ammunition that were found jeopardized the safety of PPUA members. Cantú might have consulted his lawyers, but there is evidence that

Ernesto Chacón was not in agreement with Cantú's public press announcement. The introductory notes of the report from the informational caravan of the Ramón Chacón Defense Committee, organized by Concha Chacón, Narciso Aleman, and Chacón's brother, indicated that Ernesto Chacón traveled to Guerrero to talk with "some persons." "They agreed with the analysis regarding Mario Cantú. That taking the party's name in vain is a serious thing, but they [party leadership] will take care of it. Ernesto had gone to San Antonio to talk to Cantú; according to Chacón, Cantú indicated that he did not want to be involved any more."[99] It is just as likely that Cantú did talk with *las gentes* before making these public statements, but we must also consider the possibility that he was grandstanding. Given what appears to be Cantú's contentious politics within the Chicano movement, particularly in south Texas and San Antonio, and his desire to continue to be a key player in politics, his intentions and words have to be placed within their local, statewide, and international contexts. In any case, Cantú, Chacón, and the PPUA were at risk. Cantú's statements caused concern within the Chicana/o community in San Antonio. George Velásquez of La Universidad de los Barrios commented, "His public statements on behalf of his one-man organization spread confusion. He undercut us [other movement organizations]."[100]

A letter written to Lucio Blanco (Cantú's alias) dated February 8, 1974, shed light on how the PPUA viewed Cantú's press conference, as well as on his future role in the party. The letter was drafted during the Second Congress of the PPUA, held in Puebla on January 10, 1974.[101] The letter was delivered by "compañera Lucena" and begins by emphasizing the dangerous conditions in Mexico, the urgency of the struggle, and the necessity of gathering all resources. The letter then explained that Lucena was commissioned to obtain the largest amount of money possible, and that given the dangerous circumstances and risks involved, all precautions should be taken to ensure her safety. As for the relationship between the PPUA and Blanco, "the comrade also had the mission of explaining the changes in your function that was decided at the second congress, that you have been designated a Delegate on the Council of Relations."[102] Finally, the Central Committee requested that Blanco put Lucena in contact with "los Primos del Norte," demonstrating that the contacts with Chicanos in the United States went beyond Texas.[103] As this letter makes apparent, the PPUA did not seem to have an opinion on Cantú's press conference, or at least the opinion did not warrant mentioning. It may have been that they did not have sufficient infor-

mation about the conference itself. But what is obvious from the letter is the important role that Cantú played in helping to finance the
PPUA, and the function that the PPUA understood Cantú to play. For
the Ramón Chacón Defense Committee, Cantú's press conference did
not help Chacón's chances for freedom.

SECOND CONFRONTATION WITH ECHEVERRÍA: "THE LITTLE FASCIST"

Again using the press conference as a means to build solidarity, Cantú
announced on Saturday, September 4, 1976, that he would protest Echeverría's pending visit to San Antonio for the opening ceremonies of the
Mexican Trade Fair to be held the following Tuesday and Wednesday.
He would be joined in the protest by Socialist Worker's Party US sena-
torial candidate Pedro Vásquez, Franklin García of the International
Meatcutters Association, and others. Speaking personally and on behalf of the Comité por la Defensa Física y Moral de los Presos Políticos en México (Committee for the Physical and Moral Defense of
Mexico's Political Prisoners), Cantú compared human rights violations
in Mexico to flagrant violation of rights in parts of Europe, Africa, and
Latin America. He then condemned Echeverría's collaboration with
the CIA: "We feel we have a special responsibility to speak out because
the CIA and the U.S.-based transnational corporations have in the past
been deeply involved in violations of human rights in various parts of
the world and today are deeply involved in Mexico with President Echeverría and the PRI [Institutional Revolutionary Party]."[104] Citing the research of former CIA bureau chief Philip Agee, whose book *Inside the
CIA* named Echeverría as a CIA asset with the code name Litempo 2,
Cantú said, "Torture is widespread in Mexico's prisons, and many political prisoners simply 'disappear.'"[105] In the rest of his remarks, Cantú
gave a historical account of the violence during the Echeverría presidency, including a list of individual names and the prisons in which
they were being held. Cantú then made six demands: (1) instate freedom
of the press; (2) instate freedom for all political prisoners, including
Ramón Chacón; (3) end the torture against political prisoners and US
citizens; (4) grant freedom for political exiles, including allowing Mario
Menéndez, editor of *¿Por Qué?*, to return to Mexico; (5) locate the disappeared; and (6) end the "attacks against the autonomy of universities. An
end to imprisonment and assassination of professors who oppose the
policies of the PRI."[106] Finally, Cantú announced, "We will be present

to greet Echeverría [on his pending visit], not in an *abrazo* [embrace] of friendship, but with a conscience and picket signs that repudiate the atrocities taking place in Mexico."[107] Manuel Rodriguez, a CASA member, announced that CASA would also protest his presence: "We are protesting the fact that Echeverría comes here not as a representative of the Third World countries or the Mexican people, but representing the captains of industry and the foreign investment stronghold."[108] The consul general of Mexico, stationed in San Antonio, swiftly responded to Cantú's allegations: "Mr. Cantú must have serious social, ideological or ethnic frustrations to so insult a country that is not his and which he does not even know. To assert that in Mexico we have political prisoners is to lie deliberately and reflects his hatred of everything coming from Mexico, with the possible exception of the Mexican workers he employs and reportedly pays less than the minimum wage."[109] The consul added, "For this reason I denounce categorically Mr. Cantú's bad will and his prejudice against Mexico whose only fault is to have given him the same blood as his parents."[110] This was the context of the confrontation between Cantú and Echeverría.

At around 8:30 p.m. on Tuesday, September 7, Cantú was standing with a group of some fifteen or twenty protesters and holding a sign that said "Free Political Prisoners" as Echeverría left the dedication of the Mexican government's tourism office in San Antonio's Guenther Hotel.[111] Joining Cantú and the protestors was John Stanford, longtime leader of the Texas Communist Party, and Robert Marbrito, formerly with Students for a Democratic Society. As Cantú began shouting, he was immediately grabbed by security guards, who pulled his jacket over his head. Momentarily stopped, Cantú advanced toward Echeverría when the guard released him. Echeverría simultaneously moved toward Cantú. As they came face to face, Echeverría took Cantú's sign, tore it in half, and called him a "pequeño joven fascista" (little fascist).[112] Returning the "fascist" insult, Cantú then held an impromptu press conference to announce he was canceling the protest for the rest of the week in light of the violence. "[Echeverría] demonstrated to the world that he's a fascist," Cantú said. "He should be responsive. He has the attitude of a dictator, like in Chile."[113] Pedro Vásquez denounced what he called an "assault" by Echeverría: "This act of violence only serves to expose the real face of Echeverría's regime. The Socialist Workers party campaign joins the Chicano movement in protesting this flagrant violation of democratic rights."[114]

The following morning at a breakfast sponsored by the Mexican American Organizations of Texas, Reies López Tijerina said to Echeverría, "I welcome you here in the name of 15 million Chicanos. I bring you an embrace from all the Chicanos of the U.S. and I apologize to the President in the name of Chicanos for the incident which happened last night on San Antonio streets."[115] Also present, and speaking positively of Echeverría, was Zavala County judge José Angel Gutiérrez. Grateful for Echeverría's visit, Gutiérrez commented, "Echeverría has more interest and foresight into the Chicano problem than any other Mexican President and any other U.S. President, including Ford and Nixon."[116]

Before Echeverría's visit, Cantú had been trying to convince Gutiérrez to set up a meeting with Echeverría to discuss the issue of the torture of Chacón and Solis in Mexico. At a conference at St. Mary's University in the summer of 1976, Cantú and Antonio Orendain, an organizer with the Texas Farm Workers Union, requested that Gutiérrez talk with Echeverría about Chacón's case or set up a meeting during the time of the visit.[117] Gutiérrez was already planning to meet with Echeverría and agreed to support Cantú if he would agree not to protest against Echeverría during the visit. For Cantú, this was unacceptable. He later criticized Gutiérrez and Reies López Tijerina for not supporting the protest against Echeverría: "The night of the protest, Reies López Tijerina is giving an excuse to Echeverría in the name of 15 million Chicanos, saying that I am not a Chicano. This demonstrates clearly the opportunism and the people should ask Reies and José Angel what are the personal benefits that they receive. I directly accuse Reies and Gutiérrez of being agents of the Mexican government inside the Chicano movement."[118] These were serious allegations, but so was the charge that Echeverría was complicit in the kidnapping, torture, and murder of social movement activists in Mexico. For Chicana/o activists who were making similar accusations about the US government, the embrace of the Mexican president went against the international solidarity inspired by Marxist anti-imperialist politics.

After Chacón's arrest, the Mexican government stepped up its war against the PPUA. Despite increased surveillance and repeated confrontations, arrests, and imprisonments, Medrano did not reappear until two years later—this time in a grand public fashion. On October 7, 1978, a little over five years since the army's invasion of La Jaramillo, some six hundred campesinos self-organized as the Asociación

Indígena de Autodefensa Campesina (Indigenous Association of Farmer Self-Defense, or AIAC).[119] Armed with shotguns, rifles, and machetes, they occupied some eighteen hundred hectares of land near Tuxtepec, Oaxaca (fig. 5.2). Leopoldo Degives, Daniel López Nelio, and Florencio Medrano were its leaders, while the organizational support came from the Unión General de Obreros y Campesinos de México (General Workers and Farmers Union of Mexico, or UGOCM) and the Coalición Obrero Campesino Estudiantil del Istmo (Student, Worker, Farmer Coalition of the Isthmus, or COCEI).[120]

Cantú organized a news crew from NBC to travel to Mexico and film the invasion, while freelance reporter Dick Reavis covered it for the magazine *Texas Monthly* (fig. 5.3). Cantú represented the group "US Solidarity with the People of Mexico—Liga Ricardo Flores Magón."[121] In an interview shortly after the land invasion, Cantú explained his

FIGURE 5.2. A note on the back of this photo reads: "Meeting of villagers to talk about PPUA plans. Medrano was not there. Near Tuxtepec, 1977 . . ." Dick J. Reavis Papers, box 2, folder 10. Courtesy of the Benson Latin American Collection, University of Texas at Austin.

FIGURE 5.3. Mario Cantú and Florencio "el Güero" Medrano, near Tuxtepec, 1977. Dick J. Reavis Papers, box 2, folder 4. Courtesy of the Benson Latin American Collection, University of Texas at Austin.

role: "Let's say I am the link between the revolutionary movement and the press here in the US. . . . This is very important because it was the first time that something like this had been done between the Chicano Movement and the Revolutionary Movement in Mexico."[122] Cantú finished the interview in his provocative style. "If they [PPUA] need money or guns and if I can I will give it to them. My participation is to arm the people of Mexico, protect them, and defend the sovereignty of Mexico."[123]

EUROPEAN COMMITTEE IN SOLIDARITY WITH THE CHICANO PEOPLE

Cantú's participation in the events in Oaxaca violated the terms of his probation for the charges stemming from a raid on his restaurant and his arrest for "shielding" undocumented workers in June of 1976.[124] Cantú returned to Texas briefly in November. Instead of staying in San

Antonio, however, he went to self-exile in France in late December.[125] In an interview conducted after his return, Cantú explained:

> [I left to] continue the struggle without confrontation. . . . I didn't leave because I intended to stay away. I had a plan. When I got subpoenaed, I already had a plan, I knew what I was risking . . . under probation. It wasn't the first time. I had been a couple of times [to Mexico]. Went to Europe to carry out a campaign in Europe to denounce violence against Chicanos in the US; and violence of the Mexican government against social actors and the existence of political prisoners.[126]

In a statement from Paris, Cantú outlined the reasons for his self-imposed exile:

> I am unwilling to continue to tolerate the restrictions on my freedom of speech and freedom of movement placed on me by the United States government and I am unwilling to place the question of my going to prison in the hands of a federal judge whose racism and blatant disregard for justice is a proven fact, not only to the public but also to his peers—to his fellow lawyers and judges. It is clear to me that should I present myself before the court . . . I will immediately be taken into custody and sent to prison. My offense will be to have exercised my right and obligation to speak out against the injustices and atrocities heaped upon the people of Mexico by the Mexican and United States governments. If any additional proof of these atrocities is needed, it will be forthcoming within the next two weeks when the findings of a recent study by the Human Rights Commission of the United Nations [are] made public. I have therefore made the decision for which I alone am responsible, to leave the United States so that I can continue to participate in the struggle to build a more humane society.[127]

Cantú traveled across Europe in 1978 and 1979, meeting contacts set up by Judith Reyes of FARO and working closely with Isaías Rojas, a writer for ¡Por Qué?, the popular and controversial political publication edited by Mario Menéndez that the DFS shut down in 1974.[128] Rojas had been kidnapped by the Brigada Blanca and forced into exile in Rome in 1976. There, Cantú, Rojas, and other Mexican and Latin American exiles founded the Comité en Solidaridad con el Pueblo Mexicano (Committee in Solidarity with the People of Mexico).[129] This group of exiled activists also organized the European Committee in Solidarity with the

Chicano People (ECSCP) that had affiliated groups in Spain, France, England, Italy, and Germany and published *¡El Otro Por Qué?* as an extension of the original magazine shut down by the Mexican government.[130] With the support of Amnesty International, Daniel Jacoby of the International Federation for the Defense of the Rights of Man, and US allies like Angela Davis, who traveled to the Basque Country to support the ECSCP, they took the issue of human rights violations of Mexican immigrants, political prisoners in Mexico, and police brutality against Chicanas/os to the international arena.[131]

According to journalist Dick Reavis, "[Cantú] was the last spokesman for a generation of Mexican Americans whose outlook on San Antonio had been formed in the years between the Mexican Revolution and World War II. In that era, before military bases were a key to the city's economy—and before the rush of Anglos in uniform—San Antonio was a northern Monterrey. In Mario's view, Mexican Americans were not interlopers in the life of either the United States or Mexico; they were the captives of both nations." Reavis is accurate to an extent. By placing Cantú within what is referred to as the Mexican American Generation, while at the same time comparing San Antonio to Monterrey in the industrial north of Mexico, we see how Cantú placed the relationship between the United States and Mexico within the context of US economic and foreign policy—an unequal relationship that created the conditions for labor migration across the northern Mexican border.

While self-exiled in France, Cantú learned of the death of his friend and comrade Florencio "el Güero" Medrano. There are differing accounts of Medrano's death. What is certainly true is that after he gave an interview to Francisco Salinas Ríos of the magazine *Revistas de Revistas* in October 1978, the military circle began to close in on him and his unit. Operating in the area of Tuxtepec, Oaxaca, Medrano was killed on March 26, 1979.[132] The DFS documents as well as the *Informe Histórico* state that Medrano was shot during a confrontation with the military and died two days later.[133] The *Austin American-Statesman* reported that Medrano was fatally wounded in a "shootout with private security guards protecting a large plantation near the village of San Ysidro Progreso, north of Oaxaca."[134] A document published in Madrid on April 20, 1979, by the ECSCP brings the two stories together, stating that Medrano's death was the result of the "military, preventative police and the DFS, reinforced by bands of para-military police forces of the *caciques* in the zone."[135] In 1979, Cantú returned to San Antonio from France to face parole violation charges. Mexican human rights activist

Rosario Ibarra de Piedra traveled to San Antonio to testify on Cantú's behalf, demonstrating the extent of his networks.

CONCLUSION

As a way to provide a unique understanding of nationalism and international solidarity at the intersection of US and Mexican Cold War politics, this chapter emphasized a transnational perspective that cuts across ethnic and area studies approaches by focusing on state violence and geopolitics on the one hand, and ideological influences, social movements, and processes of political radicalization on the other. It has taken us from the federal prison cells in Leavenworth, Kansas, to the torture room of the DFS in Monterrey, Mexico; from the urban streets of San Antonio to the rural landscapes of Cuernavaca; and from Magonista-inspired Chicano revolutionaries in south Texas to a Maoist-inspired Mexican People's Army spread across southern Mexico.

Though this chapter has been about organizations, movements, events, and connections, Cantú, Chacón, and Medrano are at the center of this story but are not the story themselves. In recounting their lives, the intention is to highlight the movements in which they took part and to emphasize that the 1970s were an active time for political movements. People continued to organize, resist domination, and create community in the midst of shifting economic and political terrain. Given the national and international networks of the Chicana/o movement at the time, specifically connections between the Chicana/o movement, the black underground, AIM, and the Puerto Rican independence movement, the connections with radical and revolutionary social movements in Mexico, Latin America, and other continents are broader and more extensive than represented here. For these Chicanos, solidarity meant armed struggle for socialism in Mexico and the United States. It meant representing the struggles of political movements in Mexico in protests, press conferences, and festivals in the United States, revealing the truth about US-Mexican relations and the violence of the Mexican government against political actors. Solidarity meant providing resources for political movements in Mexico and Latin America, as well as for elements of the Third World Left in the United States. Solidarity meant circulating struggles through networks in the United States, inviting artists and political organizers to visit and exchange ideas with political movements. It meant providing material

resources to make revolution in Mexico. Solidarity meant directly joining these efforts, and it meant working primarily with other men.

Cantú was a controversial figure in San Antonio politics. Chacón
was less public about his politics—even after his release. Interviews
and the little that has been written about Cantú attest that the maxim
that you either loved him or hated him might be a bit extreme. Supporting so many political movements with resources and publicity, Cantú's
restaurant gave him a different type of economic freedom that allowed
for different risks—with consequences that might have appeared to be
individual, but were incurred by an entire movement. When Cantú was
under indictment for charges stemming from the raid on his restaurant,
a broad swath of the political and religious leaders in San Antonio came
to his public support. Though he worked with different movements,
he worked alone or with few people, primarily if not exclusively men.
Cantú created a variety of organizations that generally included no
more than a handful of people. His public statements were brash and
bold. Whether he was contesting Mexican politics, directly challenging presidents, or critiquing other male leaders in the Chicano movement, Cantú seemed oblivious to the consequences. Given the nature
of his statements—calling out foreign governments for human rights
violations, directly challenging sitting presidents in public, supporting revolutionary movements with guns and ammunition—his words
could be seen as a mechanism of protection. This can be an effective
strategy for reaching particular political goals, animating an audience,
and bringing attention to an issue. Cantú's pronouncements, as demonstrated by the response of other San Antonio activists, did not necessarily attract widespread support from Chicano movement leaders,
nor did they attract many women to the struggle. At the same time,
these may not have been Cantú's goals. Solidarity for Cantú, Chacón,
raúlrsalinas, and others took many forms. Their actions place them in a
long line of *contrabandistas* running guns and other products between
the United States and Mexico, and specifically between Texas and Latin
America.[136]

Chacón, Cantú, and raúlrsalinas (though he figures less in this narrative) were all politicized while serving time in federal prisons. Puerto
Rican and African anticolonialism was combined with a Mexican an-
archist/Marxist perspective forged in prison in the context of a burgeoning Chicana/o movement. When these men came out of prison,
it was like a blast from a cannon. Older than the "youth" of the move-

ment, and having survived the retaliation from guards and wardens for their prison organizing and learned the exigencies of the "hole," their loss of freedom changed how they measured risk and danger, how they understood what could be taken from them. These were hard men, and they worked in solidarity, often with other hard men. The experience of organizing inside prison, and the revolutionary political imagination that emerged from these experiences, influenced how and with whom these men collaborated.

PUENTE DE CRISTAL (CRYSTAL BRIDGE): MAGDALENA MORA, THE 1975 TOLTECA STRIKE, AND INSURGENT FEMINISM

Caminábamos dóciles
en un Puente de cristal
y la lucha nos encontró.

Obediently we walked
over a crystal bridge
and struggle found us.

LUCHA CORPI, PUENTE DE CRISTAL[1]

BUILDING ON THE PREVIOUS chapter and extending the analysis of international solidarity of the Chicana/o Left to labor organizing, this chapter examines radical insurgent feminism as a way to think about how cross-border solidarity can be created within a political space, such as a factory of a transnational corporation. Through collective organizing with documented and undocumented workers, "a political tradition that contest[ed] the social relations of production and reproduction" was cultivated. Through leadership, direct negotiation, and taking of the struggle from the factory to the community, "women who articulate[d] these sentiments call[ed] for Chicana [and Mexicana] self-determination which encompasse[d] a struggle against both personal and institutional manifestations of racial discrimination, patriarchy, and class exploitation."[2] Mexican workers have a long history of organizing in the fields and factories of the agricultural world, garment industries, and other US labor sectors. From pecan shellers in San Antonio in the 1930s to cigar workers in Florida in the 1940s, to garment workers in Los Angeles and agricultural workers throughout the twentieth century, struggles led by Mexican women with leftist-inspired politics have been militant and creative, disrupting political power and challenging gender roles in politics and the personal sphere. As discussed in chapter 1, labor solidarity across borders between people of Mexican descent dates back to the nineteenth century. Solidarity through the creation of cross-border organizations, newspaper articles and editorials denouncing injustices, organized protests, and alliances with other US workers—white, black, or Asian—has characterized the longer history of the Chicana/o-Mexicana/o Left. This chapter emphasizes not only the public political activity but also the social relationships behind the emergence of solidarity.

On Tuesday, May 13, 1975, workers at the Tolteca Foods factory in Richmond, California, organized a strike. Most of the workers were women from Mexico, many of whom were undocumented. S&W Fine Foods, a subsidiary of the Canadian transnational corporation IMASCO, had recently purchased the family-owned factory in Richmond. After the change in ownership, working conditions worsened and pay increases disappeared. Union representation was ineffectual at a time when anti-immigration laws were making job security and organizing initiatives all the more urgent. After defending their strike with their bodies—several of the women were injured when the only Anglo truck driver at Tolteca attempted to break the strike by ramming his truck through the picket line—the workers won many of their demands.

The Tolteca strike was significant for a number of reasons. The largely female and undocumented labor force successfully organized a strike at a transnational company at a time when the labor movement was struggling to survive the first onslaught of neoliberal economic policies. The leaders who emerged during the struggle sidestepped the union representatives and, drawing on their own experiences, developed a culture of leadership and organizing that nurtured their "own terms of humanity."[3] Taking their meetings from the union hall to the community center, they expanded the political discussion to include issues that directly affected undocumented women outside of the workplace, while locating their struggle in an international context of labor organizing. Organizing as undocumented women, and in concert with other groups of undocumented women, provided new ways of conceptualizing community-based labor struggles. As leaders within the movement that emerged from the strike, local Marxist activists and organizers (members of the Centro de Acción Social Autónomo [CASA] and the October League) were instrumental both in organizing community support in the San Francisco Bay area for the strike and in supporting the Tolteca workers.

One of these participants was Magdalena Mora, a student leader at the University of California, Berkeley who eventually joined CASA. Mora was born in 1952 in Tlalpujahua, Michoacan, Mexico. Her father, Magdaleno, worked as a campesino, factory worker, and miner, and was a leader in the local labor movement during the 1930s and 1940s. Her mother, Esther, worked and raised Magdalena and her brothers, always encouraging their educational development. Migrating to the United States in 1965 at the age of thirteen, Magdalena Mora worked in the agricultural fields and cannery industry in San Jose, California, and attended Abraham Lincoln High School, where she was a member of the Mexican American Youth Organization (MAYO) and UMAS (United Mexican American Students). A short story, "Un día en el fil de cebolla" (One Day in the Onion Field), which she wrote for a class with the renowned Mexican writer Juan José Arreola when he was a visiting writer in UC Berkeley's Chicano Studies program, revealed Mora's literary talents.[4] Her father's political organizing and her mother's support for her intellectual development influenced Mora's political activism in the 1970s. She was "a model of Chicana activism" according to Chicana historian Vicki Ruiz.[5] Drawing from this political foundation while studying at UC Berkeley, Mora became active in the Chicano movement at a statewide level, graduating with a degree in economics in 1975. "[Maggie] had been born with an intellectual awareness, sharpened by her and her family's experiences in the fields and later in the barrio," her close friend Lucha Corpi wrote. "She had since [her youth] the ability to see and the will to do something about the conditions, systems (the establishment) that kept her parents and so many others from getting a fair deal in life."[6] After working with "a propaganda collective in the Bay Area," Prensa Sembradora, Mora joined the San Jose/Oakland CASA in 1974 during a transitional period that accompanied the merging of the Committee to Free Los Tres and CASA in 1975. Mora, a key organizer for CASA of the Tolteca Foods strike, served on the Political Commission and wrote articles and editorials for the CASA newspaper, Sin Fronteras (fig. 6.1).

Four years later, she returned to higher education to attend graduate school in history at the University of California, Los Angeles. That same year, she was diagnosed with a malignant brain tumor. Mora continued writing—cofounding and publishing El Foro del Pueblo along with CASA member Carlos Vásquez and publishing academic articles—and editing one of the first anthologies focusing on the lives and experiences of Mexican women workers.[7] In April 1981, Mora returned to Tlal-

FIGURE 6.1. Magdalena Mora, second from left, Teotihuacan, Mexico. Image courtesy of Gregorio Mora-Torres.

pujahua, Mexico. A month later she was given a ceremonial burial as per town tradition. In "Raíz Fuerte que no se Arranca," a memorial program in her honor, historian Devra Weber explained, "Magdalena was a fighter. She saw and understood the potential in people. This motivated her political work and her struggle for a society in which that potential could be realized."[8] Adelaida Del Castillo dedicated her book *Between Borders: Essays on Mexicana/Chicana History* to her comrade: "Magdalena Mora, activist, author, once a student who worked with, researched and wrote about Mexican women and the Mexican working class. She wrote of the interrelation of national and international factors in the formations of the Mexican working class and the importance of these factors in the historical development of the southwestern United States."[9] As CASA member Carlos Vásquez wrote:

She fought for life . . . not only because she was a vibrant young woman struck down in her intellectual and physical prime, but because she understood that we have reached a stage in this country when all people are fighting for life—against pollution, environmental abuse, and careless disposal practices. In her two-year bout with diagnosed brain cancer, she fought back using all of nature's weapons and learned of the strength in nature's food before corporate man gets a hold of it.[10]

Focusing on Mora's political analysis and politics of solidarity, her anticapitalist perspective, and how her analysis was informed by her own life experiences as a farmworker, student organizer, and journalist, this chapter describes how relations with those in power were transformed through the organization and struggles of undocumented Mexican women enacting radical feminist socialist dreams.[11] In particular, it discusses enacting solidarity; connecting along issues of class exploitation, gender, and nation; and the organizing of undocumented women—doing so through the lens of the Tolteca strike, with much of the narrative adapted from Mora's own research article on the strike published in 1981 as part of her graduate work. Mora's research centered on the emerging leadership and the diverse political issues discussed within organizing spaces created outside of the factory floor and union hall, in community centers, parks, homes, and neighborhoods (fig. 6.2).

In recovering these stories, the goal is to also place Mora within this historical narrative, both to emphasize her involvement, dedication, and writings and to contextualize her participation as an important example of activist research and critical inquiry that antagonizes the dominating relationships universities and academic research can have with communities and people. The chapter then examines Mora's articles and editorials published in CASA's newspaper, *Sin Fronteras*.

The poetic accompaniment woven into this chapter is a gift from the award-winning Chicana writer Lucha Corpi. "Puente de Cristal," dedicated to Mora and read at a commemoration of her life in Los Angeles in May 1981, marks a series of layered moments, repetitions, and remembrances.[12] Emphasizing an epistemology that includes these poetics of resistance, the poem is also a gesture toward the "intertextual conversations" that mixed-genre forms of writing create and make possible. Given that "forms and contents are dialectically related . . . new innovative forms of writing were imperative and indicative of new forms of political subjectivities. . . . The diverse forms Chicanas invented to 'speak themselves' into poetic and political discourses [testify] to a new sense

FIGURE 6.2. Left to right: Carlos Vásquez, Madgalena Mora, Hortensia Busi Allende, Luis Juárez, Maria Elena Durazo, Evelina Fernández, Maria Inez Quiñones. Image courtesy of Gregorio Mora-Torres.

of creative agency."[13] Or put another way, it is a dialogue across geopolitical and historical topographies highlighting the creative means of survival and human dignity at the center of a politics of solidarity that animated a decolonial imaginary among self-identified Chicana/o--Mexicana/o leftists.

Se desgarró el capullo
y a punto cero calculado
el ojo sibílico apuntó.

Grito de lucha
en el campo
en la fábrica
en mi yo
en el tuyo
al extraño
al compañero.

The bud tore loose
and the sybil's eye
aimed at zero.

Battle cry
in the fields
in the factory
in my self
in yours
to the stranger
to the friend.

DECOLONIAL IMAGINARIES: *SIN FRONTERAS*

Examining the historical terrain and epistemological limitations of
the Chicano historical imagination by tracing a genealogy of ideas and
repetitions that uncover contested histories of feminism in the Chicano movement, Emma Pérez identified the colonial imaginary. With
specific regard to the dominating influence of nationalisms, race, capitalism, and heteropatriarchy within the historiographical literature,
Pérez's theoretical, heuristic, and political insight reveals how violent
legal and pedagogical structures have influenced the writing of US and
Chicano history. These same dynamics also help explain why we know
so little about the Chicana/o Left. Building on the work of the Chicana
intellectuals Antonia I. Castañeda, Vicki Ruiz, Deena González, Chela
Sandoval, Gloria Anzaldúa, and many others, the colonial imaginary
"already leaves something out, leaves something unsaid, leaves silences
and gaps that must be uncovered."[14] Pérez provides the alternative perspective that the decolonial imaginary, "that interstitial space where
different politics and social dilemmas are negotiated," is located "between that which is colonialist and that which is colonized."[15] Sexing
of the colonial imaginary can uncover fugitive wills by focusing on process rather than masculine event, or the process to event.[16] For Pérez,
meaningful consideration of Chicana and Chicano borderland subjects
requires the awareness that "despite geo-political borders, those of us
who study Chicanas and Chicanos face historiographic dilemmas regarding the placement of people who, although Mexican or mixed Native American by birth, entered a unique double bind as a diasporic
yet colonized race in the nineteenth-century United States."[17] Yet heed
her warning: "We must also remember the irony that the colonized

may also become like their invaders, assimilating a colonial mindset. This colonial mentality accepts the dominant culture, gender class, and sexuality as normal, natural, and good."[18] The dominant culture also strives to define and police the politics of international solidarity—from state and privatized philanthropy to study abroad, volunteerism, and the Peace Corps—and even economic development, human rights, and US aid can be interpreted as solidarity. Consider that solidarity is situated on the border between colonizers and colonized, that it can explicate in less obvious and insidious ways the relationship of power between structurally unequal partners. Solidarity emerges and is defined in struggle. It can also challenge and redefine relationships between different actors, sometimes taking time, trust, and situated experiences to create an alternate relationship or perhaps change the conditions of domination and injustice. Solidarity involves not only shared conditions of oppression and domination but also shared experiences in the struggle to create different possible outcomes.

> Sólo entre el silencio
> preciso de dos puertas
> pueden mantenerse
> crisálidas eternas.

> Only in the precise
> silence of two doors
> can the chrysalid
> sleep forever.

The Mexican population in California experienced substantial growth during Magdalena Mora's childhood. A study by the California Division of Fair Employment Practices identified that of the five southwestern states where the majority of Mexicans lived, California's Spanish-surnamed population was growing the most rapidly, increasing by 88.1 percent from 1950 to 1960, and by an additional 50.4 percent between 1960 and 1970.[19] By the time Mora graduated from Berkeley, in 1974, and joined CASA, she already had a variety of political experiences with student (high school and university) and farmworker organizing in the Bay area. Mora developed a multivocality with Prensa Sembradora and as a short-story author.[20] Members of Prensa Sembradora were central to Mora's political and intellectual development, introducing her to writing for a public audience, collective analysis and critique, and the

Chicana/Chicano *rasquache* sensibility and do-it-yourself aesthetic.[21] With a literary voice from writing short stories, Mora's pen increasingly developed into an important weapon in her arsenal of struggle.

CASA was founded in 1968 as a mutual aid (*mutualista*) organization, but its deeper organizational and ideological roots can be traced to the late nineteenth century. It is important to place the *mutualista* movement within the longer genealogy of ways that people of Mexican descent have organized to survive conditions not of their own making. Community-based mutual aid organizations (*sociedades mutualistas*) were basically groups of workers and their families that came together to help each other and to create a sense of community. Their common ground was often ethnic or racial ties, religious or political beliefs, geography, proximity, or labor. The focus was on survival in times of crisis and community building through shared struggles and experiences. Consider that mutual-aid societies were a form of self-defense and survival for nonwhite communities during a time of racial apartheid. Workers and families would pool their money in the event of a medical emergency or death, as well as for cultural celebrations. Communities were made through *mutualistas* as people came together to make and carry out decisions, organize events, or support each other in times of personal, economic, or social crisis. Some *mutualistas* offered educational opportunities, while others were a form of trade union, organizing for labor and civil rights. For example, in 1917 in San Antonio, Morelos Mutua de Panaderos, a group of bakers and one of the six labor *mutualistas* in the area, organized a yearlong strike eventually mediated by the US Department of Labor. La Gran Liga Mexicanista de Beneficencia y Protección, a *mutualista* based in Laredo, Texas, and La Agrupación Protectiva Mexicana of San Antonio, both founded in 1911, organized for equal educational opportunities for Mexican American children, and against lynchings and police violence. During the following decade, La Liga Protectora Mexicana, the successor organization to La Agrupación, worked with farmworkers and tenant farmers. In California in 1931, the Comité de Vecinos de Lemon Grove filed a desegregation lawsuit against the local school district. Some *mutualistas* had Ladies Auxiliary clubs. Women also organized their own mutual-aid organizations. In Texas, the Club Femenino Orquidia was organized in San Antonio, while the Sociedad Josefa Ortiz de Domínguez—named after Josefa Ortiz, "La Corregidora," the conspirator and supporter of independence from Spain at whose home revolutionaries met—continued the tradition of radical organizing in Laredo along the border with Mexico. Located throughout the southwestern United States as well as in Indiana, Chicago, Washington State, Idaho, and Kansas, these organizations were important in the lives of Mexicans and Mexican Americans through the late nineteenth and early twentieth centuries. *Mutualistas* in Mexico and the United States, particularly along the border in Texas and Arizona, supported each other and provided important networks of communication and solidarity.[22] Though a combination of state violence, capitalist changes in production, white supremacy, and the Great Depression devastated these organizations, the influence of the *mutualista* model continued after World War II and into the 1960s and 1970s with the founding of the Hermandad General de Trabajadores (HGT) in 1951 and the founding and expansion of CASA in 1968 and 1975, respectively.[23]

While the origins and history of the transformations within CASA have been told elsewhere (see chapter 1), the emergence of CASA-HGT in 1968 was a direct result of activists recognizing the need for a new political formation to engage the current political establishment.[24] The precursor of CASA-HGT was the Hermandad Mexicana Nacional, founded in San Diego. Bert Corona and Soledad Alatorre, both longtime labor and community workers with strong ties to the organized political Left in the United States, particularly the Communist Party USA (CPUSA), worked with CASA-HGT.[25] In 1974 a shift occurred in the leadership, direction, and ideology of CASA: "Graduate students, undergraduates, and young professionals launched an ambitious agenda for what they considered a new and improved CASA. In addition to running the service center, they would educate the public through their newspaper, *Sin Fronteras*, organize workers into trade unions, and fortify themselves through research and study groups, openly Marxist in orientation."[26]

"Women who lived and breathed and worked the movement" brought up issues of women's participation and gender oppression within CASA, an organization of "men and women [who] saw themselves as Marxist–Leninists struggling for the liberation of Chicano/Mexicano working class in the United States and Mexico."[27] Women's analysis was published in *Sin Fronteras*, which invoked the radical imagination of the anarcho-syndicalist Partido Liberal Mexicano (PLM) (commonly referred to as Magonistas, after Ricardo and Enrique Flores Magón). The PLM organized workers in the US Southwest and throughout Mexico, launched a guerrilla war against the Mexican state from north of the US-Mexican border, and, as Pérez demonstrates, inspired "third-space feminism" in the socialist Yucatan peninsula in Mexico.[28] In their writings and organizing efforts, CASA members Mora, Evelina Márquez, Evelina Fernández, Irma García, Isabel H. Rodríguez, Margarita Ramírez, Elsa Rivas, Gilda Rodríguez, Maria Elena Durazo, Andrea Elizalde, Diane Factor, Jana Adkins, Teresa Rentería, and Patricia Vellanoweth articulated feminist insurgencies as a political practice, insisting on the importance of creating spaces (editorial, organizational, and personal) for Mexican and Chicana women to participate in the political debate, in turn challenging the "male nationalisms" of the movement.[29] Magdalena Mora and the other women in charge of *Sin Fronteras*, like the largely female staff of *El Grito del Norte* in New Mexico in the 1970s, were part of an inherited tradition of revolutionary women involved in the PLM on the northern side of the border, including Sara Estela Ramírez in Laredo, Texas, the Villarreal sisters in San Antonio, and Blanca Moncaleano, Teresa Arteago, and Maria Talavera in Los Angeles. All of them contributed to the revolution's agenda as revolutionists, activists, and journalists.[30] *Sin Fronteras* focused on news and analysis about political and labor movements in Mexico and Latin America, and on Third World struggles in general. Scathing editorials and investigative articles allowed the writers, especially Mora, to take aim at the various forces of oppression.

The organizations' political framework from 1975 through 1978 was described by members as "a genuinely revolutionary mass organization functioning under principles of democratic centralism, guided by the theory of Marxist-Leninism, and lighted by the revolutionary spirit of our most courageous and anti-imperialist people." The shift was partly a result of CASA-HGT merging with El Comité to Free Los Tres (CTFLT). The CTFLT emerged as the defense committee for Alberto Ortiz, Juan Fernández, and Rodolfo Sánchez, who were accused of robbing and shooting a drug dealer, Bobby Parker, who turned out to be an undercover agent of the US Bureau of Narcotics and Dangerous Drugs in 1971 (though it was not known at the time that Parker was working undercover). Women in the CTFLT participated in the Committee to Stop Forced Sterilizations (CSFS), organized in the early 1970s to end this genocidal, eugenicist procedure conducted on Chicanas and Mexicanas at the University of Southern California–Los Angeles County Medical Center. CSFS was part of a national movement led by women of color: Puerto Ricans (Young Lords Party in New York), Native Americans, and African Americans organized committees and pushed legislation to end this national practice.[31] CTFLT was also influenced by

Casa Carnalismo, an organization committed to expelling drug dealers from the Pico Gardens–Aliso Village projects in East Los Angeles.[32] The experiences of women working with CSFS in Los Angeles and with the propaganda collective Prensa Sembradora in the Bay Area, a cadre that included Mora, Isabel H. Rodríguez, Evelina Márquez, and Maria Elena Durazo, also influenced the trajectory of CASA, first in San José/Oakland and later in Los Angeles with the production of *Sin Fronteras* in 1975.[33]

Though comprising self-defined Marxist-Leninists, post-1974 CASA "became imbued with some of cultural nationalism's male identification, which partially informed CASA's vision of 'the woman question.'" As a result, "the women in CASA thus existed as women and as Marxists in a movement dominated by cultural nationalist ideology."[34] This had direct consequences for the organization: "CASA members, including women, saw women's issues as an equal part of the class struggle and did not see the need to separate them, like women in the feminist movement. However, a difference existed between the theoretical desire for the equal participation of women in all aspects of the organization and its actual practice."[35]

Caminábamos dolientes
en un Puente de cristal
entre dos puertos.

Painfully we walked
over a crystal bridge
between two doors.

THE TOLTECA STRIKE

Mora, along with other members of the Prensa Sembradora, joined the San José/Oakland chapter of CASA shortly before that collective folded in 1974–1975. In this section, I focus on Mora's participation in organizing the strike, which she discussed in the posthumously published article "The Tolteca Strike: Mexican Women and the Struggle for Union Representation." As Mora explains in the introductory paragraph, "The analysis is based on the observations of Carlos Vásquez and this writer, and on numerous interviews, personal notes, union and company memoranda, and on 'La Expresíon Libre' (Free Speech), a newsletter produced by the workers."[36] "The Tolteca Strike" began with an overview of the labor conditions at the Tolteca Foods factory in Richmond and CASA's role in promoting trade union education and the organization of immigrant workers. Many of the workers at Tolteca were long-term employees, and many of the women had shop-floor organizing experience dating back to at least 1969, when "they invited the AFL-CIO culinary Workers Union, Local No. 595 to represent them."[37] Four years later, the union had done little to help the workers, as "speed-ups, immigration raids, discretionary firings, substandard wages, and unsafe working conditions went unchallenged."[38] Workers began to look elsewhere for support. CASA members and other allies offered a more nuanced and effective strategy for organizing: "The assistance took the form of active participation in support activities, research, and political and labor education. . . . A group of twelve people, including several women and their husbands, two CASA representatives [including Mora], and one member of the October League[,] was to provide leadership throughout the strike."[39]

Through interviews, discussion, and reflection, Mora gathered insight into the everyday lives and daily struggles of these women, and the relationships between their identities as workers, wives, women, and organizers. In examining the social and labor history of undocumented women workers who were also mothers, feminists, editorialists, and public speakers, Mora emphasized leadership as being relational and collective, based on everyday experience:

> Essential factors in a successful rank and file movement will be its leadership capacity, commitment, militancy, and ability to unify and communicate with the various groups of workers. A group of women emerges as activist within the organizing process. Their consistency and individual abilities qualified them for the important roles they assumed prior to and during the strike. These women became known in their departments and shifts. They were the most informed and the quickest to react to the abuses in the factory.[40]

Emphasizing the dynamic militancy of the worker meetings, the analysis led to clear objectives that included "improvement of working conditions, a new contract, the ousting of the plant supervisor, and the formation of a workers' organization that would fight for their rights and reform the union."[41] Discussing "union business" meant engaging in issues concerning immigration law and documentation status, as well as state repression and women's rights. Reports about struggles in other countries provided the opportunity for people to learn together and from each other. These organizing meetings enabled participants to give collective meaning to their own struggles. In circulating organizing knowledge, new social relations emerged from the meetings, where "workers were encouraged to participate and take responsibility [to provide] information for other workers in their department and shifts about the discussions, meetings, and other activities."[42]

After S&P Foods took control of Tolteca in 1974, workers immediately organized, and by late spring of 1975 they had attended numerous meetings to convince their representative to take their concerns to the union leadership, and later to demand that they be allowed to participate in the process of organizing and negotiations. The union representative ignored their concerns during the first general meeting, in March 1975. The deadline for the new contract was May 13. As the date approached, workers considered petitioning to join Local No. 6 of the International Longshoremen's and Workers Union, but intraunion politics limited this option. The primary issue in the internal union struggle concerned self-determination, dignity, and respect; whether the workers themselves could define, represent, and protect their own interests; and whether undocumented workers would be a key component of a strong labor movement, union democracy, and community formation.

Community members—two of whom were CASA militants— supported the union leadership in their own internal development and in their strategy for engaging with the company. Mora's article emphasizes a number of emerging leaders "recognized as negotiators, public speakers, and organizers, particularly Esperanza [who] was the central figure."[43] Respected by her coworkers and *comadres*,[44] Esperanza was a unifying force. Having been involved in organizing labor at Tolteca since 1969, "she was impartial and refused to get involved in subjective discussions and personal judgments about the other workers. This gave credence and strength to her decisions and minimized the divisions and conflicts existing among the workers." Collective decision making and specific organizing strategies created the space and possibility to learn and practice different types of participation and leadership, which in turn framed a new context for negotiating the terms of their humanity and their engagement. For example, Olivia played a key role in the contract negotiations between the union and the company. Alicia organized the night shift, "[most] difficult of all since discipline and alertness were at a lower level" and connections between these women had to overcome the added challenges. Hortencia gave public talks at schools, union halls, and community centers, emphasizing links between the Tolteca struggle and other labor movements in the United States, and taking the struggle to other arenas in the social factory beyond the workplace. The support from community organizations, students, and their families expanded the support that the Tolteca workers relied on and cultivated. All of the strike leaders shared responsibility for speaking on the radio, giving public interviews and public presentations, and writing in the union's paper, *La Expresión Libre*. Hortencia, whose "development was an example of this process of liberation," encouraged other women to organize: "This is international women's year and what have you done? Nothing, so do not say you have. There is still time, you have many reasons to struggle, you have power and intelligence, struggle for yourself and for your compañeras."[45]

The new leaders convened meetings outside of labor and capitalist spaces, shifting the energy of the struggle from the union hall to the community center and forcing the union to respond to the needs of women in their own neighborhoods. Community-based meetings expanded the discussion of issues, providing the possibility of including issues of the neighborhood and home in the union organizing efforts: "Meetings were not restricted to union business. Issues on immigration, [police and INS] repression, international women's day, and reports of other labor struggles were also part of the agenda." The meetings also provided the opportunity to organize cultural and educational events for the larger community and the family members of striking workers: "Performances by cultural groups and films on social issues were shown at the meetings," engaging audiences in a politics of solidarity.[46] Inspired by the Zapatista uprising in Chiapas, Mexico, in 1994, Chicana mother, activist, and scholar Michelle Téllez offers a useful definition of autonomous spaces and how they offered new possibilities: "Autonomous spaces [are] those places where voices are no longer suppressed, where creative energies are shared, and the lives of those who have been silenced by race, class, and gender oppression are valued and restored. In these contexts, rules of power are renegotiated, critiques of the current system are articulated, and resistance is encouraged."[47]

On May 13, 1975, the week following May Day and almost a year after organizing began, about 150 workers decided to go on strike, despite the fact that the Contra Costa Labor Council (CCLC) did not sanction the decision. Forced to hold an emergency meeting that day, the CCLC listened to a delegation of women from the independent democratic faction in the union, "where their call for support was an emotionally stirring scene. Women showed scarred hands and faces caused by factory accidents" as the physical evidence of premature death and violence from capitalism on the bodies of human beings.[48] Their scarred bodies testified to abusive working conditions, exploitative management, physical danger, and staggering wage differentials. Shortly after the council sanctioned the strike, a phone call "informed the workers that the machinery was being removed from the factory."[49] To avoid a "runaway shop," the strikers put their bodies on the line. The first driver refused to drive through the picket line, and a second (white) driver was summoned who did drive through the picketers. As Olivia wrote in *La Expresión Libre*, "The strikers were determined not to let the truck in regardless of the number of policemen that were called in to stop us." After the first truck driver turned back, "the only male [A]nglo truck driver at Tolteca drove the truck through the line hitting several of the picketing workers."[50]

The vehicular assault by the truck driver occurred while the company obtained a temporary restraining order and the union representative "Jim C" made another agreement behind the workers' backs. This pushed the strike committee to commit to constant security, with community supporters and members of the molders' union helping to mount a round-the-clock vigil. The committee also worked to get the courts to sanction the strike and enforce an injunction preventing the company from moving the equipment. By the third day, control of the factory was complete. When the owner, William Wakefield, attempted to enter along with office workers, supervisors, and scabs, they were stopped at the picket line. "Angry and frustrated," according to Mora, "[Wakefield's] opposition was reduced to threats. Workers who previously trembled at the sight of him proudly marched in front of him." By the end of the first week, the organized workers were clearly in control, and "a higher level of political awareness was demonstrated throughout the strike. Discussions on the role of women in society, trade unionism, racism, police repression, immigration and socialism were some of the issues discussed while women were on picket duty."[51] The role of the Immigration and Naturalization Service (INS) in enforcing labor law was discussed, with some suggesting that undocumented workers should not risk arrest by picketing, but most supporting undocumented workers' fight to defend their rights and dignity.

Three weeks after the strike began, an international union representative from Mexico replaced the Anglo union representative. A new S&W Fine Foods representative replaced Wakefield, and a new contract was signed that "basically filled some gaps that should have been covered in the first contract in 1969." As Mora wrote, the improvement in the contract, though significant, was directly related to "the formation of class consciousness, and the development of leadership and organization among the Tolteca women [that] were products of their political work."[52] This political work involved organizing their peers, learning about labor law and economic history as well as public speaking and negotiating, working as a collective for each other's rights, and in the process redefining their relationship to work, each other, and their families and communities. Perhaps occupying one of the most disempowered and oppressed structural positions in a capitalist labor structure, undocumented migrant Mexican women successfully challenged a multinational corporation and the incorrigible obstinacy, sexism, and arrogance of labor unions during the 1970s, when capitalism shifted away from a Keynesian approach to planned economic development to a neoliberal form of accumulation by dispossession.[53]

Abrió sus piernas la noche
El arco ofendido cedió
y se fertilizó
la semilla guerrillera
entre el abrir y cerrar.

Night opened her legs
The wounded arc gave way
and the seed of war
quickened
between the opening and the shutting.

SIN FRONTERAS "A LO CONCRETO"

As a way to highlight how solidarity was reflected in struggles such as the Tolteca strike, this section examines specific elements in five commentaries published between 1975 and 1977. Beginning in September 1975, shortly after the CASA summer convention and the shift in the organizing campaign in Richmond to the struggle over the implementation of the contract agreement, the pages of Sin Fronteras also changed focus. The analysis was on issues facing Mexican workers, the Mexican community in the United States, international labor struggles, anticolonial wars, and cases of political prisoners. In these first issues, Mora—now relocated to Los Angeles—wrote editorials and critical articles reporting on labor strikes, international solidarity, the CIA's infiltration of the American Federation of Labor–Congress of Industrial Organizations (AFL-CIO), women's organizing, labor struggles in Mexico, farmworkers' struggles, and a number of other national and international issues.

In the first issue, Mora inaugurated an editorial column, "a lo concreto."[54] The goal was to discuss "questions on the economies of the United States and Mexico . . . to clarify the basis of these economies, how they function and what are the results with the purpose of leading us to understand them and to understand the position of Mexican workers and all workers within these economies. This is necessary for workers to determine the role they will play in the transformation of this basic aspect of society."[55] In subsequent editorials, Mora explained how taxation is a form of class struggle, linking the regressive taxing of the working class to corporate tax breaks, particularly for corporations profiting from war industries on the one hand and the defunding of social programs that directly affected working-class communities on the other. Mora outlined how unemployment and rising profits were a direct result of the antiworker policies of the Gerald Ford administration that, in turn, led to the falling of real wages and spending power of the working class. Mora used everyday examples, many perhaps from her own life, to make these processes accessible in English and Spanish to working Mexican men and women. In each editorial, Mora not only provided examples and analysis but also made calls to action. From organizing unions and demanding policy changes, specifically the redistribution of the social wage, to organizing against national anti-immigrant policy, Mora used this platform to educate and agitate a "cooperative subject."

In the 1976 editorial "Eastland Bill Reestablished Bracero Program," Mora discussed the relationship between immigration law, history, and capitalist exploitation, particularly the Eastland and Rodino bills in California (these would lead in 1986 to the Simpson-Rodino federal bill, otherwise known as the Immigration Reform and Control Act [IRCA]) and their relation to the binational labor agreement known as the Bracero Program. CASA continued the organizing work against anti-migrant legislation that Hermandad had begun in the early 1970s, specifically against the 1971 Dixon-Arnett bill in California. Mora argued that these bills promised to make immigration agents of all employers. In addition, they would eliminate the provisions requiring employers to prove there was a need for migrant labor as a backdoor way to create the conditions for a reinstitution of the infamous Bracero Program.[56]

As Mora emphasized, the arguments behind these bills were no different than the reasons given for the Bracero Program. As "virtual rented slaves," Mora wrote, "Mexican worker[s] cannot permit the reestablishment of the Bracero Program, a system of institutionalized slavery." Mora noted an important effect the Bracero Program had on the possibility for organizing workers across borders, even if they shared similar cultural or national histories: "The consequences of this program have been very regressive for the economic progress and unity of the Mexican people. It has fomented the division and mistrust between the Mexicans born in Mexico and those in the U.S." Mora's analysis is insightful (if not incite-ful), as it located and identified how a state of quasi-legal existence (braceros had no rights to organize) created the inevitable conditions for exploitation that constituted the primary labor practice of racial capitalism. Mora concluded, "The only solution to these problems that daily affect our lives is the cooperation and struggle for vindication of the working class, *the struggle for the rights of the Mexican people*" (emphasis added).[57]

Mora analyzed Mexican labor and transnational capital in a December 1976 article, "Conditions Prepared for a New Bracero Program," which linked a critique of domestic social policies to foreign trade policy: "The defeat of Proposition 14, the Bakke decision and the Eilberg law are events whose effects will be the definite setback of the political, economic and social development of the Mexican people." Proposition 14 was a statewide initiative put forth by the United Farm Workers to protect California's landmark 1975 farm labor law from agribusiness; the *University of California Board of Regents v. Bakke* (affirmative action) decision challenged the use of race as a variable in affirmative action programs; and the Eilberg law, signed by President Jimmy Carter in 1977 (just one of many proposals that would be woven together as Plan Carter), had provisions that would divide families, set limits on migration specifically from Mexico, and undermine workers' power.[58] In her June 1977 editorial "Carter's Grand Deception," Mora argued, "Carter's present policy represents the strategy of the bourgeoisie, to combat the economic crisis and the growing social conflicts which endanger the existence of the capitalist system." For Mora and CASA, the domestic policies toward workers, Mexicans, and undocumented people conditioned the possibility of a new bracero program. After explaining the close collaboration among agribusiness, bankers, oil companies, and the California Farm Bureau against Proposition 14, she linked these political forces to the push for a contract-labor system for migrant agricultural workers. Here, Mora highlighted the ideological relationship between challenges to affirmative action in the United States, the possible organizing power of undocumented labor, and the crisis of capitalism. Mora concluded by invoking the necessity for wideranging progressive alliances, solidarity, and cooperative projects: "In the face of this situation, our people's only solution is ceaseless effort to organize amongst all sectors of our people. We must build student and trade union organizations, democratic and civil rights organizations, organizations for economic survival that will produce amongst our people a spirit of struggle and the understanding of the need for broad unity in action confronting these attacks will still greater determines [sic] and the will to defeat them."[59]

In these three editorials, Mora not only addressed her analysis to the Mexican community (as for CASA, Chicanas/os did not exist) but also invoked a "cooperative subject," a class struggle that emerged from the linking of knowledge about exploitation and survival to self-activity and collective organizing as political tactics, using solidarity of shared conditions and shared cultures to create new possibilities. The intersections of social movements and cross-border solidarity as well as an insurgent feminism inspired Mora's politics: "The alternative must definitely be the development of a strategy which will promote and mobilize working class interests and the interests of victims of the current crisis. Total opposition and resistance is necessary. Consumer groups which will organize and fight against shortages, organization against cutbacks in social services, struggles against labor bureaucrats and struggle within the unions to oppose militarism, struggles to create socially beneficial jobs, must all be intensified. These mass movements are part of the solution."[60] Not only did Mora inform readers, but by emphasizing certain elements and processes and asking questions of the capitalist state from a worker's perspective within an international context, she provided a historical analysis of the relationship between labor law, capitalist reproduction, and militarism, connections that were targets for organizing and points of possible solidarity.

While supporters of Olga Talamante were pressuring the State Department and the US Embassy in Buenos Aires through a grassroots campaign organized by her parents, and supporters of Ramón Chacón continued to pressure the Mexican government for his release, both framing their campaigns in the context of the US support for conservative governments as an issue of human rights, CASA and other organizations across the United States challenged President Ford, then Carter, on a number of issues, particularly those relating to US-Mexican relations in areas such as economic development, migration, border issues, water rights, and human rights. Mora clearly stated CASA's position: "The undocumented worker is an integral part of the working class and cannot be separated from the class struggle. The strengthening of the working class takes place in the struggles against the capitalist in collective and individual acts of resistance in the factories, unions and courts."[61] Mora demanded that the mainstream labor movement, particularly the AFL-CIO, open and expand its definition of workers to include migrant undocumented labor, and to see its own interests tied in with the strength of the organized power of undocumented workers.

In 1977, the National Labor Relations Board challenged the efficacy of Section 2805 of the California Labor Code, which allowed the INS, with the consent of the AFL-CIO, to raid workplaces. Recognizing the pro-undocumented stance of California locals from the Teamsters, United Steelworkers, and United Furniture Workers unions in support of rescinding the California code, Mora explained, "It is important to emphasize that the movements which succeeded in bringing about the NLRB decision is important in the development of a united and independent workers movement since it is a victory against the racist, anti-immigrant policies of the AFL-CIO."[62] Undocumented workers were not only central to the power of working-class organizing but also the catalyst for a global movement. Mora located the "vital role" of the Mexican worker "in the development of this country's economic empire, particularly in the agricultural and mining industries" as a context for emphasizing that "historically, the Mexican and agricultural worker has developed methods of struggle which has provided him with a political vision and the organizational direction needed to combat exploitation and oppression."[63]

Mora's position concerning the centrality of US imperialism—and corporate/state collusion—in any analysis of capitalism was determined and clear. In an editorial titled "Latin American Workers Confront AFL-CIO Intervention," Mora sets her target: "In Latin America the class struggle against Yankee imperialism must have as a base the alliance and solidarity of the proletariat of the continent guided by an international consciousness. That is the only guarantee for a profound and effective anti-imperialist strategy."[64] Explaining the role of large transnational corporations in maintaining US economic hegemony abroad while destroying social movements within the United States, she cites examples like International Telegraph and Telephone in Chile, Del Monte and United Fruit in Central America, and General Motors and Anaconda (mining) as part of the Rockefeller empire, linking their political connections with government officials, particularly the founding of the American Institute for Free Labor Development (AIFLD) in 1962 with support from the CIA. As Mora explained, "The main purpose of the AIFLD is to put a stop to the working class organizations and unions of the Latin American proletariat, conduct the ideological fight against the Cuban Revolution, rechannel the strength of the workers' movement toward a procapitalist stand and divide the movement with anti-imperialist tendencies." Mora then brings the international analysis home to the local level, reporting on how the Council for Latin American Advancement (CLAA) attempted to destroy the organizing efforts of Juan Chacón in the steel industry. Mora cites the work of ex–CIA agent Philip Agee's book *Inside the Company*, where he exposed Jack Otero, former president of the CLAA, as a CIA agent, pointing out, "In the opinion of various Mexican trade unionists, the CLAA does not serve the interest of the Mexican Worker, and is simply a nest of CIA agents even though it might include honest elements."[65]

In each of these examples, Mora connected the working-class movement in the United States to anti-imperialist struggles in Latin America, emphasizing the local possibilities of organizing work and the importance of political solidarity: "The working class of the U.S., an imperialist country, has the immediate task of confronting the monopolies and the militaristic and aggressive policies of the yankee state on a massive level. Only a limited, militant and organized workers movement can carry out such an important task. . . . It is only through a rank-and-file movoement [sic] that a true revolutionary working class movement will develop with the class consciousness and capacity to fight for political power with the dominant class."[66] Naming how organized state violence within the United States was linked to state repression outside its borders exposed the intellectual, political, and economic connections between these institutions, the links that, for the Chicana/o or Mexicana/o Left, undergird imperialism and racial capitalism in the United States.

Giró el humo rojo
en la médula del viento
formando punto a punto
el fénix dialéctico.

Red smoke whirled
in the medula of the wind
forming, point by point,
the dialectic phoenix.

Women have always "organized against the almost routine violence that shapes their lives," writes Kimberlé Crenshaw.[67] Referring to the black radical tradition, H. L. T. Quan explains that women within the movement "are the plotters of history. They are women of substance, of imagination, a formidable social force, women who would kill and wage revolutions against the state and the world economy."[68] At the same time, as Blackwell clarifies concerning the masculine influence of the Chicano movement, "the political speech of the movement was gendered, as was the vernacular movimiento culture, meetings, and rallies. The culture of political meetings was largely the culture of the 'vatos,' or street warriors, reflecting the way the youth movement idealized the street warrior as a form of resistance, though it was also, incidentally, a subaltern form of masculinity."[69] The masculinist elements of political leadership and the gendered division of labor characterized the organization Mora joined: "CASA was absolutely male dominated, very macho in the attitude of the leadership."[70] This was particularly true, according to Laura Pulido, concerning discussions of political theory and the direct link to perceived or socialized characteristics of leadership, which became moments "for the performance of masculinity and male competition."[71] This gendered characterization of charismatic leadership and division of labor is one way to understand the dynamics and context of Pulido's explanation for Mora's ability to navigate this terrain and challenge men on their theoretical assumptions. "Because they were more comfortable and therefore more proficient in theoretical debate, which was highly valued by CASA," writes Pulido, "men were more likely to emerge as leaders. In fact, few women were acknowledged as leaders. Virtually all interviewees recognized Mora as brilliant and as one of the few women able to compete with men theoretically. Because she could stand her own ground in political debates, she was accorded a degree of respect not given to other women, although she still suffered from the 'emotional abuse' that other women experienced in their personal relationships."[72] The role of women was never simple, and always contested: "[Women] clearly occupied a subordinated role—though one punctuated by moments of strong female leadership."[73] Exerting pressure to change cultures of organizing, "the personal, professional and political trajectories of CASA members reveal that they were conscious of women's issues and struggles."[74]

These multiple insurgencies gave meaning to larger movement strategies, as Marisela Chávez explains: "CASA figures into an analysis of the development of Chicana feminisms by defying the dichotomy of two opposing groups of women, the 'feministas' and the 'loyalists.' . . . The women in CASA provide a concrete example of how women active in the Chicano movement engendered multiple and competing visions of feminisms depending on their individual experiences, even though they did not fit the definition of feministas."[75] As we recognize how leadership is influenced by assumptions, performances, and power relationships, the lives and political militancy of Mora (and Rodríguez, Márquez, Durazo, and Ramírez), as well as the Tolteca leaders Esperanza, Alicia, Hortencia, and Olivia, provide new grammars of gendered resistance. Insurgent feminists insisted that organizing be collective and centered on a critique of capitalism, while also challenging structural and personal oppressions both shared and generative. It should provide an alternative historical construction and another way to understand political solidarity: "Multiple and competing notions about Chicanas and Feminists existed precisely because Chicanas active in the movement were not a homegrown lot."[76]

The Chicana/o Left and the politics of solidarity are conditioned by time and geography, gender and nationalism. In this chapter I have moved toward honoring the ways of knowing, learning, and sharing that are the catalytic experiences which define struggle and survival. It is an attempt to engage in a dialogue with history and historical actors about solidarity and insurgent feminism. The collective emphasis is on the lived experiences of creative survival, what people brought with them (1) when forced to move against their will to a new, foreign, hostile place; (2) when forced (often by law enforcement as well as economic conditions) to work in unsafe and exploitative labor settings or endure the violence of state health care workers; and (3) when they confronted the ways that structures of domination and control—across lines of gender, sexuality, nation, race, and class—play out in social relations. But being forced does not equal consent, consensus, or acquiescence. How people survived together; how that togetherness was forged in struggle with what people brought with them in their hearts and minds and memories; and how those struggles were passed on to create the possibility for radical traditions—these form a past that remains relevant in the present. Insurgent feminists demonstrate the ways that people complicate and mitigate the impact of structures of domination.

In 1980, Magdalena Mora and Alelaida R. Del Castillo coedited the anthology *Mexican Women in the United States: Struggles Past and Present*, cowriting the introduction, "Sex, Nationality and Class: La Obrera Mexicana." It remains a classic anthology documenting the social, political, and economic struggles and experiences of women, one of a number of "other early collections of feminist histories."[77] Recovering the stories that Mora narrated—not only stories of her own life, but also those of others who inspired her—perhaps helps us to think about the relationships among experience, memory, knowledge production, community resistance, and transformation. Mora evoked solidarity in her analysis and actions, while solidarity inspired her political imaginary. She wrote about women and men she organized with, knew well, and struggled next to. She was a vital force in both the Bay Area and Los Angeles. As historian Devra Weber said, "Magdalena was a fighter. She saw and understood the potential in people. This motivated her political work and her struggle for a society in which that potential could be realized."[78]

Y yo por primera vez
dejé que mi palabra
apuntara hacia esenciales.

And for the first time
I allowed my word
to turn to essentials.

As Michelle Téllez explains, "bridging the world of the academy and community demands that we *crear puentes*, create bridges—of struggle—that are made of feelings, pasts (not only histories) and transformation."[79] Today, Mora would be considered a revolutionary activist, scholar, theorist, creative writer, poet, organizer, and cultural worker, creating bridges and revealing how the differences among the working class are a political illusion. Engaging the contradictions between the university and community, unions and undocumented workers, Chicanas/Chicanos and Mexicanas/Mexicanos, different trajectories of the Chicana/Chicano movement, and the internationalist Third World Left, Mora invoked solidarity in all its myriad forms.[80] Perhaps what is most significant is how she navigated these intersecting political traditions and organizations, enacting a political imagination of the both/ and perspective rather than either/or, or as Téllez proposes, invoking Chela Sandoval, "the co-existence of seemingly contradictory ideas."[81] As Ruíz writes, for Mora, her community was a place "she never left."[82]

On Saturday, June 13, 1981, her friends and comrades gathered in Los Angeles to honor and celebrate Mora's life. "Raiz Fuerte que no se Arranca: The Life of a Luchador," read the program title that announced a celebration of her life as a "socialist, worker, feminist." Carlos Vázquez, director of *El Foro del Pueblo*, provided the opening and closing words; Nora Sierra, editor of *Mazorca*, offered a biographical sketch, followed by Rob Brown singing "Somos" and a presentation of the film *The Chicano: A Working People*, directed by Richard Soto. The participants represented a broad base of the radical Left in Los Angeles that created a politics of solidarity with Mexico, Cuba, Latin America, Asia, and Africa, as well as other Third World peoples in the United States. The very organization of the program reflected the deep cultural roots of ritual and *testimonio* as central to remembering and honoring the life of our friends and comrades in struggle. *Testimonios* came from Rosa Moreno from the Brigada Antonio Maceo, a group of young Cuban-Americans that organized trips to Cuba to learn firsthand about the revolution; José Jácques y Medina, a 1968 political activist in Mexico targeted by US authorities for deportation, represented the IBGW; UCLA Chicano historian Juan Gómez-Quiñones; Chole Alatorre from La Hermandad Mexicana; and Cal State Northridge Chicano Studies professor Rodolfo Acuña. Chuy Pérez then remembered Mora through music, leading a chorus of "Hasta la Patagonia." Lucha Corpi read her "Poemas para Magdalena." Bert Corona (also representing La Hermandad Mexicana) and Carlos Vásquez concluded the evening.

In music, documentary footage, poetry, and testimonies from "Maggie's" friends and comrades, Mora's life was remembered through the contributions from the people who inspired and inflamed her politics, accompanied her personal journey, and influenced her theories about change and struggle. Corpi, honoring the life, influence, and inspiration of Mora, wrote her friend the poem "Puente de cristal" that has accompanied us in this essay.[83] In a reminiscence thirty years after

Mora's death, Corpi, like Mahmoud Darwish,[84] reminds historians that the poets write pasts still present:

Although I was about five years older than her, we were the best of friends . . . she was an outstanding scholar and indefatigable activist. There was also a sweetness in her and a great desire to enjoy life in the smallest of ways, the ordinary ways we usually take for granted— though she didn't think much of cleaning the stove or cooking for that matter. But she loved music and dancing and having a glass of wine while she had dinner with us and we talked about her work and mine. I went to see her in San José a week before she made her last journey with her family to her hometown. And already having lost most of her eyesight and being in terrible pain, she was, however, still working to support the Tolteca workers' strike in San José. I still miss her terribly.

CONCLUSION

Magdalena Mora—like Olga Talamante and the editorial collective of *El Grito del Norte*—applied an analysis of state violence, capitalism, and US imperialism to advance arguments for political activity grounded in a politics of international solidarity. Through their writings and actions, Mora and her counterparts "showed that state violence directed at peoples of color [and particularly peoples of Latin America] not only defines U.S. democracy but also provides an insidious blueprint for U.S. imperial designs."[85] Magdalena Mora and the female cadre of CASA were part of a longer tradition of revolutionary women of Mexican descent in the United States who were firmly grounded in an internationalist trajectory of Mexicana/Chicana feminism: "Drawing from the Mexican roots of Chicana feminism, as suggested by Ruiz and Pérez, Chicana feminism has historically had not just a border consciousness (Anzaldúa) but a cross-border consciousness that reflects Chicana feminist commitment to international solidarity."[86] Combining labor organizing, women's leadership and vision, activist research, and an internationalist perspective, the Tolteca strike marks a significant moment in Mexican, Chicana, and US labor history. At a time when the labor movement was struggling to survive the recomposition of capital,[87] the largely female and undocumented labor force successfully organized a strike at a transnational company that shifted the relations of power by enlisting the social factory in the struggle against an oppressive factory system.

By connecting US domestic and foreign policy to poverty and violence across the continent, insurgent feminists found similarities in political movements with internationalist tendencies by emphasizing the political practices of people in struggle. Simultaneously, in the political imaginaries of the Tolteca leaders, Mora, and CASA members, we get a clear picture of feminism-in-nationalism: "Ultimately, after an early period of Chicana feminisms, many activists abandoned nationalist claims and nationalist imaginaries to create alternative ways of belonging *between and beyond nationalist frames*. They imagined a way out of nationalism that crossed national and racial/ethnic divides, and their critique signaled the coming of a post-nationalist critique that resonated with many other feminist and queer activists." As Blackwell reminds us, "Early Chicana feminism was characterized by an explicit challenge to gender hierarchy, sexual coercion, and violence. . . . While they shared these views with other feminists, their approach and agenda differed in that they did not view gender as the primary source of oppression, a practice reserved for those privileged enough to see race as invisible or naturalized by their dominant social position."[88] Between and beyond nationalist frames that inherited and cultivated a trajectory of international solidarity, there were evolving, overlapping, and sometimes contradictory perspectives. At the same time, "while early Chicana feminism did not always develop an antidiscrimination stance toward non-normative sexualities and genders or link homophobia and sexism in its critique of patriarchy, it, like other early women of color feminisms, laid the foundation for other 'intersectional' paradigms of gay, lesbian, bisexual, transgender, and queer to emerge."[89]

Insurgent feminism, community-based militancy, international solidarity, and labor organizing played central roles in the longer story of the *movimiento* and must be understood as contested places within the Chicana/o Left. These stories expand how we understand political struggle and the continuation of these struggles, from the antisterilization organizing among Third World women in California to the continued focus on community health and human rights by Chicana feminists, radical Chicana/o Queers, and Chicana/o leftists, who advance a political imaginary that continues to connect the local and the global, while understanding that capitalism and patriarchy are localized not only in communities but on the body.[90]

SOLIDARITY/BEYOND SOLIDARITY

Revolutionary dreams erupt out of political engagement; collective social movements are incubators of new knowledge.
ROBIN D. G. KELLEY, *FREEDOM DREAMS*

IN THE PRECEDING PAGES we have learned about oppositional theater, revolutionary gunrunners, insurgent feminists, peasant guerrillas, radical undocumented workers, and the organizations and individuals that imagined revolution and a politics of solidarity in Greater Mexico. What emerges is a unique understanding of nationalism and internationalism at the intersection of US, Mexican, and Latin American Cold War politics. By finding common cause in shared political struggles, those who worked to build international solidarity were able to connect movements and people across borders. Their stories demonstrate the political astuteness of activists who understood that their local or regional grassroots anticapitalist struggles for civil, human, and economic rights were part of larger organized struggles across the globe. By engaging in and connecting with these larger struggles, political movements in Mexico and Latin America further internationalized the trajectory and imaginary of the Chicana/o movement, particularly the Chicana/o Left. Contemporary solidarity politics like Chicana/o support for the Zapatista movement in Chiapas, Mexico, or for the Bolivarian revolution in Venezuela, for example, demonstrate the longer historical evolution and political and cultural genealogy of these internationalist anti-imperialist struggles, as well as the impulse to go beyond solidarity and create "dignified alternatives."[1]

Connecting the Chicana/o Left to the larger Chicana/o movement, and to the Mexican and Latin American Left, through a politics of solidarity and people's theater, these histories "[afford] us the opportunity to think beyond the familiar binaries that structure most understandings of the sixties and seventies—cultural nationalism versus civil rights; race versus class; domestic versus international; political activism versus cultural representation."[2] Chicana/o identity was not homogenous, and the Chicana/o Left and the cultural politics of imagining and experimenting with hybrid forms, collective creativity, and political context fostered a changing sense of Chicanisma/o. In creating organizations, political cadres, cultural movements, aesthetic innovations, and a diverse and varied politics of solidarity, the Chicana/o Left also replicated patriarchal and heteronormative organizing cultures. At the same time, the critique of racial capitalism, US imperialism (primarily but not exclusively in Latin America), and state violence in US domestic and foreign policy distinguished Chicano/a or Mexicana/o leftists from the Chicana/o movement, even as they shared a critique of US racism and police brutality.[3] This is one of the major legacies of Chicana/o leftists for Latin American politics—their idea of a radical critique of state violence as central to racial capitalism.

The Chicano/a movement influenced the Mexican Left by helping to reorient its gaze northward, complicating the simplistic and pragmatic understanding of the political importance of Mexicans living in the United States while offering a different analysis of imperialism that included Chicana/o solidarity. The "Carta de Lecumberri" (chapter 2), the MEChA chapter at the UNAM, and the thematic influence—not simply of migration, but of anti-imperialism within the "belly of the beast"—on artistic production and political imaginaries were a result of direct engagement with different elements of the Chicano/a movement through the 1970s.[4] "Our consciousness, our language, our resistance to injustice, our art, theater, and music of the Chicano Movement," writes Chicana historian Antonia Castañeda, "were shaped by the duality of being of the histories and cultures of both the United States and of the Americas writ large."[5]

The state terror of the FBI's COINTELPRO operations devastated political movements in the United States, including the Chicana/o movement. The expansion of the criminal justice regimes, combined with the militarization of the police, both funded by the Law Enforcement Administration Assistance (LEAA), led to the incarceration of huge numbers of poor people and people of color beginning in the late 1970s.[6] Economic attrition disguised in discourses of smaller government and self-help gained ideological traction during these years. The abandonment of the social welfare state and the social wage happened just at the moment when historically marginalized communities had finally, after decades of struggles, gained (limited) civil, social, and economic rights.[7] A nascent color-blind racism characterized the transition from "the conservative 1960s" to the even more repressive neoliberal 1970s and 1980s.[8] In the context of the deep structural crisis of racial capitalism, struggles for economic, social, and political rights intensified in the 1970s, as did the concentration of revolutionary-oriented movements across the Américas, including Chicana/o América, as people connected to various domestic and foreign policies in their political analysis and activity.[9] They also intentionally created alternate ways of engaging across political and cultural borders. If the Cold War "Yankee Nightmare" was solidarity among peoples across the Americas, then the nightmare was within US borders as well as beyond them.

The political imaginary of the Chicano movement produced a variety of imaginaries for Mexico. More specifically, the internationalist experience of the Chicana/o Left produced an imagined Mexico through their understanding of political connections and anti-imperialist analysis that led them to make connections across borders. For many Chicanas and Chicanos, traveling to Mexico as part of a political or cultural gathering was their first direct experience of the birthplace of their parents — or perhaps of their own birthplace before migrating to the United States. This coming-home narrative was complicated, but it was powerful in influencing the ideas that some Chicanos/as had about Mexico, Latin America, and themselves. How Chicanas/os imagined Mexico and acted on those imaginaries, holding close the idea that imagination can come from experience, is influenced by time and circumstance. This imaginary is also influenced by a relationship to Mexico, whether through family, literature, history, or even silences and absences. Depending on their experiences, family structure, or place of residence and birth, the relationship to Mexico was different. So while some Chicanas/os had personal narratives that related to Mexico as their birthplace or that of their parents or grandparents, different experiences influenced expectations and responses. The Chicana/o movement looked to Mexico (and Latin America) as a cultural wellspring and homeland, and while the Chicana/o Left shared these traits, it looked instead to socialist, revolutionary, and radical political and cultural movements. Sheila Contreras reminds us that Mexico existed in the minds of Chicanas/os before they actually stepped foot in Mexico, and that their imagination of going home, an exceptionalist narrative, could be framed only from somewhere outside of Mexico: "The tie to Mexico is filial — one of kinship, blood ties, and a shared history of conquest and oppression. The *idea of Mexico* exudes comfort; if *feels* like home. When you are on *this* side that is." In other words, "nostalgia for the homeland of Mexico [occurred] only within the borders of the United States."[10] Solidarity cannot be based on nostalgia. Though solidarity can transform political meanings and people, it was about building militant convivial cultures that were catalyzed by passion, emotion, creativity, and revolt. These cross-border political engagements influenced "Chicana/o solidarity efforts with the leftist and indigenous peoples of Latin America, and their activism in defense of undocumented immigrants, contribut[ing] to Chicana/o activists' self-perception as a trans-national community and people."[11]

There were Chicana/o leftists in all parts of the country where there was Chicana/o movement activity. People of Mexican descent dissented against the economic, political, and social status quo, embracing Marxist politics and extending solidarity across borders. While not everyone agreed or even got along politically or personally, and while organizations too did not always agree, they did come together around issues of anticapitalism and leftist-inspired political imaginaries—even as their responses, solutions, ideas, and "freedom dreams" were not the same.[12] In the imaginary of revolution we can see a nascent antiglobalization critique. The early 1970s were a pivotal time in the acceleration of social, political, and economic crisis resulting from social movements that centered international solidarity of the previous decades. The Chicana/o Left in the 1970s added to this acceleration.

The influence of leftist ideas within the Chicana/o movement did not end with the 1970s or as a consequence of a politics of war and attrition in the domestic and foreign policies of the Republican Party during the 1980s. Washington war hawks, in an attempt to recover from defeats in Southeast Asia, looked to Latin America and the Middle East as the newest fronts of the anticommunist, procapitalist struggles. Through the 1970s and 1980s, Chicanas/os-Latinas/os organized support and worked in solidarity for movements in Chile, Argentina, Central America, Palestine, and South Africa.[13]

People, organizations, ideas, and political struggles provide a bridge of continuity between the Chicana/o Left of the 1970s and the 1990s/2000s, and along that bridge—often on the backs of women of color—traveled the challenges and contradictions of the political movements of the time.[14] There are important direct connections between the Chicana/o leftist politics and imaginaries of the 1970s and the

Chicana/o support for the Ejercito Zapatista de Liberación Nacional (EZLN) over the last twenty years. The politics of going beyond solidarity emerges in the context of the Chicana/o-Zapatista solidarity community in Greater Mexico.

On January 1, 1994, the day that the North American Free Trade Agreement (NAFTA) officially went into effect, the EZLN launched an armed uprising against the Mexican state. The largely indigenous movement occupied municipal administrations in a number of towns in the southeastern Mexican state of Chiapas, declaring war on the government of Carlos Salinas de Gortari and the neoliberal economic policies implemented since 1982. Twelve days later, after multiple casualties and deaths on both sides, and in response to hundreds of thousands of mobilized citizens in Mexico and internationally, a cease-fire was declared. The EZLN withdrew from the towns, and the Mexican government agreed to negotiations.

The Zapatista base communities in Chiapas exist in the midst of the everyday pressures and violence of a low-intensity war waged by the Mexican state. Military troops, paramilitary groups, and federal, state, and local policing authorities occupy the state of Chiapas. Violations of basic human and environmental rights, racial and gender discrimination, constitutional changes to land rights, and acute economic disparities were central reasons for the uprising of 1994 and are a shared characteristic of grassroots mobilizations across the globe—from Chiapas to Seattle to Indonesia and Africa. Yet the Zapatista communities are not simply mobilized against the neoliberal Mexican state; they are redefining their relationship to the state as well as the balance between politics, culture, and rights, between economic policies and environmental concerns, and, most notably, between meanings of citizenship and indigenous identity. The appearance of the Zapatistas and their demands for democracy, liberty, respect, land, dignity, and autonomy resonated throughout Mexico and the world. Not wanting power for themselves, the Zapatistas struggle to exist as indigenous and as Mexican, to create political spaces where new ideas can be discussed, agreed upon, and enacted. As Subcomandante Marcos explains:

> We believe that revolutionary change in Mexico will not be the product of *only* one type of action. That is, it will not be, in a strict sense, an armed revolution or a peaceful revolution. It will be, primarily, a revolution resulting from struggle on various social fronts, with many methods, under different social forms, with varying degrees of commit-

ment and participation. And its result will not be that of a triumphant party, organization or alliance of organizations with its specific social proposal, but rather a chance for a democratic space for resolving the confrontation among diverse political proposals. This democratic space for resolution will have three fundamental premises that are now historically inseparable: democracy, in order to decide upon the dominant social proposal; the liberty to subscribe to one or another proposal; and justice, to which all proposals should conform (January 20, 1994).[15]

The Zapatista struggle and their creative political strategies have invigorated a global movement "against Neoliberalism and for Humanity," providing examples of a politically sophisticated movement that is inspirational rather than dogmatic, intuitive instead of programmatic, and that asks questions more often than it imposes solutions.[16] The Zapatistas have placed political autonomy and dignity "at the center of [their] oppositional thought" and called for a revolutionary politics of listening "that mean[s] learning to talk as well, not just explaining things in a different way but thinking them in a different way."[17]

The EZLN has identified two time periods central to the emergence of their political ideas. In 1982, five urban-based and intellectually trained revolutionaries, a cadre of the Fuerzas de Liberación Nacional (FLN) in existence since 1969, took to the isolated mountains of Chiapas to learn to live in the jungle and connect with indigenous populations.[18] The FLN cadre hoped to foment and support a revolutionary leftist-inspired uprising. The cadre soon learned how unprepared they were to survive in the jungle without support. They also realized that the indigenous Maya of the region had been in struggle for five hundred years and already had their own ways of knowing and resisting. Soon there were only three people left. In 1983, a small cadre of three indigenous and three mestizo activists founded the EZLN. These initial encounters of shared ideas of struggle and freedom between those with different political analyses and positions would lead, over the next nineteen years, to the next significant event before the public uprising on January 1, 1994.

The second important moment in the Zapatista revolution came in 1993, when the Women's Revolutionary Laws were passed after much discussion and disagreement in all Zapatista communities.[19] As references for revolutionary movements, the laws have been defended and enacted vigorously by the EZLN in its struggles to renegotiate gender roles within Zapatista communities. These demands for dignity, the right to control one's body, to participate in political activities and community governance, to health, nutrition, and education, to freedom from violence and the right to be in the revolutionary army—these inspired political movements and women across the globe.[20] Chicanas/os in Zapatista-inspired organizations used these laws as a basis for renegotiating gender roles within leftist organizing circles. Furthermore, like the insurgent feminists discussed elsewhere in this book, the Women's Revolutionary Laws reoriented political culture within Zapatista solidarity movements in Chicana/o communities. Some of the Chicana/o political formations that developed critiques on the limitations of solidarity, and ideas on how to go beyond it to where *everything* is possible, were inspired by how these two movements challenged assumptions of leadership and revolution, reinvigorated struggles for autonomy, and asserted the importance of women's rights and participation.[21]

Over the past twenty years, the Zapatistas have inspired leftists and antiauthoritarian politics across the globe through innovative and revolutionary political projects like Intergalactic Encuentros (gatherings that convened people from across the globe), democratic political fronts, and La Otra Campaña in 2006, as well as collective educational, health, and economic projects within autonomous Zapatista territory. In addition, communiqués from the EZLN have specifically reached out to the Chicana/o-Mexicana/o communities. When La Otra Campaña convened groups in Tijuana, Mexico, in 2006, the gathering included participants from the Mexican descent community: "No one will speak for them, no one will speak for the *Mexicanos* or *Mexicanas* or the Chicanos on the other side; instead, they will construct their own space, defend it, speak for themselves, explain the reasons why they are there, the difficulties that they face, and what they have been able to construct as rebelliousness and resistance on that other side."[22] For folks who are inspired by the ideas and politics of Zapatismo, "the Zapatistas have been celebrated as armed communities able to open vital and vibrant political spaces for a collective interrogation of out-dated political practice and renewed efforts towards social justice."[23] In this sense Zapatismo can be understood as a "political and cultural practice" that simultaneously asks questions about going beyond solidarity.[24]

Consider that going beyond solidarity "does not mean abandoning the responsibilities and challenges of sincere solidarity work."[25] It might mean recognizing how "solidarity effort[s] can easily reproduce paternalism and hierarchy within the organization and between the organization and the constituency being served," what Subcomandante

Marcos called the "Cinderella Syndrome."[26] Going beyond solidarity means building a politics of *encuentro*, local assemblies, local knowledge, creative intergenerational projects, and local forms of justice (restorative/community) that are as much an experiment as they are a project, a work in progress. Going beyond solidarity, urban Zapatismo as one example, means understanding that a politics of solidarity is essentially a political "challenge" to "struggle for a world of dignity, to localize struggles and community based power, centering community health and surviving the violence of the state, of capitalism, of patriarchal heteronormativity."[27] It is about not only being against capitalism or political marginalization, but also determining the terms of engagement with the state (even as that means disengagement) and creating the conditions that make possible something else perhaps best characterized by the idea of "One No, Many Yeses."[28] Yet "rather than emphasize networks as our only organizing objective, we might also imagine solidarity with the Zapatistas as an imagined community, a collective effort to define obligations that are rooted in locally placed culture generating knowledge about what works across generations," instead of only a politics of engagement with people in struggle somewhere else.[29]

There are numerous examples of Chicana/o political and cultural work inspired by the EZLN, many of which have explicitly pushed for a politics going beyond solidarity. For example, Estacíon Libre, a group of people of color from across the United States inspired by the EZLN, and the group El Kilombo Intergalactico in Durham, North Carolina, have reimagined solidarity as a political tool that is the "practice of democracy" emphasizing encounter, assembly, creativity, and rebellion. Estación Libre (EL) led delegations to Zapatista communities in the late 1990s and early 2000s. Organizing out of the "Orange House" in the colonial city of San Cristóbal de las Casas, the group was critical of the "Zapatourismo" that Subcomandante Marcos would refer to as the "Cinderella Syndrome." EL facilitated *encuentros* between people from progressive and leftist organizations and the EZLN communities, as well as among these same US-based activists.[30] El Kilombo emerged in the context of EL delegations and local conditions in Durham, coming together "after the historic antiwar movement which preceded the US invasion of Iraq, and in the midst of a floundering and disoriented US Left and a disenfranchised population. As students, migrants, and other members of the community we realized that we shared common problems . . . as well as common enemies. . . . We started by opening a social center, a space for encounter, where people could come together, not only to find things and services they need, but to meet each other and to talk about creating things they desired."[31] The ARMA Collective in Los Angeles continues the work of EL, taking delegations of organizers and artists to Chiapas, and "is part of the urban Zapatismo work that began shortly after the uprising. We attempt to walk together not only with the Zapatistas, but with other groups who align themselves with the notion of dignity and community healing. Our goal is to engage in a transformative process of decolonization through the principles of Zapatismo. We create a variety of workshops, curricula, delegations and gatherings that help us find alternatives to the status quo."[32]

Political activists and artists from the Los Angeles area immediately engaged the Zapatista movement after that first day of January 1994. In 1997, as a result of three years of artists and activists traveling to and living in Zapatista communities, the Encuentro Chicano-Zapatista sobre La Cultura, Arte y la Autonomía emerged as a way to deepen these connections.[33] Invoking the political and cultural imaginary of the 1974 Quinto Festival/Primer Encuentro, Chicanas/os and Latinas/ os in the Los Angeles area created autonomous cultural projects in Los Angeles, San Jose, Oakland, San Francisco, San Diego, and other parts of California. These projects included but were not limited to the Eastside Café Echospace in El Sereno, the South Central Farm in Vernon, Mujeres de Maiz in Highland Park, and La Casa del Pueblo in Echo Park. When scholar-activist Pablo Gonzalez, who was involved in Estacíon Libre and a participant in many of these movement spaces, reflected on what he calls "Chicana/o urban Zapatismo" in Los Angeles, he noted, "Autonomy in Los Angeles is a difficult project. There are so many obstacles that face poor working class communities of color on a daily basis that make autonomy such a distant horizon. These autonomous spaces have laid the groundwork for autonomy's possibility and for dignity's revolt."[34] Autonomy and Leftist politics in Los Angeles, as mentioned in chapter 1, have a long, long history across the nineteenth and twentieth centuries. Specifically, the direct connections between the Chicana/o Left in the 1970s, Chicana/o engagement with the EZLN, and the subsequent autonomous projects in Los Angeles draw from a political genealogy dating back to the late nineteenth century.

Acción Zapatista (AZ) in Austin, Texas, and later in Humbolt and the San Francisco Bay Area, and the Universidad de La Tierra projects in California are other examples of a politics going beyond solidarity. AZ emerged from the Comité en Solidaridad con Chiapas in Austin in 1996. The *comité* had brought together a group of Chicanas/os convening gatherings under the idea "derrumbando Fronteras" in the early 1990s with the Barrio Student Resource Center (Austin) and a group of activist students that met at a local watering hole, the Hole in the Wall. AZ pushed the question of what it meant to go beyond solidarity through pamphlets that circulated communiqués and political analysis, theater projects for youth, organizing efforts with custodial workers and students, and issues of prisoners' rights and police brutality. In the 2000s, AZ expanded to California. In the Bay Area and San Diego, Chicanas/os and Latinas/os organized various virtual campuses of Uni-Tierra Califas, described as "a local project somewhere in-between network and collective pedagogies that is also a project of strategic conviviality and a Zapatismo beyond Chiapas. . . . UT Califas engages a collective subject as part of an epistemological struggle inspired by Indigenous autonomy currently underway throughout Latin America."[35] An autonomous intellectual/research and political organizing project directly connected to local communities in struggle, Uni-Tierra Califas offers a political praxis of community knowledge, convivial research, and assemblies to strengthen already existing cultures of survival and organize against the continued onslaught of state violence—particularly at the hands of the police strategies of low-intensity warfare (a critique that emerged from analyzing political conditions in Chiapas).[36] A related collective project, the Center for Convivial Research and Autonomy (also out of the Bay Area), is engaged with mapping police violence and organizing with the families of people affected by police violence, using community-based, collective, and convivial research as a basis for organizing.

International solidarity and a resurgent Chicana/o Left political imaginary have done more than create political organizations. The Encuentro Chicano-Zapatista sobre La Cultura, Arte y la Autonomía in 1997 was one iteration of how culture and political struggles continue to be intimately linked. The Son Jarocho musical movement is a recovery of a musical style and cultural genealogy from the Mexican coast, particularly Veracuz, but by extension it is also a movement where the African diaspora meets indigenous Mexico through Chicana/o artivistas.[37] Hip Hop is an international language for political struggle as much as a commodified cultural form that capitalism captures for profit. MCs, DJs, and musical poets from Chicana/o, Latina/o, and Latin American backgrounds have connected struggles through an urban art form created in the early 1970s cultural mix originating in the Bronx, New York, and in turn deeply influenced by the Caribbean rhythms and innovative creativity of the black diaspora.[38] Reclaiming dignity and claiming an openly leftist political orientation, Zapatista-influenced music collectives, community mural projects, radio collectives programs, and intergenerational poetry groups are forms of cultural resistance and political movement that continue the tradition of cultural workers redefining the creative process and cultural politics, as well as cultures of political organizing. Finally, for Chicanos like Byron Shane Chubbuck (indigenous name: Oso Blanco), incarcerated at Leavenworth Federal Penitentiary, where Ramón Chacón, Mario Cantú, and raúlrsalinas were politicized in the late 1960s, solidarity meant revolutionary expropriations of banks in the United States to provide munitions support for the EZLN.

The genius of the Chicana/o movement and the Chicana/o Left is the insistence—before Lenin and the postnational turn in American studies, respectively—on emphasizing the relationship between colonialism and empire. The experience of surviving state violence can create a collective community, where the meaning of justice is related to trauma and healing as much as it is to collectively organizing to transform the social conditions that allowed and made possible state violence in the first place. The people and organizations in this book were just as much a part of anticolonial, Third World liberation struggles as they were integral to labor struggles, prisoners' rights activism, university-based protests, and women's, indigenous, and antiracist movements in the United States.[39] "We Raza are not alone. We have allies all over this country, all over the world—in America, Asia, Africa, even in Europe," wrote Betita Martínez and Enriqueta Longeaux y Vásquez in 1974. "We all step up now to have our day in the world court of humanity and you have no choice but to bow. For your whip is gone, it has become my sword. *Tu riata es mi espada*—your whip is my sword."[40] Or as Olga Talamante believed, "Chicana was really an inclusive term, that it really included all of Latin America."[41]

Revolutionary imaginaries are as much about political activities, ideologies, and organizations, the form and content that contextualize political contestation, as they are about how revolution was imagined, how that imagination was cultivated through collective activity, and how collectivity could affect social relations and political power. Imagining revolution was as much about reorganizing social relationships, challenging structures of domination and state violence, and organizing people's power as it was about how culture is intimately and intricately always political, and how politics is fought in the realm of culture. Politics can be about both naming what is killing us and creating the conditions of possibility for changing society and creating a different world.[42] Asking questions beyond solidarity can amplify these organized forces. Culture can communicate these amplifications and organize the imaginary toward direct action. Organization of people (rather than simply organizations) can aggregate direct action into new social relations and convivial institutions. Going beyond solidarity means asking questions about how to make possible the impossible, prefiguring society in the politics and art of political movements, and reclaiming and catalyzing a genealogy of organizing that fosters self-activity, autonomy, and creative survival and living.

INTRODUCTION

1. I use "Chicana/o movement" and "Chicana/o Left" instead of "Chicano movement" because the inflected forms are commonly accepted in the field and more inclusive of the historical reality. I also use "Chicano(s)" and "Chicana(s)" to refer to individuals or groups. I retain the word "Chicano" when quoting sources or discussing groups that used the term as part of their names.

2. Robin D. G. Kelley, *Freedom Dreams: The Black Radical Imagination* (Boston: Beacon, 2002).

3. Jorge Mariscal, *Brown-Eyed Children of the Sun: Lessons from the Chicano Movement, 1965-1975* (Albuquerque: University of New Mexico Press, 2005), 90.

4. Robin D. G. Kelley, "Foreword," in Cedric J. Robinson, *Black Marxism: The Making of the Black Radical Tradition* (Chapel Hill: University of North Carolina Press, 2000), xv.

5. Américo Paredes, *A Texas-Mexican Cancionero: Folksongs of the Lower Border* (Austin: University of Texas Press, 1995), xiv.

6. Américo Paredes, *"With His Pistol in His Hand": A Border Ballad and Its Hero* (Austin: University of Texas Press, 1958); Benedict Anderson, *Imagined Communities: Reflections on the Origin and Spread of Nationalism* (London: Verso, 1983).

7. José Rabassa, "Pre-Columbian Pasts and Indian Presents in Mexican History," *Disposition* 19, no. 46 (1994): 245–270; Alexandra Minna Stern, "From Mestizophilia to Biotypology: Racialization and Science in Mexico, 1920–1960," in *Race and Nation in Modern Latin America*, ed. Nancy P. Applebaum, Anne S. Macpherson, and Karin Alejandra Rosemblatt (Chapel Hill: University of North Carolina Press, 2003), 187–210; Estelle Tarica, *Inner Life of Mestizo Nationalism* (Minneapolis: University of Minnesota Press, 2008); Jesus Antonio Machuca, "Nacion, Mestizaje y Racismo," in *Nacion, Racismo e Identidad*, ed. Alicia Castellanos Guerrero and Juan Manuel Sandoval Palacios (Mexico City: Nuestro Tiempo, 1998), 37–74.

8. See Josefina Saldaña-Portillo, *The Revolutionary Imagination in the Americas and the Age of Development* (Durham, NC: Duke University Press, 2003); Alex Kashnabish, *Zapatismo beyond Borders: New Imaginations of Political Possibility* (Toronto: University of Toronto Press, 2008).

9. Sonia E. Alvarez, Evelina Dagnino, and Arturo Escobar, *Cultures of Politics/ Politics of Cultures: Re-Visioning Latin American Social Movements* (Boulder, CO: Westview, 1998), 7.

10. Maylei Blackwell, *¡Chicana Power! Contested Histories of Feminism in the Chicano Movement* (Austin: University of Texas Press, 2011).

11. Aurora Levins Morales, *Medicine Stories: History, Culture, and the Politics of Integrity* (Boston: South End, 1999).

12. Vijay Prashad, "Second-Hand Dreams," *Social Analysis* 49 (Summer 2005): 2.

13. Blackwell, *¡Chicana Power!*; Laura Pulido, *Black, Brown, Yellow, and Left: Radical Activism in Los Angeles* (Berkeley: University of California Press, 2006);

Mario T. García, *Memories of Chicano History: The Life and Memories of Bert Corona* (Berkeley: University of California Press, 1994).

14. George Lipsitz, *Time Passages: Collective Memory and American Popular Culture* (Minneapolis: University of Minnesota Press, 2001), 84.

15. George Lipsitz, "Not Just Another Social Movement," in *Just Another Poster: Chicano Graphic Arts in California*, ed. Chon Noriega (Seattle: University of Washington Press, 1991), 84; Alicia Schmidt Camacho, *Migrant Imaginaries: Latino Cultural Politics in the U.S.-Mexico Borderlands* (New York: New York University Press, 2008), 26.

16. Fernando Calderón and Adela Cedillo, *Challenging Authoritarianism in Mexico: Revolutionary Struggles and the Dirty War, 1964–1982* (New York: Routledge, 2011).

17. Carlos Cantú, "*Colegio Jacinto Treviño*: The Rise and Fall of the First Chicano College," *Journal of South Texas* 19 (2008–2009): 33–51.

18. Pulido, *Black, Brown, Yellow, and Left*; Marisela R. Chávez, "'We Lived and Breathed and Worked the Movement': The Contradictions and Rewards of Chicana/Mexicana in el Centro de Acción Social Autónomo-Hermandad General de Trabajadores (CASA-HGT), Los Angeles, 1975–1978," in *Las Obreras: Chicana Politics of Work and Family*, ed. Vicki L. Ruiz and Chon Noriega (Los Angeles: UCLA Chicano Studies Research Center Publications, 2000), 83–105.

19. Manolo Callahan, "Zapatismo beyond Chiapas," in *Globalize Liberation: How to Uproot the System and Build a Better World*, ed. D. Solnit (San Francisco: City Lights Books, 2004), 217–228.

20. Jordan T. Camp, "Blues Geographies and the Security Turn: Interpreting the Housing Crisis in Los Angeles," *American Quarterly* 64, no. 3 (September 2012): 543–570.

21. Inderpal Grewal, *Transnational America: Feminisms, Diasporas, Neoliberalisms* (Durham, NC: Duke University Press, 2005); Nick Dyer-Witheford, *Cyber-Marx: Cycles and Circuits of Struggle in High-Technology Capitalism* (Urbana: University of Illinois Press, 1999). See also Winfried Fluck, Donald E. Pease, and John Carlos Rowe, eds., *Re-Framing the Transnational Turn in American Studies* (Hanover, NH: Dartmouth University Press, 2011); Schmidt Camacho, *Migrant Imaginaries*; Laura Briggs, Gladys McCormick, and J. T. Way, "Transnationalism: A Category of Analysis," *American Quarterly* 60, no. 3 (September 2008): 625–648; Sandyha Shukla and Heidi Tinsman, eds., *Imagining Our Americas: Toward a Transnational Frame* (Durham, NC: Duke University Press, 2007); Shelley Fisher Fishkin, "Crossroads of Cultures: The Transnational Turn in American Studies," Presidential Address to the American Studies Association, November 12, 2004, *American Quarterly* 57, no. 1 (March 2005): 17–57.

22. Chris Cameron, interview with Robin D. G. Kelley, "20 Year Anniversary Roundtable on Robin D. G. Kelley, *Race Rebels*: Author Interview," December 7, 2014, http://aaihs.org/20-year-anniversary-roundtable-on-robin-d-g-kelley-race-rebels-author-interview/.

23. Pulido, *Black, Brown, Yellow, and Left*, 180.

24. Frank B. Wilderson III, "Prison-Slave as Hegemony's Silent Scandal," *Social Justice* 30, no. 2 (2003): 18–28.

25. Cherríe Moraga, "Queer Aztlán: The Re-formation of Chicano Tribe," in *The Last Generation*, by Moraga (Boston: South End, 2003), 145–174; Luis Álvarez, *The Power of the Zoot: Youth Cultures of Resistance during World War II* (Berkeley: University of California Press, 2008); Jennifer Jihye Chun, George Lipsitz, and Young Shin, "Intersectionality as a Social Movement Strategy," *Signs* 38, no. 4 (Summer 2013): 917–940.

26. Joan Wallach Scott, "The Evidence of Experience," *Critical Inquiry* 17, no. 4 (Summer 1991): 773–797.

27. Denise A. Segura and Beatriz M. Pesquera, "'There Is No Going Back': Chicanas and Feminism," in *Chicana Critical Issues*, ed. Norma Alarcón et al. (Berkeley, CA: Third Woman Press, 1993), 99, reprinted in *Chicana Feminist Thought: The Basic Historical Writings*, ed. Alma García (New York: Routledge, 1997): 301–302; Denise A. Segura and Beatriz M. Pesquera, "Chicana Political Consciousness: Renegotiating Culture, Class, and Gender with Oppositional Practices," *Aztlán: A Journal of Chicano Studies* 24, no. 1 (Spring 1999): 1–32.

28. George Katsiaficas, *The Imagination of the New Left: A Global Analysis of 1968* (Boston: South End, 1999); Jeremi Suri, *Power and Protest: Global Revolution and the Rise of Détente* (Cambridge, MA: Harvard University Press, 2003).

29. Harry Cleaver, "The Inversion of Class Perspective in Marxian Theory: From Valorization to Self-Valorization," in *Open Marxism*, vol. 2: *Theory and Practice*, ed. Werner Bonefeld and Richard Gunn (London: Pluto, 1992), 106–144.

30. Mario Montano, "Notes on the International Crisis," *Zerowork* 1 (1975), reprinted in *Midnight Oil: Work, Energy, War, 1973–1992*, ed. Midnight Notes Collective (New York: Autonomedia, 1992), 115–142; Antonio Negri, "Marx on the Cycle and on Crisis," in *Revolution Retrieved: Selected Writings on Marx, Keynes, Capitalist Crisis and New Social Subjects, 1967–83*, by Negri (Red Notes: London, 1988), 47–90; Dyer-Witheford, *Cyber-Marx*; Mario Tronti, "The Strategy of the Refusal," in *Autonomia: Post-Political Politics*, ed. Sylvère Lotringer and Christian Marazzi (Boston: Semiotext(e), 1980), 28–35; and Zerowork, "Introduction to Zerowork 1," in *Midnight Oil: Work, Energy, War, 1973–1992*, ed. Midnight Notes Collective (Brooklyn: Autonomedia, 1992), 109–114.

31. Stuart Hall with Bill Swartz, "Society and State, 1880–1930," in *The Hard Road to Renewal: Thatcherism and the Crisis of the Left*, by Hall (New York: Verso, 1988), 96, quoted in Ruth Wilson Gilmore, *Golden Gulag: Prisons, Surplus, Crisis, and Opposition in Globalizing California* (Berkeley: University of California Press, 2007), 54.

32. Manuel Callahan, "In Defense of Conviviality and the Collective Subject," *Polis: Revista LatinoAmericano* (2012): 3, http://polis.revues.org/8432; Annie Paradise, "Militarized Policing and Resistance in the Social Factory: The Battle for Community Safety in the Silicon Valley" (PhD diss., California Institute for Integral Studies, 2015), http://cril.mitotedigital.org/projects.

33. Erik S. McDuffie, *Sojourning for Freedom: Black Women, American Communism, and the Making of Black Left Feminism* (Durham, NC: Duke University Press, 2007).

34. John Holloway, "Urban Zapatismo," *Humboldt Journal of Social Relations* 29, no. 1 (2005): 6–37.

35. To speak of involvement and participation is not to create hierarchies or to

traffic in competitive language comparing political actions with regard to their supposed radical public nature or level of newspaper coverage; instead, to do so is related to the intentions and reasons for choosing to participate and involve oneself in a political situation (by joining an organization, performing theater on the street, or moving to another country to engage in strident militancy).

36. See Jared Sexton, "People-of-Color-Blindness: Notes on the Afterlife of Slavery," *Social Text* 28, no. 2 103 (Summer 2010): 31–56; Wilderson, "Prison-Slave as Hegemony's Silent Scandal."

37. Pulido, *Black, Brown, Yellow, and Left*, 180.

38. H. L. T. Quan, "Geniuses of Resistance: Feminist Consciousness and the Black Radical Tradition," *Race and Class* 47, no. 2 (2005): 39–53; Chandra Mohanty, *Feminism without Borders: Decolonizing Theory, Practicing Solidarity* (Durham, NC: Duke University Press, 2003).

39. Mariarosa Dalla Costa and Selma James, *The Power of Women and the Subversion of the Community* (Bristol, UK: Falling Wall, 1972); Mario Tronti, "Social Capital," *Telos* 17 (1973): 98–121; Tronti, "The Strategy of Refusal," in *Working Class Autonomy and the Crisis: Italian Marxist Texts of the Theory and Practice of a Class Movement: 1964–1979*, ed. Red Notes (London: Red Notes and CSE Books, 1979), 7–22.

40. Kelley, *Race Rebels*.

41. Tanalís Padilla, *Rural Resistance in the Land of Zapata: The Jaramillista Movement and the Myth of the Pax-Priísta, 1940–1962* (Durham, NC: Duke University Press, 2008), 17.

CHAPTER 1: CARTOGRAPHIES OF THE CHICANA/O LEFT

1. Laura Pulido, *Black, Brown, Yellow, and Left: Radical Activism in Los Angeles* (Berkeley: University of California Press, 2006), 3.

2. José Montoya, *In Formation: 20 Years of Joda* (San Jose, CA: Chusma House, 1992), 245.

3. Alan Eladio Gómez, "Feminism, Torture, and the Politics of Chicana/Third World Solidarity: An Interview with Olga Talamante," *Radical History Review* 101 (Spring 2008): 160–178.

4. This paramilitary organization received training in the United States after the incident. Kate Doyle, "'Los Halcones': Made in the USA," *Proceso* 1388, June 8, 2003, 36–42.

5. Olga Talamante, telephone interview by author, San Francisco, June 15, 2004.

6. Gaye Theresa Johnson, *Spaces of Conflict, Sounds of Solidarity: Music, Race, and Spatial Entitlement in Los Angeles* (Berkeley: University of California Press, 2013), xiii. According to the Chicano ethnomusicologist Estevan Azcona, "The song is basically a ranchera, or is based on that form. The melodic instrument is the requinto, the accompanying instruments are guitar and tololoche [similar to an upright bass] . . . Jose is the most likely composer. The arrangement, however, was by Rudy Carrillo, the requinto player." The composition was also an experimental arrangement, "what Jose and most of the movement songwriters were doing when they took traditional/popular forms, like the ranchera, and transformed those songs into political tools." This was an important change influenced by the new forms of

artistic creativity and production. The quotations are from email correspondence with Azcona.

7. Ella María Díaz, "The Necessary Theater of the Royal Chicano Air Force," *Aztlán: Journal of Chicana/o Studies* 38, no. 2 (2013): 41–70; Jorge Huerta, *Necessary Theater: Six Plays about the Chicano Experience* (Houston: Arte Público, 1989). For a brilliant history of *movimiento* music, see Estevan Azcona, "Movements in Chicano Music: Performing Culture, Performing Politics, 1965–1979" (PhD diss., University of Texas at Austin, 2008).

8. Shifra M. Goldman, "A Public Voice: Fifteen Years of Chicano Posters," *Art Journal* 44, no. 1 (Spring 1984): 50–57.

9. Elizabeth Sutherland Martínez, *The Youngest Revolution: A Personal Report on Cuba* (New York: Dial Press, 1969).

10. Maylei Blackwell, *¡Chicana Power! Contested Histories of Feminism in the Chicano Movement* (Austin: University of Texas Press, 2011).

11. Luis Álvarez, *The Power of the Zoot: Youth Cultures of Resistance during World War II* (Berkeley: University of California Press, 2008).

12. Alicia Schmidt Camacho, *Migrant Imaginaries: Latino Cultural Politics in the U.S.-Mexico Borderlands* (New York: New York University Press, 2008), 25. Paraphrasing Cornelius Castoriadis, Schmidt Camacho explains the social imaginary as "[that which] represents a symbolic field in which people come to understand and describe their social being . . . social relations must first be imagined in order to be comprehended and acted on" (5).

13. Robin D. G. Kelley, *Freedom Dreams: The Black Radical Imagination* (Boston: Beacon, 2002).

14. Christina Heatherton, "University of Radicalism: Ricardo Flores Magón and Leavenworth Penitentiary," *American Quarterly* 66, no. 3 (2014): 576.

15. Beth Bailey and David Farber, "Introduction," in *America in the Seventies* (Lawrence: University Press of Kansas, 2004), 4.

16. Harry Cleaver, "The Inversion of Class Perspective in Marxian Theory: From Valorization to Self-Valorization," in *Open Marxism*, vol. 2: *Theory and Practice*, ed. Werner Bonefeld and Richard Gunn (London: Pluto, 1992).

17. For an analysis of this literature, see Robin D. G. Kelley, "Looking Extremely Backward: Why the Enlightenment Will Only Lead Us into the Dark," in *Yo' Mama's Disfunktional! Fighting the Culture Wars in Urban America* (Boston: Beacon, 1997), 103–124.

18. See Bailey and Farber, *America in the Seventies*.

19. Jacquelyn Dowd Hall, "The Long Civil Rights Movement and the Political Uses of the Past," *Journal of American History* 91, no. 4 (March 2005): 1233–1263.

20. Carol Anderson, *Eyes Off the Prize: The United Nations and the African American Struggle for Human Rights, 1944–1955* (Cambridge, UK: Cambridge University Press, 2003). See also Mary L. Dudziak, *Cold War Civil Rights: Race and the Image of American Democracy* (Princeton, NJ: Princeton University Press, 2002); Robin D. G. Kelley, *Hammer and Hoe: Alabama Communists during the Great Depression* (Chapel Hill: University of North Carolina Press, 1990); Timothy B. Tyson, *Radio Free Dixie: Robert F. Williams and the Roots of Black Power* (Chapel Hill: University of North Carolina Press, 1999); Peniel E. Joseph, *Waiting 'Til the Midnight Hour: A Narrative History of Black Power in America* (New York: Henry Holt,

2007). For a brilliant study of transatlantic, multiracial, working-class alliances and solidarities in the seventeenth and eighteenth centuries, see Peter Linebaugh and Marcus Rediker, *The Many-Headed Hydra: Sailors, Slaves, Commoners, and the Hidden History of the Revolutionary Atlantic* (Boston: Beacon, 2000).

21. George Katsiaficas, *The Imagination of the New Left: A Global Analysis of 1968* (Boston: South End, 1999).

22. Aurora Levins Morales, *Medicine Stories: History, Culture, and the Politics of Integrity* (Boston: South End, 1999), 67-78; Álvarez, *Power of the Zoot*, 8-9; John Holloway, "Dignity's Revolt," in *Zapatista! Reinventing Revolution in Mexico*, ed. John Holloway and Eloína Peláez (London: Pluto, 1998), 159-198; Manuel Callahan, "Why Not Share a Dream? Zapatismo as Political and Cultural Practice," in *Zapatismo as Political and Cultural Practice*, special issue, *Humboldt Journal of Social Relations* 29, no. 1 (2005): 6-37; Gustavo Esteva, Madhu S. Prakash, and Dana L. Stuchul, "A Pedagogy for Liberation to Liberation from Pedagogy," in *Rethinking Freire: Globalization and the Environmental Crisis*, ed. C. A. Bowers and Frédérique Apffel-Marglin (Mahwah, NJ: Lawrence Erlbaum Associates, 2005), 13-30; Jared Sexton, "People-of-Color-Blindness: Notes on the Afterlife of Slavery," *Social Text* 28, no. 2 103 (Summer 2010): 31-56.

23. Marisela R. Chávez, "Despierten hermanas y hermanos: Women, the Chicano Movement, and Chicana Feminisms in California" (PhD diss., Stanford University, 2005), 27.

24. Jorge Mariscal, *Brown-Eyed Children of the Sun: Lessons from the Chicano Movement, 1965-1975* (Albuquerque: University of New Mexico Press, 2005), 182.

25. Pauli Murray and Mary O. Eastwood, "Jane Crow and the Law: Sex Discrimination and Title VII," *George Washington Law Review* 34, no. 2 (1965): 232-256.

26. Mariscal, *Brown-Eyed Children*, 7.

27. Lee Bebout, *Mythohistorical Interventions: The Chicano Movement and Its Legacies* (Minneapolis: University of Minnesota Press, 2011), 3.

28. Ibid.

29. Ibid.

30. Raúl Coronado, *A World Not to Come: A History of Latino Writing and Print Culture* (Cambridge, MA: Harvard University Press, 2013).

31. Mariscal, *Brown-Eyed Children*, 15-16.

32. Robert T. Rodríguez, *Next of Kin: The Family in Chicano/a Cultural Politics* (Durham, NC: Duke University Press, 2009), 4, 7.

33. Mariscal, *Brown-Eyed Children*.

34. Schmidt Camacho, *Migrant Imaginaries*; Emma Pérez, *The Decolonial Imaginary: Writing Chicanas into History* (Bloomington: Indiana University Press, 1999).

35. For critiques of the heteropatriarchal norms assumed in "los planes," see, for example, Angie Chambram-Denersesian, "I Throw Punches for My Race, but I Don't Want to Be a Man: Writing Us—Chica-nos (Girl, US)/Chicanas—into the Movement Script," in *Cultural Studies*, ed. Lawrence Grossberg, Cary Nelson, and Paula Treichler (New York: Routledge, 1991), 81-95.

36. Bebout, *Mythohistorical Interventions*, 5.

37. Alma M. Martínez, "Un Continente, Una Cultura? The Political Dialectic for a United Chicano, Mexican and Latin American Popular/Political Theatre Front, Mexico City, 1974" (PhD diss., Stanford University, 2006), 40.

38. Annalise Orleck and Lisa Gayle Hazirjian, *The War on Poverty: A New Grassroots History, 1964-1980* (Athens: University of Georgia Press, 2011).

39. Cynthia A. Young, *Soul Power: Culture, Radicalism and the Making of a U.S. Third World Left* (Durham, NC: Duke University Press, 2006), 13.

40. See Cedric J. Robinson, *Black Marxism: The Making of the Black Radical Tradition* (Chapel Hill: University of North Carolina Press, 2000); Linebaugh and Rediker, *Many-Headed Hydra*; Frank A. Guridy, "From Solidarity to Cross-Fertilization: Afro-Cuban/African American Interaction during the 1930s and 1940s," *Radical History Review* 87 (Fall 2003): 19–48. See also Penny M. Von Eschen's *Race against Empire: Black Americans and Anticolonialism, 1937-1957* (Ithaca, NY: Cornell University Press, 1997); Cary Fraser, "An American Dilemma: Race and Realpolitik in the American Response to the Bandung Conference, 1955," in *Window on Freedom: Race, Civil Rights, and Foreign Affairs, 1945-1988*, ed. Brenda Gayle Plummer (Chapel Hill: University of North Carolina Press, 2003), 115–140; Christopher J. Lee, *Making a World after Empire: The Bandung Moment and Its Political Afterlives* (Athens: Ohio University Press, 2010).

41. Young, *Soul Power*, 3.

42. Vijay Prashad, *The Darker Nations: A People's History of the Third World* (New York: New Press, 2007), xv.

43. Young, *Soul Power*, 14.

44. Lorena Oropeza, *¡Raza Si! ¡Guerra No! Chicano Protest and Patriotism during the Vietnam War Era* (Berkeley: University of California Press, 2005).

45. William D. Carrigan and Clive Webb, *Forgotten Dead: Mob Violence against Mexicans in the United States, 1848-1928* (Oxford, UK: Oxford University Press, 2013); Edward J. Escobar, *Race, Police, and the Making of a Political Identity: Mexican Americans and the Los Angeles Police Department, 1900-1945* (Berkeley: University of California Press, 1999).

46. Gustavo Licón, "¡La Union Hace La Fuerza! (Unity Creates Strength!): M.E.Ch.A." (PhD diss., University of Southern California, 2009), 70.

47. See Alan Knight, "Empire, Hegemony and Globalization in the Americas," *NACLA Report on the Americas* 39, no. 2 (September/October 2005): 8–11. See also Patrick Wolfe, *Settler Colonialism and the Transformation of Anthropology: The Politics and Poetics of an Ethnographic Event* (New York: Cassell, 1999); Lorenzo Veracini, *Settler Colonialism: A Theoretical Overview* (New York: Palgrave Macmillan, 2010); Jared Sexton, "The Vel of Slavery—Tracking the Figure of the Unsovereign," *Critical Sociology* 2014: 1–15.

48. Greg Grandin, *Empire's Workshop: Latin America, the United States, and the Rise of the New Imperialism* (New York: Metropolitan Books, 2006), 25.

49. Licón, "¡La Union Hace La Fuerza!," 79.

50. Kelley, *Hammer and Hoe*, 2.

51. See Blackwell, *¡Chicana Power!*

52. See Claudio Lomnitz, *The Return of Comrade Ricardo Flores Magón* (New York: Zone Books, 2014); Chaz Bufe and Mitchell Cowen Verter, eds., *Dreams of Freedom: A Ricardo Flores Magón Reader* (Oakland, CA: AK Press, 2006); Emilio Zamora, *The World of the Mexican Worker in Texas* (College Station: Texas A&M University Press, 1994).

53. Devra Weber, "Keeping Community, Challenging Boundaries: Indigenous

Migrants, Internationalist Workers, and Mexican Revolutionaries, 1900–1920," in *Mexico and Mexicans in the Making of the United States*, ed. John Tutino (Austin: University of Texas Press, 2011), 208–235.

54. Pérez, *Decolonial Imaginary*; Blackwell, *¡Chicana Power!*

55. Vicki Ruiz, *From Out of the Shadows: Mexican Women in Twentieth-Century America* (New York: Oxford University Press, 2008), 81.

56. Johnson, *Spaces of Conflict*, 4.

57. Mario T. García, *Mexican Americans: Leadership, Ideology, and Identity, 1930–1960* (New Haven, CT: Yale University Press, 1991), 146–150.

58. Ibid., 153; Lorenzo Meyer, *Mexico and the United States in the Oil Controversy, 1917–1942* (Austin: University of Texas Press, 1997); Kevin J. Middlebrook, *The Paradox of Revolution: Labor, the State, and Authoritarianism in Mexico* (Baltimore: Johns Hopkins University Press, 1995).

59. García, *Mexican Americans*, 154; Erik S. McDuffie, *Sojourning for Freedom: Black Women, American Communism, and the Making of Black Left Feminism* (Durham, NC: Duke University Press, 2011); Bull V. Mullen, *Popular Fronts: Chicago and African-American Cultural Politics, 1935–46* (Urbana: University of Illinois Press, 1999).

60. Mark A. Weitz, *The Sleepy Lagoon Murder Case: Race Discrimination and Mexican-American Rights* (Lawrence: University Press of Kansas, 2010).

61. Denise A. Segura and Beatriz M. Pesquera, "'There Is No Going Back': Chicanas and Feminism," in *Chicana Critical Issues*, ed. Norma Alarcón et al. (Berkeley: Third Woman Press, 1993), 106.

62. García, *Mexican Americans*, 199.

63. Ibid., 201.

64. Ibid.

65. Summary culled from Mario T. García, *Memories of Chicano History: The Life and Narrative of Bert Corona* (Berkeley: University of California Press, 1994).

66. Ibid.; Ruíz, *From Out of the Shadows*; David Gutiérrez, *Walls and Mirrors: Mexican Americans, Mexican Immigrants, and the Politics of Ethnicity* (Berkeley: University of California Press, 1995).

67. Antonia Castañeda, "We Shall Not Be Moved": The Chicano Movement and Solidarity with Chile," talk presented at Trinity University, San Antonio, Texas, February 20, 2014.

68. I understand the origin of the theorizations of the national question to reside with Lenin, not Joseph Stalin. The argument provided by Leon Trotsky and the urgent distinction emphasized by Yolanda Alaniz and Megan Cornish in an important work that summarizes the national question with regard to Chicana/o history convincingly demonstrate that Lenin should be credited as the originator of the theory. Joseph Stalin, *Marxism and the National Question* (Calcutta: New Book Centre, 1975); Leon Trotsky, *Stalin: An Appraisal of the Man and His Influence* (New York: Grosset and Dunlap, 1940); Yolanda Alaniz and Megan Cornish, *Viva La Raza: A History of Chicano Identity and Resistance* (Seattle: Red Letter, 2008), 23–78.

69. Stalin, *Marxism and the National Question*, 21.

70. Alaniz and Cornish, *Viva La Raza*.

71. García, *Mexican Americans*, 154.

72. Arnoldo García, "Toward a Left without Borders: The Story of the Center

for Autonomous Social Action—General Brotherhood of Workers," *Monthly Review* 54, no. 3 (July-August 2002): 69–78; Ernesto Chávez, *"¡Mi Raza Primero!": Nationalism, Identity, and Insurgency in the Chicano Movement in Los Angeles, 1966-1978* (Berkeley: University of California Press, 2002); Pulido, *Black, Brown, Yellow, and Left*; García, *Memories of Chicano History*.

73. Pulido, *Black, Brown, Yellow, and Left*, 131.

74. On ATM, see Licón, "¡La Union Hace La Fuerza!"; Max Elbaum, *Revolution in the Air: Sixties Radicals Turn to Lenin, Mao, and Che* (New York: Verso, 2002), 114, 196, 199, 234–235, 271, 300. In 1978, ATM joined with I Wor Kuen, a Marxist-Leninist revolutionary formation founded in 1969 and consisting of activists from various Asian nationalities, to form the League of Revolutionary Struggle (Marxist-Leninist). See League of Revolutionary Struggle, *Statements on the Founding of the League of Revolutionary Struggle* (Oakland, CA: Getting Together Publications, 1978); Elbaum, *Revolution in the Air*; Fred Ho, "Fists of Revolution: The Revolutionary History of I Wor Kuen/League of Revolutionary Struggle," in *Legacy to Liberation: Politics and Culture of Revolutionary Asian Pacific America*, ed. Fred Ho, Carolyn Antonio, Diane Fujino, and Steve Yip (Oakland, CA: AK Press, 2000), 3–14.

75. Licón, "¡La Union Hace La Fuerza!," 18.

76. Pulido, *Black, Brown, Yellow, and Left*, 131.

77. Ibid.

78. Chávez, *¡Mi Raza Primero!*, 109.

79. Pulido, *Black, Brown, Yellow, and Left*, 132.

80. Licón, "¡La Union Hace La Fuerza!," 132.

81. August Twenty-Ninth Movement, "Casa Attacks on the Chicano Movement," pamphlet, CASA Collection, box 25, folder 8, p. 2, quoted in Pulido, *Black, Brown, Yellow, and Left*, 132.

82. Communist Collective of the Chicano Nation, "Report to the Communist Collective of the Chicano Nation on the Chicano National-Colonial Question," 1973, https://www.marxists.org/history/erol/ncm1a/cccn/introduction.htm.

83. Alan Eladio Gómez, "'Nuestras vidas corren casi paralelas': Chicanos, Puerto Rican Independentistas, and the Prison Rebellion Years at Leavenworth, 1969-1972," in *Behind Bars: Latinos/as and Prison in the United States*, ed. Suzanne Oboler (New York: Palgrave-MacMillan, 2008), 67–96.

84. Salinas began to write his name in lowercase letters, as his pen name, while in Leavenworth prison in the late 1960s.

85. Alan Eladio Gómez, "Resisting Living Death at Marion Federal Penitentiary, 1972," *Radical History Review* 96 (Fall 2006): 58–86; Dan Berger, *Captive Nation: Black Prison Organizing in the Civil Rights Era* (Chapel Hill: University of North Carolina Press, 2014); Daniel Chard, "Rallying for Repression: Police Terror, 'Law-and-Order' Politics, and the Decline of Maine's Prisoners' Rights Movement," *The Sixties: A Journal of History, Politics and Culture* 5, no. 1 (2012); Victoria Law, *Resistance behind Bars: The Struggles of Incarcerated Women* (Oakland, CA: PM Press, 2009).

86. Oropeza, *¡Raza Si! ¡Guerra No!*, 97.

87. Mariscal, *Brown-Eyed Children*, 88.

88. Dan Georgakas and Marvin Surkin, *Detroit, I Do Mind Dying* (Boston: South End, 1998); Victor M. Rodríguez, "Boricuas, African Americans, and Chicanos in the

222 NOTES TO PAGES 39-45

'Far West': Notes on the Puerto Rican Pro-Independence Movement in California, 1960s–1980s," in *Latino Social Movements: Historical and Theoretical Perspectives*, ed. Rodolfo D. Torres and George Katsiaficas (New York: Routledge, 1999), 79–110.
    89. Mariscal, *Brown-Eyed Children*, 294n86.

CHAPTER 2: MEXICO, ANTICOMMUNISM, AND THE CHICANA/O MOVEMENT

1. Tanalís Padilla, *Rural Resistance in the Land of Zapata: The Jaramillista Movement and the Myth of the Pax-Priísta, 1940–1962* (Durham, NC: Duke University Press, 2008), 210.
    2. Ernesto Vigil, *The Crusade for Justice: Chicano Militancy and the Government's War on Dissent* (Madison: University of Wisconsin, 1999); José Angel Gutiérrez, *The Making of a Chicano Militant: Lessons from Cristal* (Madison: University of Wisconsin Press, 1999); Email correspondence with Narciso Alemán, June 5, 2006.
    3. "Investigación Social y Política de los Problemas Actuales en las Comunidades Mexicoamericanas (Chicanos)," especially 11–204–1, folder 8–30, Movimiento Chicano, Archivo General de la Nación, Ramo Dirección Federal de Seguridad, Mexico City, cited in Nydia A. Martínez, "The Struggles of Solidarity: Chicana/o-Mexican Networks, 1960s–1970s," special issue on Border Studies, *Social Sciences* 4, no. 3 (2015): 526.
    4. Philip Agee, *Inside the Company: CIA Diary* (New York: Farrar Straus & Giroux, 1975).
    5. Oval Office, conversation no. 735-1, cassette nos. 2246–2248, June 15, 1972, 10:31 a.m.–12:10 p.m. Audio of this and other recordings have been archived at http://www.gwu.edu/~nsarchiv/NSAEBB/NSAEBB95/.
    6. Sergio Aguayo Quezada, *El Panteón de los Mitos: Estados Unidos y nacionalismo mexicano* (Mexico City: Colegio de México, 1998), 200.
    7. The text presented here uses the words of a translator included in the transcription.
    8. Oval Office, conversation no. 735-1.
    9. Ibid.
    10. Bettina Aptheker, *Morning Breaks: The Trial of Angela Davis*, 2nd ed. (Ithaca, NY: Cornell University Press, 1999).
    11. Memorias de la Secretaría de Relaciones Exteriores, México 1971–1972, 1973–1974, pp. 51–111, quoted in Arturo Santamaría Gómez, *La Política entre México y Aztlán: Relaciónes Chicano Mexicanas del 68 a Chiapas 94* (Sinaloa, Mexico: Universidad Autónoma de Sinaloa and California State University, Los Angeles, 1994), 54.
    12. Saidiya Hartman, *Scenes of Subjection: Terror, Slavery, and Self-Making in Nineteenth Century America* (New York: Oxford University Press, 1997).
    13. Lesley Gill, *The School of the Americas: Military Training and Political Violence in the Americas* (Durham, NC: Duke University Press, 2004); Alfred McCoy, *A Question of Torture: CIA Interrogation, from the Cold War to the War on Terror* (New York: Metropolitan Books, 2005); John Dinges, *The Condor Years: How Pinochet and His Allies Brought Terrorism to Three Continents* (New York: New Press, 2004); Richard H. Immerman, *The CIA in Guatemala: The Foreign Policy of Intervention* (Austin: University of Texas Press, 1982); Ross Gelbspan, *Break-ins, Death*

Threats, and the FBI: The Covert War against the Central America Movement (Boston: South End, 1991).

14. Micol Seigel, "Nelson Rockefeller in Latin America: Global Currents of U.S. Prison Growth," *Comparative American Studies* (forthcoming).

15. Christina Heatherton, *The Color Line and the Class Struggle: The Mexican Revolution, Internationalism, and the American Century* (Berkeley: University of California Press, forthcoming).

16. Michael Flamm, *Law and Order: Street Crime, Civil Unrest, and the Crisis of Liberalism in the 1960s* (New York: Columbia University Press, 2007); Sean Cunningham, *Cowboy Conservatism: Texas and the Rise of the Modern Right* (Lexington: University of Kentucky Press, 2010); Jeffrey Haas, *The Assassination of Fred Hampton: How the FBI and the Chicago Police Murdered a Black Panther* (Chicago: Lawrence Hill Books, 2009); Ward Churchill and Jim Vander Wall, *Agents of Repression: The FBI's Secret Wars against the Black Panther Party and the American Indian Movement* (Boston: South End, 1988).

17. See Chandan Reddy, *Freedom with Violence: Race, Sexuality, and the US State* (Durham, NC: Duke University Press, 2011) on the relationship between violence, the state, sexuality, and democracy.

18. Kevin Middlebrook, *The Paradox of Revolution: Labor, the State, and Authoritarianism in Mexico* (Baltimore: Johns Hopkins University Press, 1995); Padilla, *Rural Resistance*.

19. Gustavo Esteva, *La Batalla de México Rural* (Mexico City: Siglo XXI, 1980); Ilan Bizberg, "La transformación del regimen politico mexicano: entre el pluralismo y el neocorporativismo," in *México: una agenda para fin del siglo*, ed. Alberto Aziz Nassiff (Mexico City: La Jornada, 1996), 175–190; Bizberg, *Modernization and Corporatism in Government/Labor Relations* (Mexico City: Colegio de México, 1990); Middlebrook, *Paradox of Revolution*.

20. Fernando Calderon and Adela Cedillo, *Challenging Authoritarianism in Mexico: Revolutionary Struggles and the Dirty War, 1964-1982* (New York: Routledge, 2001); Padilla, *Rural Resistance*.

21. Padilla, *Rural Resistance*; Aurora Loyo Brambila, *El movimiento magisterial de 1958 en México* (Mexico City: Era, 1980); Loyo Brambila, *El movimiento ferrocarrilero en México, 1958-1959* (Mexico City: Era, 1980).

22. Padilla, *Rural Resistance*, 220.

23. Greg Grandin, *Empire's Workshop: Latin America, the United States, and the Rise of the New Imperialism* (New York: Metropolitan Books, 2006), 10.

24. Ibid., 188.

25. Kate Doyle, Comisión Nacional de los Derechos Humanos México: *Informe Especial Sobre las Quejas en Materia de Desapariciones Forzadas Ocurridas en la Decada de los 70 y Principios de los 80*, Anexo I, "Gráficas," no. 10, http://www.cndh.org.mx/Principal/document/informe/index.html.

26. Details are summarized from Raúl Álvarez Garín, *La Estela de Tlatelolco* (Mexico City: Ithaca, 2002); Carey, *Plaza of Sacrifices: Gender, Power, and Terror in 1968 Mexico* (Albuquerque: University of New Mexico Press, 2007); and Raúl Jardón, *El Espionaje contra el Movimiento Estudiantil: Los documentos de la Dirección Federal de Seguridad y las agencies de inteligencia estadounidense en 1968* (Mexico City: Editorial ITACA, 2003).

27. Jaime Pensado, *Rebel Mexico: Student Unrest and Authoritarian Political Culture during the Long Sixties* (Stanford, CA: Stanford University Press, 2013).

28. Héctor Anaya, *Los parricidas del 68: la protesta juvenil* (México: Plaza y Janes, 1998); Sergio Zermeño, *México, una democracia utopica: el movimiento estudiantil del 68* (México: Siglo XXI, 1978).

29. Pensado, *Rebel Mexico*; Lessie Jo Frazier and Deborah Cohen, "Defining the Space of Mexico '68: Heroic Masculinity in the Prison and 'Women' in the Streets," *Hispanic American Historical Review* 83, no. 4 (2003): 617–660.

30. See Garín, *La Estela de Tlatelolco*, especially 139–166.

31. Carey, *Plaza of Sacrifices*, 61.

32. Garín, *La Estela de Tlatelolco*, 77.

33. Mariano Leyva Dominguez, interview by author, Ocotopec, Morelos, Mexico, November 16, 2004.

34. Pensado, *Rebel Mexico*, 231.

35. Padilla, *Rural Resistance*, 11.

36. See, for example, Juilio Scherer García and Carlos Monsiváis, *Parte de Guerra: Tlatelolco 1968 — Documentos Del General Marcelino García Barragán: Los Hechos y la Historia* (Mexico City: Nuevo Siglo/Aguilar, 1999).

37. Garín, *La Estela de Tlatelolco*, 77.

38. "En los sesenta había en México una izquierda joven, y poco numeroso, sin inserción social y política consistente, pero inquieta, estudiosa y decidida." Ibid., 146. Thanks to de la maza peréz tamayo for the translation.

39. Pensado, *Rebel Mexico*, 232; Garin, *La Estela de Tlatelolco*, 122.

40. Pensado, *Rebel Mexico*, 232.

41. See Sergio Aguayo Quezada, *El Panteón de los Mitos: Estados Unidos y nacionalismo mexicano* (Mexico City: Colegio de México, 1998); for a sound hagiography, see Enrique Krauze, *Mexico: A Biography of Power, A History of Modern Mexico, 1910–1996* (New York: Harper Perennial, 1998). For Echeverría's description of his past, see Oval Office, conversation no. 735-1.

42. Aguayo Quezada, *El Panteón*, 194.

43. Gilberto López y Rivas, "¿SEDENA? a forma paramilitares?" *La Jornada*, September 28, 2001; Kate Doyle, "'Los Halcones': Made in the USA," *Proceso* 1388, June 8, 2003, 36–42.

44. Aguayo Quezada, *El Panteón de los Mitos*, 194; Carlos Tello, *La Política Económica en México, 1970–1976* (Mexico City: Siglo XXI, 1979).

45. Fernando Calderón and Adela Cedillo, *Challenging Authoritarianism in Mexico: Revolutionary Struggles and the Dirty War, 1964–1982* (New York: Routledge, 2011), 9.

46. Padilla, *Rural Resistance*, 14.

47. Dan Berger, ed., *The Hidden 1970s: Histories of Radicalism* (New Brunswick, NJ: Rutgers University Press, 2009).

48. Greg Grandin, *The Last Colonial Massacre: Latin America in the Cold War* (Chicago: University of Chicago Press, 2004), 11.

49. Hector Camin and Lorenzo Meyer, *In the Shadow of the Mexican Revolution: Contemporary Mexican History, 1910–1989*, translated by Luis Alberto Fierro (Austin: University of Texas Press, 1993).

50. Ibid.; Joshua Rubenstein, *Leon Trotsky: A Revolutionary's Life* (New Haven, CT: Yale University Press, 2011).

51. Calderon and Cedillo, *Challenging Authoritarianism in Mexico*, 5.

52. Manuel Buendía, *La CIA en México* (México: Océano, 1983). Until the CIA station in Baghdad was built in 2007, the largest installation was in Mexico.

53. Jefferson Morely, "LITEMPO: The CIA's Eyes on Tlatelolco," National Security Archive Electronic Briefing Book no. 204, National Security Archive, 2006, http://www2.gwu.edu/~nsarchiv/NSAEBB/NSAEBB204/.

54. "Las históricas relaciónes entre México y la Cuba son, de buena medida, una leyenda que ambos naciones han promovido incansablemente desde 1959." Kate Doyle, "Archivos Abiertos," *Proceso*, March 2, 2003, 37.

55. "Ofrece nuevas evidencias de que la tolerancia de Estados Unidos hacia la intransigencia de México estuvo basado en un pacto secreto que hicieron los jefes de Estado mexicano con su contrapartes de Washington." Ibid., 39.

56. In regard to the Mexico Project of the National Security Archives, see the National Security Archive, George Washington University, http://www.gwu.edu/~nsarchiv/mexico/.

57. Camín and Meyer, *In the Shadow of the Mexican Revolution*.

58. Santamaría Gómez, *La Política entre México y Aztlán*, 32.

59. Francisco Balderrama, *In Defense of La Raza, the Los Angeles Mexican Consulate, and the Mexican Community, 1929 to 1936* (Tucson: University of Arizona Press, 1982).

60. Ibid., 34.

61. Jorge Mariscal, *Brown-Eyed Children of the Sun: Lessons from the Chicano Movement, 1965–1975* (Albuquerque: University of New Mexico Press, 2005), 59.

62. "Los primeros esfuerzos visibles y productivos para agremiar a los trabajadores indocumentados que emprendieron los activistas chicanos coincidieron con los movimientos estudiantiles, campesinos y obreros posteriors al 68 mexicano que en su conjunto propiciaron una atmósfera para el acercamiento de los *dos Méxicos*" [author's emphasis]. Santamaría Gómez, *La Política entre México y Aztlán*, 95.

63. Interview with Antonio Rodríguez, October 15, 1990, in Santamaría Gómez, *La Política entre México y Aztlán*, 38.

64. "Se relacionó con los comités de lucha de la UNAM, y particularmente con el de la *Facultad de Derecho*. Las asambleas de los universitarios mexicanos y las visitas a ejidos y colonias populares fueron para los jóvenes chicanos un 'gran aprendizaje.'" Santamaría Gómez, *La Política entre México y Aztlán*, 38–39. Gómez gathers his narrative from his interview with Antonio Rodríguez, later of CASA.

65. Handwritten notes of a conversation with Rubén Solis, San Antonio, June 14, 2005, in possession of the author.

66. Santamaría Gómez, *La Política entre México y Aztlán*, 37.

67. Ibid., 32.

68. Ibid.

69. *La Raza* 1, no. 9 (September 1972): 3, 7.

70. I have not been able to clarify whether the delegation that traveled to Texas was the same group that protested, or whether the group had received permission or managed to organize their trip through other means. Letter from "Two Chicanas,

MEChA—University of California in San Diego," July 11, 1972, printed in *La Raza* 1, no. 9 (September 1972): 3. The record indicates that a group from San Antonio (and possibly Los Angeles) went in response to Echeverría's invitation. The "Two Chicanas" explain that they arrived on June 26. It is unclear if there was coordination between these two delegations.

71. Letter from "Two Chicanas," 3. In a postscript, the authors explain why they have chosen to remain anonymous and encourage readers to get involved. Students arrested in 1968 were paroled in May 1971, shortly before the Halconazo.

72. Ibid.

73. José Revueltas, *México 68: Juventud y revolución* (Mexico City: Era, 1978).

74. "Chicanos y mexicanos están unidos por una herencia histórica común y por una justa lucha en contra de un opresor común. Estamos luchando en contra de un enemigo que arrebató una parte de nuestro Territorio Nacional y que condenó a un sector de nuestro pueblo a vivir bajo un Gobierno extranjero." Loose sheet photocopy, July 11, 1972, RSPA. It appears to be a copy of *El Grito del Norte*, but it is quite impossible to tell.

75. "Message to the Chicano Delegation Visiting Mexico City," printed in *La Raza* 1, no. 9 (September 1972): 3.

76. Ibid.

77. Ibid., 7.

78. David G. Gutiérrez, *Walls and Mirrors: Mexican Americans, Mexican Immigrants, and the Politics of Ethnicity* (Berkeley: University of California Press, 1995).

79. Mario Cantú, interview with Linda Fregoso, March 5, 1980, *Onda Latina: The Mexican American Experience*, University of Texas at Austin, http://www.laits .utexas.edu/onda_latina/program?sernum=000535499&theme=Social%20Issues.

80. Gutiérrez, *Making of a Chicano Militant*, 237.

81. *Caracol* (San Antonio) 2, no. 3, (November 1975), 6.

82. Members of LRUP would travel to Cuba and Libya in the 1970s.

83. Sylvia Orozco, "The View of Chicanos in Mexico," interview with Armando Gutiérrez, May 24, 1979, *Onda Latina: The Mexican American Experience*, University of Texas at Austin, http://www.laits.utexas.edu/onda_latina/program?sernum =000534549&term=.

84. Gutiérrez interview, quoted in Armando Navarro, *La Raza Unida Party: A Chicano Challenge to the U.S. Two-Party Dictatorship* (Philadelphia: Temple University Press, 2000), 255; Gutiérrez, *Making of a Chicano Militant*, 180–183.

85. María Rosa Garcia-Acevedo, "Return to Aztlan: Mexican Policy Design toward Chicanos," in *Chicanas/Chicanos at the Crossroads: Social, Economic, and Political Change*, ed. David R. Maciel and Isidro D. Ortiz (Tucson: University of Arizona Press, 1996), 139.

86. Gutiérrez, *Making of a Chicano Militant*, 238.

87. Ibid., 224.

88. Ibid., 232.

89. Oval Office, conversation no. 735-1.

90. Ibid.

CHAPTER 3: NUEVO TEATRO POPULAR ACROSS THE AMÉRICAS

1. Alma M. Martínez, "Un Continente, Una Cultura? The Political Dialectic for a United Chicano, Mexican and Latin American Popular/Political Theatre Front, Mexico City, 1974" (PhD diss., Stanford University, 2006), 248.

2. "La base fundamental de su actividad es: 'la comunicación entre los diferentes movimientos y agrupaciónes teatrales y culturales a fin de romper las barreras tradicionalmente impuestas entre nuestros países.'" "Frente Latino Americano de Trabajadores de la Cultura," *Comunicado* no. 1, August 1, 1972, Archivos Mascarones, Universidad Nahuatl Collection (hereafter AM, UNC). The document was signed by sixteen men and three women: Atehualpa del Cioppo (Uruguay); Augusto Boal (Brasil); Enrique Buenaventura (Colombia); Liber Forti (Bolivia); Milton Schinca (Uruguay); Jesús Franco and Germán Cobo (Colombia); Clemente Izaquirre (Venezuela); Mario Delgado and Luis Nieto (Perú); Maria Gignacco, Evandelina Carrieiro, and Oswauldo Grande (Argentina); Paulo Antillano (Chile); and Ilonka Vargas and Ulises Estrella (Ecuador).

3. Andre Gunder Frank, *Capitalism and Underdevelopment in Latin America: Historical Studies of Chile and Brazil* (New York: Monthly Review Press, 1967); Ramón Grosfoguel, "Developmentalism, Modernity, and Dependency Theory in Latin America," *Nepantla: Views from the South* 1, no. 2 (2000): 372.

4. "En el plano económico-político, el intensive saqueo de nuestras riquezas naturales combínanse con la permanencia del monocultivo, junto a la arcaica estructura latifundista, surge una industrialización con deformadas tendencies centradas en la constitución de grandes monopolios multinacionales y las dominantes inversions extranjeras. Cuanto más crece la renta nacional de nuestros países, mayor es la irregularidad en la distribución: la explotación del trabajo del pueblo aumenta cada vez más. Esta situación interea, en primer lugar, a las grandes corporaciónes extranjeras (en su mayor parte norteamericanas) y en sugundo lugar a las burguesías locales intermediaries, quienes para mejor cumplir su función, se constituyen en gobiernos sirvientes y dictaduras facistas." "Frente Latino Americano de Trabajadores de la Cultura," 1–2.

5. Por diez días, Manizales se convierte en un centro cultural del país y, en los que hace el teatro, de la America Latina. . . . Pero para los cientos de personas que vienen al festival, para los participantes y grandes sectores de la población, especialmente los trabajadores que abren los locales de sus sindicatos a las representaciones, sus casas a los 'artistas,' la fiesta tiene un significado profundo, algo que esta también en la esencia del teatro: Manizales es un lugar donde se hace posible, quizá tan solo por unos minutos, quizá por más, una communion: un encuentro." Victor Fuentes, "El Festival de Manisales," *Chicano Theatre Three* (Spring 1974): 45–48. Unless otherwise noted, the summary comes from this article. The quotation is from p. 45.

6. "Hay entre los grupos de América Latina gran interes por conocer nuestro Teatro, del que se tiene bastante referencia. Es de esperar que en los proximos festivales acuda una representación chicana." Ibid., 48.

7. Diana Taylor, *Theatre of Crisis: Drama and Politics in Latin America* (Lexington: University Press of Kentucky, 1991), 20–21.

8. Martínez, "Un Continente, Una Cultura?" chap. 3.

9. Victor Fuentes, "La creación colectiva del Teatro Experimental del Cali," in *Popular Theater for Social Change in Latin America*, ed. Gerardo Luzuriaga (Los Angeles: UCLA Latin American Center Publications, 1978), 347.

10. Paul Gilroy, *Small Acts: Thoughts on the Politics of Black Cultures* (London: Serpent's Tail Press, 1994).

11. Donald H. Frischman, *El Nuevo Teatro Popular en México* (Mexico City: Instituto Nacional de Belles Artes, 1990), 28 (emphasis in the original).

12. As Diana Taylor points out, for example, "Civic disobedience, resistance, citizenship, gender, ethnicity, and sexual identity [to which I'd add nation] are rehearsed and performed daily in the public sphere." Taylor, *The Archive and the Repertoire: Performing Cultural Memory in the Americas* (Durham, NC: Duke University Press, 2003), 3.

13. Taylor, *Theatre of Crisis*, 3, 8.

14. Ibid., 8.

15. Ibid., 6.

16. Alma Martínez's dissertation, "Un Continente, Una Cultura?," should be consulted by anyone interested in this time period. Though we cover much of the same ground, the primary differences between her work and mine are that I focus more on events in Mexico before and after the festival and examine the declassified intelligence documents, which not only demonstrate the extent to which movements were monitored and infiltrated but also provide access to a plethora of materials collected by the informants and/or agents. In addition, I focus on the founding of CLETA and Mexican theater history and rely on different interviews at different times. Martínez's work is invaluable, as she was a participant and is also a trained actress and deeply engaged scholar on Chicana/o theater.

17. Yolanda Broyles-González, *El Teatro Campesino: Theater in the Chicano Movement* (Austin: University of Texas Press, 1994), xiii.

18. Martínez, "Un Continente, Una Cultura?," 111.

19. Jack Hirschman, ed., *Art on the Line: Essays by Artists about the Point Where Their Art and Activism Intersect* (Willimantic, CT: Curbstone, 2002).

20. NTP emerges during the time period that Diana Taylor defines as "theatre of crisis." While NTP and theatre of crisis are not synonymous, as the former contextualizes the latter, both generated diverse voices, aesthetics, and creativity. Taylor points out that "theatre of crisis [and by extension NTP] is not, however, a cohesive and straightforward theater of the oppressed." Taylor, *Theatre of Crisis*, 8.

21. Taylor, *Theatre of Crisis*, 64–92.

22. Augusto Boal, *Hamlet and the Baker's Son: My Life in Theatre and Politics* (New York: Routledge, 2001).

23. Martínez, "Un Continente, Una Cultura?," 120.

24. See Taylor, *Theatre of Crisis*, 96–147.

25. Colin Chambers, ed., *The Continuum Companion to Twentieth Century Theatre* (New York: Continuum, 2006), 495.

26. Frischman, *El Nuevo Teatro Popular in México*; Judith A. Weiss, ed., *Latin American Popular Theatre: The First Five Centuries* (Albuquerque: University of New Mexico Press, 1993); Gerardo Luzuriaga, *Introducción a las teorías latinoamericanas del teatro* (Puebla: Universidad Autónoma de Puebla, 1990).

27. Martínez, "Un Continente, Una Cultura?," 19.

28. Roy Eric Xavier, "Politics and Chicano Culture: Luis Valdez and El Teatro Campesino, 1964–1990," in *Chicano Politics and Society in the Late Twentieth Century*, ed. David Montejano (Austin: University of Texas Press, 1999), 175–200.

29. Jorge A. Huerta, "The Influences of Latin American Theatre on Chicano Theater," in *Mexican American Theatre: Then and Now*, ed. Nicolás Kanellos (Houston: Arte Público Press, 1983), 70.

30. Martínez, "Un Continente, Una Cultura?," 22.

31. Ibid.

32. Yvonne Yarbro-Bejarano, "The Female Subject in Chicano Theater: Sexuality, 'Race,' and Class," in *Performing Feminisms: Feminist Critical Theory and Theatre*, ed. Sue-Ellen Case (Baltimore: Johns Hopkins University Press, 1990), 131.

33. Yolanda Broyles-González, *El Teatro Campesino: Theatre in the Chicano Movement* (Austin: University of Texas Press, 1994).

34. Ibid., 74.

35. See Luis Álvarez, *The Power of the Zoot: Youth Cultures of Resistance during World War II* (Berkeley: University of California Press), 2008.

36. Jorge A. Huerta, "En Torno," *Chicano Theatre One* (Spring 1973): 3.

37. For a full list of TENAZ *teatros* in 1974, see Martínez, "Un Continente, Una Cultura?" Appendix C, 279–282. See also Maureen Dolan, "Chicano Theatre in Transition: The Experience of El Teatro de la Esperanza" (PhD diss., University of Glasgow, 2012).

38. Broyles-Gonzalez, *El Teatro Campesino*, 75.

39. Huerta, "En Torno," 3.

40. See Broyles-Gonzáles, *El Teatro Campesino*, on this point.

41. Martínez, "Un Continente, Una Cultura?," 3.

42. Ibid.

43. Mariano Leyva Dominguez, interview by author, Ocotopec, Morelos, Mexico, November 16, 2004.

44. "Los Mascarones de México," in *Chicano Theatre Two: Special Festival Issue*, TENAZ (Summer 1973): 18.

45. Martha Ramirez-Oropeza, "Two Examples of Art Challenging Political Times: '10 de Junio' Teatro Mascarones and 'Danzas Indígenas,' Judith Baca Monument," paper for Humanities 390, Urban Zapatismo, Los Angeles, California State University–Northridge, February 2006, 1–2. Copy of document in author's possession.

46. Ibid., 2.

47. Alan Eladio Gómez, "'Nuestras vidas corren casi paralelas': Chicanos, Puerto Rican Independentistas, and the Prison Rebellion Years at Leavenworth, 1969–1972," in *Behind Bars: Latino/as and Prison in the United States*, ed. Suzanne Oboler (New York: Palgrave-Macmillan, 2008), 67–96.

48. "Nosotros a principio, no quieriamos ir a los Estado Unidos por lo que implicaba, por todo lo que implicaba que allá estaban los imperialistas y como todavia no nos dabamos cuenta que había una parte de nuestros hermanos de aquí de México, de todo México. Y despúes vimos la importancia que tenía el haber estado allá, no. Y al llegar a San Diego, a me empecé a dar cuenta de los símbolos, de la importancia que tiene las cuestiónes indígenas, si. Y desde allí empecé a interesarme más por la ... porque me interesaba una parte de que la cuestión del teatro y poesía que era lo que más manejabamos, me importaba la poesía indígena, pero digo allá fue en donde

recobré más de mi identidad, con los compañeros Chicanos. Lo más importante de todo esto fue que nos retroalimentábamos. O sea, nosotros no íbamos a competir con nadie, ni a criticar, o sea, fue un encuentro muy padre no. Que los dos aprendimos de muchas cosas." Fernando Hernández, interview by author, Ocotepec, Mexico, November 16, 2004.

49. Ernesto Reyes, interview by author, Mexico City, July 27, 1999.

50. "*Cabrón*," literally a male goat, implies "the best or strongest" within the context of hypermasculinity: relentless, an alpha male, tough, without remorse, and steeped in pride. "*Más*" means more. So the two together mean "the strongest."

51. Undated flyer, "Los Mascarones," Archivos Mascarones, Universidad Nahuatl, Ocotepec, Morelos, Mexico, hereafter cited as AM, UNA. The performers included Mariano Leyva, Lourdes Gay, Enrique Vallejo, Fernando Hernández, Eduardo Lopez, Rodrigo Galicia, Javier Luna, Isidrio Rico, Lourdes Gutierrez, Juan Gaytan, Guillermo Gonzalez, and Jose Manuel Galvan.

52. Flyer, "MEChA Sacramento State College," 1970, AM, UNA.

53. "Creemos que para el pueblo de México y el sector estudiantil que tener oportunidad de ver su teatro sera mur grato poder apreciar por primera vez sus expresiones dramáticas que hablar de todo un pueblo, cuyas raices son nuestros también." Letter from Jorge A. Villamil, Subdirector of the Preparatoria Popular, June 10, 1971, AM, UNA.

54. Letter from Guadalupe Saavedra to Mariano Leyva, November 4, 1971, AM, UNA.

55. Undated letter from Leonardo J. Maestas, Director of Master's Candidates, Colegio Jacinto Treviño, AM, UNA.

56. Letter from John Dauer AFSC, San Antonio, October 15, 1972, AM, UNA.

57. Memorandum on "Los Mascarones," US Department of Justice, FBI, San Antonio, Texas, September 24, 1971, MCP, Benson Latin American Collection, box 1, folder 5.

58. Reyes interview. On CLETA see Weiss, *Latin American Popular Theatre*; Frederico Campbell, "A 10 Años de CLETA, dos líneas: trabajor o no con el Estado," *Proceso* 370 (December 5, 1983): 58–59; and Huerta, "Influences of Latin American Theater," 64–77.

59. Ismael Colmenares, interview by author, Mexico City, November 24, 2004.

60. Hernández interview.

61. Liliana García Sánchez, *Judith Reyes, una mujer de canto revolucionario* (Mexico City: Redez, 2007); Judith Reyes, *La otra cara de la patria: Testimonio de una mujer revolucionaria, militante y canta-autora* (Mexico: Redez, 2007); Martín Martínez Rodríguez, *Cancionero Subversivo: José de Molina Petet de la Canción Libertaria* (Mexico City: Ediciones Tequiani, 2005). Molina composed a song, "Canto a Florencio Medrano," about the land takeover discussed in chapter 6.

62. Colmenares interview. The first members were Ismael "Mailo" Colmenares, José Martínez, José Ramón Castillo, and Armando Vélez. See Eric Zolov, *Refried Elvis: The Rise of the Mexican Counterculture* (Berkeley: University of California Press, 1999).

63. The "Letter from Lecumberri" proclaimed "unconditional solidarity" for the primarily female workforce on strike against the Grupo Industrial InterAmericano, a transnational firm based in Italy. The following people signed the letter as part of

CARM: Leopoldo Ayala, poet; Sayd Berumen, photographer; Carlos Bracho, actor; Susana Campos, painter; Salvador Carballeda, musician; Pilar Castañeda, painter; Guillermo Ceniceros, painter; Gerardo de la Torre, writer; Mario Díaz, painter; Jose Dugong, painter; Enrique Escalona, cinematographer; Miguel Flores, writer; Isabel Fraire, poet; Manuel Fuentes, sculptor; Bryon Galvez, painter; Jose Garcia, painter; Victor Gochez, painter; Ester Gonzalez, painter; José Hernández Delgadillo, painter; Jaime Hernández Lino, musician; Miguel Hernández Urban, painter; Marcos Huerta, painter; Efraín Hurmúndez, photographer; Ricardo Infante, painter; Carlos Jurado, painter; Humberto Kubli, painter; Jaime Labastida, poet; Jesus Martinez, engraver; Oscar Menéndez, cinematographer; Alfredo Meneses, painter; José de Molina, compositor; Beatriz Munch, actress; Carlos Nakatuni, painter; Thelma Nava, poet; Claudio Obregón, actor; Amparo Ochoa, singer; Carlos Olachea, painter; Armando Ortega, sculptor; Jorge Perezvega, painter; Héctor Polanco, architect; Javier Quiñones, musician; Fanney Rable, painter; Pataricia Rinón Gallardo, musician; Mario Salinas, musician; Carlos Sánchez Cuara, musician; Jaime Agosto Shelley, poet; René Villanueva, painter; Efrain Vivar, sculptor; Armoando Zaya, musician; "and many others." This project awaits a dutiful oral historian.

64. Mercedes Nieto, interview by author, Mexico City, November 6, 2004.

65. "Porque tratrabamos realmente de imponer un punto de vista de tú a tú con el varon, a ver. A mi, yo me acuerdo en muchas ocasiones en las asambleas me callaban, no? [looking at her partner, Abraham Vidales]. [imitating male] Ay, ya va a hablar esa, que no sé que. Pues lo siento, me dejan hablar porque me toca hablar porque yo había pedida la palabra. A lo mejor politicamente no estoy muy lograda todavia, en eso tiempo muchos menos. Nos faltaba estudia mucho. Ver las cosas. Quieriamos, sobre toda, aprender a vivir de otra forma. Inclusivo eso se daba tambíen en el foro. Cuando nosotras quieriamos manifestar algo, [imitating male] 'este, no, no, no, si no sabes de que estas hablando.' Aunque no sepa necesito hablarlo porque aquí es donde me esta molestando este asunto y necesitamos hablarlo. A lo mejor todavía no me sé echar los rollos que ustedes echan, ni me interesa. [imitating voice again] 'Pero hay cuestíones que se deben manejar, que estamos viendo que ustedes van por el terreno equivocado. Por allí no es la situacíon. Y no estan viendo esta e otra opción. No esta viendo esta e otra consecuencía.' Y era difícil, era muy difícil todavia de tartar de dar marcha atras sobre situacíones." Nieto interview.

66. Ching-In Chen, Jai Dulani, and Leah Lakshmi Piepzna-Samarasinha, eds., *The Revolution Starts at Home: Confronting Intimate Violence within Activist Communities* (New York: South End Press, 2011).

67. "Manifesto del Teatro Nacional de Aztlán," El Cuarto Festival de Teatro Chicanos en San Jose, California, June 24, 1973, published on the inside cover of *Chicano Teatro Three* (Spring 1974).

68. Ibid.

69. Quoted in Martínez, "Un Continente, Una Cultura?," 54.

70. "El nombre que se iba a llevar la organización, a mi me salió, se me occurio, dijé yo, 1848 . . . son una tenacidad, y entonces en tenaz veia yo TEatro NAcional de Aztlán, TENAZ, le dijé a Luis [Valdez], TENAZ, el tiene que llevar TENAZ, porque estedes han sido tenazes, porque han aguantado y han tenido una tenacidad de Huitzilopochtli." Leyva Dominguez interview. Huitzilopochtli is the Aztec god of war, "blue hummingbird on the left," and is represented by the sun.

71. Mariano Leyva and Fernando Hernández interviews.

72. Interview with Mariano Leyva cited in Martínez, "Un Continente, Una Cultura?," 59.

73. "Los Mascarones ya son muy conocidos por toda la Chicanada y han sido una verdadera inspiración para nuestra gente aqui." Betita Martinez, *El Grito del Norte* (Fariview/Espanola, N.M.), June 12, 1972, AM, UNA.

74. Ibid. "This is a rebirth; from the old comes the new. Theater is a mirror and spirit of the movement. In the mirror of Tezcatlipoca [Aztec deity] that illuminates the evil we are surrounded by; it is in the spirit of Quetzalcoatl that we find the goodness and hope of la Raza. Theater is the voice of the barrios, of the community, of those from below, the humble-ones, the rasquachis."

75. "Los Trabajadores del TENAZ are committed to a way of Life/Struggle ayudandole a la gente a entender el porque de sus problemas sociales individuales and to search for solutions. Que sea nuestro Teatro el arco iris humano: let it create Teatro para . . . niños, jovenes, viejos, mujeres, estudiantes, obreros, campesinos y hasta para los tapados. Debe nutrirse de las raices culturales de nuestros antepasados para sembrar semillas de liberacion en el presente y para cosechar en el futuro la Victoria de nuestros pueblos." Ibid.

76. "Manifesto del Teatro Nacional de Aztlán," El Cuarto Festival de Teatro Chicanos en San Jose, California, June 24, 1973, published on the inside cover of *Chicano Teatro Three* (Spring 1974).

77. Martínez, "Un Continente, Una Cultura?," 37. For a description of his first meeting with Segura, see Alejandro Murguía, *The Medicine of Memory: A Mexica Clan in California* (Austin: University of Texas Press, 2010), 128–129.

78. Martínez, "Un Continente, Una Cultura?," 39. See also Gustavo Segade, *Chicano indigenismo: Alurista and Miguel Meléndez M* (n.p., 1975); Sheila Marie Contreras, *Blood Lines: Myth, Indigenism, and Chicana/o Literature* (Austin: University of Texas Press, 2008).

79. Martínez, "Un Continente, Una Cultura?," 41.

80. Obituary, *Guadalupe Cultural Center Newsletter*, San Antonio, October 1997.

81. Martínez, "Un Continente, Una Cultura?," 44. See also Andrés Segura, "The Path of Quetzalcoatl," Deganawidah-Quetzalcoatl University, Davis, California, 1977, http://www.youtube.com/watch?v=GwXMc2VP9y8; Murguía, *Medicine of Memory*.

82. Martínez, "Un Continente, Una Cultura?," 37.

83. Gaye Theresa Johnson, *Spaces of Conflict, Sounds of Solidarity: Music, Race, and Spatial Entitlement in Los Angeles* (Berkeley: University of California Press, 2013), xii.

84. I want to be careful not to impose false unities through the concept of NTP. It helps to explain as much as it might obscure. Taylor argues, "In Latin America, theatre can more effectively undermine oppressive forces than can other art forms . . . theatre is live; live actors affect live audiences in unforeseeable ways; each performance would have to be policed in order to ensure that actors did not deliver a line or make a gesture that would communicate a politically prohibited message to its audience." Taylor, *Theatre of Crisis*, 5.

85. Jill Dolan, *Utopia in Performance: Finding Hope at the Theater* (Ann Arbor: University of Michigan Press, 2005).

CHAPTER 4: "SOMOS UNO PORQUE AMÉRICA ES UNA"

1. Annette Oropeza, interview by Alicia Muñoz, Oakland, California, October 23, 1998, cited in Alicia Muñoz Cortes, "The Struggle of the Mujeres to Liberate Olga Talamante, a Political Prisoner" (PhD diss., San Jose State University, 1999), 106.

2. Mercedes Nieto, interview by author, Mexico City, November 6, 2004.

3. Jaime Pensado, *Rebel Mexico: Student Unrest and Authoritarian Political Culture during the Long Sixties* (Stanford, CA: Stanford University Press, 2013).

4. Greg Grandin, *Empire's Workshop: Latin America, the United States, and the Rise of the New Imperialism* (New York: Metropolitan Books), 2006.

5. Vicki Ruiz, *From Out of the Shadows: Mexican Women in Twentieth-Century America* (Oxford, UK: Oxford University Press, 2008).

6. María Acosta, interview by Bill Berkowitz, October 1976, Olga Talamante Defense Committee Interview Collection, quoted in Muñoz Cortes, "Struggle of the Mujeres," 105.

7. "Junta del Comité Organizador de TENAZ (CLETA)," March 12, 1974, loose sheet; Memorandum from TENAZ Organizing Committee in Mexico to TENAZ Central Organizing Committee, Regional Representatives, Mexico City, March 19, 1974, Archivos Mascarones, Universidad Nahuatl, Ocotopec, Morelos, Mexico, hereafter cited as AM, UNA. On March 21 Maria del Carmen Nieva Lopez, an anthropology professor, was able to use her contacts to secure Teotihuacán, a fortuitous event given the difficulties in establishing communication with the director of the Anthropology Museum.

8. "Junta del Comité Organizador de TENAZ (CLETA)," March 12, 1974, AM, UNA.

9. Letter from L. Espinoza, October 9, 1973, included in the notes from the TENAZ Final Coordinating Committee meeting, copy in author's possession.

10. "Festival '74 Organizing Committee Report," undated loose sheet, two pages, AM, UNA.

11. "Acta de la reunión de octubre 9 de 1973," Oficina del TENAZ-CLETA-FLATC, two pages, AM, UNA.

12. Letter from O. Gutierrez de Velasco P., Jefe del Departamento de Tráfico de Pasajeros, Ferrocarriles Nacionales de México to Mariano Leyva, June 13, 1974, AM, UNA.

13. Alma M. Martínez, "Un Continente, Una Cultura? The Political Dialectic for a United Chicano, Mexican and Latin American Popular/Political Theatre Front, Mexico City, 1974" (PhD diss., Stanford University, 2006), 167.

14. Ibid., 168.

15. O. Gutierrez de Velasco P. to Mariano Leyva, June 13, 1974; Carta de J. M. Salgado, Superintendente de Tráfico, Ferrocarril Sonora Baja California, S.A. de C.V. to Sr. Luis P. Bravo C., Jefe de Estación, Mexicali, B.C., June 19, 1974, copy in author's possession.

16. Carta de La Comision para la Alimentación del V Festival de los Teatros Chicanos 1er Encuentro Latinamericano to C. Lic. Jorde de la Vega Dominguez, Director General de CONASUPO, undated, copy in author's possession.

17. Lourdes Pérez Gay y Silvia Sandoval de la La Comisión para la Alimentación del V Festival de los Teatros Chicanos 1er Encuentro Latinamericano to Sr. Abel

234 NOTES TO PAGES 99-104

Boza, Administrador de la Unidad Tlatelolco, February 26, 1974, copy in author's possession.

18. "Programa de alimentación del V Festival de los Chicanos 1er Encuentro Latinoamericano," de La Comision para la Alimentación del V Festival de los Teatros Chicanos 1er Encuentro Latinamericano, undated loose sheet.

19. "Será un momento histórico para México y para el Chicano quien está en la búsqueda de sus raíces, y de lo universal dentro de lo específico." Katia Pana, Counseling Psychologist and Lecturer, Merrill College, University of California-Santa Barbara, to CLETA-UNAM, February 25, 1974, AM, UNA.

20. "Que para uds. [CLETA] y para Latino America, este encuentro de teatros de un triunfo más y un buen paso para una union mas profunda . . ." Mario Matollana, "El Quetzal" Movimiento Artístico del Pueblo, San Jose, California, to "Estimados Compañeros," April 11, 1974, AM, UNA.

21. "Como organizacion cultural educativa, pensamos que este evento tendra importancia para nuestra Raza aqui en Aztlan en que se confrontaran? Con sus raices culturales/historicas." Antonio Perales, Director, Artistas del Centro Cultural de la Gente, San Jose, California, to CLETA-UNAM, April 17, 1974, AM, UNA.

22. "La capital de México, la tierra de nuestras raizes [sic], para compartir con el pueblo de México el mensaje de unidad y amor que todos los carnales y carnalas Chicanos trairan en sus corazones." Luis Valdez, Director of El Centro Campesino Cultural, San Juan Bautista, California, to CLETA-UNAM, May 1, 1974, AM, UNA.

23. Mariano Leyva Dominguez, interview by author, Ocotopec, Morelos, Mexico, November 16, 2004.

24. Martínez, "Un Continente, Una Cultura?," 160.

25. TENAZ, "El Quinto Festival de los Teatros Chicanos," Chicano Theatre Three (Spring 1974): 3.

26. Ibid., 4.

27. Ibid., 5.

28. Ibid.

29. Yolanda Broyles-González, El Teatro Campesino: Theater in the Chicano Movement (Austin: University of Texas Press, 1994), 80.

30. Ibid., 6.

31. The CCH system was a product of the university movement of 1968. Conceived by Pablo Gonzalez Cassanova and put into action by coalitions of students, university professors, and social activists, the original idea was to create eleven high school campuses across Mexico City with open curriculums that were to be individually designed by the students themselves. A state version of the Prepa Populares (Popular High Schools), they became a threat to the regime as students were learning a career while also receiving preparation in political analysis. The original plan to build eleven schools was halted at five. See Ismael "Mailo" Colmenares, interview by author, Mexico City, November 14, 2004. Colmenares is currently the coordinator of culture for all the CCH schools in Mexico City.

32. Leyva Dominguez interview; Enrique Cisneros, interview by author, Mexico City, November 17, 2004.

33. "Seven page report," March 7, 1974, IPS, folder 1887, box 6520, Archivo Histórico de la Nación, Mexico City, hereafter cited as AGN. According to the newspaper Excelsior, there were two thousand participants. Excelsior, March 8, 1974, p. 17. Per-

haps the 250 cited in the surveillance report referred to the number of participants affiliated with CLETA that were part of the larger demonstration.

34. IPS, folder 1887, box 6520, AGN.

35. Cesar del Angel Fuentes, Veracruz, to Guillermo Bonfil Batalla, Mexico City, May 6, 1974, photocopy in author's possession.

36. Fernando Hernández, interview by author, Ocotepec, Mexico, November 16, 2004; Carlos Tello, *La Política Económica en México, 1970–1976* (Mexico City: Siglo XXI, 1979); Américo Saldívar, *Ideología y política del estado mexicano, 1970–1976* (Mexico City: Siglo XXI, 1980); Carlos Bazdresch and Santiago Levy, "Populism and Economic Policy in Mexico, 1970–1982," in *The Macroeconomics of Populism in Latin America*, ed. Rudiger Dornbusch and Sebastian Edwards (Chicago: University of Chicago Press, 1991), 223–262.

37. "La Presidencia apoya lo más posible con la única condición de que los Chicanos se lleven una Buena impression del gobierno que dirige el nacionalista Luis Echeverría." Quoted in Enrique Cisneros, *Si me permiten actuar* (Mexico City: CLETA, n.d.), 67.

38. Leyva Dominguez interview.

39. Cisneros interview.

40. Cisneros, *Si me permiten actuar;* Cisneros interview; Hernández interview. According to Hernández, the money was for land improvements.

41. Martínez, "Un Continente, Una Cultura?," 169. Martínez is summarizing an interview with Eduardo Gómez, "a member of ETC from 1971–1973 and Grupo Los Mascarones from 1973–1975."

42. "¿Tú también vienes a marearnos con eso de Quetzalcoatl y la Virgen de Guadalupe?" Cisneros, *Si me permiten actuar*, 66.

43. "Los Chicanos son como niños a quienes sería injusto quitarles la vision romántica del México prehispánico; sería como despojarlos de la única paleta que tienen." Ibid.

44. "Agudizó las contradicciones internas de CLETA, que se habia originado por el coqueteo que Mariano Leyva tenía con el naciente Partido Socialista de los Trabajadores (the PST), relación que se tradujo en manipuleos y acciones que contravenían los lineamientos internos de nuestra organización." Ibid.

45. Ibid., 67.

46. We are one because America is one.

47. Martínez, "Un Continente, Una Cultura?," 167.

48. Ibid.

49. "Quinto Festival de los Teatros Chicanos y I Encuentro Latinoamericano," DFS, June 22, 1974, box 2713, AGN. Surveillance photographs from the IPS—some thirty in number—bear witness to what was a festive scene.

50. "In one example, when the compañeros arrived by train, los Chicanos, they (Los Mascarones) hid the flags made by CLETA themselves, for the 'horrible crime of being red,' the same as the PST flags, and for them [CLETA] that was the clear and undeniable proof of the supposed manipulation that they blamed on Los Mascarones (even though Los Mascarones had nothing to do with the flag situation." Cisneros, *Si me permiten actuar*, 67.

51. "Poniendo en peligro, irresponsablemente la realización del Festival. Otro hecho salta a la vista: la ignorancia y falta de preparación política de estos 'activistas'

manejados provocativamente, al pasar por alto que en México, los llamados presos politicos, actualmente, no solo son de izquierda, sino también . . . de derecha." Ibid.

52. "Al iniciarse el primer día del Festival bloqueraon (Los Mascarones) a la base de CLETA, ocultándoles la fecha de la llegada del primer contingende de compañeros chicanos a la estación de Buenavista de Ferrocarriles, reservándose el 'derecho de saberlo.' Sin embargo sí lo comunican a la dirección de PST para que, ante la prensa, aparezca dicho partido como organizador del Festival. Pero también ese día se inicia la Guerra abierta [my emphasis], la base de CLETA descubre la deshonesta acción de 'Los Mascarones' y comienza por desaparecer cientos de banderas rojas símbolo del sucio partido, cerrando además el Foro Isabelino." "Lo que es y lo que parece ser la expulsion de Mascarones," *Los Chidos* 34–36, cited in Cisneros, *Si me permiten actuar*, 69.

53. *La noche triste*, from the Spanish settler colonial perspective, refers to the defeat of the Spanish conquistador Hernan Cortés by Aztec warriors on June 30, 1520, at Tenochtitlán.

54. Teresa González, "Quinto Festival de los Teatros Chicanos/Primer Encuentro Latinoamericano," *Caracol* 1 (September 1974): 4.

55. This summary is from Martínez, "Un Continente, Una Cultura?," 175–176.

56. Ibid., 178. Martínez is citing an interview with Gómez.

57. "Fifth Festival of the Chicano Theatres, First Encounter of Latin American Theatres," undated, CLETA-TENAZ Organizing Committee, AM, UNA. I provide the English version of this document with the exception of a few key words and phrases that lose their original meaning in translation. The original documents are in English and Spanish, and not in the language-switching format that I am using.

58. Photocopy in author's possession. RIUS had previously engaged Chicanos in the United States in 1970 when a copy of *Los Agachados* was sent to Chicano *pintos* at Leavenworth Prison by Mario Cantú—who had recently been released. Members of CORA (Chicanos Organizados Revolucionarios de Aztlán), a group of politicized *pintos* who organized study groups, published a newspaper and corralled the political unrest at the prison during that time (as part of a larger wave of prison rebellions in the United States) into organized resistance, responded to the cartoon by drawing and narrating their own strip, with characters culled from the *pintos* at Leavenworth.

59. "V Festival de Teatros Chicanos y I Encuentro Latinoamericano," DFS, June 24, 1974, box 2713, AGN.

60. Quoted in Juan González, "Quinto Festival Chicano/Primer Encuentro Latinoamericano," *El Tecolote* 4, no. 8 (August 1974): 35.

61. "V Festival de Teatros Chicanos y I Encuentro Latinoamericano," DFS, June 24, 1974, box 2713, AGN.

62. "Festival Schedule," loose sheets in AM, UNA.

63. Ibid.

64. Theodore Shank, "A Return to Mayan and Aztec Roots," *Drama Review* 18 (1974): 66.

65. González, *Caracol*, 4.

66. Ibid., 4.

67. "V Festival de Teatros Chicanos y I Encuentro Latinoamericano," DFS, June 24, 1974, box 2713, AGN; "Festival Schedule."

68. Ibid. See also Juan Bruce-Novoa and C. May Gamboa, "Tiempovillo: Para-

guayan Experimental Theatre," *Latin American Theatre Review* 8, no. 2 (Spring 1975): 75–83.

69. "V Festival de Teatros Chicanos y I Encuentro Latinoamericano," DFS, June 24, 1974, box 2713, AGN.

70. Yvonne Yarbro-Bejarano, "The Female Subject in Chicano Theater: Sexuality, 'Race,' and Class," in *Performing Feminisms: Feminist Critical Theory and Theatre*, ed. Sue-Ellen Case (Baltimore: Johns Hopkins University Press, 1990), 139.

71. "V Festival de los Teatros Chicanos y I Encuentro Latinoamericano," DFS, June 26, 1974, box 2712, AGN; "Hoy tuvó lugar la obra," IPS, June 28, 1974, folder 73, box 6520, AGN.

72. "V Festival de los Teatros Chicanos y I Encuentro Latinoamericano," DFS, June 28, 1974, box 2712, AGN; "Hoy en el Teatro 'Jorge Negrete,'" IPS, June 29, 1974, folder 73, box 6520, AGN.

73. "V Festival de los Teatros Chicanos y I Encuentro Latinoamericano," DFS June 30, 1974, box 2712, AGN.

74. Ibid.

75. "V Festival de los Teatros Chicanos y I Encuentro Latinoamericano," DFS, July 3, 1974, box 2710, AGN; "V Festival de los Teatros Chicanos y I Encuentro Latinoamericano," IPS, July 4, 1974, box 2710, AGN.

76. "V Festival de los Teatros Chicanos y I Encuentro Latinoamericano," DFS, July 4, 1974, box 2710, AGN.

77. Patricia Cabrera López, *Pensamiento, cultura y literatura en América Latina* (Mexico City: UNAM, 2004), 291.

78. Literally "Alarm!" *Alarma* is a popular tabloid newspaper with consistent images of graphic violence, accidents, murders, and sensationalized news.

79. "Las señoras fufurufas y seudorevolucionarias de Amnistía Internaciónal" and "Varios de los integrantes de Amnistía salieron de la sala vomitando," Cisneros, *Si me permiten actuar*, 58.

80. Ibid., 59.

81. "Influyeron hondamente al resto de los integrantes de la organización." Ibid.

82. "Los centros de educación les enseñan a los alumnus los como respetar a la Bandera Nacional, para que después vean como es pisoteada junto con el pueblo por parte de las autoridades." "El Grupo 'Zopilote' de San Luis," IPS, July 1, 1974, folder 73, box 6520, AGN; "El Grupo de Teatro Chicano Paraguay," IPS, July 9, 1974, folder 73, box 6520, AGN; "El Grupo 'Triangulo' de Teatro Chicano de Colombia," IPS, July 10, 1974, folder 73, box 6520, AGN.

83. "Recalcando que [the bone] da poder e impunidad y al finalizar, el que lo recoge, se suicida." "V Festival de los Teatros Chicanos y I Encuentro Latinoamericano," DFS, June 30, 1974, box 2712, AGN.

84. "V Festival de los Teatros Chicanos y I Encuentro Latinoamericano," DFS, June 28, 1974, box 2712, AGN.

85. "V Festival de los Teatros Chicanos y I Encuentro Latinoamericano," DFS, June 30, 1974, box 2712, AGN. The children's theater group Nopalera from CLETA-UNAM postponed their performance in order to give the Vendedores Ambulantes the opportunity to perform.

86. "V Festival de los Teatros Chicanos y I Encuentro Latinoamericano," DFS,

June 30, 1974, box 2712, AGN; "Hoy, en la continuación," IPS, July 30, 1974, folder 73, box 6520, AGN.

87. "Mientras Augusto Boal se alucinó, otros afirmaban que eso no era teatro." Cisneros, *Si me permiten actuar*, 77.

88. "Disseminate culture at the popular level, which is why the forum was originally created." Caja 1887/73/6520, IPS, AGN.

89. Juan González, "Quinto Festival Chicano/Primer Encuentro Latinoamericano," 31.

90. María Josefina Saldaña-Portillo, *The Revolutionary Imagination in the Americas and the Age of Development* (Durham, NC: Duke University Press, 2003).

91. I will briefly describe the discussions. For a more detailed account of all the plays, see Martínez, "Un Continente, Una Cultura?"

92. I have re-created the following section from recordings of the discussions kept in the Mascarones archive in Cuernavaca, Mexico. Of the seventeen tapes, I have only been able to access, identify, and log five. These discussions are taken primarily from tape seventeen.

93. Martínez, "Un Continente, Una Cultura?," 193. See also Nicolás Kanellos, *Hispanic Literature of the United States: A Comprehensive Reference* (Westport, CT: Greenwood, 2003), 271.

94. Martínez, "Un Continente, Una Cultura?," 202–203.

95. Ibid., 205.

96. Ibid.

97. Ibid.

98. Ibid., 210.

99. Cisneros, *Si me permiten actuar*, 73–74.

100. "Demasiado local, no visualizando en forma conjunta los problemas de toda la raza hispanoamericana." "Sintesis," IPS, July 1, 1974, box 2710, AGN, 21; "Panorama General," DFS, July 1, 1974, box 2710.

101. Quoted in Martínez, "Un Continente, Una Cultura?," 213.

102. Ibid., 216.

103. "Entonces, viene la dictadura facista y los compañeros de este teatro Chileno estan muertos, estan presos, o estan perseguidos. Aqui viene un problema: En el Peru hay el peligro del facismo, en el Brazil el facismo, y en mi país Ecuador, hay el peligro del facismo. Entonces, la gente de teatro no es solamente gente de teatro, tiene que seleccionar su acción, tiene que seleccionar sus posibilidades de decir las cosas en el poco tiempo que nos queda. De allí compañeros, que el teatro no es un fin. El teatro no es el ultimo ojectivo que nosotros podemos obtener, sino en medio de nuestro proceso de nuestra acción como hombres politicos, el teatro es una manera, es precisamente esa manera de que esa verdad se transmita. Cúal verdad? La verdad del pueblo." Ulises Estrella, audio recording, 1974, AM, UNA.

104. Unidentified Chicano, audio recording 17, Mexico City, 1974, AM, UNA.

105. Ibid.

106. Ibid.

107. Ibid.

108. Quoted in Martínez, "Un Continente, Una Cultura?," 217.

109. Ibid.

110. Ibid., 223.

111. Mariano Leyva, audio recording 17, Mexico City, 1974, AM, UNA.

112. "Aunque con la ideología equivocada, es posible hacer un arte extaordinario." Ibid.

113. "Rompimiento total con la religion y las tradiciónes, cosa que él y muchos que pensaban igual no estaban dispuestos a hacerlo." "Sintesis," IPS, July 1, 1974, box 2710, AGN, 22; "Panorama General," DFS, July 1, 1974, box 2710, AGN.

114. Martínez, "Un Continente, Una Cultura?," 225.

115. Ibid. See also Susana D. Castillo, "Festivales De Teatro En América," Latin American Theater Review 8, no. 1 (1974): 75–78.

116. Teresa González, Caracol (San Antonio), 4. See also María Teresa Marrero, "From El Teatro Campesino to the Gay 1990s: Transformations and Fragments in the Evolution in Chicana/O Latina/O Theater and Performance," in The State of Latino Theater in the United States, ed. Luis Ramos-García (New York: Routledge, 2002), 39–66.

117. "Allí habria que ver si nos unimos para desunirnos, ¿ó que pasó? Porque allí fue en un rompimiento entre la cuestíon de las gentes, de los radicales de América del Sur que tenian cementada la cuestíon del marxismo-leninismo, y no alcanzaron a entender porque Luis Valdez hacia estas cuestíones religiosas." Hernández interview.

118. Broyles-González, El Teatro Campesino, 120.

119. Juan Bruce-Novoa and C. May Gamboa, "El Quinto Festival de Teatros," De Colores 2, no. 2 (1975).

120. Luis Valdez, interview by Haldun Morgan, Radio Aguascalientes Archives, September 2002, digital recording in author's possession.

121. Unidentified Chicano, audio recording 17, AM, UNA.

122. "En el Palacio de Bellas Artes," IPS, July 5, 1974, folder 73, box 6520, AGN. Given the history between CLETA and actors from the INBA, this rebuttal is understandable. Of course space may have been needed for a graduation, but it was needed for an international theater festival as well.

123. Letter from Cesar del Angel Fuentes to Guillermo Bonfil Batalla, Mexico City, May 6, 1974, AM, UNA.

124. González, Caracol (San Antonio), 5.

125. Ibid.

126. Ibid., 6.

127. IPS, June 30, 1974, folder 1887, box 6510, AGN.

128. Cisneros interview.

129. Martínez, "Un Continente, Una Cultura?," 187.

130. "Los artistas de teatro, plástica y cine que están cambiando la función social del arte al extenderlo a públicos nuevos, que buscan canales de comunicación no convencionales y abren sus obras a la participación de los espectadores." Néstor García Canclini, Arte popular y sociedad en América Latina (Mexico City: Grijalbo, 1977), 9.

131. Ibid., 10.

132. See Alan Knight, "Empire, Hegemony and Globalization in the Americas," NACLA Report on the Americas 39, no. 2 (September-October 2005): 8–12; Gilbert M. Joseph and Daniela Spenser, In from the Cold: Latin America's New Encounter with the Cold War (Durham, NC: Duke University Press, 2011).

133. Martínez, "Un Continente, Una Cultura?," 160.

134. Muñoz Cortes, "Struggle of the *Mujeres*."

135. Oropeza interview.

136. "El Festival fue hermoso. . . . Por la primera vez en la historiá del teatro de nuestro América se reunían en un mismo evento los grupos de E.E.U.U. con los del sur del Río Bravo. Todos reunidos trabajando juntos. Fueron dos semanas de intensa actividad, día y noche, noche y día había teatro, discusiones políticas, estéticas, convivencias, actos de amor; día y noche. . . . Antes hubo en México otros eventos latinoamericanos y nos dejaron enseñanzas. Después han venido grupos de los que también hemos aprendido, pero este Festival fue distinto, fue nuestro, de los teatreros de todo el continente." Cisneros, *Si me permiten actuar*, 70.

137. Valdez interview.

138. "El Primer Encuentro Latinoamericano y El Quinto Festival de Teatros Chicanos para intentar a abrazar a toda latinoamerica y parte de los estados unidos en un festival que aglutada a todas las corrientes de expresión de teatro latinoamericano independiente . . . y todos nos consideramos 'que locos,' como un grupito, unos cuantos la veintena de locos intentaron organizar un festival de este envergatura. Sin embargo, se pudo llevar acabo—verdad. Eran propuestas locas que encontraron oidos y accíon. Era una situación de dejar que todo ocuriera porque todos teniamos la intención de hacer las cosas, de llevarlos acabo. En este momento no nos cuestionamos si era politicamente corecto, sabiamos que era necesario hacerlo, dejar testimonio de las cosas que quieriamos manifestar en su momento y lo haciamos. En realidad, la línea política no nos interesaba de todo, por eso fue que logramos conjuntar a tantas corrientes de pensamiento, por eso fue que tanta gente se unío a nosotros en un momento dado." Nieto interview.

139. Kanellos, *Hispanic Literature of the United States*, 271.

140. Tomas Ybarra-Frausto, "The Chicano Movement and the Emergence of a Chicano Poetic Consciousness," *New Scholar* 6 (1977): 87; Ybarra-Frausto, "The Chicano Movement/The Movement of Chicano Art," in *Exhibiting Cultures: The Poetics and Politics of Museum Display*, ed. Ivan Karp and Steven Lavine (Washington, DC: Smithsonian Institution Press, 1993), 87.

141. Robin D. G. Kelley, *Freedom Dreams: The Black Radical Imagination* (Boston: Beacon, 2002), ix.

142. For a more extensive discussion of social majorities, see Gustavo Esteva and Madhu Prakash, *Grassroots Postmodernism: Remaking the Soils of Culture* (London: Zed Books, 1998), 18.

143. Avery Gordon, *Ghostly Matters: Haunting and the Sociological Imagination* (Minneapolis: University of Minnesota Press, 1996).

144. Martínez, "Un Continente, Una Cultura?," 191.

145. Ernest Reyes, interview by author, Mexico City, July 27, 1999.

146. Cisneros, *Si me permiten actuar*, 79.

147. "Nosotras [the women] nos opusimos desdel principio a la expulsíon de los grupos del foro. Fíjate que yo siento que eso fue una de las cuestiones que desgregaron y fue producto de las gentes infiltradas dentro del movimiento. La separacíon de los grupos, el cuestionamiento político de los grupos para que finalmente se fueron cada uno yendo por su propio camino. Que lo que hizó fue nada más dispersarlos, olarizarlos, enfrentarlos y eliminar así el movimiento. Nosotras siempre nos opusimos a estas expulsíons." Nieto interview, 2004.

148. Cisneros, *Si me permiten actuar*, 82.

149. Martínez, "Un Continente, Una Cultura?," 188.

150. Diana Taylor, *The Archive and the Repertoire: Performing Cultural Memory in the Americas* (Durham, NC: Duke University Press, 2003), 20.

151. Chon Noriega, introductory note, "Self-Help Graphics: Tomás Benitez talks to Harry Gamboa Jr.," in *The Sons and Daughters of Los: Culture and Community in L.A.*, ed. David James (Philadelphia: Temple University Press, 2003), 196.

152. Alicia Schmidt-Camacho, *Migrant Imaginaries: Latino Cultural Politics in the U.S.-Mexico Borderlands* (New York: New York University Press, 2008), 26.

CHAPTER 5: "POR LA REUNIFICACIÓN DE LOS PUEBLOS LIBRES DE AMÉRICA EN SU LUCHA POR EL SOCIALISMO"

1. Alfredo de la Torre, "Entrevista con Mario Cantú," *Caracol* 5, no. 4 (December 1978): 16.

2. Bill Towery, "Tortured in Mexico," *San Antonio Light*, October 17, 1975; "Press Release," Ramón Chacón Defense Committee, n.d., Raúl Salinas Personal Archives (hereafter cited as RSPA).

3. Ramón Tijerina, telephone interview by author, Harlingen, TX, February 25, 2015. Though several different accounts of the event exist, the general story goes that near Brownsville, Texas, in 1910, Jacinto Treviño killed a Texas Ranger and another man (his cousin—perhaps at the time of the beating or in a different incident) who together had savagely beaten Treviño's half brother. A hero to the Mexican community and a bandit to the Anglo community, Treviño was associated with a political genealogy that scared the local white residents. A popular *corrido* about Treviño's life continues to tell this story. Victor Guerra-Garza, ed., *HOJAS: A Chicano Journal of Education* (Austin: Juárez-Lincoln University, 1976). Vertical Files, Dolph Briscoe Center for American History, University of Texas at Austin.

4. "Descubren el Laredo Madriguera de la AIT," *El Norte*, October 5, 1975.

5. As Ben Olguín explains, *la pinta* is the Chicana/o vernacular [*caló*] Spanish term for prison—a truncated alliterative abbreviation of *penitencia*, the Spanish word for "penitentiary." *Pinto* is the masculine *caló* noun identifying a male prisoner. See Olguín, *La Pinta: Chicana/o Prisoner Literature, Culture, and Politics* (Austin: University of Texas Press, 2010), 23–32; quote is from p. 23.

6. Jalil Muntaqim, "On the Black Liberation Army," in *We Are Our Own Liberators: Selected Prison Writings* (Montreal: Abraham Guillen Press, 2003): 29–42; Daniel Burton-Rose, *Guerrilla USA: The George Jackson Brigade and the Anticapitalist Underground of the 1970s* (Berkeley: University of California Press, 2010); Oscar López Rivera, "A Century of Colonialism: One Hundred Years of Puerto Rican Resistance," in *Warfare in the American Homeland: Policing and Prison in a Penal Democracy*, ed. Joy James (Durham, NC: Duke University Press, 2007), 161–196; Dan Berger, *Outlaws of America: The Weather Underground and the Politics of Solidarity* (Oakland, CA: AK Press, 2006); Jeremy Varon, *Bringing the War Home: The Weather Underground, the Red Army Faction, and Revolutionary Violence in the 1960s and 1970s* (Berkeley: University of California Press, 2004).

7. Cindy Katz, "On the Grounds of Globalization: A Topography for Feminist Political Engagement," *Signs* 26, no. 4 (Summer 2001): 1229.

8. David Montejano, *Quixote's Soldiers: A Local History of the Chicano Movement, 1966–1981* (Austin: University of Texas Press, 2010), 145–148.

9. Memorandum on "Los Mascarones," US Department of Justice, FBI, San Antonio, September 24, 1971, MCP, Benson Latin American Collection, University of Texas at Austin, box 1, folder 5, hereafter cited as BLAC.

10. Richard R. Flores, *Remembering the Alamo: Memory, Modernity, and the Master Symbol* (Austin: University of Texas Press, 2002).

11. Juan Gómez Quiñones, *Sembradores: Ricardo Flores Magón y El Partido Liberal Mexicano: A Eulogy and Critique* (Monograph no. 5, Chicano Studies Center Publications, University of California, Los Angeles, 1973); Chaz Bufe and Mitchell Cowen Verter, eds., *Dreams of Freedom: A Ricardo Flores Magón Reader* (Oakland, CA: AK Press, 2006); Claudio Lomnitz, *The Return of Comrade Ricardo Flores Magón* (New York: Zone Books, 2014).

12. Thanks to Manolo Callahan for pointing out this case.

13. Christina Heatherton, "University of Radicalism: Ricardo Flores Magón and Leavenworth Penitentiary," *American Quarterly* 66, no. 3 (September 2014): 557–581.

14. Emilio Zamora, *The World of the Mexican Worker in Texas* (College Station: Texas A&M University Press, 1993); Zamora, "Chicano Socialist Labor Activity in Texas, 1900–1920," *Aztlán* 6 (Summer 1975): 221–236; Jose E. Limón, "El Primer Congreso Mexicanista de 1911: A Precursor to Contemporary Chicanismo," *Aztlán* 5 (Spring-Fall 1974): 85–117; Raquel Rosas, "(De)Sexing Prostitution: Race, Reform, and Sex Work in Texas, 1889–1920" (PhD diss., University of Texas at Austin, 2013).

15. Manuel Callahan, "This Is No War of Bandits: Los Martires de Tejas, 1913," n.d., 2–3, unpublished manuscript in author's possession.

16. Christopher Finan, *From the Palmer Raids to the Patriot Act: A History of the Fight for Free Speech in America* (Boston: Beacon, 2008); Patricia M. Hill, *Men, Mobs, and Law: Anti-Lynching and Labor Defense in US Radical History* (Durham, NC: Duke University Press, 2008).

17. Timothy Paul Bowman, "What About Texas? The Forgotten Cause of Antonio Orendain and the Río Grande Valley Farm Workers, 1966–1982," (master's thesis, University of Texas at Arlington, 2005).

18. Rodolfo Rosales, *The Illusion of Inclusion: The Untold Political Story of San Antonio* (Austin: University of Texas Press, 2000).

19. Montejano, *Quixote's Soldiers*.

20. Mario Cantú, "Confidencia de Prensa," San Antonio, 1976, p. 3, and box 2, folder 13, MCP, BLAC; "PPUA Calls Press Conference in the U.S.," English reprint of press release, *Bracero: Organo de la Liga Flores Magon* 1, no. 1 (1976): 3, box 4, folder 1, MCP, BLAC.

21. Security report, "Estado de Nuevo León," folders 19–36, L-3, DFS, Archivo General de la Nación; Ramón Tijerina, interview by author, Harlingen, Texas, February 25, 2015.

22. Heatherton, "University of Radicalism." For more on Magón's influence on Chicano prisoners at McNeil Island in the late 1960s, see Alan Eladio Gómez, *"With Dignity Intact": Rainbow Coalitions, Control Units, and Struggles for Human Rights in the US Federal Prison System, 1969–1974* (Lincoln: University of Nebraska Press, forthcoming).

23. raúlrsalinas, interview by author, Austin, Texas, June 16, 2004.

24. Alan Eladio Gómez, "'Nuestras vidas corren casi paralelas': Chicanos, Puerto Rican Independentistas, and the Prison Rebellion Years at Leavenworth, 1969–1972," in *Behind Bars: Latino/as and Prisons in the United States*, ed. Suzanne Oboler (New York: Palgrave-MacMillan, 2008); Dan Berger, *Captive Nation: Black Prison Organizing in the Civil Rights Era* (Chapel Hill: University of North Carolina Press, 2014).

25. Gómez, "Nuestras vidas corren casi paralelas"; Heatherton, "University of Radicalism."

26. Letter from raúlrsalinas to Michael Deutsch, September 16, 1972, Salinas Papers, box 6, folder 20, Special Collections, Stanford University, hereafter cited as RSP, SCSU.

27. "Letter to Mario Cantú Jr.," February 29, 1972, reprinted in *raúlrsalinas and the Jail Machine: My Weapon Is My Pen, Selected Writings*, ed. Louis Mendoza (Austin: University of Texas Press, 2006), 117–118.

28. Interview with Mario Cantú by Linda Fregoso, March 5, 1980, Longhorn Radio Network Mexican American Programs, Special Collections, Benson Latin American Collection, University of Texas at Austin.

29. Ibid.

30. Dick Reavis, "Taste for Trouble," *Texas Monthly*, January 1, 2001.

31. raúlrsalinas interview.

32. Letter from the Central Comité of the PPUA to Lucio Blanco, Puebla, Mexico, February 8, 1976, box 3, folder 1, MCP, BLAC.

33. raúlrsalinas interview.

34. Elena Poniatowska, *Fuerte es el Silencio* (Era: Mexico City, 1980).

35. Unless otherwise indicated, this summary is taken from Poniatowska, *Fuerte es el Silencio*, 206–207.

36. Ibid., 226–228.

37. Gustavo Esteva, *La Batalla en México Rural* (Mexico City: Siglo XXI, 1980), 17.

38. R. Levy et al., *Chile: An Economy in Transition* (Washington, DC: World Bank, 1980), 68; Robert Kaufman, *The Politics of Land Reform in Chile, 1950–1970: Public Policy, Political Institutions, and Social Change* (Cambridge, MA: Harvard University Press, 1972).

39. Kaufman, *Politics of Land Reform in Chile*; Midnight Notes Collective, "New Enclosures," in *Midnight Oil: Work, Energy, War, 1973–1992* (Brooklyn: Autonomedia, 1992), 317–333; Esteva, *La Batalla en México Rural*.

40. "Estado de Morelos," DFS, July 19, 100-15-1, Exp. 13 F 229, AGN. Before it was expropriated by the Crespo family, the land was a collectively "owned" *ejido* named El Salto. One of the *ejidarios* (title holders), Leovigildo Jimenez Flores, claimed to have lived there since 1942. These competing claims from the governor's family and *ejidatarios* (groups similarly disenfranchised and marginalized by the Mexican Miracle) further complicated the land struggle.

41. Tanalís Padilla, *Rural Resistance in the Land of Zapata: The Jaramillista Movement and the Myth of the Pax-Priísta, 1940–1962* (Durham, NC: Duke University Press, 2008), 9.

42. Ibid.

43. Ibid., 8.

44. Marco Belligeri, *Del agrarismo a la guerra de los pobres* (Mexico City: Casa Juan Pablos, 2003), 21; Padilla, *Rural Resistance in the Land of Zapata*, 8.

45. Alexander Aviña, *Specters of Revolution: Peasant Guerrillas in the Cold War Mexican Countryside* (Oxford, UK: Oxford University Press, 2014); Armando Bartra, *Guerrero bronco: Campesinos, ciudadanos y guerrilleros en la Costa Grande* (Mexico City: Ediciones Era, 2000); Carlos Montemayor, *Guerra en el Paraíso* (Mexico City: Era, 2000).

46. Poniatowska, *Fuerte es el Silencio*, 197.

47. Ibid., 251.

48. Ibid., 249; Dick Reavis, "My Recollections of Güero," May 12, 2002, box 1, folder 4, DRP-BLAC.

49. Poniatowska quoting someone quoting Medrano, *Fuerte es el Silencio*, 199. Poniatowska's book was published in 1980, six years after the army invasion of La Jaramillo. The book reproduced conversations and opinions by and about Medrano through people still living in the *colonia* when she did the research.

50. Ramón Pérez, *Diary of a Guerrilla* (Houston: Arte Público, 1999), 48.

51. Alfredo de la Torre, "Entrevista con Mario Cantú," *Caracol* 5, no. 4 (December 1978): 11.

52. raúlrsalinas interview.

53. Laura Castellanos, *México Armado: 1943–1981* (Mexico City: Era, 2007), 239; Poniatowska, *Fuerte es el Silencio*, 266. The delegation was actually a group that had agreed to decommission their arms as part of an agreement with Governor Crespo that military forces would not be sent to the Colonia. Either the governor never communicated this to the military or it was a political ruse to draw out the armed elements at La Jaramillo.

54. Reavis, "My Recollections of Güero."

55. Poniatowska, *Fuerte es el Silencio*, 271.

56. "Los ricos usan la violencia para explotar al Pueblo. El Pueblo usará violencia para liberar al Pueblo." "PPUA," *La Lucha del Pueblo: Organo Oficial del Partido Proletario Unido de América* 1, no. 1 (July 1975), RSPA; PPUA, "Programa General del Partido Proletario Unido de América (P.P.U.A.)," RSPA.

57. PPUA Central Committee, "¿Quienes Somos?" *La Lucha del Pueblo: Organo Oficial del Partido Proletario Unido de América* 1, no. 1 (July 1975), 1–2, RSPA.

58. Ibid., 1.

59. Ibid., 2.

60. PPUA, "Programa General del Partido Proletario Unido de América," n.d., 1.

61. Ibid., 5.

62. Ibid., 7.

63. Ibid., 9–14.

64. Shortly after this Congress, unidentified agents from the DFS, military intelligence, or both detained Eduardo Correa at his home. They sexually assaulted his wife and two daughters. His house was subsequently destroyed. Martinez Correa was then tortured by electric shocks to his body and suffered massive trauma from blows to his eyes and ears. The torture left him deaf. In the words of one of the agents, "The body has its limits. Here you talk or we make you talk." Ibid., 271.

65. Letter from Florencio "El Tio" Medrano to Mario Cantú, San Antonio, circa early 1976, box 3, folder 3, MCP, BLAC; raúlrsalinas interview.

66. raúlrsalinas interview.

67. "Organigram de PPUA," DFS, October 6, 1978, 11-249, H-50 L-1, AGN. Miguel

Enriquez Espinosa was a leader of the Movimiento de Izquierda Revolucionaria (MIR), part of the Chilean resistance movement against the Pinochet dictatorship. He was killed on October 5, 1974, after a three-hour shoot-out.

68. Alfonso Ibarra, "'Se Cumplieron la Exigencias,' Dice la Familia de la Señora Martínez Davis," *Excelsior*, December 11, 1874; "Partido Proletario Unido de América," DFS, February 6, 1976, 11-249, L 2, 92, AGN.

69. Méndez Arceo was an adherent of liberation theology and actively sought to make alliances with Catholics across the hemisphere who also favored Marxist ideas. A controversial figure within the Mexican and Latin American clerical hierarchy, Méndez Arceo was loved by his parishioners and scorned by his many detractors. Vicente Leñero, "Introduction," in Carlos Fazio, *La cruz y el martillo* (Mexico City: Joaquin Mortiz Planeta, 1988), 7.

70. Tom Davis to Sara Davis, Cuernavaca, Morelos, December 28, 1974, box 3, folder 3, Dick Reavis Papers, Benson Latin American Collection, hereafter cited as DRP, BLAC.

71. "Frente a todos, el Güero abrió [los paquetes] y empezó a contarlos. Cuando llegó a la suma de cuarenta mil dólares explicó que la mitad era para que los Chicanos organizaran el PPUA en el norte del país." Poniatowska, *Fuerte es el Silencio*, 274; "Partido Proletario Unido de América," DFS, February 6, 1976, 11-249, L 2, 92, AGN. Poniatowska is not clear about what "norte" Medrano was referring to—Monterrey and northern Mexican states or in "el norte," part of Greater Mexico. According to the DFS, the plan was to change the money in the United States in the event that the bills were marked. "Partido Proletario Unido de América," DFS, February 6, 1976, 11-249, L 2, 92, AGN.

72. Poniatowska, *Fuerte es el Silencio*, 274. On May 10, 1975, Abelardo Escamilla Suarez was kidnapped by a commando of the EPLUA in Morelos. On December 28 of the same year, Elfego Coronel Ocampo was kidnapped and then killed on January 21, 1976. The record does not give any more details about Coronel Ocampo's death. "Partido Proletario Unido de América," DFS, February 6, 1976, 11-249, L 2, 93, AGN.

73. "Descubren el Laredo Madriguera de la AIT," *El Norte*, October 5, 1975.

74. Ibid; "Abundiz y su Esposa Trasladados a Monterrey, N.L.," *El Diario de Nuevo Laredo*, October 7, 1975.

75. "Una gran cantidad de literatura subversiva." "Descubren el Laredo Madriguera de la AIT," *El Norte*, October 5, 1975. "Abundiz y su Esposa Trasladados a Monterrey, N.L.," *El Diario de Nuevo Laredo*, October 7, 1975.

76. "Buscan en EU a jefe de la AIT," *El Norte*, October 10, 1975; "Son de la Alianza Internacional de Terroristas; Son Malisimos..!" *Alarma*, October 20, 1975.

77. Lucía Rayas, "Subjugating the Nation: Women and the Guerrilla Experience," in *Challenging Authoritarianism in Mexico: Revolutionary Struggles and the Dirty War, 1964–1982*, ed. Fernando Calderón and Adela Cedillo (Routledge: New York, 2011), 167–181.

78. Towery, "Tortured in Mexico"; "Smuggling of U.S. Guns into Mexico Said Rising," *The Monitor*, October 26, 1975.

79. "Ramon Raul Chacon, Political Prisoner in Mexico," Ramón Chacón Defense Committee newsletter, n.d., RSPA; Ramón Chacón Defense Committee, "Report," n.d., 2, RSPA.

80. Towery, "Tortured in Mexico."

81. Ibid.; "Press Release," Ramón Chacón Defense Committee, n.d., RSPA.

82. "Dos de AIT quedan bien presos," *El Norte*, October 15, 1975.

83. "Monterrey, N.L.," DFS, October 3, 1973, 11-249, L 1, 18–22, AGN; "Estado de Nuevo Leon," DFS, October 3, 1973, 11-249, Exp. 1 Fs. 1–3, AGN.

84. Press release, Ramón Chacón Defense Committee, n.d., RSPA.

85. "Declaraciones de Ruben Solis García y Joaquin Vite Patiño, Presuntos Reponsables en el Contrabando de Armas," DFS, July 2, 1974, 2710, 1–13, AGN; Towery, "Tortured in Mexico." The Solis case, though very important, is beyond the scope of this chapter.

86. See Towery, "Tortured in Mexico."

87. "Mexican Torture Probe Pushed," *San Antonio Light*, December 17, 1975.

88. Ibid.; "Mario Cantú niega y apela a LEA y HK," *El Norte*, October 15, 1975; "Mario Cantú Insiste en Acusaciones de Torturas a dos Presos en México," *El Sol de Texas*, October 24, 1975.

89. "Activista Chicano Niega Acusacion de Estar Vinculado a la Guerrilla en Mexico," *El Sol de Texas*, October 17, 1975; "Smuggling of U.S. Guns into Mexico Said Rising," *The Monitor*, October 26, 1975.

90. "CIA, FBI Are Linked to Torture of 2 Men," *San Antonio Light*, October 17, 1975.

91. "Señalan Que Campaña Contra Cantú es para Atacar a Chicanos," *El Sol de Texas*, November 21, 1975.

92. "Caen Agentes de AIT aquí y en Venezuela," *El Norte*, November 20, 1975; "Documento Secreto revela plan de PUA," *El Norte*, n.d. From research and interviews, it appears that Cantú was indeed still trafficking narcotics at the same time that these events occurred. That said, there is no evidence to suggest the exchange of guns and drugs.

93. "Para correctamente informar a todo el público y esclarecer cualquier mal entendimiento que pueda existir como resultado de lo que se ha publicado en la prensa de México y los Estados Unidos." "Activista chicano hablará hoy del tráfico de armas," *San Antonio Light*, January 3, 1976.

94. Unless otherwise noted, this summary is taken from Mario Cantú, "Confidencia de Prensa," 1976, San Antonio, 3, box 2, folder 13, MCP, BLAC; "PPUA Calls Press Conference in the U.S.," English reprint of press release, *Bracero: Organo de la Liga Flores Magón* 1, no. 1 (1976), 3, box 4, folder 1, MCP, BLAC.

95. Cantú, "Confidencia de Prensa"; "PPUA Calls Press Conference in the U.S."

96. "PPUA Calls Press Conference in the U.S." Note that Chacón called the group the "Poor People's Party" rather than the "Proletarian Party."

97. Ibid. See also Alfred McCoy, *The Politics of Heroin in Southeast Asia* (New York: Lawrence Hill Books, 1983).

98. Initially, Cantú uses the abbreviation PPUA. Then he switches to UPPA. I have kept the citation as it is in the original.

99. "Ernesto Chacon viajó para Guerrero donde hablo con 'las gentes.' Estan de acuerdo sobre el analisis tocante a Mario Cantú. Que tomar el nombre del partido en vano es cosa seria, ellos se encargaran de esto. Ernesto se encuentra a este tiempo en San Antonio hablando con Mario Cantú, quien, a segun Chacón, no quiere meterse más." Ramón Chacón Defense Committee, "Report," n.d., 2, RSPA. For a similar nar-

ration of Chacón's story by the Defense Committee, see "Liberty for Ramón Raúl Chacón," Ramón Chacón Defense Committee, n.d., RSPA.

100. Quoted in Montejano, *Quixote's Soldiers*, 196.

101. PPUA, "Programa General del Partido Proletario Unido de América," 25.

102. "La compañera también tiene la mission d explicarte los cambios de tu funciones que se decidieron en el Segundo Congreso del Partido, y tral el cual has sido designado Delegado del Consejo de Relaciones." Letter from the Central Comité of the PPUA to Lucio Blanco, Puebla, Mexico, February 8, 1976, box 3, folder 1, MCP, BLAC.

103. Ibid.

104. Comité por la Defensa Física y Moral de los Presos Políticos en México, "Press Conference," September 4, 1976, Mario's Restaurant, 2–3, box 2, folder 13, MCP, BLAC.

105. Ibid.

106. Ibid.

107. David McLemore, "Echeverría to Be Picketed," *San Antonio Express-News*, September 5, 1976.

108. Ibid. This was the second time in a week that Cantú and others had blasted Echeverría. "Consul Calls Cantú Charges Lies," *San Antonio Light*, September 1, 1976.

109. "Consul Calls Cantú Charges Lies," *San Antonio Light*, September 1, 1976; "Mexican Envoy Blasts Cantú," *San Antonio Express-News*, September 1, 1976.

110. "Consul Calls Cantú Charges Lies," *San Antonio Light*, September 1, 1976.

111. "Mexican President Grabs, Rips U.S. Activist's Poster," *Los Angeles Times*, September 8, 1976.

112. Sharon Watkins, "Fascist! Angered Chief Yells," *San Antonio Light*, September 8, 1976; "Echeverría Tears Up Protest Signs," *San Antonio Light*, September 8, 1976; "Mexican President Wins Bout with Protestor," *San Antonio Express*, September 8, 1976; "Echeverría Rips Cantú's Sign Insult," *San Antonio News*, September 8, 1976; "San Antonio Picketers Anger Mexican President," *Houston Post*, September 8, 1976.

113. "Mexican President Wins Bout with Protestor," *San Antonio Express*, September 8, 1976.

114. David Salner, "Mexican President Assaults Chicano," *The Militant*, n.d., clipping, box 2, folder 11, MCP, BLAC.

115. Alan Bailey, "Echeverría Lauds Future of MexFair," *San Antonio Express*, September 8, 1976.

116. Ibid. The major Mexican daily *Excelsior* published two articles about Echeverría's visit to San Antonio. Neither one mentions the confrontation. See "La Insolvencia Internacional, Peligro Para la paz: Echeverría," *Excelsior*, September 9, 1976; "Instó Echeverría a los Chicanos a Defender sus Derechos Legalmente," *Excelsior*, September 9, 1976.

117. Ibid. Unless otherwise indicated, this summary is taken from de la Torre, "Entrevista con Mario Cantú."

118. "Esa noche de la protesta, Reies Lopez Tijerina sale dando una escusa a Echeverría en nombre de 15 milliones de Chicanos, diciendo que yo no era chicano. Eso se ve claro en oportunismo y debía preguntarle la gente a Reies y José Angel cuáles son los beneficios personales que reciben. Y los acuso yo directamente a Reies y José

Angel de ser agents del gobierno mexicano dentro del movimiento chicano." Ibid., 16. Tijerina would attend the January 1977 inauguration of president-elect José López Portillo.

119. Formerly the Frente Campesino Independiente (FCI).

120. José Coronado Pérez, "Armados con Machetes y Escopetas 600 Campesinos Toman 1,800 Hectáres," *Excélsior*, October 8, 1978. See also Jeffrey W. Rubin, "COCEI in Juchitan: Grassroots Radicalism and Regional History," *Journal of Latin American Studies* 26, no. 1 (February 1994): 109–136; Rubin, *Decentering the Regime: Ethnicity, Radicalism, and Democracy in Juchitán, Mexico* (Durham, NC: Duke University Press, 1997).

121. De la Torre, "Entrevista con Mario Cantú"; "Mario Cantú Backs Revolt," *San Antonio Light*, October 10, 1978; Press Release, United States Committee in Solidarity with the People of Mexico—Liga Ricardo Flores Magón, June 5, 1978, box 3, folder 5, MCP, BLAC; Dick Reavis, "Unreliable Witness," *Texas Monthly*, July 25, 1980, 10. It is unclear who was part of this organization, or if it was created specifically in support of this action.

122. De la Torre, "Entrevista con Mario Cantú," 16.

123. Ibid., 16. In an undated letter to Cantú, Medrano admonishes him for his statements, as "many organizations are asking us for help and we can't even solve our own problems." Letter from "El Tío" [Güero] to Mario Cantú, box 13, folder 3, DRP, BLAC.

124. On Friday, June 18, 1976, Immigration and Naturalization Services agents arrested Cantú, who was later charged with harboring and shielding undocumented workers. A series of court cases concluded with a five-year sentence. Cantú was the first person to be convicted on these charges. Though beyond the scope of this book, the case is significant for the time, the place, and the political consequences of the arrest, both for Cantú and the larger immigrants' rights movement. While on probation from his suspended sentence, Cantú traveled to Mexico.

125. "Statement by Mario Cantú," December 4, 1978, Paris, reprinted in *Caracol*, May 1979, 4.

126. Cantú interview by Fregoso.

127. "Statement by Mario Cantú," December 4, 1978, Paris.

128. Jacinto Rodríguez Munguía, *La otra guerra secreta: Los archivos prohibidos de la prensa y el poder* (Mexico City: Debate, 2007), 207–219.

129. Letter from Mario Cantú to Corky Gonzalez, May 20, 1980, box 2, folder 6, MCP, BLAC.

130. "El Movimiento Chicano Denuncia: CARTER NO RESPETA LOS DERECHOS HUMANOS," Comité Europeo de Solidaridad con El Pueblo Chicano, n.d., box 3, folder 5, MCP, BLAC.

131. "El régimen mejicano, culpable de la tragedia de los emigrantes a Estados Unidos," *Egin*, 12, box 3, folder 5, MCP, BLAC.

132. Poniatowska, *Fuerte es el Silencio*, 275–276; "Asesinan en México al Dirigente Guerrillero Florencio Medrano (Güero)," Comité Europeo de Solidaridad con el Pueblo Chicano, April 20, 1979, Madrid, box 2, folder 1, DRP, BLAC.

133. Carolina Verduzco and Ileana Chavez, *Informe histórico presentado a la sociedad mexicana: fiscalía especial FEMOS* (Mexico City: Comité 68 Pro Libertadores Democráticas, 2008), 290.

134. Larry Jolidon, "Revolutionary Dies, Mexican Rebel Leader Killed, Leaves Void among Followers," *Austin American-Statesman*, April 14, 1979.

135. "Asesinan en Mexico al dirigente guerrillero Florencio Medrano (Güero)," Comité Europeo de Solidaridad con El Pueblo Chicano, April 20, 1979, 1, box 2, folder 1, DRP-BLAC. More than twenty years after Medrano's death, I had a conversation with a comrade from Oaxaca living in Austin whose family was from this area. He shared a story from his mother, who believed that Medrano had been killed by the private guards of a wealthy rancher, but not because of a land dispute. Rather, according to this version, Medrano was killed because of love and machismo. Apparently, Medrano, who must have been in his late fifties, and the daughter of a rancher had fallen in love, and the father killed Medrano out of revenge.

136. Antonio del Conde, largely responsible for arming Fidel Castro during his time in Mexico in preparation for the attack on the Moncado Barracks in 1953, was also arrested in Texas for attempting to transport arms to Cuba through Mexico. See Antonio del Conde's self-published book, *Memorias del Yate Granma* (Mexico City, 2004). I met Conde in 2005 in Mexico City at a Tribunal Popular concerning the dirty war in Mexico.

CHAPTER 6: PUENTE DE CRISTAL (CRYSTAL BRIDGE)

1. The chapter title is from a poem by Lucha Corpi dedicated to Mora: Lucha Corpi, *Palabras de Mediodia/Noon Words*, translated by Catherine Rodríguez Nieto (Houston: Arte Público, 2001). That said, I have made two changes in my English translation.

2. Beatriz M. Pesquera and Denise A. Segura, "'There Is No Going Back': Chicanas and Feminism," in *Chicana Critical Issues, Series in Chicana/Latina Studies*, ed. Norma Alarcón et al. (Berkeley: Third Woman Press, 1993), 99; Denise A. Segura and Beatriz M. Pesquera, "Chicana Political Consciousness: Renegotiating Culture, Class, and Gender with Oppositional Practices," *Aztlán: A Journal of Chicano Studies* 24, no. 1 (Spring 1999): 1–32.

3. Cedric J. Robinson, *Black Marxism: The Making of the Black Radical Tradition*, 2nd ed. (Chapel Hill: University of North Carolina Press, 2000), 342.

4. Lucha Corpi, email correspondence with author, June 20, 2013.

5. Vicki Ruiz, *From Out of the Shadows: Mexican Women in Twentieth-Century America* (New York: Oxford University Press, 2008), 117–118.

6. Lucha Corpi, email correspondence with author, June 20, 2013.

7. Magdalena Mora and Adelaida Del Castillo, *Mexican Women in the United States: Struggles Past and Present*, Occasional Paper no. 2 (Los Angeles: Chicano Studies Research Center Publications, UCLA, 1980).

8. Weber interview, 1981, quoted in Ruíz, *From Out of the Shadows*, 118.

9. Adelaida A. Del Castillo, *Between Borders: Essays on Mexicana/Chicana History* (Los Angeles: Flor y Canto, 1981), i.

10. Carlos Vásquez, *Remembering a Revolutionary Mujer Compañera Magdalena Mora*, pamphlet produced by Editorial Prensa Sembradora, Inc., 1981, accessed February 18, 2011, http://uniondelbarrio.org/lvp/newspapers/97/janmay97/pg01.html.

11. Emma Pérez, *Decolonial Imaginary: Writing Chicanas into History* (Bloomington: Indiana University Press, 1999).

12. Avery Gordon, *Ghostly Matters: Haunting and the Sociological Imaginations* (Minneapolis: University of Minnesota Press, 1996).

13. Maylei Blackwell, *¡Chicana Power! Contested Histories of Feminism in the Chicano Movement* (Austin: University of Texas Press, 2011), 154–155. Blackwell cites A. Chabram-Denersesian, "And, Yes . . . the Earth Did Part: On the Splitting of Chicana/o Subjectivity," in *Building with Our Hands: New Directions in Chicana Studies*, ed. Adela de la Torre and Beatríz M. Pesquera (Berkeley: University of California Press, 1933), 34–56 for this insight.

14. Emma Pérez, "Queering the Borderlands: The Challenge of Excavating the Invisible and Unheard," *Frontiers: A Journal of Women's Studies* 24, no. 2/3 (2003): 123.

15. Pérez, *Decolonial Imaginary*, 7.

16. In using the term "fugitive wills," I am drawing on the work of Michael Hames-García in *Fugitive Thought: Prison Movements, Race, and the Meaning of Justice* (Minneapolis: University of Minnesota Press, 2004), and Sara Ahmed, *Willful Subjects* (Durham, NC: Duke University Press, 2014), to emphasize the ways that people written outside of the law (and humanity) create and establish freedom dreams that imagine other possibilities and prefigure those potentialities.

17. Ibid., xviii.

18. Emma Pérez, "Decolonial Critics for Academic Freedom," in *Academic Repression: Reflections from the Academic Industrial Complex*, ed. Anthony J. Nocella II, Steven Best, and Peter McLaren (San Francisco: AK Press, 2010), 365.

19. Marisela R. Chávez, "Despierten hermanas y hermanos: Women, the Chicano Movement, and Chicana Feminisms in California" (PhD diss., Stanford University, 2005), 10.

20. Marisela R. Chávez, "'We Lived and Breathed and Worked the Movement': The Contradictions and Rewards of Chicana/Mexicana Activism in El Centro de Acción Social Autónomo-Hermandad General de Trabajadores (CASA-HGT), Los Angeles, 1975–1978," in *Las Obreras: Chicana Politics of Work and Family*, ed. Vicki L. Ruiz and Chon Noriega (Los Angeles: UCLA Chicano Studies Research Center Publications, 2000).

21. For *rasquachismo*, "the irreverent and spontaneous are employed to make the most from the least," writes Amelia Mesa-Bains. See her *"Domesticana*: The Sensibility of Chicana Rasquache," in *Distant Relations: Chicano, Irish, and Mexican Art and Critical Writing*, ed. Trisha Ziff (Santa Monica, CA: Smart Art, 1996), 165–163.

Rasquachismo involves "a combination of resistant and resilient attitudes devised to allow the Chicano to survive and persevere with a sense of dignity," an "understanding of a particular aesthetic code of any particular community [. . . that] comes out of the experience of living in that community . . . you make do with what you have." Tomás Ybarra-Frausto, "Rasquachismo," interview with Latinopia Art, accessed August 28, 2011, http://latinopia.com/latino-art/latinopia-art-tomas-ybarra -frausto-rasquachismo/. In another interview, Ybarra-Frausto reflected on his first contact with Chicanos at McNeil Island: "It was very exciting. First of all because again we were, because they were such eager learners. It was like a graduate seminar . . . with brilliant students; the questions they asked were very good questions. But it was sort of like a recognition, a growing recognition about human nature, you know, the power of people is their experience and their way, the movidas, the way they figured out, and *in many ways that became the basis of my thinking later on about the aesthetics, the movidas that people, the ordinary things you do to survive.* And sometimes the theory didn't fit what we're seeing . . ." [emphasis added]. Tomás Ybarra-Frausto and Dudley Brooks, interview with author, San Antonio, February 23, 2012.

22. Julie Leininger Pycior, "Sociedades Mutualistas," *Handbook of Texas Online,* Texas State Historical Association, accessed August 16, 2011, https://tshaonline.org /handbook/online/articles/vesor; Emilio Zamora, *The World of the Mexican Worker in Texas* (College Station: Texas A&M University Press, 1993).

23. Mario García, *Memories of a Chicano History: The Life and Narrative of Bert Corona* (Berkeley: University of California Press, 1994).

24. Ernesto Chávez, *"¡Mi Raza Primero!": Nationalism, Identity, and Insurgency in the Chicano Movement in Los Angeles, 1966–1978* (Berkeley: University of California Press, 2002); Arnoldo García, "Toward a Left without Borders: The Story of the Center for Autonomous Social Action—General Brotherhood of Workers," *Monthly Review* 54, no. 3 (July–August 2002): 69–78; M. Chávez, "We Lived and Breathed"; Laura Pulido, *Black, Brown, Yellow, and Left: Radical Activism in Los Angeles* (Berkeley: University of California Press, 2006).

25. Other original founders included Francisco Amaro, María Cedillos, Juan Mariscal, and Rafail Zacarías.

26. Ruiz, *From Out of the Shadows,* 117.

27. M. Chávez, "Despierten hermanas y hermanos," 201.

28. Pérez, *Decolonial Imaginary,* 31–45.

29. M. Chávez, "We Lived and Breathed"; M. Chávez, "Despierten hermanas y hermanos"; Pulido, *Black, Brown, Yellow, and Left.*

30. Pérez, *Decolonial Imaginary,* 56.

31. Virginia Espino, "'Woman Sterilized as Gives Birth': Forced Sterilization and the Chicana Resistance in the 1970s," in *Las Obreras: Chicana Politics of Work and Family,* ed. Vicki Ruíz (Los Angeles: UCLA Chicano Studies Research Center Publications, 2002), 65–82.

32. M. Chávez, "We Lived and Breathed," 192.

33. Ibid., 211–212.

34. Ibid., 85.

35. Ibid., 86.

36. Magdalena Mora, "The Tolteca Strike: Mexican Women and the Struggle for Union Representation," in *Mexican Immigrant Workers in the U.S.,* ed. Antonio Ríos-Bustamante (Los Angeles: Chicano Studies Research Center Publications, University of California, 1981), 111.

37. Ibid.

38. Ibid.

39. Ibid., 113.

40. Ibid.

41. Ibid., 113.

42. Quote is from ibid.

43. Only first names are given in the original paper.

44. *Comadres* refers to a relationship between women that conveys deep respect and mutual support.

45. Mora, "The Tolteca Strike," 115.

46. Ibid., 114–115.

47. Michelle Téllez, "Doing Research at the Borderlands: Notes from a Chicana Feminist Ethnographer," *Chicana/Latina Studies: The Journal of Mujeres Activas en Letras y Cambio Social* 4, no. 2 (2005): 47.

48. Mora, "The Tolteca Strike," 113.

49. Ibid.

50. Ibid.

51. Ibid., 116.

52. Ibid.

53. Silvia Federici, *Caliban and the Witch: Women, the Body, and Primitive Accumulation* (New York: Autonomedia, 2005); David Harvey, *The New Imperialism* (New York: Oxford University Press, 2005).

54. Magdalena Mora, "A lo concreto: Impuestos Sin Provecho," *Sin Fronteras* 2, no. 6 (February 1976): 8.

55. Ibid.

56. The Bracero Program was a series of binational labor agreements between the United States and Mexico, beginning in 1942 and lasting until 1964. The program encouraged and facilitated migration from Mexico, while limiting the rights of workers and sanctioning their exploitation by agribusiness. See Kelly Lytle-Hernandez, *Migra! A History of the U.S. Border Patrol* (Berkeley: University of California Press, 2010).

57. Magdalena Mora, "Eastland Bill Reestablished Bracero Program," *Sin Fronteras* 2, no. 10 (June 1976): 9. I should point out that there is no analog to slavery (Frank B. Wilderson III), virtual or otherwise. This is the place where "junior partner of empire" echoes a need to fully engage the contradictions of settler colonialism, Chicana/o indigeneity, and antiblackness. For a discussion of these issues, see Jared Sexton, "People-of-Color-Blindness: Notes on the Afterlife of Slavery," *Social Text* 28, no. 2 103 (Summer 2010): 31–56; Jared Sexton, "The *Vel* of Slavery—Tracking the Figure of the Unsovereign," *Critical Sociology* (2014), http://crs.sagepub.com /content/early/2014/12/19/0896920514552535.full.pdf+html; Frank B. Wilderson III, "Prison-Slave as Hegemony's Silent Scandal," *Social Justice* 30, no. 2 (2003): 18–28; Andrea Smith, "Indigeneity, Settler Colonialism and White Supremacy," *Global Dialogue* 12, no. 2 (Summer/Autumn 2010), http://www.worlddialogue.org/content.php ?id=488.

58. Magdalena Mora, "Conditions Prepared for a New Bracero Program," *Sin Fronteras* 3, no. 4 (December 1976): 8. See David G. Gutiérrez, *Walls and Mirrors: Mexican Americans, Mexican Immigrants, and the Politics of Ethnicity* (Berkeley: University of California Press, 1995), chap. 6.

59. Mora, "Conditions Prepared for New Bracero Program."

60. Magdalena Mora, "FLOC—Unified Struggle of Agricultural Workers," *Sin Fronteras* 3, no. 11 (1977): 10.

61. Ibid.

62. Magdalena Mora, "Trade Unions Must Defend All Members," *Sin Fronteras* 3, no. 8 (April 1977): 8.

63. Magdalena Mora, "Carter's Grand Deception," *Sin Fronteras* 3, no. 10 (June 1977): 8.

64. Magdalena Mora, "Latin American Workers Confront AFL-CIO Intervention," *Sin Fronteras* 3, no. 2 (October 1976): 8.

65. Ibid. Linking the infiltration and disruptions of social movements by the CIA in collusion with labor union leadership, government bureaucrats, and the military in Latin America to disruptions of movements in the USA must be understood in the context of CASA being the target of infiltration and harassment by the FBI and the larger FBI COINTELPRO operations that were under investigation at the time.

66. Magdalena Mora, "Strong Rank and File Base Insures Genuine Worker's Movement," *Sin Fronteras* 3, no. 6 (February 1977): 8.

67. Kimberlé Crenshaw, "Mapping the Margins: Intersectionality, Identity Politics and Violence against Women of Color," *Stanford Law Review* 43, no. 6 (1993): 1241.

68. H. L. T. Quan, "Geniuses of Resistance: Feminist Consciousness and the Black Radical Tradition," *Race and Class* 47, no. 2 (2005): 48.

69. Blackwell, *¡Chicana Power!*, 66.

70. Pulido, *Black, Brown, Yellow, and Left*, 200.

71. Ibid., 199.

72. Ibid., 200.

73. Ibid., 195.

74. M. Chávez, "Despierten hermanas y hermanos," 204.

75. Ibid., 202–203.

76. Ibid., 14.

77. Blackwell, *¡Chicana Power!*, 31.

78. Quoted in Ruíz, *From Out of the Shadows*, 118.

79. Téllez, "Doing Research at the Borderlands."

80. Charles Hale, ed., *Engaging Contradictions: Theory, Politics, and Methods of Activist Scholarship* (Berkeley: University of California Press, 2008).

81. Téllez, "Doing Research at the Borderlands."

82. Ruíz, *From Out of the Shadows*, 78.

83. Teresa McKenna, *Migrant Song: Politics and Process in Contemporary Chicano Literature* (Austin: University of Texas Press, 1997), 47–48.

84. Mahmoud Darwish, "Don't Write History as Poetry," in *The Butterfly's Burden* (Port Townsend, WA: Copper Canyon, 2007), 259.

85. Cynthia A. Young, *Soul Power: Culture, Radicalism, and the Making of a US Third World Left* (Durham, NC: Duke University Press, 2006), 5.

86. Blackwell, *¡Chicana Power!*, 210.

87. On the recomposition of capital, see Harry Cleaver, "The Inversion of Class Perspective in Marxian Theory: From Valorization to Self-Valorization," in *Open Marxism*, vol. 2: *Theory and Practice* (London: Pluto, 1992).

88. Blackwell, *¡Chicana Power!*, 210–211.

89. Ibid., 211.

90. See Jena M. Loyd, *Health Rights Are Civil Rights: Peace and Justice Activism in Los Angeles, 1963–1978* (Minneapolis: University of Minnesota Press, 2014); Espino, "Woman Sterilized as Gives Birth."

EPILOGUE

1. ARMA Collective, "Who We Are," http://www.armacollective.com/?page_id =317.

2. Cynthia A. Young, *Soul Power: Culture, Radicalism, and the Making of a US Third World Left* (Durham, NC: Duke University Press, 2006), 250.

3. For an important discussion of the Chicana/o anti–Vietnam War movement and a critique of state violence, see Lorena Oropeza, *¡Raza Sí! ¡Guerra No! Chicano Protest and Patriotism during the Vietnam War Era* (Berkeley: University of California Press, 2005).

4. Marisela R. Chávez, "Pilgrimage to the Homeland: California Chicanas and International Women's Year, Mexico City, 1975," in *Memories and Migrations: Mapping Boricua and Chicana Histories*, ed. Vicki Ruiz and John Chávez (Urbana: University of Illinois Press, 2008), 170–195.

5. Antonia Castañeda, "'We Shall Not Be Moved': The Chicano Movement and Solidarity with Chile," Plática presented at Trinity University, San Antonio, February 20, 2014.

6. Michael Flamm, *Law and Order: Street Crime, Civil Unrest, and the Crisis of Liberalism in the 1960s* (New York: Columbia University Press, 2007); Michelle S. Phelps, "Rehabilitation in the Punitive Era: The Gap between Rhetoric and Reality in U.S. Prison Programs," *Law & Society Review* 45, no. 1 (2011): 33–68; Dylan Rodríguez, *Forced Passages: Imprisoned Radical Intellectuals and the U.S. Prison Regime* (Minneapolis: University of Minnesota Press, 2006).

7. Vijay Prashad, "Second-Hand Dreams," *Social Analysis* 49, no. 2 (Summer 2005): 191–198.

8. Peter Farber and Jeff Roche, *The Conservative Sixties* (New York: Peter Lang, 2003); Dan Berger, *Captive Nation: Black Prison Organizing in the Civil Rights Era* (Chapel Hill: University of North Carolina Press, 2014).

9. W. E. B. DuBois, "The African Roots of War," in *W.E.B. Du Bois: A Reader*, ed. Meyer Weinberg (New York: Harper & Row, 1970), 360–371; Jenna M. Loyd, *Health Rights Are Civil Rights: Peace and Justice Activism in Los Angeles, 1963-1978* (Minneapolis: University of Minnesota Press, 2014).

10. Sheila Marie Contreras, *Blood Lines: Myth, Indigenism, and Chicana/o Literature* (Austin: University of Texas Press, 2008), 158 (emphasis added; in original, "home" is italicized).

11. Gustavo Licón, "¡La Union Hace La Fuerza! (Unity Creates Strength!): MEChA" (PhD diss., University of Southern California, 2009), 18.

12. Robin D. G. Kelley, *Freedom Dreams: The Black Radical Imagination* (Boston: Beacon, 2002).

13. Jorge Mariscal, *Brown-Eyed Children of the Sun: Lessons from the Chicano Movement, 1965-1975* (Albuquerque: University of New Mexico Press, 2005); Antonio González, "Chicano Politics and U.S. Policy in Central America, 1979-1990," in *Chicano Politics and Society in the Late Twentieth Century*, ed. David Montejano (Austin: University of Texas Press, 1999), 154-175; Castañeda, "We Shall Not Be Moved."

14. Cherríe Moraga and Gloria Anzaldúa, eds., *This Bridge Called My Back: Writ-*

ings by Radical Women of Color (New York: Kitchen Table/Women of Color Press, 1984).

15. Subcomandante Marcos II, "Marcos to NGOs: Zapatistas Don't Want Charity, but Respect: CHIAPAS: The Thirteenth Stele—Part Two: A Death," translated by Irlandesa, in *The Speed of Dreams: Selected Writings 2001–2007*, ed. Canek and Greg Ruggiero (San Francisco: City Lights, 2007), 199–239.

16. John Holloway, "Zapatismo Urbano," *Humboldt Journal of Social Relations* 29, no. 1 (2005): 168–179.

17. John Holloway, "Dignity's Revolt," in *Zapatista! Reinventing Revolution in Mexico*, ed. John Holloway and Eloína Peláez (London: Pluto Press, 1998), 164.

18. See Gloria Muñoz Ramírez, *EZLN 20 y 10: El Fuego y La Palabra* (Mexico City: La Jornada, 2003); Adela Cedillo, "Armed Struggle without Revolution: The Organizing Process of the National Liberation Forces (FLN) and the Genesis of Neo-Zapatismo—1969–1983," in Fernando Calderon and Adela Cedillo, *Challenging Authoritarianism in Mexico: Revolutionary Struggles and the Dirty War, 1964–1982* (New York: Routledge, 2011), 148–166.

19. "Taking into account the situation of the woman worker in Mexico, the [Zapatista] revolution incorporates their just demands of equality and justice in the following Women's Revolutionary Law: 1. Women, regardless of their race, creed, color or political affiliation, have a right to participate in the revolutionary struggle in any way that their desire and capacity determine. 2. Women have the right to work and receive a just salary. 3. Women have the right to decide the number of children they have and care for. 4. Women have the right to participate in the matters of the community and to take charge if they are freely and democratically elected. 5. Women and their children have the right to primary attention in their health and nutrition. 6. Women have the right to education. 7. Women have the right to choose their partner and are not obliged to enter into marriage. 8. Women have the right to be free of violence from both relatives and strangers. Rape and attempted rape will be severely punished. 9. Women will be able to occupy positions of leadership in the organization and hold military ranks in the revolutionary armed forces. 10. Women will have all the rights and obligations which the revolutionary laws and regulations give."

20. Hilary Klein, *Compañeras: Zapatista Women's Stories* (New York: Seven Stories Press, 2015); Shannon Speed, R. Aída Hernández Castillo, and Lynn Stephen, eds., *Dissident Women: Gender and Cultural Politics in Chiapas* (Austin: University of Texas Press, 2006); Guiomar Rovira, *Mujeres de Maíz* (Mexico City: Era, 1997).

21. El Kilombo Intergalactico, *Beyond Resistance: Everything: An Interview with Subcomandante Insurgente Marcos* (Durham, NC: Paper Boat, 2007).

22. Subcomandante Marcos, "Building a Bridge of Struggle across the Border," interview with Aura Bogado, *Counterpunch*, March 10, 2006, quoted in Manuel Callahan, "Crisis and Permanent War on the U.S.-Mexico Borderlands," unpublished manuscript in author's possession, 1.

23. Callahan, "Why Not Share a Dream? Zapatismo as Political and Cultural Practice," in *Zapatismo as Political and Cultural Practice*, special issue, *Humboldt Journal of Social Relations* 29, no. 1 (2005): 7.

24. Ibid.

25. Callahan, "Why Not Share a Dream?," 16.

26. Ibid.

27. Holloway, "Zapatismo Urbano," 169.

28. See generally the writings of Gustavo Esteva.

29. Callahan, "Why Not Share a Dream?," 17.

30. SubComandante Marcos II, "Marcos to NGOs."

31. El Kilombo Intergalactico, *Beyond Resistance*, vii. See also Alex Khasnabish, *Zapatismo beyond Borders: New Imaginations of Political Possibility* (Toronto: University of Toronto Press, 2008).

32. ARMA Collective, "Who We Are."

33. "The Encuentro Chican@-Zapatista consisted of 4 days of intense dialogue on 4 major themes: Nos Encontramos, La Mujer, Using Art as an educational and political tool, and Autonomy. These themes were marked by sub-themes of Education, Salud [Health], Economía, and Struggle for Autonomy. The resolutions and workshop products were presented to the general assemblies in one or several art forms that included performance art, dance, murals, music, poetry, spoken word, and teatro. Many of the young Chican@ artists that I propose to interview for the dissertation were participants in this encuentro." Roberto Flores, "Chicano Artists and Zapatistas Walk Together Asking, Listening, Learning: The Role of Transnational Informal Learning Networks in the Creation of a Better World" (PhD diss., University of Southern California, 2007).

34. Pablo Gonzalez, "Autonomy Road: the Cultural Politics of Chicana/o Autonomous Organizing in Los Angeles, California" (PhD diss., University of Texas at Austin, 2011).

35. Manuel Callahan, "In Defense of Conviviality and the Collective Subject," *Polis: Revista LatinoAmericano* (2012): 3, http://polis.revues.org/8432.

36. For a brilliant study of community conviviality and survival resisting police violence and low-intensity war in the Bay Area, see Annie Paradise, "Militarized Policing and Resistance in the Social Factory: The Battle for Community Safety in the Silicon Valley" (PhD diss., California Institute of Integral Studies, 2015).

37. Martha Gonzalez, "Chican@ Artivistas: East Los Angeles Trenches Transborder Tactics" (PhD diss., University of Washington, 2013).

38. Jeff Chang, *Can't Stop, Won't Stop: A History of the Hip Hop Generation* (New York: Picador, 2005).

39. Young, *Soul Power*.

40. Elizabeth Sutherland Martínez and Enriqueta Longeaux y Vásquez, *Viva la Raza! The Struggle of the Mexican-American People* (New York: Doubleday, 1974), 339–340.

41. Alan Eladio Gómez, "'Nuestras vidas corren casi paralelas': Chicanos, Puerto Rican Independentistas, and the Prison Rebellion Years at Leavenworth, 1969–1972," in *Behind Bars: Latino/as and Prison in the United States*, ed. Suzanne Oboler (New York: Palgrave-Macmillan, 2008), 67–96.

42. Avery Gordon, *Ghostly Matters: Haunting and the Sociological Imagination* (Minneapolis: University of Minnesota Press, 2008).

BIBLIOGRAPHY

PRIMARY SOURCES

ARCHIVES

Archivo Histórico de la Nación, Mexico City (AGN)
Ramo Dirección Federal de Seguridad (DFS)
Ramo Dirección General de Investigaciones Políticas y Sociales (DGIPS)
Ramo Presidentes (AGN/P)
Archivos Mascarones, Universidad Nahuatl, Ocotopec, Morelos, Mexico
Nettie Lee Benson Latin American Collection, University of Texas at Austin
Mario Cantú Papers
Dick Reavis Papers
The Onda Latina Collection
Mariano Leyva, personal archive, Ocotopec, Morelos, Mexico
Mercedes Nieto, personal archive, Mexico City
raúlrsalinas, personal archive, Austin, Texas
Stanford University Library, Department of Special Collections
raúlrsalinas Papers
Centro de Acción Social Autónomo Papers
Alejandro Stewart Papers
Abraham Vidales, personal archive, Mexico City

NEWSPAPERS, NEWSLETTERS, AND PERIODICALS

Alarma (Mexico City)
Austin American-Statesman
Bracero: Organo de la Liga Flores Magón (San Antonio)
Caracol (San Antonio)
Chicano Theater (Los Angeles)
CLETA (Mexico City)
Daily Worker
Egin (Hernani, Basque Country)
El Chido (Mexico City)
El Cuamil (San Antonio)
El Día (Mexico City)
El Diario de Nuevo Laredo (Nuevo Laredo, Tamaulipas, Mexico)
El Gallo (Denver)
El Grito del Norte (Española, New Mexico)
El Malcriado (Delano, California)
El Norte (Monterrey, Mexico)
El Sol de Texas (Dallas/Ft. Worth)
El Universal (Mexico City)
Excélsior (Mexico City)
Guadalupe Cultural Center Newsletter (San Antonio)

La Jornada (Mexico City)
La Raza (Lincoln Heights, Los Angeles)
The Monitor (McAllen, Texas)
The News (San Antonio)
Periodico Oaxaca de Juárez (Oaxaca, Mexico)
¡Por Qúe? (Mexico City)
Proceso (Mexico City)
San Antonio Express-News
San Antonio Light
San Antonio Times
Sin Fronteras (San Antonio/Los Angeles)
Tecolote (San Francisco)

INTERVIEWS, VIDEOS, AND AUDIO SOURCES

Acosta, María. Interview by Bill Berkowitz, October 1976. Olga Talamante Defense Committee Interview Collection.

Brooks, Dudley. Interview with author, San Antonio, February 23, 2012.

Cantú, Mario. Interview by Linda Fregoso, Austin, Texas, March 5, 1980. Onda Latina: The Mexican American Experience, University of Texas at Austin website, http://www.laits.utexas.edu/onda_latina/program?sernum=000535499&theme=Social%20Issues.

Cisneros, Enrique. Interview by author, Mexico City, November 17, 2004.

Colmenares, Ismael. Interview by author, Mexico City, November 24, 2004.

García, Irma. Interview by author, Guanajuato, Mexico, November 13, 2004.

Hernández, Fernando. Interview by author, Ocotepec, Mexico, November 16, 2004.

Kelley, Robin D. G. Interview by Chris Cameron, "20 Year Anniversary Roundtable on Robin D. G. Kelley, *Race Rebels*: Author Interview," December 7, 2014. http://aaihs.org/20-year-anniversary-roundtable-on-robin-d-g-kelley-race-rebels-author-interview/.

Leyva Dominguez, Mariano. Interview by author, Ocotopec, Morelos, Mexico, November 16, 2004.

———. Audio recording no. 17, *Los Mascarones Archive*, Mexico City, 1974.

Moreno, Dorinda. Interview by author, Guanajuato, Mexico, November 13, 2004.

Nieto, Mercedes. Interview by author, Mexico City, November 6, 2004.

Oropeza, Annette. Interview by Alicia Muñoz, Oakland, California, October 23, 1998.

Orozco, Sylvia. "The View of Chicanos in Mexico." Interview by Armando Gutiérrez, Austin, Texas, May 24, 1979. Onda Latina: The Mexican American Experience, University of Texas at Austin website, http://www.laits.utexas.edu/onda_latina/program?sernum=000534549&term=.

Ramírez, Ana Ignacia. Interview by author, Mexico City, November 5, 2004.

Reyes, Ernesto. Interview by author, Mexico City, July 27, 1999.

raúlrsalinas. Interview by author, Austin, Texas, June 4, 2004.

———. Interview by author, Austin, Texas, June 16, 2004.

———. Interview by author, Austin, Texas, August 27, 2005.

Talamante, Olga. Telephone interview by author, San Francisco, June 15, 2004.

Tijerina, Ramón. Telephone interview by author, Harlingen, Texas, February 25, 2015.

Valdez, Luis. Interview by Haldun Morgan, September 2002, Radio Aguascalientes Archives.

Vidales, Abraham. Interview by author, Mexico City, November 6, 2004.

Ybarra-Frausto, Tomás. Interview with author, San Antonio, February 23, 2012.

BOOKS, ARTICLES, AND DISSERTATIONS

Acosta-Belén, Edna. "Reimagining Borders: A Hemispheric Approach to Latin American and U.S. Latino and Latina Studies." In *Color-Line to Borderlands: The Matrix of American Ethnic Studies*, ed. Johnnella E. Butler, 240–264. Seattle: University of Washington Press, 2001.

Affigne, Tony, and Pei-te Lien. "Peoples of Asian Descent in the Americas: Theoretical Implications of Race and Politics." *Amerasia Journal* 28, no. 2 (2002): 1–27.

Agamben, Giorgio. *Means without End: Notes on Politics*. Minneapolis: University of Minnesota Press, 2000.

———. *States of Exception*. Chicago: University of Chicago Press, 2005.

Agee, Philip. *Inside the Company: CIA Diary*. New York: Farrar Straus & Giroux, 1975.

Aguayo Quezada, Sergio. *La Charola: Una historia de los servicios de inteligencia en México*. Mexico City: Grijalbo, 2002.

———. *1968: Los archivos de la violencia*. Mexico City: Grijalbo, 1999.

———. *El Panteón de los Mitos: Estados Unidos y nacionalismo mexicano*. Mexico City: Colegio de Mexico, 1998.

Ahmed, Sarah. *Willful Subjects*. Durham, NC: Duke University Press, 2014.

Alaniz, Yolanda, and Megan Cornish. *Viva La Raza: A History of Chicano Identity and Resistance*. Seattle: Red Letter, 2008.

Albizu Campos, Pedro. *La conciencia nacional puertorriqueña*. Mexico City: Siglo XXI, 1972.

Albro, Ward S. *Always a Rebel: Ricardo Flores Magón and the Mexican Revolution*. Fort Worth: Texas Christian University Press, 1992.

Alexander, M. Jacqui, and Chandra Talpade Mohanty, eds. *Feminist Genealogies, Colonial Legacies, Democratic Futures*. New York: Routledge, 1997.

Almaguer, Tomás. "Toward the Study of Chicano Colonialism." *Aztlán* 2 (Spring 1971): 137–142.

Alvarado, Luis Felipe. "El discurso posmoderno en el texto dramatico de Hector Azar." PhD diss., University of Cincinnati, 1995.

Álvarez, Luis. *The Power of the Zoot: Youth Cultures of Resistance during World War II*. Berkeley: University of California Press, 2008.

Álvarez, Sonia, Evelyn Dagnino, and Arturo Escobar, eds. *Cultures of Politics/Politics of Cultures: Re-Visioning Latin American Social Movements*. Boulder, CO: Westview, 1998.

Anaya, Héctor. *Los parricidas del 68: la protesta juvenil*. Mexico City: Plaza y Janés, 1998.

Anderson, Carol. *Eyes off the Prize: The United Nations and the African American Struggle for Human Rights, 1944–1955*. Cambridge, UK: Cambridge University Press, 2003.

Aptheker, Bettina. *Morning Breaks: The Trial of Angela Davis.* 2nd ed. Ithaca, NY: Cornell University Press, 1999.

Araiza, Lauren. *To March for Others: The Black Freedom Struggle and the United Farm Workers.* Philadelphia: University of Pennsylvania Press, 2013.

Aussaresses, Paul. *The Battle of the Casbah: Terrorism and Counter-Terrorism in Algeria, 1955–1957.* Translated by Robert L. Miller. New York: Enigma, 2002.

Aviña, Alexander. *Specters of Revolution: Peasant Guerrillas in the Cold War Mexican Countryside.* Oxford, UK: Oxford University Press, 2014.

Azcona, Estevan César. "Movements in Chicano Music: Performing Culture, Performing Politics, 1965–1979." PhD diss., University of Texas at Austin, 2008.

Bailey, Beth, and David Farber, eds. *America in the Seventies.* Lawrence: University Press of Kansas, 2004.

Balderrama, Francisco. *In Defense of La Raza, the Los Angeles Mexican Consulate, and the Mexican Community, 1929 to 1936.* Tucson: University of Arizona Press, 1982.

Bartra, Armando. *Guerrero Bronco: Campesinos, ciudadanos y guerrilleros en la Costa Grande.* Mexico City: Ediciones Era, 1996.

Bartra, Armando, ed. *Los Herederos de Zapata: Movimientos Campesinos Posrevolucionarios en México.* Mexico City: Ediciones Era, 1985.

———. *Regenración, 1900–1918: La corriente más radical de la Revolución Mexicana de 1910 a través de su periódico de combate.* Mexico City: Ediciones Era, 1977.

Bebout, Lee. *Mythohistorical Interventions: The Chicano Movement and Its Legacies.* Minneapolis: University of Minnesota Press, 2011.

Bellingeri, Marco. *Del agrarismo armado a la Guerra de los Pobres: 1940–1974.* Mexico City: Casa Juan Pablos, 2003.

Bello, Walden. *Dark Victory: The United States, Structural Adjustment, and Global Poverty.* London: Pluto, 1994.

Belnap, Jeffrey, and Raúl Fernández, eds. *José Martí's "Our America": From National to Hemispheric Cultural Studies.* Durham, NC: Duke University Press, 1998.

Berger, Dan. *Captive Nation: Black Prison Organizing in the Civil Rights Era.* Chapel Hill: University of North Carolina Press, 2014.

———. *Outlaws of America: The Weather Underground and the Politics of Solidarity.* Oakland, CA: AK Press, 2006.

Berger, Dan, ed. *The Hidden 1970s: Histories of Radicalism.* New Brunswick, NJ: Rutgers University Press, 2010.

Bhenken, Brian D. *The Struggle in Black and Brown: African American and Mexican American Relations during the Civil Rights Era.* Lincoln: University of Nebraska Press, 2013.

Biondi, Martha. *To Stand and Fight: The Struggle for Civil Rights in Postwar New York City.* Cambridge, MA: Harvard University Press, 2003.

Bizberg, Ilan. *Modernization and Corporatism in Government/Labor Relations.* Mexico City: Colegio de Mexico, 1990.

———. "La transformación del regimen politico mexicano: Entre el pluralismo y el neocorporativismo." In *Mexico: Una agenda para fin del siglo,* ed. Alberto Aziz Nassiff, 175–190. Mexico City: La Jornada, 1996.

Blackwell, Maylei. ¡Chicana Power! Contested Histories of Feminism in the Chicano Movement. Austin: University of Texas Press, 2011.

———. "Geographies of Difference: Mapping Multiple Feminist Insurgencies and Transnational Public Cultures in the Americas." PhD diss., University of California, Santa Cruz, 2000.

Blauner, Robert. "Internal Colonialism and Ghetto Revolt." Social Problems 16 (Spring 1969): 393–408.

Boal, Augosto. Hamlet and the Baker's Son: My Life in Theatre and Politics. New York: Routledge, 2001.

———. Theatre of the Oppressed. Minnesota: TCG Books, 1985.

Bologna, Sergio. "The Tribe of Moles." In Autonomia: Post-Political Politics, ed. Sylvère Lotringer and Christian Marazzi, 36–61. New York: Semiotext(e), 1980.

Bonfil Batalla, Guillermo. México Profundo: Reclaiming a Civilization. Austin: University of Texas Press, 1996.

Bowman, Timothy Paul. "What about Texas? The Forgotten Cause of Antonio Orendain and the Río Grande Valley Farm Workers, 1966–1982." Master's thesis, University of Texas at Arlington, 2005.

Broyles-González, Yolanda. El Teatro Campesino: Theater in the Chicano Movement. Austin: University of Texas Press, 1994.

Bruce-Novoa, Juan, and C. May Gamboa. "Tiempovillo: Paraguayan Experimental Theatre." Latin American Theatre Review 8, no. 2 (Spring 1975): 75–83.

Buendía, Manuel. La CIA en México. Mexico City: Océano, 1983.

Bufe, Chaz, and Mitchell Cowen Verter, eds. Dreams of Freedom: A Ricardo Flores Magón Reader. Oakland, CA: AK Press, 2006.

Buhle, Paul, and Dan Georgakas, eds. The Immigrant Left in the United States. Albany, NY: SUNY Press, 1996.

Burton-Rose, Daniel. Guerrilla USA: The George Jackson Brigade and the Anticapitalist Underground of the 1970s. Berkeley: University of California Press, 2010.

Caban, Pedro. "The New Synthesis of Latin American and Latino Studies." In Borderless Borders: U.S. Latinos, Latin Americans, and the Paradox of Interdependence, ed. Frank Bonilla et al. Philadelphia: Temple University Press, 1998.

Cabrera López, Patricia. Pensamiento, cultura y literatura en América Latina. Mexico City: UNAM, 2004.

Calderón, Fernando, and Adela Cedillo. Challenging Authoritarianism in Mexico: Revolutionary Struggles and the Dirty War, 1964–1982. New York: Routledge, 2011.

Calderón, Roberto R. "Union, Paz y Trabajo: Laredo's Mexican Mutual Aid Societies in the 1890s." In Mexican Americans in Texas History, Selected Essays, ed. Emilio Zamora, Cynthia Orozco, and Rodolfo Rocha. Austin: Texas State Historical Association, 2000.

Callahan, Manuel. "Crisis and Permanent War on the U.S.-Mexico Borderlands." Unpublished manuscript in author's possession.

———. "In Defense of Conviviality and the Collective Subject." Polis: Revista Latino-Americano 2012: 3. http://polis.revues.org/8432.

———. "Mexican Border Troubles: Social War, Settler Colonialism, and the Production of Frontier Discourses, 1848–1880." PhD diss., University of Texas at Austin, 2003.

———. "This Is No War of Bandits: Los Martires de Tejas, 1913." Unpublished manuscript in author's possession.

———. "Why Not Share a Dream? Zapatismo as Political and Cultural Practice." In *Zapatismo as Political and Cultural Practice*, special issue, *Humboldt Journal of Social Relations* 29, no. 1 (2005): 6–37.

———. "Zapatismo beyond Chiapas." In *Globalize Liberation: How to Uproot the System and Build a Better World*, ed. D. Solnit, 217–228. San Francisco: City Lights Books, 2005.

Camin, Héctor Aguilar, and Lorenzo Meyer. *In the Shadow of the Mexican Revolution: Contemporary Mexican History, 1910–1989*. Translated by Luis Alberto Fierro. Austin: University of Texas Press, 2010.

Camp, Jordan T. "Blues Geographies and the Security Turn: Interpreting the Housing Crisis in Los Angeles." *American Quarterly* 64, no. 3 (September 2012): 543–570.

Campos Gómez, Eleazar, and Lucio Cabañas. *Lucio Cabañas y el Partido de los Pobres: Una Experiencia Guerrillera en Mexico*. Mexico City: Editorial Nuestra America, 1987.

Carey, Elaine. *Plaza of Sacrifices: Gender, Power, and Terror in 1968 Mexico*. Albuquerque: University of New Mexico Press, 2007.

Carrigan, William D., and Clive Webb. *Forgotten Dead: Mob Violence against Mexicans in the United States, 1848–1928*. Oxford, UK: Oxford University Press, 2013.

Castañeda, Antonia. "Introduction: Gender on the Borderlands." *Frontiers: A Journal of Women Studies* 24 (2003): xi–xix.

———. "'We Shall Not Be Moved': The Chicano Movement and Solidarity with Chile." Talk presented at Trinity University, San Antonio, February 20, 2014.

Castellanos, Laura. *Mexico Armado: 1943–1981*. Mexico City: Era, 2007.

Castillo, Susan D. "Festivales De Teatro En América." *Latin American Theater Review* 8, no. 1 (1974): 75–78.

Chabram-Dernersesian, Angie. "I Throw Punches for My Race, but I Don't Want to Be a Man: Writing Us—Chica-nos (Girl, US)/Chicanas—into the Movement Script." In *Cultural Studies*, ed. Lawrence Grossberg, Cary Nelson, and Paula Treichler, 81–95. New York: Routledge, 1991.

Chakrabarty, Dipesh. *Provincializing Europe: Postcolonial Thought and Historical Difference*. Princeton, NJ: Princeton University Press, 2000.

Chambers, Colin, ed. *The Continuum Companion to Twentieth Century Theater*. New York: Continuum, 2006.

Chang, Jeff. *Can't Stop, Won't Stop: A History of the Hip Hop Generation*. New York: Picador, 2005.

Chard, Daniel. "Rallying for Repression: Police Terror, 'Law-and-Order' Politics, and the Decline of Maine's Prisoners' Rights Movement." *The Sixties: A Journal of History, Politics and Culture* 5, no. 1 (2012).

Chávez, Ernesto. *"¡Mi Raza Primero!": Nationalism, Identity, and Insurgency in the Chicano Movement in Los Angeles, 1966–1978*. Berkeley: University of California Press, 2002.

Chávez, Marisela R. "Despierten hermanas y hermanos: Women, the Chicano Movement, and Chicana Feminisms in California." PhD diss., Stanford University, 2005.

———. "Pilgrimage to the Homeland: California Chicanas and International

Women's Year, Mexico City, 1975." In *Memories and Migrations: Mapping Boricua and Chicana Histories*, ed. Vicki Ruiz and John Chávez, 170–195. Urbana: University of Illinois Press, 2008.

———. "'We Lived and Breathed and Worked the Movement': The Contradictions and Rewards of Chicana/Mexicana in El Centro de Acción Social Autónomo-Hermandad General de Trabajadores (CASA-HGT), Los Angeles, 1975–1978." In *Las Obreras: Chicana Politics of Work and Family*, ed. Vicki L. Ruiz and Chon Noriega, 83–105. Los Angeles: UCLA Chicano Studies Research Center Publications, 2000.

Chen, Ching-In, Jai Dulani, and Leah Lakshmi Piepzna-Samarasinha, eds. *The Revolution Starts at Home: Confronting Intimate Violence within Activist Communities*. Boston: South End, 2011.

Chun, Jennifer Jihye, George Lipsitz, and Young Shin. "Intersectionality as a Social Movement Strategy." *Signs* 38, no. 4 (Summer 2013): 917–940.

Churchill, Ward, and Jim Vander Wall. *Agents of Repression: The FBI's Secret Wars against the Black Panther Party and the American Indian Movement*. Boston: South End, 1988.

Churchill, Ward, and Jim Vander Wall, eds. *The COINTELPRO Papers: Documents from the FBI's Secret Wars against Dissent in the United States*. Boston: South End, 1990.

Cilia Olmos, David. *Carpizo y la CNDH: La otra cara de la Guerra Sucia*. Mexico City: Editorial Comuna, 2002.

Cisneros, Enrique. *Si me permiten actuar*. Mexico City: CLETA, n.d.

Cleaver, Harry. "The Inversion of Class Perspective in Marxian Theory: From Valorization to Self-Valorization." In *Open Marxism*, vol. 2: *Theory and Practice*. London: Pluto, 1992.

———. "Nature, Neoliberalism, and Sustainable Development: Between Charybdis and Scylla?" Paper prepared for the Fourth Ecological Meeting on Economy and Ecology, Instituto Piaget, Viseu, Portugal, April 17–19, 1997.

———. "The Uses of an Earthquake." *Midnight Notes* 9 (1988): 10–14.

Cleaver, Kathleen, and George Katsiaficas, eds. *Liberation, Imagination, and the Black Panther Party: A New Look at the Panthers and Their Legacy*. New York: Routledge, 2001.

Communist Collective of the Chicano Nation. "Report to the Communist Collective of the Chicano Nation on the Chicano National-Colonial Question." 1973. https://www.marxists.org/history/erol/ncm-1a/cccn/introduction.htm.

Contreras, Sheila Marie. *Blood Lines: Myth, Indigenism, and Chicana/o Literature*. Austin: University of Texas Press, 2008.

Corona, Bert. "La Raza Unida Party and the 'Illegal Alien' Scare." Speech delivered at Mi Raza Primero Conference, Muskegon, MI, January 22, 1972. New York: Pathfinder, 1972.

Coronado, Raúl. *A World Not to Come: A History of Latino Writing and Print Culture*. Cambridge, MA: Harvard University Press, 2013.

Corpi, Lucha. *Palabras de Mediodia / Noon Words*. Houston: Arte Público, 2001.

Crenshaw, Kimberlé. "Mapping the Margins: Intersectionality, Identity Politics and Violence against Women of Color." *Stanford Law Review* 43, no. 6 (1993): 1241–1301.

Cunningham, David. *There's Something Happening Here: The New Left, the Klan, and FBI Counterintelligence*. Berkeley: University of California Press, 2004.

Dalla Costa, Mariarosa, and Selma James. *The Power of Women and the Subversion of the Community*. Bristol, UK: Falling Wall, 1972.

Darwish, Mahmoud. *The Butterfly's Burden*. Port Townsend, WA: Copper Canyon, 2007.

de la Torre, Alfredo. "Entrevista con Mario Cantú." *Caracol* 5, no. 4 (December 1978): 16.

Del Castillo, Adelaida A. *Between Borders: Essays on Mexicana/Chicana History*. Los Angeles: Flor y Canto, 1981.

Delgado, Alvaro. *El Ejército de Dios: Nuevas revelaciones sobre la extrema derecha en México*. Mexico City: Plaza y Janés, 2004.

———. *El Yunque: La Ultraderecha en el poder*. Mexico City: Plaza y Janés, 2003.

Dinges, John. *The Condor Years: How Pinochet and His Allies Brought Terrorism to Three Continents*. New York: New Press, 2004.

Dolan, Jill. *Utopia in Performance: Finding Hope at the Theater*. Ann Arbor: University of Michigan Press, 2005.

Dolan, Maureen. "Chicano Theatre in Transition: The Experience of El Teatro de la Esperanza." PhD diss., University of Glasgow, 2012.

Doyle, Kate. Comisión Nacional de los Derechos Humanos Mexico: *Informe Especial Sobre las Quejas en Materia de Desapariciones Forzadas Ocurridas en la Decada de los 70 y Principios de los 80*. Anexo I, "Gráficas," no. 10. http://www.cndh.org.mx/sites/all/doc/Informes/Especiales/2001_Desapariciones70y80.pdf.

———. "La 'diplomacia tranquila' de Estados Unidos," *Proceso* 1384 (May 11, 2003): 20.

———. "Human Rights and the Dirty War in Mexico." *National Security Archives*, May 11, 2003. http://nsarchive.gwu.edu/NSAEBB/NSAEBB89/.

———. "La Operación Intercepción: Los peligros del unilateralismo." *Proceso* 1380 (April 13, 2003): 44–48.

———. "Archivos abiertos." *Proceso* (March 2, 2003): 37.

———. "'Los Halcones': Made in the USA." *Proceso* 1388 (June 8, 2003): 36–42.

Dudziak, Mary L. *Cold War Civil Rights: Race and the Image of American Democracy*. Princeton, NJ: Princeton University Press, 2002.

Dyer-Witheford, Nick. *Cyber-Marx: Cycles and Circuits of Struggle in High-Technology Capitalism*. Urbana: University of Illinois Press, 1999.

Elbaum, Max. *Revolution in the Air: Sixties Radicals Turn to Lenin, Mao, and Che*. London: Verso, 2002.

El Kilombo Intergalactico. *Beyond Resistance: Everything: An Interview with Subcomandante Insurgente Marcos*. Durham, NC: Paper Boat, 2007.

Escobar, Edward J. *Race, Police, and the Making of a Political Identity: Mexican Americans and the Los Angeles Police Department, 1900–1945*. Berkeley: University of California Press, 1999.

Esperanza, Aparicio, et al. *Voces de la preparatoria popular*. México City: Plaza y Janés, 2007.

Espino, Virginia. "'Woman Sterilized as Gives Birth': Forced Sterilization and the Chicana Resistance in the 1970s." In *Las Obreras: Chicana Politics of Work and*

Family, ed. Vicki Ruiz (Los Angeles: UCLA Chicano Studies Research Center Publications, 2002), 65–82.

Esteva, Gustavo. *La batalla en México rural*. Mexico City: Siglo XXI, 1980.

Esteva, Gustavo, and Madhu S. Prakash. *Grassroots Postmodernism: Remaking the Soils of Cultures*. London: Zed Books, 1998.

Esteva, Gustavo, Madhu S. Prakash, and Dana L. Stuchul. "From A Pedagogy for Liberation to Liberation from Pedagogy." In *Rethinking Freire: Globalization and the Environmental Crisis*, ed. C. A. Bowers and Apffel-Marglin, 13–30. Mahwah, NJ: Lawrence Erlbaum Associates, 2005.

Farber, Peter, and Jeff Roche. *The Conservative Sixties*. New York: Peter Lang, 2003.

Fazio, Carlos. *La cruz y el martillo*. Mexico City: Joaquin Mortiz Planeta, 1988.

Fein, Seth. "New Empire into Old: Making Mexican Newsreels the Cold War Way." *Diplomatic History* 28, no. 5 (2004): 201.

Ferreira, Jason. "All Power to the People: A Comparative History of 'Third World' Radicalism in San Francisco, 1968–1974." PhD diss., University of California, Berkeley, 2003.

Ferreira da Silva, Denise. *Toward a Global Idea of Race*. Minneapolis: University of Minnesota Press, 2007.

Finan, Christopher. *From the Palmer Raids to the Patriot Act: A History of the Fight for Free Speech in America*. Boston: Beacon Press, 2008.

Fishkin, Shelley Fisher. "Crossroads of Cultures: The Transnational Turn in American Studies." Presidential Address to the American Studies Association, November 12, 2004. *American Quarterly* 57, no. 1 (March 2005): 17–57.

Flamm, Michael. *Law and Order: Street Crime, Civil Unrest, and the Crisis of Liberalism in the 1960s*. New York: Columbia University Press, 2007.

Flores, Richard R. *Remembering the Alamo: Memory, Modernity, and the Master Symbol*. Austin: University of Texas Press, 2002.

Flores, Roberto. "Chicano Artists and Zapatistas Walk Together Asking, Listening, Learning: The Role of Transnational Informal Learning Networks in the Creation of a Better World." PhD diss., University of Southern California, 2007.

Fluck, Winfried, Donald E. Pease, and John Carlos Rowe, eds. *Re-Framing the Transnational Turn in American Studies*. Hanover, NH: Dartmouth University Press, 2011.

Frank, Andre Gunder. *Capitalism and Underdevelopment in Latin America: Historical Studies of Chile and Brazil*. New York: Monthly Review Press, 1967.

Fraser, Carey. "An American Dilemma: Race and Realpolitik in the American Response to the Bandung Conference, 1955." In *Window on Freedom: Race, Civil Rights, and Foreign Affairs, 1945–1988*, ed. Brenda Gayle Plummer, 115–140. Chapel Hill: University of North Carolina Press, 2003.

Frazier, Lessie Jo, and Deborah Cohen. "Defining the Space of Mexico '68: Heroic Masculinity in the Prison and 'Women' in the Streets." *Hispanic American Historical Review* 83, no. 4 (2003): 617–660.

Fregoso, Rosa Linda. "Reproduction and Miscegenation on the Borderland: Mapping the Maternal Body of Tejanas." In *Chicana Feminisms: A Critical Reader*, ed. Gabriela F. Arredondo, Aida Hurtado, Norma Klahn, Olga Najera-Ramirez, and Patricia Zavella, 324–348. Durham, NC: Duke University Press, 2003.

Frente Latino Americano de Trabajadores de la Cultura. *Comunicado* no. 1. August 1, 1972.

Frischman, Donald H. *El Nuevo Teatro Popular en México*. Mexico City: Instituto Nacional de Belles Artes, 1990.

Fuentes, Victor. "El Festival de Manisales." *Chicano Theatre Three* (Spring 1974): 45–48.

——. "La creación colectiva del Teatro Experimental del Cali." In *Popular Theater for Social Change in Latin America*, ed. Gerardo Luzuriaga, 338–349. Los Angeles: UCLA Latin American Center Publications, 1978.

Galeano, Eduardo. *Open Veins of Latin America: Five Centuries of the Pillage of a Continent*. New York: Monthly Review Press, 1997.

García, Arnoldo. "Toward a Left without Borders: The Story of the Center for Autonomous Social Action—General Brotherhood of Workers." *Monthly Review* 54, no. 3 (July–August 2002): 69–78.

García, Ignacio M. *Chicanismo: The Forging of a Militant Ethos among Mexican Americans*. Tucson: University of Arizona Press, 1997.

García, Mario T. "*La Frontera*: The Border as Symbol and Reality in Mexican-American Thought." In David G. Gutiérrez, *Between Two Worlds: Mexican Immigrants in the United States*, 175–212. Wilmington, DE: SR Books, 1996.

——. *Memories of Chicano History: The Life and Narrative of Bert Corona*. Berkeley: University of California Press, 1994.

——. *Mexican Americans: Leadership, Ideology, and Identity, 1930–1960*. New Haven, CT: Yale University Press, 1991.

Garcia-Acevedo, María Rosa. "Return to Aztlán: Mexican Policy Design toward Chicanos." In *Chicanas/Chicanos at the Crossroads: Social, Economic, and Political Change*, ed. David R. Maciel and Isidro D. Ortiz, 130–155. Tucson: University of Arizona Press, 1996.

García Canclini, Néstor. *Arte popular y sociedad en América Latina*. Mexico City: Grijalbo, 1977.

García Sánchez, Liliana. *Judith Reyes, una mujer de canto revolucionario*. Mexico City: Redez, 2007.

Garín, Raúl Álvarez. *La Estela de Tlatelolco*. Mexico City: Ithaca, 2002.

Gelbspan, Ross. *Break-ins, Death Threats, and the FBI: The Covert War against the Central America Movement*. Boston: South End, 1991.

Georgakas, Dan, and Marvin Surkin. *Detroit, I Do Mind Dying*. Boston: South End, 1998.

Gill, Lesley. *The School of the Americas: Military Training and Political Violence in the Americas*. Durham, NC: Duke University Press, 2004.

Gilroy, Paul. *Small Acts: Thoughts on the Politics of Black Cultures*. New York: Serpent's Tail, 1994.

Goldman, Shifra M. "A Public Voice: Fifteen Years of Chicano Posters." *Art Journal* 44, no. 1 (Spring 1984): 50–57.

Goldman, Shifra, and Tomás Ybarra-Frausto. *Arte Chicano: A Comprehensive Annotated Bibliography of Chicano Art, 1965–1981*. Chicano Studies Library Publications Unit, University of California, Berkeley, 1985.

Gómez, Alan Eladio. "Feminism, Torture, and the Politics of Chicana/Third World

Solidarity: An Interview with Olga Talamante." *Radical History Review* 101 (Spring 2008): 160–178.

———. "'Nuestras vidas corren casi paralelas': Chicanos, Puerto Rican Independentistas, and the Prison Rebellion Years at Leavenworth, 1969–1972." In *Behind Bars: Latino/as and Prison in the United States,* ed. Suzanne Oboler, 67–96. New York: Palgrave-Macmillan, 2008.

———. "Resisting Living Death at Marion Federal Penitentiary, 1972." *Radical History Review* 96 (Fall 2006): 58–86.

———. "The Student Strike: UNAM." Master's thesis, University of Texas at Austin, 2002.

———. *"With Dignity Intact": Rainbow Coalitions, Control Units, and Struggles for Human Rights in the US Federal Prison System, 1969–1974.* Lincoln: University of Nebraska Press, forthcoming.

Gómez Quiñones, Juan. *Sembradores: Ricardo Flores Magon y El Partido Liberal Mexicano: A Eulogy and Critique.* Monograph no. 5, Chicano Studies Center Publications, University of California, Los Angeles, 1973.

González, Antonio. "Chicano Politics and U.S. Policy in Central America, 1979–1990." In *Chicano Politics and Society in the Late Twentieth Century,* ed. David Montejano, 154–175. Austin: University of Texas Press, 1999.

González, Martha. "Chican@ Artivistas: East Los Angeles Trenches Transborder Tactics." PhD diss., University of Washington, 2013.

Gonzalez, Pablo. "Autonomy Road: The Cultural Politics of Chicana/o Autonomous Organizing in Los Angeles, California." PhD diss., University of Texas at Austin, 2011.

Gordon, Avery. *Ghostly Matters: Haunting and the Sociological Imagination.* Minneapolis: University of Minnesota Press, 1996.

Gosse, Van. *Rethinking the New Left: An Interpretative History.* New York: Palgrave Macmillan, 2005.

Grandin, Greg. *Empire's Workshop: Latin America, the United States, and the Rise of the New Imperialism.* New York: Metropolitan Books, 2006.

———. *The Last Colonial Massacre: Latin America in the Cold War.* Chicago: University of Chicago Press, 2004.

Grewal, Inderpal. *Transnational America: Feminisms, Diasporas, Neoliberalisms.* Durham, NC: Duke University Press, 2005.

Grosfoguel, Ramón. "Developmentalism, Modernity, and Dependency Theory in Latin America." *Nepantla: Views from the South* 1, no. 2 (2000): 347–374.

Grosfoguel, Ramón, Nelson Maldonado-Torres, and José David Saldívar, eds. *Latin@s in the World-System: Decolonization Struggles in the 21st Century U.S. Empire.* Boulder, CO: Paradigm, 2006.

Grow, Michael. *U.S. Presidents and Latin American Interventions: Pursuing Regime Change in the Cold War.* Lawrence: University of Kansas Press, 2008.

Guerra-Garza, Victor, ed. *HOJAS: A Chicano Journal of Education.* Austin: Juárez-Lincoln University, 1976.

Guha, Ranajit. "The Prose of Counter-Insurgency." In *Selected Subaltern Studies,* ed. Ranajit Guha and Gayatri Chakravorty Spivak, 45–88. New York: Oxford University Press, 1988.

Guidotti-Hernández, Nicole M. *Unspeakable Violence: Remapping U.S. and Mexican National Imaginaries.* Durham, NC: Duke University Press, 2011.

Guridy, Frank A. "From Solidarity to Cross-Fertilization: Afro-Cuban/African American Interaction during the 1930s and 1940s." *Radical History Review* 87 (Fall 2003): 19–48.

Gutiérrez, David G. "*Sin Fronteras?* Chicanos, Mexican Americans, and the Emergence of the Contemporary Immigration Debate, 1968–78," in David G. Gutiérrez, *Between Two Worlds: Mexican Immigrants in the United States,* 175–212. Wilmington: SR Books, 1996.

——. *Walls and Mirrors: Mexican Americans, Mexican Immigrants, and the Politics of Ethnicity.* Berkeley: University of California Press, 1995.

Gutiérrez, José Angel. *The Making of a Chicano Militant: Lessons from Cristal.* Madison: University of Wisconsin Press, 1998.

Haas, Jeffrey. *The Assassination of Fred Hampton: How the FBI and the Chicago Police Murdered a Black Panther.* Chicago: Lawrence Hill Books, 2009.

Hahn, Peter L., and Mary Ann Heiss, eds. *Empire and Revolution: The United States and the Third World since 1945.* Columbus: Ohio State University Press, 2001.

Hale, Charles, ed. *Engaging Contradictions: Theory, Politics, and Methods of Activist Scholarship.* Berkeley: University of California Press, 2008.

Hall, Jacquelyn Dowd. "The Long Civil Rights Movement and the Political Uses of the Past." *Journal of American History* 91, no. 4 (March 2005): 1233–1263.

Hall, Stuart, and Bill Swartz. *The Hard Road to Renewal: Thatcherism and the Crisis of the Left.* New York: Verso, 1988.

Hames-García, Michael. *Fugitive Thought: Prison Movements, Race, and the Meaning of Justice.* Minneapolis: University of Minnesota Press, 2004.

Hart, John Mason. *Anarchism and the Mexican Working Class, 1860–1931.* Austin: University of Texas Press, 1987.

——. *Empire and Revolution: The Americans in Mexico since the Civil War.* Berkeley: University of California Press, 2002.

Hartman, Saidiya. *Scenes of Subjection: Terror, Slavery, and Self-Making in Nineteenth-Century America.* New York: Oxford University Press, 1997.

Harvey, David. *The New Imperialism.* New York: Oxford University Press, 2005.

Heatherton, Christina. *The Color Line and the Class Struggle: The Mexican Revolution, Internationalism, and the American Century.* Berkeley: University of California Press, forthcoming.

——. "University of Radicalism: Ricardo Flores Magón and Leavenworth Penitentiary." *American Quarterly* 66, no. 3 (2014): 557–581.

Hernández, Inés. "Sara Estela Ramirez Legacy." *Western Women Writers* 6, no. 1 (Spring 1989): 13–26.

Hernández Padilla, Salvador. *El Magonismo: Historia de una pasión libertaria, 1900–1912.* Mexico City: Era, 1999.

Hill, Rebecca N. *Men, Mobs, and Law: Anti-Lynching and Labor Defense in U.S. Radical History.* Durham, NC: Duke University Press, 2008.

Hirschman, Jack, ed. *Art on the Line: Essays by Artists about the Point Where Their Art and Activism Intersect.* Willimantic, CT: Curbstone, 2002.

Ho, Fred. "Fists of Revolution: The Revolutionary History of I Wor Kuen/League of Revolutionary Struggle." In *Legacy to Liberation: Politics and Culture of Revolu-*

tionary Asian Pacific America, ed. Fred Ho, Carolyn Antonio, Diane Fujino, and Steve Yip, 3–14. Oakland, CA: AK Press, 2000.

Hodges, Donald C. *Mexican Anarchism after the Revolution*. Austin: University of Texas Press, 1995.

Holloway, John. *Change the World without Taking Power: The Meaning of Revolution Today*. London: Pluto, 2002.

———. "Dignity's Revolt." In *Zapatista! Reinventing Revolution in Mexico*, ed. John Holloway and Eloína Peláez, 159–198. London: Pluto, 1998.

———. "Zapatismo Urbano." *Humboldt Journal of Social Relations* 29, no. 1 (2005): 168–179.

Huerta, Jorge A. "En Torno." *Chicano Theatre One* (Spring 1973): 3.

———. "The Influences of Latin American Theater on Chicano Theater." In *Mexican American Theater: Then and Now*, ed. Nicolas Kanellos, 68–77. Houston: Arte Público, 1983.

———. *Necessary Theater: Six Plays about the Chicano Experience*. Houston: Arte Público, 1989.

Illich, Ivan. "To Hell with Good Intentions." An address by Monsignor Ivan Illich to the Conference on Inter-American Student Projects (CIASP) in Cuernavaca, Mexico, April 20, 1968. http://www.swaraj.org/illich_hell.htm.

Immerman, Richard H. *The CIA in Guatemala: The Foreign Policy of Intervention*. Austin: University of Texas Press, 1982.

Jardón, Raúl. *El Espionaje contra el Movimiento Estudiantil: Los documentos de la Dirección Federal de Seguridad y las agencies de inteligencia estadounidense en 1968*. Mexico City: Editorial ITACA, 2003.

Johnson, Benjamin H. *Revolution in Texas: How a Forgotten Rebellion and Its Bloody Suppression Turned Mexicans into Americans*. New Haven, CT: Yale University Press, 2009.

Johnson, Gaye Theresa. *Spaces of Conflict, Sounds of Solidarity: Music, Race, and Spatial Entitlement in Los Angeles*. Berkeley: University of California Press, 2013.

Joseph, Gilbert M., Catherine C. Legrand, and Ricardo D. Salvatore, eds. *Close Encounters of Empire: Writing the Cultural History of U.S.–Latin American Relations*. Durham, NC: Duke University Press, 1998.

Joseph, Gilbert M., and Daniela Spenser. *In from the Cold: Latin America's New Encounter with the Cold War*. Durham, NC: Duke University Press, 2011.

Joseph, Peniel E. *Waiting 'Til the Midnight Hour: A Narrative History of Black Power in America*. New York: Henry Holt, 2007.

Kanellos, Nicolas. *Hispanic Literature of the US: A Comprehensive Reference*. Westport, CT: Greenwood, 2003.

Kaplan, Amy, and Donald E. Pease, eds. *Cultures of United States Imperialism*. Durham, NC: Duke University Press, 1994.

Katsiaficas, George. *The Imagination of the New Left: A Global Analysis of 1968*. Boston: South End, 1987.

Kaufman, Robert. *The Politics of Land Reform in Chile, 1950–1970: Public Policy, Political Institutions, and Social Change*. Cambridge, MA: Harvard University Press, 1972.

Kazanjian, David. *The Colonizing Trick: National Culture and Imperial Citizenship in Early America*. Minneapolis: University of Minnesota Press, 2003.

Kelley, Robin D. G. "Foreword." In Cedric J. Robinson, *Black Marxism: The Making of the Black Radical Tradition*, xv. Chapel Hill: University of North Carolina Press, 2000.

———. *Freedom Dreams: The Black Radical Imagination*. Boston: Beacon, 2002.

———. *Hammer and Hoe: Alabama Communists during the Great Depression*. Chapel Hill: University of North Carolina Press, 1990.

———. *Yo' Mama's Disfunktional! Fighting the Culture Wars in Urban America*. Boston: Beacon, 1997.

Khasnabish, Alex. *Zapatismo beyond Borders: New Imaginations of Political Possibility*. Toronto: University of Toronto Press, 2008.

Klein, Hilary. *Compañeras: Zapatista Women's Stories*. New York: Seven Stories Press, 2015.

Knight, Alan. "Empire, Hegemony, and Globalization in the Americas." *NACLA Report on the Americas* 39, no. 2 (September/October 2005): 8–12.

Krauze, Enrique. *Mexico: Biography of Power: A History of Modern Mexico, 1910–1996*. New York: Harper Perennial, 1998.

Lamb, Ruth Stanton. *Mexican Theatre of the Twentieth Century: Bibliography and Study*. Claremont, CA: Ocelot, 1975.

Latorre, Guisela. *Walls of Empowerment: Chicana/o Indigenist Murals of California*. Austin: University of Texas Press, 2008.

Law, Victoria. *Resistance behind Bars: The Struggles of Incarcerated Women*. Oakland, CA: PM Press, 2009.

League of Revolutionary Struggle. *Statements on the Founding of the League of Revolutionary Struggle*. Oakland, CA: Getting Together Publications, 1978.

Lee, Christopher J. *Making a World after Empire: The Bandung Moment and Its Political Afterlives*. Athens: Ohio University Press, 2010.

Leo Grande, William M. *Our Own Backyard: The United States in Central America, 1977–1992*. Chapel Hill: University of North Carolina Press, 1998.

Licón, Gustavo. "¡La Union Hace La Fuerza! (Unity Creates Strength!): MEChA." PhD diss., University of Southern California, 2009.

Limón, Jose E. "El Primer Congreso Mexicanista de 1911: A Precursor to Contemporary Chicanismo." *Aztlán* 5 (Spring-Fall 1974): 85–117.

Linebaugh, Peter, and Marcus Rediker. *The Many-Headed Hydra: Sailors, Slaves, Commoners, and the Hidden History of the Revolutionary Atlantic*. Boston: Beacon, 2000.

Lipsitz, George. *American Studies in a Moment of Danger*. Minneapolis: University of Minnesota Press, 2001.

———. *Time Passages: Collective Memory and American Popular Culture*. Minneapolis: University of Minnesota Press, 2001.

Lomnitz, Claudio. *The Return of Comrade Ricardo Flores Magón*. New York: Zone Books, 2014.

Lopez, Jaime. *10 Años de Guerrillas en México 1964-1974*. Mexico City: Editorial Posada, 1974.

López Rivera, Oscar. "A Century of Colonialism: One Hundred Years of Puerto Rican Resistance." In *Warfare in the American Homeland: Policing and Prison in a Penal Democracy*, ed. Joy James, 161–196. Durham, NC: Duke University Press, 2007.

López y Rivas, Gilberto. "¿SEDENA forma paramilitares?" *La Jornada*, September 28, 2001.

Loyd, Jena M. *Health Rights Are Civil Rights: Peace and Justice Activism in Los Angeles, 1963–1978*. Minneapolis: University of Minnesota Press, 2014.

Loyo Brambila, Aurora. *El movimiento ferrocarrillero en México, 1958–1959*. Mexico City: Era, 1980.

———. *El movimiento magisterial de 1958 en México*. Mexico City: Era, 1980.

Luzuriaga, Gerardo. *Introducción a las teorías latino-americanas del Teatro*. Puebla: Universidad Autónoma de Puebla, 1990.

Lytle-Hernandez, Kelly. *Migra! A History of the U.S. Border Patrol*. Berkeley: University of California Press, 2010.

Mabry, Donald. *The Mexican University and the State: Student Conflicts, 1910–1971*. College Station: Texas A&M University Press, 1982.

Machuca, Jesus Antonio. "Nacion, Mestizaje y Racismo." In *Nacion, Racismo e Identidad*, ed. Alicia Castellanos Guerrero and Juan Manuel Sandoval Palacios, 37–74. Mexico City: Nuestro Tiempo, 1998.

MacLachlan, Colin M. *Anarchism and the Mexican Revolution: The Political Trials of Ricardo Flores Magón in the United States*. Berkeley: University of California Press, 1991.

Mallon, Florencia. "Barbudos, Warriors, and Rotos: The MIR, Masculinity, and Power in the Chilean Agrarian Reform, 1965–1974." In *Changing Men and Masculinities in Latin America*, ed. Matthew C. Gutmann, 179–215. Durham, NC: Duke University Press, 2003.

Mariscal, Jorge. *Brown-Eyed Children of the Sun: Lessons from the Chicano Movement, 1965–1975*. Albuquerque: University of New Mexico Press, 2005.

Marrero, María Teresa. "From El Teatro Campesino to the Gay 1990s: Transformations and Fragments in the Evolution in Chicana/o Latina/o Theater and Performance." In *The State of Latino Theater in the United States*, ed. Luis Ramos-García, 39–66. New York: Routledge, 2002.

Martínez, Alma M. "Un Continente, Una Cultura? The Political Dialectic for a United Chicano, Mexican and Latin American Popular/Political Theatre Front, Mexico City, 1974." PhD diss., Stanford University, 2006.

Martínez, Elizabeth. "A View from Nuevo Mexico: Recollections of the *Movimiento* Left." *Monthly Review* 54, no. 3 (July-August 2002): 79–86.

Martínez, Elizabeth Sutherland. *The Youngest Revolution: A Personal Report on Cuba*. New York: Dial, 1969.

Martínez, Elizabeth Sutherland, and Enriqueta Longeaux y Vásquez. *Viva la Raza: The Struggle of the Mexican-American People*. New York: Doubleday, 1974.

Martínez Rodríguez, Martín. *Cancionero Subversivo: José de Molina Petet de la canción libertaria*. Mexico City: Ediciones Tequiani, 2005.

Marx, Karl. *The Grundrisse: Foundations of the Critique of Political Economy*. New York: Penguin Classics, 1993.

Mbembe, Achille. "Necropolitics." *Public Culture* 15, no. 1: 12.

McCoy, Alfred. *A Question of Torture: CIA Interrogation, from the Cold War to the War on Terror*. New York: Metropolitan Books, 2005.

McDuffie, Erik S. *Sojourning for Freedom: Black Women, American Communism, and the Making of Black Left Feminism.* Durham, NC: Duke University Press, 2011.

McGirr, Lisa. *Suburban Warriors: The Origins of the New American Right.* Princeton, NJ: Princeton University Press, 2001.

McKenna, Teresa. *Migrant Song: Politics and Process in Contemporary Chicano Literature.* Austin: University of Texas Press, 1997.

Medina, Jorge. *Universidad, política y sociedad.* Mexico City: Juan Pablos, 1978.

Medina Valdes, Gerardo. *Operación 10 de Junio.* Mexico City: Editorial Jus, 1972.

Mendiola, Tacho, Jr., and Max Martínez. *Chicano-Mexico Relations.* Mexican American Studies Monograph no. 4. Houston: Mexican American Studies Program, University of Houston–Houston Park, 1986.

Menjívar, Cecilia, and Néstor Rodríguez, eds. *When States Kill: Latin America, the U.S., and Technologies of Terror.* Austin: University of Texas Press, 2005.

Mesa-Bains, Amelia. "*Domesticana*: The Sensibility of Chicana Rasquache." In *Distant Relations: Chicano, Irish, and Mexican Art and Critical Writing,* ed. Trisha Ziff, 165–163. Santa Monica, CA: Smart Art, 1996.

"Message to the Chicano Delegation Visiting Mexico City." *La Raza* 1, no. 9 (September 1972): 3.

Meyer, Lorenzo. *Mexico and the United States in the Oil Controversy, 1917–1942.* Translated by Muriel Vasconcellos. Austin: University of Texas Press, 1997.

Middlebrook, Kevin J. *The Paradox of Revolution: Labor, the State, and Authoritarianism in Mexico.* Baltimore: Johns Hopkins University Press, 1995.

Midnight Notes Collective, ed. "Introduction to Zerowork 1." In *Midnight Oil: Work, Energy, War, 1973–1992,* 109–114. Brooklyn, NY: Autonomedia, 1992.

———. *Midnight Oil: Work, Energy, War, 1973–1992.* Brooklyn, NY: Autonomedia, 1992.

———. "New Enclosures." In *Midnight Oil: Work, Energy, War, 1973–1992.* Brooklyn, NY: Autonomedia, 1992.

Mignolo, Walter D. "Capitalism and Geopolitics of Knowledge: Latin American Social Thought and Latino/a American Studies." In *Critical Latin American and Latino Studies,* ed. Juan Poblete, 32–75. Minneapolis: University of Minnesota Press, 2003.

———. *The Idea of Latin America.* London: Blackwell, 2005.

Mohanty, Chandra Talpade. *Feminism without Borders: Decolonizing Theory, Practicing Solidarity.* Durham, NC: Duke University Press, 2003.

Montano, Mario. "Notes on the International Crisis." *Zerowork* 1 (1975). Reprinted in *Midnight Oil: Work, Energy, War, 1973–1992,* ed. Midnight Notes Collective, 115–142. Brooklyn, NY: Autonomedia, 1992.

Montejano, David. *Anglos and Mexicans in the Making of Texas, 1836–1986.* Austin: University of Texas Press, 1986.

———. *Quixote's Soldiers: A Local History of the Chicano Movement, 1966–1981.* Austin: University of Texas Press, 2010.

Montemayor, Carlos. *Guerra en el Paraiso.* Mexico City: Era, 2000.

———. *Los Informes Secretos.* Mexico City: Joaquín Mortiz, 1999.

Montoya, José. *In Formation: 20 Years of Joda.* San Jose, CA: Chusma House, 1992.

Mora, Magdalena. "A lo concreto: Impuestos sin provecho." *Sin Fronteras* 2, no. 6 (February 1976): 8.

———. "Carter's Grand Deception." *Sin Fronteras* 3, no. 10 (June 1977): 8.

———. "Conditions Prepared for a New Bracero Program." *Sin Fronteras* 3, no. 4 (December 1976): 8.

———. "Eastland Bill Reestablished Bracero Program." *Sin Fronteras* 2, no. 10 (June 1976): 9.

———. "FLOC—Unified Struggle of Agricultural Workers." *Sin Fronteras* 3, no. 11 (July 1977): 10.

———. "Latin American Workers Confront AFL-CIO Intervention." *Sin Fronteras* 3, no. 2 (October 1976): 8.

———. "Strong Rank and File Base Insures Genuine Worker's Movement." *Sin Fronteras* 3, no. 6 (February 1977): 8.

———. "The Tolteca Strike: Mexican Women and the Struggle for Union Representation." In *Mexican Immigrant Workers in the U.S.*, ed. Antonio Ríos-Bustamante, 111–117. Los Angeles: Chicano Studies Research Center Publications, University of California, 1981.

———. "Trade Unions Must Defend All Members." *Sin Fronteras* 3, no. 8 (April 1977): 8.

Mora, Magdalena, and Adelaida Del Castillo. *Mexican Women in the United States: Struggles Past and Present.* Occasional Paper no. 2. Chicano Studies Research Center Publications, University of California, Los Angeles, 1980.

Moraga, Cherríe. *The Hungry Woman: A Mexican Medea.* Albuquerque: West End, 1997.

———. "Queer Aztlán: the Re-formation of Chicano Tribe." In Moraga, *The Last Generation*, 145–174. Boston: South End, 2003.

Moraga, Cherríe, and Gloria Anzaldúa, eds. *This Bridge Called My Back: Writings by Radical Women of Color.* New York: Kitchen Table/Women of Color Press, 1984.

Morales, Aurora Levins. *Medicine Stories: History, Culture, and the Politics of Integrity.* Boston: South End, 1999.

Morely, Jefferson. "LITEMPO: The CIA's Eyes on Tlatelolco." National Security Archive Electronic Briefing Book no. 204. National Security Archive, 2006. http://www2.gwu.edu/~nsarchiv/NSAEBB/NSAEBB204/.

Mullen, Bill V. *Afro-Orientalism.* Minneapolis: University of Minnesota Press, 2004.

———. *Popular Fronts: Chicago and African-American Cultural Politics, 1935–46.* Urbana: University of Illinois Press, 1999.

Muñoz Cortes, Alicia. "The Struggle of the Mujeres to Liberate Olga Talamante, a Political Prisoner." Master's thesis, San Jose State University, 1999.

Muñoz Ramírez, Gloria. *EZLN 20 y 10: El Fuego y La Palabra.* Mexico City: La Jornada, 2003.

Muntaqim, Jalil. *We Are Our Own Liberators: Selected Prison Writings.* Montreal: Abraham Guillen Press, 2003.

Murguía, Alejandro. *The Medicine of Memory: A Mexica Clan in California.* Austin: University of Texas Press, 2002.

Murray, Pauli, and Mary O. Eastwood. "Jane Crow and the Law: Sex Discrimination and Title VII." *George Washington Law Review* 34, no. 2 (1965): 232–256.

"National Chicano Conference: Repression Workshop." *El Gallo: La Voz de la Justicia* 10, no. 2 (March–April 1978): 2.

Navarro, Armando. *La Raza Unida Party: A Chicano Challenge to the U.S. Two-Party Dictatorship.* Philadelphia: Temple University Press, 2000.

Negri, Antonio. *Marx beyond Marx: Lessons on the Grundrisse.* Brooklyn, NY: Autonomedia, 1991.

———. "Marx on the Cycle and on Crisis." In Negri, *Revolution Retrieved: Selected Writings on Marx, Keynes, Capitalist Crisis and New Social Subjects, 1967–83,* 47–90. London: Red Notes, 1988.

Noriega, Chon. Introductory note to "Self-Help Graphics: Tomás Benitez Talks to Harry Gamboa Jr." In *The Sons and Daughters of Los: Culture and Community in L.A.,* ed. David James, 47–90. Philadelphia: Temple University Press, 2003.

Olguín, B. V. *La Pinta: Chicana/o Prisoner Literature, Culture, and Politics.* Austin: University of Texas Press, 2010.

Orleck, Annalise, and Lisa Gayle Hazirjian. *The War on Poverty: A New Grassroots History, 1964–1980.* Athens: University of Georgia Press, 2011.

Oropeza, Lorena. *¡Raza Si! ¡Guerra No! Chicano Protest and Patriotism during the Vietnam War Era.* Berkeley: University of California Press, 2005.

Oshinsky, David. *Worse than Slavery: Parchman Farm and the Ordeal of Jim Crow Justice.* New York: Free Press, 1996.

Padilla, Tanalís. *Rural Resistance in the Land of Zapata: The Jaramillista Movement and the Myth of the Pax-Priísta, 1940–1962.* Durham, NC: Duke University Press, 2008.

Paradise, Annie. "Militarized Policing and Resistance in the Social Factory: The Battle for Community Safety in the Silicon Valley." PhD diss., California Institute for Integral Studies, 2015.

Paredes, Américo. *A Texas-Mexican Cancionero: Folksongs of the Lower Border.* Austin: University of Texas Press, 1995.

———. *"With His Pistol in His Hand": A Border Ballad and Its Hero.* Austin: University of Texas Press, 1958.

Paul, Carlos. "Falleció ayer Daniel Manrique Arias, creador del movimiento Tepito Arte Acá." *La Jornada* (Mexico City), August 23, 2010. http://www.jornada.unam.mx/2010/08/23/cultura/a10n1cul.

Payne, Charles. *I've Got the Light of Freedom: The Organizing Tradition and the Mississippi Freedom Struggle.* Berkeley: University of California Press, 1995.

Pensado, Jaime. *Rebel Mexico: Student Unrest and Authoritarian Political Culture during the Long Sixties.* Stanford, CA: Stanford University Press, 2013.

Pérez, Emma. "Decolonial Critics for Academic Freedom." In *Academic Repression: Reflections from the Academic Industrial Complex,* ed. Anthony J. Nocella II, Steven Best, and Peter McLaren, 364–373. San Francisco: AK Press, 2010.

———. *The Decolonial Imaginary: Writing Chicanas into History.* Bloomington: Indiana University Press, 1999.

———. "Queering the Borderlands: The Challenge of Excavating the Invisible and Unheard." *Frontiers: A Journal of Women's Studies* 24, nos. 2/3 (2003): 122–131.

Pérez, Ramón. *Diary of a Guerrilla.* Houston: Arte Público, 1999.

Phelps, Michelle S. "Rehabilitation in the Punitive Era: The Gap between Rhetoric and Reality in U.S. Prison Programs." *Law & Society Review* 45, no. 1 (2011): 33–68.

Pineda Ochoa, Fernando. *En Las Profundidades del MAR (El oro no llegó de Moscú).* Mexico City: Plaza y Valdes, 2003.

Poblete, Juan, ed. *Critical Latin American and Latino Studies*. Minneapolis: University of Minnesota Press, 2003.

Poniatowska, Elena. *Fuerte es el Silencio*. Mexico City: Era, 1980.

Prashad, Vijay. *The Darker Nations: A People's History of the Third World*. New York: New Press, 2007.

———. "Second-Hand Dreams." *Social Analysis* 49, no. 2 (Summer 2005): 191–198.

Pulido, Laura. *Black, Brown, Yellow, and Left: Radical Activism in Los Angeles*. Berkeley: University of California Press, 2006.

Quan, H. L. T. "Geniuses of Resistance: Feminist Consciousness and the Black Radical Tradition." *Race and Class* 47, no. 2 (2005): 39–53.

Rabasa, José. "Pre-Columbian Pasts and Indian Presents in Mexican History." *Disposition* 19, no. 46 (1994): 245–270.

Rabe, Stephen G. *The Killing Zone: The United States Wages Cold War in Latin America*. New York: Oxford University Press, 2011.

———. *The Most Dangerous Area in the World: John F. Kennedy Confronts Communist Revolution in Latin America*. Chapel Hill: University of North Carolina Press, 1999.

Ramirez-Oropeza, Martha. "Two Examples of Art Challenging Political Times: '10 de Junio' Teatro Mascarones and 'Danzas Indígenas,' Judith Baca Monument." Paper for Humanities 390, Urban Zapatismo, California State University–Northridge, February 2006.

Ramos Zavala, Raúl, and Arturo Gámiz García. *El tiempo que nos toco vivir . . . y otros documentos de la guerrilla en México*. Mexico City: Editorial Huasipungo, 2003.

Rayas, Lucía. "Subjugating the Nation: Women and the Guerrilla Experience." In *Challenging Authoritarianism in Mexico*, ed. Fernando Calderón and Adela Cedillo, 167–181. Routledge: New York, 2011.

Reavis, Dick. "Taste for Trouble." *Texas Monthly*, January 1, 2001.

———. "Unreliable Witness." *Texas Monthly*, July 25, 1980.

Reddy, Chandan. *Freedom with Violence: Race, Sexuality, and the US State*. Durham, NC: Duke University Press, 2011.

René de Dios Corona, Sergio. *La Historia que no pudieron borrar: La Guerra Sucia en Jalisco, 1970–1985*. Guadalajara: La Casa del Mago, 2004.

Revueltas, José. *México 68: Juventud y revolución*. Mexico City: Era, 1978.

Reyes, Judith. *La otra cara de la patria: Testimonio de una mujer revolucionaria, militante y canta-autora*. Mexico City: Redez, 2007.

Robinson, Cedric J. *Black Marxism: The Making of the Black Radical Tradition*. 2nd ed. Chapel Hill: University of North Carolina Press, 2000.

Rodríguez, Dylan. *Forced Passages: Imprisoned Radical Intellectuals and the U.S. Prison Regime*. Minneapolis: University of Minnesota Press, 2006.

———. "'Social Truth' and Imprisoned Radical Intellectuals." *Social Justice* 30, no. 2 (2003): 66–80.

Rodríguez, Robert T. *Next of Kin: The Family in Chicano/a Cultural Politics*. Durham, NC: Duke University Press, 2009.

Rodríguez, Victor M. "Boricuas, African Americans, and Chicanos in the 'Far West': Notes on the Puerto Rican Pro-Independence Movement in California, 1960s-1980s." In *Latino Social Movements: Historical and Theoretical Perspec-*

tives, ed. Rodolfo D. Torres and George Katsiaficas, 79–110. New York: Routledge, 1999.

Rodríguez Munguía, Jacinto. *La otra guerra secreta: Los archivos prohibidos de la prensa y el poder.* Mexico City: Debate, 2007.

Rosales, Rodolfo. *The Illusion of Inclusion: The Untold Political Story of San Antonio.* Austin: University of Texas Press, 2000.

Rosas, Raquel. "(De)Sexing Prostitution: Race, Reform, and Sex Work in Texas, 1889–1920." PhD diss., University of Texas at Austin, 2013.

Rovira, Guiomar. *Mujeres de maíz.* Mexico City: Era, 1997.

Rubenstein, Joshua. *Leon Trotsky: A Revolutionary's Life.* New Haven, CT: Yale University Press, 2011.

Rubin, Jeffrey W. "COCEI in Juchitán: Grassroots Radicalism and Regional History." *Journal of Latin American Studies* 26, no. 1 (February 1994): 109–136.

———. *Decentering the Regime: Ethnicity, Radicalism, and Democracy in Juchitán, Mexico.* Durham, NC: Duke University Press, 1997.

———. "State Policies, Leftist Oppositions, and Municipal Elections: The Case of COCEI in Juchitán." In *Electoral Patterns and Perspectives in Mexico,* ed. Arturo Alvarado, 127–160. Monograph Series 22. Center for US-Mexican Studies, University of California, San Diego, 1987.

Ruiz, Vicki. *From Out of the Shadows: Mexican Women in Twentieth-Century America.* New York: Oxford University Press, 1998.

Saldaña-Portillo, María Josefina. *The Revolutionary Imagination in the Americas and the Age of Development.* Durham, NC: Duke University Press, 2003.

Sanders, Sara Katherine. "The Mexican Student Movement of 1968: National Protest Movements in International and Transnational Contexts." In *Human Rights and Transnational Solidarity in Cold War Latin America,* ed. Jessica Stites Mor, 74–98. Madison: University of Wisconsin Press, 2013.

Sandos, James. *Rebellion in the Borderlands: Anarchism and the Plan of San Diego, 1904–1923.* Norman: University of Oklahoma Press, 1992.

Santamaría Gómez, Arturo. *La izquierda mexicana y los trabajadores indocumentados.* Culiacán: Universidad Autónoma de Sinaloa, 1988.

———. *La política entre México y Aztlán.* Culiacán: Universidad Autónoma de Sinaloa, 1994.

Scherer García, Julio, and Carlos Monsiváis. *Los patriotas: de Tlatelolco a la guerra sucia.* Mexico City: Aguilar, 2004.

———. *Parte de guerra: Tlatelolco 1968 — documentos del General Marcelino García Barragán: Los Hechos y la Historia.* Mexico City: Nuevo Siglo/Aguilar, 1999.

———. *Parte de Guerra II: Los rostros del 68.* Mexico City: Aguilar, 2002.

Schmidli, William Michael. *The Fate of Freedom Elsewhere: Human Rights and U.S. Cold War Policy toward Argentina.* Ithaca, NY: Cornell University Press, 2013.

Schmidt Camacho, Alicia. *Migrant Imaginaries: Latino Cultural Politics in the U.S.-Mexico Borderlands.* New York: New York University Press, 2008.

Schulman, Bruce J. *The Seventies: The Great Shift in American Culture, Society, and Politics.* Cambridge, MA: Da Capo, 2002.

Scott, James C. *Domination and the Arts of Resistance: Hidden Transcripts.* New Haven, CT: Yale University Press, 1990.

———. *Weapons of the Weak: Everyday Forms of Peasant Resistance*. New Haven, CT: Yale University Press, 1987.

Segade, Gustavo. *Chicano Indigenismo: Alurista and Miguel Meléndez M.* N.p., 1975.

Segura, Andres. "The Path of Quetzalcoatl." Deganawidah-Quetzalcoatl University, Davis, CA, 1977. http://www.youtube.com/watch?v=GwXMc2VP9y8.

Segura, Denise A., and Beatriz M. Pesquera. "Chicana Political Consciousness: Renegotiating Culture, Class, and Gender with Oppositional Practices." *Aztlán: A Journal of Chicano Studies* 24, no. 1 (Spring 1999): 1–32.

———. "'There Is No Going Back': Chicanas and Feminism." In *Chicana Critical Issues*, ed. Norma Alarcón et al., 95–115. Berkeley, CA: Third Woman Press, 1993.

Sexton, Jared. "People-of-Color-Blindness: Notes on the Afterlife of Slavery." *Social Text* 28, no. 2 103 (Summer 2010): 31–56.

———. "The *Vel* of Slavery—Tracking the Figure of the Unsovereign." *Critical Sociology* (2014). http://crs.sagepub.com/content/early/2014/12/19/0896920514552535 .full.pdf+html.

Shank, Theodore. "A Return to Mayan and Aztec Roots." *Drama Review* 18 (1974): 66.

Shaughness, Nicola. *Applying Performance: Live Art, Socially Engaged Theatre and Affective Practice*. New York: Palgrave-Macmillan, 2012.

Smith, Andrea. "Indigeneity, Settler Colonialism and White Supremacy." *Global Dialogue* 12, no. 2 (Summer–Autumn 2010). http://www.worlddialogue.org/content .php?id=488.

Solis Mimendi, Antonio. *Jueves de corpus sangriento (revelaciónes de un halcon)*. Mexico City: Alfaro Hermanos, 1975.

Speed, Shannon, R. Aída Hernández Castillo, and Lynn Stephen, eds. *Dissident Women: Gender and Cultural Politics in Chiapas*. Austin: University of Texas Press, 2006.

Stalin, Joseph. *Marxism and the National Question*. Calcutta: New Book Centre, 1975.

Stern, Alejandra Minna. "From Mestizophilia to Biotypology: Racialization and Science in Mexico, 1920–1960." In *Race and Nation in Modern Latin America*, ed. Nancy P. Appelbaum, Anne S. Macpherson, and Karin Alejandra Rosemblatt, 187–210. Chapel Hill: University of North Carolina Press, 2003.

Subcomandante Marcos II. "Marcos to NGOs: Zapatistas Don't Want Charity, but Respect: CHIAPAS: The Thirteenth Stele—Part Two: A Death." Translated by Irlandesa. In *The Speed of Dreams: Selected Writings 2001–2007*, ed. Canek and Greg Ruggiero, 199–239. San Francisco: City Lights, 2007.

Suri, Jeremi. *Power and Protest: Global Revolution and the Rise of Détente*. Cambridge, MA: Harvard University Press, 2003.

Tarica, Estelle. *Inner Life of Mestizo Nationalism*. Minneapolis: University of Minnesota Press, 2008.

Taylor, Diana. *The Archive and the Repertoire: Performing Cultural Memory in the Americas*. Durham, NC: Duke University Press, 2003.

———. *Theatre of Crisis: Drama and Politics in Latin America*. Lexington: University Press of Kentucky, 1991.

Téllez, Michelle. "Doing Research at the Borderlands: Notes from a Chicana Feminist Ethnographer." *Chicana/Latina Studies: The Journal of Mujeres Activas en Letras y Cambio Social* 4, no. 2 (2005): 46–70.

Tello, Carlos. *La política económica en México, 1970–1976*. Mexico City: Siglo XXI, 1979.

TENAZ. "El Quinto Festival de los Teatros Chicanos." *Chicano Theatre Three* (Spring 1974): 3.

Torres, Andrés, and José E. Velázques, eds. *The Puerto Rican Movement: Voices from the Diaspora*. Philadelphia: Temple University Press, 1998.

Trejo, Rubén. *Magonismo: utopia y revolución, 1910–1013*. Mexico City: Cultura Libre, 2005.

Tronti, Mario. "Social Capital." *Telos* 17 (1973): 98–121.

———. "The Strategy of Refusal." In *Working Class Autonomy and the Crisis: Italian Marxist Texts of the Theory and Practice of a Class Movement: 1964–1979*, ed. Red Notes, 7–21. London: Red Notes and CSE Books, 1979.

Trotsky, Leon. *Stalin: An Appraisal of the Man and His Influence*. New York: Grosset and Dunlap, 1940.

Truett, Samuel, and Elliott Young, eds. *Continental Crossings: Remapping U.S.-Mexico Borderlands History*. Durham, NC: Duke University Press, 2004.

Tyson, Timothy B. *Radio Free Dixie: Robert F. Williams and the Roots of Black Power*. Chapel Hill: University of North Carolina Press, 1999.

Underiner, Tamara. "Notes from the Ivory Labyrinth of Solitude." *Theatre Journal* 56, no. 3 (October 2004): 449–452.

Valtonen, Pekka. "Political Discourse, the State and the Private Sector in Mexico, 1940–1982." Paper presented at the XVII Jornadas de Historia Económica, University of Tucumán Argentina, September 22, 2000.

———. "Reflecting on Tlatelolco: 27 Years Later, La Lucha Continua." *¡LA VERDAD!* July–September 1995.

Varon, Jeremy. *Bringing the War Home: The Weather Underground, the Red Army Faction, and Revolutionary Violence in the 1960s and 1970s*. Berkeley: University of California Press, 2004.

Vásquez, Carlos. *Remembering a Revolutionary Mujer Compañera Magdalena Mora*. Pamphlet produced by Editorial Prensa Sembradora, Inc., 1981. Accessed February 18, 2011. *http://uniondelbarrio.org/lvp/newspapers/97/janmay97/pg01.html*.

Veracini, Lorenzo. *Settler Colonialism: A Theoretical Overview*. New York: Palgrave Macmillan, 2010.

Verduzco, Carolina, and Ileana Chavez. *Informe histórico presentado a la sociedad mexicana: fiscalía especial FEMOS*. Mexico City: Comité 68 Pro Libertadores Democráticas, 2008.

Viego, Antonio. *Dead Subjects: Toward a Politics of Loss in Latino Studies*. Durham, NC: Duke University Press, 2007.

Vigil, Ernesto B. *The Crusade for Justice: Chicano Militancy and the Government's War on Dissent*. Madison: University of Wisconsin Press, 1999.

Von Eschen, Penny M. *Race against Empire: Black Americans and Anticolonialism, 1937–1957*. Ithaca, NY: Cornell University Press, 1997.

Weber, Devra. "Keeping Community, Challenging Boundaries: Indigenous Migrants, Internationalist Workers, and Mexican Revolutionaries, 1900–1920." In *Mexico and Mexicans in the Making of the United States*, ed. John Tutino, 208–235. Austin: University of Texas Press, 2011.

Weiss, Judith A., ed. *Latin American Popular Theatre: The First Five Centuries*. Albuquerque: University of New Mexico Press, 1993.

Weitz, Mark A. *The Sleepy Lagoon Murder Case: Race Discrimination and Mexican-American Rights*. Lawrence: University Press of Kansas, 2010.

Wilderson, Frank B., III. "Prison-Slave as Hegemony's Silent Scandal." *Social Justice* 30, no. 2 (2003): 18–28.

Wilson Gilmore, Ruth. "Globalisation and U.S. Prison Growth: From Military Keynesianism to Post-Keynesian Militarism." *Race and Class* 40, nos. 2–3 (1998/99): 175.

Wolfe, Patrick. *Settler Colonialism and the Transformation of Anthropology: The Politics and Poetics of an Ethnographic Event*. New York: Cassell, 1999.

Xavier, Roy Eric. "Politics and Chicano Culture: Luis Valdez and El Teatro Campesino, 1964–1990." In *Chicano Politics and Society in the Late Twentieth Century*, ed. David Montejano, 175–200. Austin: University of Texas Press, 1999.

Yarbro-Bejarano, Yvonne. "The Female Subject in Chicano Theater: Sexuality, 'Race,' and Class." In *Performing Feminisms: Feminist Critical Theory and Theatre*, ed. Sue-Ellen Case, 131–149. Baltimore: Johns Hopkins University Press, 1990.

Ybarra-Frausto, Tomás. "The Chicano Movement and the Emergence of a Chicano Poetic Consciousness." *New Scholar* 6 (1977): 87.

——. "The Chicano Movement/The Movement of Chicano Art." In *Exhibiting Cultures: The Poetics and Politics of Museum Display*, ed. Ivan Karp and Steven Lavine, 128–150. Washington, DC: Smithsonian Institution Press, 1993.

——. "Rasquachismo." Interview with Latinopia Art. Accessed August 28, 2011. http://latinopia.com/latino-art/latinopia-art-tomas-ybarra-frausto-rasquachismo/.

Young, Cynthia A. *Soul Power: Culture, Radicalism, and the Making of a US Third World Left*. Durham, NC: Duke University Press, 2006.

Young, Elliot. *Catarino Garza's Revolution on the Texas-Mexico Border*. Durham, NC: Duke University Press, 2004.

Zamora, Emilio. "Chicano Socialist Labor Activity in Texas, 1900–1920." *Aztlán* 6 (Summer 1975): 221–236.

——. "Mutualist and Mexicanist Expressions of a Mexican Political Culture in Texas." In *Mexican Americans in Texas History: Selected Essays*, ed. Emilio Zamora, Cynthia Orozco, and Rodolfo Rocha, 83–101. Austin: Texas State Historical Association, 2000.

——. *The World of the Mexican Worker in Texas*. College Station: Texas A&M University Press, 1993.

Zermeño, Sergio. *México, una democracia utopica: el movimiento estudiantil del 68*. Mexico City: Siglo XXI, 1978.

Zolov, Eric. *Refried Elvis: The Rise of the Mexican Counterculture*. Berkeley: University of California Press, 1999.